Biography today

Biography Today

**Profiles
of People
of Interest
to Young
Readers**

2000
Annual
Cumulation

Laurie Lanzen Harris
Executive Editor

Cherie D. Abbey
Co-Editor

Omnigraphics

*615 Griswold Street
Detroit, Michigan 48226*

Laurie Lanzen Harris, *Executive Editor*
Cherie D. Abbey, *Co-Editor*
Sheila Fitzgerald, Kevin Hillstrom, Laurie Hillstrom, and
Sue Ellen Thompson, *Sketch Writers*
Joan Margeson and Barry Puckett, *Research Associates*

Omnigraphics, Inc.

* * *

Peter E. Ruffner, *Senior Vice President*
Matthew P. Barbour, *Vice President — Operations*
Laurie Lanzen Harris, *Vice President — Editorial*
Thomas J. Murphy, *Vice President — Finance*
Jane J. Steele, *Marketing Coordinator*
Kevin Hayes, *Production Coordinator*

* * *

Frederick G. Ruffner, Jr., Publisher

ISBN 0-7808-0410-4

The information in this publication was compiled from the sources cited and
from other sources considered reliable. While every possible effort has been
made to ensure reliability, the publisher will not assume liability for damages
caused by inaccuracies in the data, and makes no warranty, express or im-
plied, on the accuracy of the information contained herein.

This book is printed on acid-free paper meeting the ANSI Z39.48 Standard.
The infinity symbol that appears above indicates that the paper in this book
meets that standard.

Printed in the United States

Contents

5

Preface

Biography Today is a magazine designed and written for the young reader—
ages 9 and above—and covers individuals that librarians and teachers tell
us that young people want to know about most: entertainers, athletes, writers, illustrators, cartoonists, and political leaders.

The Plan of the Work

The publication was especially created to appeal to young readers in a format they can enjoy reading and readily understand. Each issue contains approximately 10 sketches arranged alphabetically. Each entry provides at least
one picture of the individual profiled, and bold-faced rubrics lead the reader
to information on birth, youth, early memories, education, first jobs, marriage and family, career highlights, memorable experiences, hobbies, and
honors and awards. Each of the entries ends with a list of easily accessible
sources designed to lead the student to further reading on the individual
and a current address. Obituary entries are also included, written to provide
a perspective on the individual's entire career. Obituaries are clearly marked
in both the table of contents and at the beginning of the entry.

Biographies are prepared by Omnigraphics editors after extensive research,
utilizing the most current materials available. Those sources that are generally available to students appear in the list of further reading at the end of
the sketch.

New Index

A new index now appears in all *Biography Today* publications. In an effort to
make the index easier to use, we have combined the **Name** and **General
Index** into one, called the **General Index**. This new index contains the
names of all individuals who have appeared in *Biography Today* since the series began. The names appear in bold faced type, followed by the issue in
which they appeared. The General Index also contains the occupations, nationalities, and ethnic and minority origins of individuals profiled. The
General Index is cumulative, including references to all individuals who have
appeared in the *Biography Today* General Series and the *Biography Today*
Special Subject volumes since the series began in 1992.

In a further effort to consolidate and save space, the Birthday and Places of Birth Indexes will be appearing only in the September issue and in the Annual Cumulation.

Our Advisors

This publication was reviewed by an Advisory Board comprised of librarians, children's literature specialists, and reading instructors so that we could make sure that the concept of this publication — to provide a readable and accessible biographical magazine for young readers — was on target. They evaluated the title as it developed, and their suggestions have proved invaluable. Any errors, however, are ours alone. We'd like to list the Advisory Board members, and to thank them for their efforts.

Sandra Arden, *Retired*
Assistant Director
Troy Public Library, Troy, MI

Gail Beaver
Ann Arbor Huron High School Library
and the University of Michigan School
of Information and Library Studies
Ann Arbor, MI

Marilyn Bethel
Pompano Beach Branch Library
Pompano Beach, FL

Eileen Butterfield
Waterford Public Library
Waterford, CT

Linda Carpino
Detroit Public Library
Detroit, MI

Helen Gregory
Grosse Pointe Public Library
Grosse Pointe, MI

Jane Klasing, *Retired*
School Board of Broward County
Fort Lauderdale, FL

Marlene Lee
Broward County Public Library System
Fort Lauderdale, FL

Judy Liskov
Waterford Public Library
Waterford, CT

Sylvia Mavrogenes
Miami-Dade Public Library System
Miami, FL

Carole J. McCollough
Wayne State University School of
Library Science, Detroit, MI

Deborah Rutter
Russell Library, Middletown, CT

Barbara Sawyer
Groton Public Library and Information
Center, Groton, CT

Renee Schwartz
School Board of Broward County
Fort Lauderdale, FL

Lee Sprince
Broward West Regional Library
Fort Lauderdale, FL

Susan Stewart, *Retired*
Birney Middle School Reading
Laboratory, Southfield, MI

Ethel Stoloff, *Retired*
Librarian, Birney Middle School
Southfield, MI

Our Advisory Board stressed to us that we should not shy away from controversial or unconventional people in our profiles, and we have tried to follow their advice. The Advisory Board also mentioned that the sketches might be useful in reluctant reader and adult literacy programs, and we would value any comments librarians might have about the suitability of our magazine for those purposes.

New Series

In response to suggestions from our readers, we have expanded the *Biography Today* family of publications. So far, we have published special subject volumes in the following categories: **Artists, Authors, Scientists and Inventors, Sports Figures, and World Leaders.** Each of these hardcover volumes is approximately 200 pages in length and covers about 10 individuals of interest to young readers.

Your Comments Are Welcome

Our goal is to be accurate and up-to-date, to give young readers information they can learn from and enjoy. Now we want to know what you think. Take a look at this issue of *Biography Today*, on approval. Write or call me with your comments. We want to provide an excellent source of biographical information for young people. Let us know how you think we're doing.

And here's a special incentive: mail or fax us the names of people you want to see in *Biography Today*. If we include someone you suggest, your library wins a free issue, with our thanks.

And take a look at the next page, where we've listed those libraries and individuals that will be receiving a free copy of this issue for their suggestions.

Laurie Harris
Executive Editor, *Biography Today*
Omnigraphics, Inc.
615 Griswold Street
Detroit, MI 48226
Fax: 1-800-875-1340

Congratulations!

Congratulations to the following individuals and libraries, who received a free copy of *Biography Today* for suggesting people who appeared in 2000:

Sarah Beam, Woodville, OH
Sarah Bordelon, Denton, TX
Jessica Carter, Oak Park, MI
Central Montcalm Middle
 School, Stanton, MI
Charlene Chan, Scarsdale, NY
Anna Chernova,
 San Francisco, CA
Creekside Elementary,
 Stockton, CA
Andrea Cushing, Concord, CA
Amelia Evert, Orinda, CA
N.L. Fletcher, The Dalles, OR
Jacquelyn Ford,
 Chicago Heights, IL
Erica Freeburg, Brookfield, IL
Erin Galligan, Riverhead, NY
Kally Goodwin, Liberal, KS
Jennifer Herrera, Arevada, CA
Ghazala Irshad, Decatur, IL

Amber Janatik,
 Michigan City, IN
Danny Johnson, Clinton
 Township, MI
Gabriela Magda,
 Middle Village, NY
Augusta Malvagno,
 Middle Village, NY
Christina Naylor, Detroit, MI
Keane Ng, San Francisco, CA
Long Pham, Vancouver, WA
Mimy Poon, San Lorenzo, CA
Jessica Slater, Tolleson, AZ
Heather Snead, Oxon Hill, MD
Justine Sobering,
 Wading River, NY
Chao Thao, Stockton, CA
Rob Tunnell, Monroe, CA
Angela Marie Zamora,
 Kenosha, WI

Christina Aguilera 1980-

American Singer
Grammy-Award Winner for Best New Artist

BIRTH

Christina Maria Aguilera (ah-gee-LAIR-ah) was born on
December 18, 1980, in Staten Island, New York, just a short
ferry ride from Manhattan. Her father, Fausto Aguilera, is a
U.S. Army sergeant who was born in Ecuador. Her mother,
Shelly Fidler Aguilera, is an Irish-American who was training
to become a Spanish translator when she met Christina's fa-
ther and who now runs her daughter's web site and fan club.
Christina has a sister Rachel, who is 13.

When Christina was seven, her parents divorced and her mother moved the two girls to Wexford, Pennsylvania, the Pittsburgh suburb where she had grown up. She met and married a paramedic there named James Kearns, adding a stepbrother, Casey, and a stepsister, Stephanie, to Christina's family. With her new husband, James Kearns, she also had another child — Christina's half brother, Robert Michael.

YOUTH

As the daughter of a career Army officer, Aguilera spent her first several years living wherever her father's assignments took the family — including Texas, New Jersey, Florida, and Japan. But singing was already an important part of her life. Aguilera's mother remembers her daughter singing to herself for hours in the bathtub, using a shampoo bottle as her microphone, or lining up all her stuffed animals and using them as her audience. "Singing was always my outlet, my form of release," Aguilera explains. "It made me feel connected to myself, even though my surroundings kept changing."

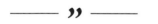

> "Singing was always my outlet, my form of release. It made me feel connected to myself, even though my surroundings kept changing."

After she saw *The Sound of Music*, the 1965 film starring Julie Andrews based on the Rodgers and Hammerstein musical, Aguilera memorized the lyrics and began singing songs from the movie. Her first public performance was on a city bus in Pittsburgh, where she sang the film's title song to a busload of strangers. By the time she was six or seven, she was singing at family events and neighborhood block parties, and then people started asking her to perform at weddings. At age eight Aguilera sang Whitney Houston's hit song "The Greatest Love of All" on "Star Search," a show that gave talented young people a chance to perform in front of a live audience on national television. Although she lost to an older boy, Aguilera spent the money she'd received as runner-up on a small, portable public address system that she could use to perform anywhere she wanted.

At age 11, Aguilera sang "The Star-Spangled Banner" at a Pittsburgh Penguins' ice hockey game in the Civic Arena — the youngest person ever to do so. She went on to sing the national anthem at every home game during the 1992 hockey season, when the Penguins won the Stanley Cup, and at Pirates and Steelers games as well. The director of a Pittsburgh theater company remembers Aguilera from local talent showcases he used to run. "The thing about her was that she wasn't just a cute little girl with a big little girl's voice," he said. "She was a little girl with an adult voice."

Shelly, Aguilera's mother, understood her daughter's need to perform and shared her love of music. When she was 16, Shelly had traveled all over Europe as a violinist with the Youth Symphony Orchestra, so she didn't think it at all strange that her daughter often opened her window and serenaded strangers on the street. And when she saw a notice in the newspaper that there would be an open audition in Pittsburgh for "The New Mickey Mouse Club," it was Shelly who asked, "Do you want to try out?"

The original "Mickey Mouse Club" show aired back in the 1950s, but since then there have been several spinoff shows. Aguilera was one of more than 15,000 aspiring Mouseketeers who showed up to audition for the third spinoff, to be shown on the Disney Channel. She was one of four selected to shoot an audition tape. But because she was only 10 at the time, she was told that she was too young to be on the show.

EDUCATION AND FIRST JOBS

For Aguilera, her school and work experiences didn't combine very well. Her appearance on "Star Search" triggered so much resentment among her elementary school classmates that she was forced to change schools.

"Going to a public school in a small town and not being around kids who did what I did made me feel like an outsider. The jealousy got really bad. People just felt threatened."

"Going to a public school in a small town and not being around kids who did what I did made me feel like an outsider," she says. "The jealousy got really bad. People just felt threatened." Someone even slashed the tires on her mother's car.

Aguilera's difficulties with her peers were destined to get worse. Two years after her audition for "The New Mickey Mouse Club," Disney executives contacted her and invited her to try again. This time she ended up with a five-year contract, which meant that her family had to move into an apartment in Orlando, Florida, from May until late October, when all the episodes for the coming year were filmed. She had to give up softball and volleyball, her favorite summer sports, and her Newfoundland dog, who was too big for the Florida apartment. But Aguilera soon discovered that

the experience she gained as a Mouseketeer was well worth the sacrifices she'd made. Disney provided her with singing, dancing, and acting lessons, and gave her a chance to perform in front of a live audience at Disney World's MGM Studios. Most of all, she says, "It was great to be around other kids who were as passionate about their careers as I was." Her fellow Mouseketeers included several teens who would go on to make a name for themselves as entertainers—including pop singer Britney Spears, actress Keri Russell (who stars in "Felicity"), and Justin Timberlake and J.C. Chasez (from 'N Sync).

At this point in her career, Aguilera lived in Orlando for half the year, then Pennsylvania for the other half. While in Florida, she was tutored three hours a day at the "Mouseketeer Bungaloo." Then, it was back to Pennsylvania, where she was a student at Marshall Middle School in North Allegheny. By the end of eighth grade, however, when Aguilera was appearing on television regularly, it became clear that her success was making her an outcast among her peers. She would be sitting in class with them one minute, and then they would go home and see her performing on TV. Sometimes they would ask her to sing for them, and if she did, they'd accuse her of showing off. If she didn't, however, they would think she was too good for them. "It made me an introvert," Aguilera recalls. But it also made her more determined than ever "to prove to myself that I could make this dream happen."

"The New Mickey Mouse Club" was canceled after Aguilera's second season. When she returned to Wexford, she knew that she could never fit in with her old friends and classmates again. So she left school, and her mother and a tutor took over the job of educating her. This arrangement gave her more freedom to travel and to focus on her career as a singer, which is what she decided she really wanted to do with her life. She earned her high school diploma in 1998.

CAREER HIGHLIGHTS

"Reflection"

During her two years as a Mouseketeer, Aguilera caught the attention of Steve Kurtz, who asked if he could be her manager. Kurtz sent a demo tape of her singing to RCA Records. "She was fearless," recalls an RCA executive. "She had perfect intonation and command of her instrument that normally you would see in someone a lot older." RCA decided to take a chance and sign her to a "demo deal," which wasn't the same as a full record deal but meant that they would work with her to develop an album and, if they liked the result, sign her.

Around this same time, Kurtz found out that Disney was looking for singers to record the soundtrack for *Mulan*, a full-length animated feature film. *Mulan* was the story of a young Chinese girl who saves her aged father from going to war by disguising herself as a warrior and taking his place in the Imperial Army. Kurtz told Aguilera that they had to get a demo tape to Disney right away, so she recorded herself singing "I Wanna Run to You" on a boom-box in her living room. She chose this song because it proved her ability to hit a high E above middle C—something Disney was specifically looking for. After listening to the tape, Disney chose Aguilera to sing "Reflection," the soundtrack's lead song and the perfect showcase for her emotional singing style and unusual vocal range.

The same week that "Reflection" was nominated for a Golden Globe award for "Best Original Song in a Motion Picture," RCA signed Aguilera to a seven-album contract. She was only 17.

"Genie in a Bottle"

In 1998, Aguilera started recording her first solo album with RCA, *Christina Aguilera*. It combined pop tunes with ballads and rhythm-and-blues-style songs, similar to the type of music performed by Mariah Carey and Whitney Houston. The first single to be released (in June 1999) was "Genie in a Bottle." The song was actually a last-minute addition to the album, and it wasn't one of Aguilera's favorites, since she felt it didn't demand much of her as a singer. But RCA believed that it would be a major hit, and as it turned out, they were right: "Genie in a Bottle" climbed almost immediately to No. 3 on the "Billboard Hot 100" chart and was No. 1 within a month. It stayed there for five weeks, joining Ricky Martin's "Livin' La Vida Loca" and Jennifer Lopez's "If You Had My Love" as the longest-running No. 1 singles of 1999. Aguilera received some criticism for the song's suggestive lyrics, although she insisted that "it's not about sex. It's about self-respect [and] not giving in to temptation until you're respected."

> *Aguilera wants to be "an all-round entertainer. I want to act, make films, make albums, do whatever I can."*

Songwriter Steve Kipner, who co-wrote "Genie in a Bottle," says he was impressed with Aguilera during their recording sessions because she didn't need any coaching on how to improvise the song's complex rhythm-and-blues lines, a skill he generally associates with more mature artists. "She's internalized all the riffs from Chaka Khan to Etta James to Mariah [Carey] and made them her own," he says. But Aguilera is the first to admit that making her first album was a learning experience. Her impulse was to belt out the song from the opening bars, but she learned that it was more effective if she kept her voice soft at first, allowing its strength and volume to build gradually.

The album received mixed reviews. Many critics favorably compared Aguilera's voice to those of Mariah Carey, Whitney Houston, and Celine Dion. But they were often less enthusiastic about the songs themselves, which were seen as being "fluff" or too generic. When the album went on to sell more than five million copies, though, Aguilera's childhood dream of being recognized wherever she went suddenly seemed to be coming true.

Aguilera and Enrique Iglesias performing at the 2000 Super Bowl.

Mademoiselle magazine named her one of its top people to watch in the new millennium, and *Ladies' Home Journal* chose her as one of the Most Fascinating Women of '99. She appeared on "The Tonight Show with Jay Leno," "Total Request Live," MTV's New Year's Eve special, and the 1999 "Christmas in Washington" special, where she performed for President and Mrs. Clinton. She also sang a duet with Enrique Iglesias during the Super Bowl half-time show. But most exciting to Aguilera was winning the Grammy Award for Best New Artist in February 2000. Also nominated was her fellow Mouseketeer, Britney Spears, to whom Aguilera has often been compared because of their similarity in age and background.

Aguilera's Plans

Aguilera considers herself more of a vocalist than a pop singer. "If music becomes too pop, I lose interest," she explains. "I need to be challenged." Her ballads reveal a mature voice that draws as much from the classic blues singers she grew up listening to, such as Billie Holliday and Etta

17

Aguilera holds her trophy for Best New Artist at the 2000 Grammy Awards.

James, as it does from more contemporary artists, such as Whitney Houston and Mariah Carey. She is able to convey a wide range of emotion in her singing, and her crystalline voice has lots of shading and a soulful ring that sets her apart from other teen vocalists. RCA executive Ron Fair refers to her as "our Streisand" — comparing her to Barbra Streisand, whose popularity has spanned three decades — because he believes that she has a very long career ahead of her. Aguilera herself wants to be "an all-round entertainer. I want to act, make films, make albums, do whatever I can."

Although she is reluctant to talk about her father, with whom she has little contact, Aguilera would like to visit Ecuador, his homeland, some day. She grew up listening to her parents speak Spanish and is currently working on a Spanish album that capitalizes on both her Ecuadorian heritage and the recent surge of interest in Latino artists and music. She is also working on a Christmas album.

MAJOR INFLUENCES

As a child, Aguilera enjoyed going to used record stores with her mother and grandmother to find old Billie Holliday records. Her mother also exposed her to the work of Etta James and B.B. King. "Blues was definitely a huge influence on me," she says. "It's probably my first musical love. I just connect with it somehow." Her favorite blues singer is Etta James, whose song "At Last" she often performs in concert.

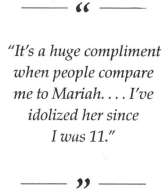

"It's a huge compliment when people compare me to Mariah. . . . I've idolized her since I was 11."

Mariah Carey is another singer whom Aguilera has always admired. "It's a huge compliment when people compare me to Mariah. . . . I've idolized her since I was 11," she says. One of her goals is to record a duet with Carey some day.

HOME AND FAMILY

Aguilera keeps an apartment on Manhattan's Upper West Side, but she still considers her real home to be her basement bedroom in Wexford, Pennsylvania. She spends most of her time in hotels while she is recording or performing, and goes back to Wexford to visit her family whenever she gets a chance. But she has lost contact with most of her former friends and classmates there. In fact, when Aguilera attended her local high school's senior prom last year, she was greeted with hostile stares from some of the other girls, who left the dance floor when the DJ started spinning her hit song, "Genie in a Bottle." "It was kind of sad," Aguilera comments. "All I want to do is be normal. But really, it's other people who won't let me be that way."

In general, Aguilera says that fame takes some time to get used to. She says that it can be "hard to be 18 and be in this business. Your album is huge, and these people 20 years your senior are seeing you as a product. That can be scary. I just wanted to make music, and all of a sudden it was all about this package—what your look was going to be. All these decisions are being made for you."

There is no boyfriend in her life right now, and Aguilera admits that her current work schedule makes it almost impossible to maintain a serious relationship. But she would like to meet "an artistically creative guy" some day who is also in the music business. "I think it's important that your partner understand what you do for a living," she says. "Music is so important to me that I want to share that with someone who feels it as much as I do."

CREDITS

Christina Aguilera, 1999

HONORS AND AWARDS

Grammy Award: 2000, for Best New Artist

FURTHER READING

Books

Golden, Anna Louise. *Christina Aguilera,* 2000
Robb, Jackie. *Christina Aguilera: An Unauthorized Biography,* 1999

Periodicals

Boston Globe, Jan. 14, 2000, Arts section, p.D13
Entertainment Weekly, Sep. 17, 1999, .31
Los Angeles Times, July 26, 1999, Entertainment section, p.1
New York Times, Sep. 6, 1999, p.E1
People, Sep. 27, 1999, p.75
Rolling Stone, Aug. 19, 1999, p.36; Oct. 28, 1999, p.52
Teen People, Dec. 1999-Jan. 2000, p.92
Time, Aug. 16, 1999, p.69; Sep. 27, 1999, p.75;Mar. 6, 2000, p.70
Washington Post, Feb. 13, 2000, p.G1
YM, Dec. 1999-Jan. 2000, p.74; Feb. 2000, p.70

ADDRESS

RCA Records
1540 Broadway
New York, NY 10036

WORLD WIDE WEB SITES

http://www.peeps.com/christina
http://www.christina-a.com

K.A. Applegate 1956-

American Children's Writer
Author of the *Animorphs* Series

EARLY LIFE

Katherine Alice Applegate was born in 1956 in Michigan. The creator of the *Animorphs* series is almost as mysterious as her books: most facts about her early life, including her parents, siblings, childhood, education, and marital status, are unavailable. In fact, Applegate avidly guards her privacy, as she explains here. "I'm afraid I'm a very reclusive, private person," she says. "I usually refuse even to do interviews. I like being anonymous and unrecognized." In comments published on the web site of Scholastic, her publisher, Applegate has spoken at length about her work. But she has also said that her desire for privacy is based on her belief that her readers should focus on the books, not on the writer. "I think that a book should be for the reader to enjoy without having to decide whether they like the author or not. The book is what's important, not the writer as an individual human being."

Still, Applegate has given out a little bit of background on her early life. When she was a child, the greatest love of her life was animals. "I had the usual suburban menagerie — lots of dogs and cats," she recalled. "But my claim to fame was gerbils. I started with just Sandy and Max. They didn't waste any time starting a family, so I used to sell baby gerbils." She also enjoyed reading books that featured animals, like *Dr. Doolittle* and *Charlotte's Web.*

During high school, Applegate turned her love for animals into a job in a veterinarian's office. "I ran lab tests, cleaned cages, assisted in surgery," she noted. "I even bathed cats. You learn fast that claws are sharp!" She always knew that she wanted to be either a veterinarian or a writer when she grew up. She finally decided that she could express her feelings about animals through writing as well as by treating them as a vet. "Eventually, I realized that, as a writer, I could spend time not only with cats and dogs and the occasional ferret, but with *any* animal under the sun — and perhaps a few from the galaxy down the road," she explained.

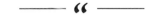

"Characters start as something I invent. That is, they start off with a few basic personality traits. Over time they evolve. . . . [Each of the] characters started off as a basic sketch, and with each book became more developed. After awhile, the characters seem to be running themselves, with me just kind of watching and going 'hmmm.'"

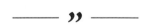

But it took Applegate a while to get started as a writer. "To be honest with you, when I got out of college I was totally clueless. I had no idea what I wanted to be." In the meantime she worked at a variety of jobs, including as a typist and a waitress, but found that she was not very good at any of them. "Then one day I just thought 'okay, that's about enough wasted time, Katherine, how about growing up and getting a life?'" She was about 30 when she decided to become a writer. "It was just a question of

finally getting serious about it," she stated. "It turns out that in order to become a writer, you actually have to start writing." She started out by writing a couple of romance novels for adults. And once she began writing, she discovered that she loved her work. But she admits that she still finds it difficult to concentrate sometimes.

CAREER HIGHLIGHTS

Since becoming a full-time writer, Applegate has written over 100 books on a wide range of subjects, from picture books for children to romance novels for adults. She has used different pseudonyms on many of her works. She wrote adult romance novels for Harlequin as Katherine Kendall. She wrote picture books for Disney as A.R. Plumb and as Nicholas Stevens. She wrote a horse series called Silver Creek Riders as Beth Kincaid. She was also one of the writers for the Sweet Valley Twins series, which is published under the name of the series creator, Francine Pascal (for more information on Pascal, see the entry in *Biography Today Authors,*Vol. 6).

In addition, Applegate wrote two series of romance novels for older teens. One series, called Making Out, features a group of lifelong friends, now in high school, who live on the fictional Chatham Island off the coast of Maine. The books tell about their experiences with falling in love. Another series, called Summer, features a high-school senior named Summer Smith and the ongoing exploits in her love life.

Animorphs

Applegate first became famous as the author of the *Animorphs* series. But before she actually wrote any of the *Animorphs* books, she started out by creating a "series bible." It was a loose-leaf binder that contained an overview of the series, ideas on style, outlines for plots, biographies of the characters, descriptions of the aliens, and sample chapters. For the characters, she found photographs of people that evoked her idea of the person. Then she filled out a form for each character. The form had a whole list of categories. One category was called "in a phrase," which is intended to sum up the person in just a few words. For the character Jake, for example, the phrase was "regular guy turned reluctant hero." Some of the other categories on her character forms were role in the group, role in the series, looks, personality, family, hobbies, age, and grade in school. After creating the series bible for *Animorphs*, Applegate sent it in to Scholastic. They liked it and decided to publish the series.

Applegate also created pronunciations for some of the difficult and invented words that she likes to use: Hork (rhymes with cork) Bajir (buh-JEER), Visser (rhymes with kisser), Tobias (toe-BYE-us), Elfangor (ELF-un-gore) Sirinial (sir-RIN-ee-ul) Shamtul (sham-TOOL), Ket Halpek (ket hal-PEK), Andalite (AN-duh-lite).

Animorphs is a science fiction series in which Applegate has created a complicated universe of different species and their history. Each new book reveals just a little bit more of that universe. Each book is written from the perspective of one of the main characters and describes the group's adventures from his or her point of view. The books are suspenseful, as the characters battle evil aliens, but they're funny, too.

The *Animorphs* series focuses on five friends — Jake, Rachel, Cassie, Marco, and Tobias. These five teenagers get special powers to help them save

—— " ——

"When Tobias becomes a hawk, I want the reader to see the world as a hawk might see it — to soar on the warm breezes and hurtle toward the ground to make a kill. When Marco becomes an ant, I want to convey the ant's lack of individuality, his blind world of sight and touch. When Cassie becomes a dolphin, I want the reader to feel the water rushing past, to experience what it must be like to leap from the cold ocean into warm sky."

—— " ——

the human race, the planet Earth, and in fact the whole universe from evil aliens, the Yeerks. When the series begins, the five teens take a shortcut home one day, even though their parents had warned them never to go that way. Passing by the construction site for a new mall, they meet Elfangor, a wounded member of a friendly alien race known as the Andalites. Elfangor and his ship had crash-landed on Earth during a space battle with the Yeerks. Before he dies, the Andalite Elfangor gives the five teenagers special powers to help them save the planet. Later in the series, the five teens are joined by Ax, an Andalite who helps them in their battle against the Yeerks.

Yeerks are an alien species from another planet who are trying to take control of the universe. Yeerks look like slugs. They're basically blind and deaf, and they use sonar to "see." Yeerks are able to take control of most species—including humans—by entering the ear and wrapping around the brain. Humans who are taken over by Yeerks are called controllers. Controllers still look and act like the original people, but everything they say and do is being controlled by the Yeerks. As the *Animorphs* series begins, Yeerks have already defeated many other races from other planets. Now they are trying to conquer all the people on Earth as part of their quest to control the universe.

> "When I invented Animorphs, I thought it would be too complex, too hard-to-follow for a wide readership. I thought it might be a sort of small-scale cult hit. Animorphs *fans have proven me wrong. I'm glad.* Animorphs *fans are the smartest, coolest fans any writer could ever hope to have. I am very grateful."*

The Characters

Each of the main characters in the *Animorphs* books shows a distinct personality. Jake, the leader of the group, is decisive and a peacemaker; Rachel, the first to take action, is brave and bold, even reckless; Cassie the environmentalist, animal lover, and pacifist, is always trying to solve problems without fighting; Marco, the self-preservationist, is funny and reluctant to fight; and Tobias, the quiet loner, is a human who has turned into a red-tailed hawk. But all the characters have grown over time, as Applegate explains here. "Characters start as something I invent. That is, they start off with a few basic personality traits. Over time they evolve. . . . [Each of the] characters started off as a basic sketch, and with each book became more developed. After awhile, the characters seem to be running themselves, with me just kind of watching and going 'hmmm.'"

Applegate has also said that her feelings about the different characters have changed over time. "Usually I find Marco the most fun to write because I like his rather complicated world view, the mix of humor and ruthlessness and fundamental decency. As for a favorite character, I like and dislike them all at different times. Sometimes they get on my nerves. Just like real people. There will be times I can't stand Jake or Cassie or Ax, and other times I think they're the best. Depends on how much trouble I'm having writing their scenes."

"Lately Jake has been getting on my nerves because I haven't been as pleased with the two most recent Jake books. So, I blame him. If my next Jake book is really good, I'll love Jake again. I haven't been 'mad' at Marco yet, but each of the others has caused me trouble at one time or another. Cassie is the character I use to get into deeper issues, so I tend to like her for that reason."

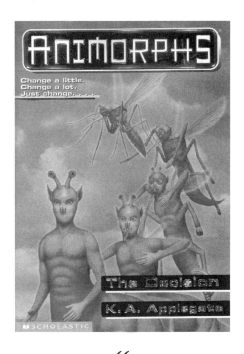

"Morphing" into Animals

The five teenagers in the *Animorphs* books all have special powers, which they got from the Andalite Elfangor, to help them fight against the Yeerks. They are able to "morph," or transform

—— " ——

"Climbing into the head of an animal is like climbing into the head of another human being. It becomes pure imagination."

—— " ——

themselves into any creature they wish simply by touching a member of that species. They use their powers to morph into a hawk, gorilla, elephant, tiger, wolf, cockroach, dolphin, several types of birds, and a variety of other animals. Once they take an animal form, they are able to use the special abilities of that animal to fight the Yeerks. In fact, the whole story of the series centers on their ability to morph into different animal forms to battle the Yeerks.

Applegate uses realistic details in the books to help readers understand what it would be like to become a different species. "When Tobias becomes a hawk, I want the reader to see the world as a hawk might see it — to soar on the warm breezes and hurtle toward the ground to make a kill," she ex-

plained. "When Marco becomes an ant, I want to convey the ant's lack of individuality, his blind world of sight and touch. When Cassie becomes a dolphin, I want the reader to feel the water rushing past, to experience what it must be like to leap from the cold ocean into warm sky."

Applegate does a great deal of research in order to create accurate descriptions of the various animals. She has a large library of books about animals at home. She also talks to zoologists and veterinarians who spend time observing and interacting with the animals. "The zoo guys are the best, because they observe the animals all day long. And sometimes I go out into the field. When I was writing about Tobias becoming a hawk, I went to a raptor center where they rehabilitate injured birds. I spent time with the birds, and with a falconer, and a vet. But after a certain point, it's just guessing," she admitted. "Climbing into the head of an animal is like climbing into the head of another human being. It becomes pure imagination."

Ongoing Success

It takes Applegate a little less than a month to write each *Animorphs* book. She writes about six pages a day for 23 or 24 days, and spends a few days rewriting. Then she starts the outline for the next book. A new *Animorphs* book usually comes out each month. To date, she has published 37 books in the *Animorphs* series, plus several related titles. These include *The Andalite Chronicles* (1997), which tells the story of Elfangor before the *Animorphs* series begins; *The Hork-Bajir Chronicles* (1998), which tells the history of the enslavement of the Hork-Bajir race; *Visser* (1999), which tells the story of how Eva became Visser One; and three volumes to date in the *Megamorphs* series, which tell about an adventure from several points of view, with each of the main characters taking turns in telling their part of the story.

The *Animorphs* books have become a huge hit. Critics have praised them for making kids want to read and talk about books, and kids love them.

Within a short time, *Animorphs* became the basis for a live-action TV series on Nickelodeon and for a set of transformer toys, and new books in the series continue to appear regularly. In fact, the success of the series has surprised Applegate. As she says, "When I invented *Animorphs*, I thought it would be too complex, too hard-to-follow for a wide readership. I thought it might be a sort of small-scale cult hit. *Animorphs* fans have proven me wrong. I'm glad. *Animorphs* fans are the smartest, coolest fans any writer could ever hope to have. I am very grateful."

Applegate says that there are two things she hopes her readers gain from her books: "I hope my books help give them respect and awe for the natural world. Animals are at least as incredible and amazing as any alien species. The other thing is that in the books, it's up to kids to save the world. In life, that's true as well."

The Future of *Animorphs*

Applegate was once questioned about her plans for the future of the series. "Hah, like I'm going to tell you? No way. You have to keep reading the books. But I'll tell you this: the adventure has just begun. And any time you think you know how it will turn out, guess again, because I am going to do my best to surprise you, scare you, and amaze you," she said.

> “
>
> *"I LOVE teasing, tricking, surprising, upsetting, scaring, infuriating, and challenging readers. I LOVE thinking you'll blow milk out of your noses because I've made you laugh. My goal is to make it impossible for you to put down an* **Animorphs** *book. I want to do all this and still present you with serious, important things to think about."*
>
> ”

"There are two things that make writing *Animorphs* really fun. Number one: they pay me a lot of money. Number two: I really, really enjoy sitting here at my computer, and typing away on a book and thinking 'Oh, now this is going to rock their worlds. This is gonna make 'em scream. This is gonna make them laugh. And when they get to this part they are going to stay up all night reading because they can't put it down."

"I LOVE teasing, tricking, surprising, upsetting, scaring, infuriating, and challenging readers. I LOVE thinking you'll blow milk out of your noses

because I've made you laugh. My goal is to make it impossible for you to put down an *Animorphs* book. I want to do all this and still present you with serious, important things to think about."

EverWorld

After writing many *Animorphs* books, Applegate decided to create a companion series. After writing so many science fiction stories, she wanted to try something new: a fantasy series with contemporary characters, set both in a fantasy environment and in the real world. And she also wanted to try writing about slightly older characters with different problems than those faced in the *Animorphs* series. So she created *EverWorld*. Applegate has published four books in the *EverWorld* series so far: *Search for Senna* (1999), *Land of Loss* (1999), *Enter the Enchanted* (1999), and *Realm of the Reaper* (1999).

A thousand years ago, the gods of myth and legend—from Norse, Greek, Aztec, Egyptian, and other cultures—decided to abandon the real world and create a new universe, *EverWorld.* This parallel universe, where magic rules, contains dragons and trolls and elves and wizards. *Ever World* existed for 1,000 years, but now it is under attack by mythological gods belonging to alien civilizations.

Trying to escape these alien gods, the Norse god of destruction, Loki, has broken through the barrier between the two worlds and seized a Midwestern high-school girl, Senna, who has some sort of power that makes her a bridge between the two universes. Possession of Senna would allow all the mythological gods, dragons, and elves of *EverWorld* to break through the barrier between the universes and enter the real world, bringing along immeasurable turmoil for humans. When Loki seizes Senna, she carries four others along with her to *EverWorld*: David, April, Jalil, and Christopher. Together, they must hold on to Senna, keep her from falling into evil hands, and learn how to deal with the gods. But because they live in two worlds simultaneously, *EverWorld* and the real world, the heroes also face the everyday realities of high-school life, with all the problems and challenges that brings.

BEING A ROLE MODEL

Once, Applegate was asked whether she considered herself a role model. Here's how she responded. "I certainly hope not. I have doubts about making any 'celebrity' a role model. You only know about a celebrity by what they do for a living, or what some press agents sells to a newspaper. You don't know them as actual people. If you want a role model, find a real person: a parent or teacher. The job of a human being is to be a good human being, not to be Michael Jordan or Britney Spears or, on a much lower scale, me. Find a real person, a person who gets up and goes to work and works hard and is decent to other people and kind to you. That's a role model."

"I hope my books help give them respect and awe for the natural world. Animals are at least as incredible and amazing as any alien species. The other thing is that in the books, it's up to kids to save the world. In life, that's true as well."

ADVICE TO YOUNG WRITERS

Applegate once gave this advice to kids interested in becoming writers. "Step A is to read. The best way to become a writer later in life is to be a reader now. Step B is to write. Read anything, write anything. Write absolutely terrible stuff, it doesn't matter. Writing anything—trying to tell any story—will teach you how to write. Especially if you take your first draft, and write a second draft and a third, fourth, and so on. Writing doesn't just come pouring out of your head ready to go. You have to work on it, repeat it, try again. . . . "

"You cannot possibly fail to learn something from any writing you do. Doesn't matter if it's fiction, nonfiction, poetry, love notes, whatever. Any time you put words on paper (or monitor) you learn a tiny bit more about writing. So write. You can't get published unless you write something. Took me about a decade to figure that out."

Applegate also offers this important piece of advice. "Rewrite. Everyone, when they're young, thinks writing is about inspiration, like the words will all just appear in the precisely right way on the page. That's not how it works. Writing isn't an ecstatic vision that pops into your head. Not generally, anyway. It's more like gardening. There's a lot of weeding involved."

HOME AND FAMILY

Applegate has acknowledged that she has a young son named Jake, but she hasn't talked about Jake's father. They live in the Minneapolis-St. Paul area of Minnesota, along with their two cats. Applegate works in her home office, a large room on the top floor of her house that has a desk, an easy chair, bookshelves, and a bed in case she wants to take a nap.

HOBBIES AND OTHER INTERESTS

In her spare time, Applegate enjoys traveling, reading, gardening, and playing the cello. But her favorite activity is shopping. "My first career choice," she says, "involved someone just magically paying me to go shopping. That never worked out."

SELECTED WRITINGS

Animorphs

1. *The Invasion*, 1996
2. *The Visitor*, 1996
3. *The Encounter*, 1996
4. *The Message*, 1996
5. *The Predator*, 1996
6. *The Capture*, 1997
7. *The Stranger*, 1997
8. *The Alien*, 1997
9. *The Secret*, 1997
10. *The Android*, 1997
11. *The Forgotten*, 1997
12. *The Reaction*, 1997
13. *The Change*, 1997
14. *The Unknown*, 1998
15. *The Escape*, 1998
16. *The Warning*, 1998
17. *The Underground*, 1998
18. *The Decision*, 1998
19. *The Departure*, 1998

20. *The Discovery*, 1998
21. *The Threat*, 1998
22. *The Solution*, 1998
23. *The Pretender*, 1998
24. *The Suspicion*, 1998
25. *The Extreme*, 1999
26. *The Attack*, 1999
27. *The Exposed*, 1999
28. *The Experiment*, 1999
29. *The Sickness*, 1999
30. *The Reunion*, 1999
31. *The Conspiracy*, 1999
32. *The Separation*, 1999
33. *The Illusion*, 1999
34. *The Prophecy*, 1999
35. *The Proposal*, 1999
36. *The Mutation*, 1999
37. *The Weakness*, 2000

Other Titles Related to *Animorphs*

The Andalite Chronicles, 1997
The Hork-Bajir Chronicles, 1998
Visser, 1999
Megamorphs 1: The Andalite's Gift, 1997
Megamorphs 2: In the Time of Dinosaurs, 1998
Megamorphs 3: Elfangor's Secret, 1999

EverWorld

1. *Search for Senna*, 1999
2. *Land of Loss*, 1999
3. *Enter the Enchanted*, 1999
4. *Realm of the Reaper*, 1999

FURTHER READING

Periodicals

Chicago Tribune, Mar. 9, 1998, News section, p.2
Dallas Morning News, Feb. 22, 1999, p.C3
Denver Post, Oct. 27, 1997, p.F10
Kansas City Star, Apr. 14, 1998, p.E1

Publishers Weekly, Nov. 3, 1997, p.36
Toronto Sun, Mar. 7, 1998, Lifestyle section, p.34
USA Today, Sep. 25, 1997, p.D8
Washington Post, June 1, 1998, p.B3

Other

"All Things Considered" Transcript, National Public Radio (NPR)
    broadcast, Jan. 7, 1998

ADDRESS

Scholastic Inc.
555 Broadway
New York, NY 10012

WORLD WIDE WEB SITES

http://www.scholastic.com/animorphs
http://www.scholastic.com/everworld

Lance Armstrong 1971-

American Professional Bicycle Racer
Survived Testicular Cancer and Came Back to Win the
1999 and 2000 Tour de France

BIRTH

Lance Edward Armstrong was born on September 18, 1971,
in Plano, Texas. He was the only child born to Linda (Mooney-
ham) Walling, a manager at a telecommunications firm, and
Eddie Gunderson, a route manager for a newspaper company. Lance's mother was just 17 years old when he was born,
and his parents separated shortly afterward. His last contact
with his biological father came when he was three.

YOUTH

After Lance's parents got divorced, his mother struggled to raise him on her own. They depended on each other and grew very close. "She instilled all her drive, motivation, and toughness in me," he noted. When Lance was six, his mother married Terry Armstrong, who adopted him and changed his last name. But he never got along with his stepfather, and he was relieved when his mother's second unhappy marriage ended in divorce during his teen years.

Lance enjoyed playing sports as a boy. But he soon realized that he was not very good at agility sports like football. So he focused on endurance sports like running and swimming instead. His mom supported him by driving him to countless swim practices and cross-country meets. When he was 14, Armstrong saw the Ironman Triathlon competition on television. In triathlons, athletes compete in a three-part race that involves swimming, bicycling, and running. Armstrong was fascinated by the triathlon and thought, "Someday I'm going to do that."

> *Armstrong once said this about his mother: "She instilled all her drive, motivation, and toughness in me."*

Armstrong took up bicycling in order to compete in triathlons. Along with a friend, he would regularly ride 60 miles north from Plano through the desert to the Oklahoma border, then turn around and ride back. Whenever he ran out of water or had a flat tire on his bike, he would call his mom to come pick him up.

Before long, Armstrong was one of the top young triathletes in the country. At 17, he won the U.S. sprint triathlon championship, which featured a 1,000-meter swim, 15-mile bike ride, and a three-mile run. When he repeated as champion the following year, people across the nation began to take notice.

But despite his success in triathlons, Armstrong started thinking about concentrating in one event. "One problem with the triathlon was that I didn't like the swimming all that much," he related. "It seemed everyone went into the water at the same time, thrashed around, and pretty much came out of the water at the same time. Then, on the bike, everyone was drafting, staying close together. [Drafting is staying behind another rider, who blocks the wind and lessens the resistance.] So the race basically became a 10-kilometer run, which was my worst part. I looked at what I did best, what I liked best. Riding the bicycle. I went with that."

EDUCATION

Armstrong attended the public schools in Plano. He spent all of his free time training for running, swimming, and triathlon competitions. During his years at Plano East High School, he would run for an hour each day with the cross-country team, then ride his bike for two more hours. Every other day, he would add a half hour of swimming to his workout.

When Armstrong was a senior in high school, officials from the U.S. national cycling team invited him to join the team. They had recognized his potential as a cyclist while watching him compete in triathlon competitions. But Plano school officials refused to let Armstrong graduate if he left school early to train with the national team. As a result, he withdrew from high school and spent the spring of his senior year training as a cyclist. In 1990, he placed 11th in the world amateur road-race championship. He also completed his course work at Bending Oaks Academy, a private school in Dallas, and earned his high school diploma.

CAREER HIGHLIGHTS

Shortly after graduating from high school, Armstrong moved to Austin, Texas. He felt that the hills around the city would benefit his training. He also liked Austin's reputation as a center of the folk-rock music scene. The following year, Armstrong competed in the Tour DuPont, the most important stage bicycle race in the United States. Stage races, along with classics, are the two types of bicycle road races. Stage races can last several weeks and cover as much as 2,000 miles. Each day is a separate race, or stage, and there are separate winners for each stage. Each rider's times are totaled for all the stages throughout the event, and the overall winner is the person who rode the whole race in the fastest time. Classic races, including the World Championship, are one-day events. In the 1991 Tour DuPont, Armstrong covered 1,085 miles in 11 days. Although he finished in the middle of the pack, he did well for someone so young and inexperienced. In fact, some people began comparing him to Greg LeMond, the great American cyclist who won the prestigious Tour de France three times.

During his early career, Armstrong became known not only for his cycling ability, but also for his confidence and outspoken manner. He admitted that some of his fellow riders viewed him as "cocky and brash" or even "an arrogant little punk," but claimed that "it's just self-confidence and a desire to win."Whenever someone tried to compare him to LeMond, he replied: "I'm not the next Greg LeMond; I'm the first Lance Armstrong."

The pressure of high expectations took a toll on Armstrong during the 1992 season. He found it difficult to make the transition from being an exciting new prospect to being one of the favorites to win. His first struggle came at the 1992 Summer Olympics in Barcelona, Spain. He entered the 115-mile cycling road race event as one of the top American medal hopefuls, but he placed a disappointing 14th. Immediately after the Olympics, he turned professional and signed a contract to race for the Motorola team.

> *In his first professional race, Armstrong finished dead last out of 111 riders, and the crowd booed when he crossed the finish line. "I was 30 minutes off the back, and it was pissing rain. It was raining so hard it hurt. But I had to finish. I didn't do it to impress anyone, just to finish. It goes back to my mother. She didn't raise a quitter."*

But disaster struck during his first professional race, the San Sebastian Classic in Spain. He finished dead last out of 111 riders, and the crowd booed when he crossed the finish line. "I was 30 minutes off the back, and it was pissing rain. It was raining so hard it hurt. But I had to finish,"he recalled. "I didn't do it to impress anyone, just to finish. It goes back to my mother. She didn't raise a quitter." Following this disappointing start, Armstrong nearly ended his professional racing career before it had hardly begun. He thought about giving up and going home, but he finally decided to finish the season. Later that year, he placed second in the Championship of Zurich, a world cup race held in Switzerland.

Winning the World Championship

Armstrong began living up to his potential in 1993. He started the year by placing second overall in the Tour DuPont. Then he earned $1 million in prize money for winning the "triple crown" racing series in the United States, which included the U.S. national championship.

In July 1993, Armstrong made his first appearance in the Tour de France. The Tour de France is a grueling, three-week race that takes competitors through 2,000 to 2,600 miles of rolling countryside, mountains, and val-

Armstrong rides past the Arc de Triomphe in Paris during the 20th and final stage of the Tour de France cycling race on July 25, 1999.

leys. The race mixes backbreaking ascents up steep hills with potentially fatal 70-mile-per-hour descents. Even for the very best professional cyclists, the Tour de France presents an incredible challenge to their physical and mental well-being.

At this point in his career, Armstrong had established himself as one of the best single-day racers in the world. But his coaches knew that he was not yet a strong enough climber to handle the multiple climbs of the Tour de France. So he approached his first Tour de France as a learning experience, planning to compete in the first two weeks and then drop out before the worst of the climbs. Armstrong surprised many observers by winning an early stage of the race, becoming one of the youngest people ever to do so. But then he left France to concentrate on training for other events.

In August 1993, Armstrong won a 160-mile road race in Norway and was crowned the world champion of professional bicycling. The race took place in a heavy rainstorm, which caused Armstrong to crash twice. But in an exciting finish, he passed three other riders during the last lap to claim the victory. As he approached the finish line, he punched the air, blew kisses to fans, and bowed to acknowledge the applause. Afterward, Armstrong was invited to meet King Harald V of Norway. But he refused to see the king until his mother was allowed to join him. "I probably came on pretty strong, but man, I don't check my mom at the door," he stated. "I don't care who it is."

Armstrong's 1994 season was still successful, though it featured fewer individual wins than he had achieved in 1993. He found that wearing the rainbow jersey awarded to the world champion made other competitors focus their efforts on beating him. "It changed my role in the sport, and I probably wasn't prepared for that," he explained. "I expected to win everything, and I didn't." Armstrong did finish second in both the San Sebastian Classic and the Tour DuPont that year. He also made a second appearance in the Tour de France, again dropping out before the end, and finished seventh in the world championships.

Armstrong came back strong in 1995, winning the Tour DuPont and completing the Tour de France for the first time. This race was difficult for him emotionally, as one of his teammates died from a head injury suffered during a crash. But Armstrong managed to win one stage and ended up 36th overall. Later that year, he earned a satisfying victory at the San Sebastian Classic, the race where he had finished dead last in his professional debut.

Diagnosed with Testicular Cancer

As the 1996 season began, it looked like it would be Armstrong's year. He repeated as the Tour DuPont champion and won the San Sebastian Classic for a second consecutive year. By May, the International Cycling Union ranked him as the top professional cyclist in the world. He also made a strong showing in the early stages of the Tour de France before illness forced him to pull out. Armstrong also competed in the 1996 Summer Olympics in Atlanta, Georgia. In fact, he was one of the favorites at the Games, which permitted professional cyclists to compete for the first time. But he missed winning an Olympic medal, finishing a disappointing sixth in the time trials and 12th in the road race. Shortly after the Olympics, he signed a $2 million contract with one of the top French cycling teams, Cofidis.

Around the time of the Olympics, Armstrong started feeling tired. He also noticed some pain and swelling in one of his testicles, but he thought it came from spending too many hours on the saddle of his bike. In late September, however, he began coughing up blood. He then became alarmed and saw a doctor about his condition. On October 3, 1996, doctors diagnosed him with an advanced case of testicular cancer. "I thought, 'I'm 25 years old. I'm one of the best in my sport. Why would I get cancer?'" he recalled. "I felt bulletproof."

The next day, the doctors performed surgery to remove the cancerous testicle. But the news soon got worse instead of better. Tests showed that the cancer had spread into his abdomen and lungs. In fact, Armstrong had dozens of tumors—ranging from the size of marbles to the size of golf balls—scattered throughout his body. The doctors told him that he probably would have died within a couple of months if he had not received treatment when he did.

But Armstrong soon faced yet another blow. Another test showed that the cancer had spread to his brain. He was almost relieved to hear this last diagnosis. "On Day 1, I was told I had cancer; on Day 5, told it was worse than they thought; on Day 12, they said it was even worse than that," he noted. "On Day 12, they found it on the brain, and once they found it there, then I thought it can't get worse than that." At this point, his doctors gave him a 50-50 chance of survival. But he was determined not only to survive, but also to return to competitive cycling. "I'm determined to fight this disease, and I will win," he stated. "I intend to ride again as a pro cyclist."

> *In 1996, doctors diagnosed him with an advanced case of testicular cancer. "I thought, 'I'm 25 years old. I'm one of the best in my sport. Why would I get cancer?' I felt bulletproof."*

Throughout his battle with cancer, Armstrong chose treatments with the hope of returning to his career as a top bicycle racer. Instead of attacking his brain tumors with radiation, which can affect the sense of balance, he chose to undergo surgery. Armstrong then endured four rounds of chemotherapy at the Indiana University Medical Center in Indianapolis. During chemotherapy, doctors administered harsh chemicals to kill the cancerous cells in his lungs and abdomen. Armstrong selected a chemotherapy drug that produced more severe side effects in the short term but would be less likely to diminish his lung capacity. He lost his hair and 15 pounds of muscle during the treatments.

While he was undergoing treatment for cancer, Armstrong continued riding his bike to stay in shape. But he also took time off to focus on other things he enjoyed. For example, he did some landscaping around his

Armstrong poses with his wife, Kristin (left), and his mother, Linda (right), on the Champs Elysees in Paris after the final stage of the 1999 Tour de France.

home in Austin, went fishing in Alaska, played in charity golf tournaments, and accompanied the rock band the Wallflowers on a national concert tour. "This year has put a lot of things in perspective for me, as a person and a professional cyclist, as an athlete and a human," he said. "This year has meant more to me than any other of my 26 years. I'm a better person for it now."

Launching a Comeback

By October 1997 — a year after his initial diagnosis — it appeared that the treatments had been successful. Armstrong's cancer had been cured. Doctors gave him a clean bill of health with only a 2 percent chance of recurrence. But despite this positive news, Cofidis dropped him from the team. Several of his other sponsors turned away from him as well. But such doubts only made Armstrong more determined to regain his strength and return to top form as a professional cyclist. "This sport didn't believe in me. This sport didn't return our phone calls. I had a team that, at the worst time in my life, completely wanted to forget about me," he recalled. "If I'm in a race and look around and see all the riders who didn't return our calls, they are going to race against a different Lance Armstrong."

Armstrong eventually took a pay cut to join an American cycling team sponsored by the U.S. Postal Service. He began training hard for his comeback. "I'm attempting one of the biggest comebacks, if not the biggest comeback, in the history of sport," he stated, "taking into account the severity of my illness, the aggressiveness of my treatment, and how long I've been away, and putting all that into a sport I consider to be the hardest sport in the world."

For Armstrong, returning to his former level of competition would not only prove something to himself and his former sponsors, but also to cancer patients everywhere. "My life doesn't revolve around cycling. My goal is not to race bikes and make a living," he explained. "It's to prove to the cancer community, to patients and their families, that you can go through the whole realm of the disease and return to a normal life, whether you're a teacher, a trucker, a mayor, or a professional cyclist."

While he was undergoing treatment for cancer, Armstrong took time off to focus on other things he enjoyed. "This year has put a lot of things in perspective for me, as a person and a professional cyclist, as an athlete and a human. This year has meant more to me than any other of my 26 years. I'm a better person for it now."

The 1999 Tour de France

As Armstrong worked his way back into competitive cycling, he began to notice that he was even better than before. The weight loss had given him a leaner body that was easier to crank up steep hills. The experience also improved his outlook, leaving him more serious, mature, and focused. After winning some short stage races and finishing fourth in the world championships in 1998, he decided to work towards winning the Tour de France in 1999.

Competitors had always considered Armstrong capable of taking individual stages in the Tour. They doubted that he could win the entire race, though, because he had never proven himself on the grueling mountain climbs. But it was a different Lance Armstrong who showed up in 1999. He and his teammates spent several weeks in Europe before the race began, training exclusively on the steep, mountainous sections of the course. The Tour de France, along with many other road races, is a team event, and Armstrong's teammates would play a crucial role. Armstrong was the "lead"rider, or best cyclist, for the U.S. Postal Service team. The job of the other cyclists on the team was to ride in front of him for most of each day's race to protect him from the wind. That would allow Armstrong, as lead cyclist, to draft, staying behind his teammates where there would be less resistance. He would be able to conserve his energy and pull out to the front later.

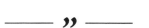

"My life doesn't revolve around cycling. My goal is not to race bikes and make a living. It's to prove to the cancer community, to patients and their families, that you can go through the whole realm of the disease and return to a normal life, whether you're a teacher, a trucker, a mayor, or a professional cyclist."

Armstrong won the short prologue that opened the Tour de France on July 4 in dramatic fashion, smashing the course record set by five-time champion Miguel Indurain. He thus staked an early claim to the yellow jersey, or *maillot jaune* in French, that is awarded to the leading rider in the race. As expected, Armstrong surrendered the leader's jersey later in the week, when sprint specialists dominated the flat portions of the course. But then he shocked many competitors by reclaiming the lead for good on July 13, during the first major climbing stage in the Alps.

Stage 9 of the Tour de France consisted of six major climbs over 132 miles. During the final seven-mile climb to the mountaintop finish, Armstrong closed a 32-second gap to catch two of the best climbers in the world, Ivan Gotti and Fernando Escartin. Then he pedaled right past the amazed competitors and opened up a commanding lead. As the U.S. Postal Service team car pulled up next to him, he looked over and said, "How do you like them apples?" Stage 9 turned out to be the turning point in the race. By the end of the stage, Armstrong led his closest competitor by over six minutes.

Disturbed by Drug Rumors

As it became clear that Armstrong was the man to beat in the 1999 Tour de France, French newspapers began printing rumors that he was using illegal performance-enhancing drugs. Some even suggested that the treat-

Lance, Kristin, and son Luke, November 1999.

ments he had received for cancer unfairly helped his performance. Although he was upset by the rumors, Armstrong knew that the Tour had been disrupted by a drug scandal the previous year, when several top competitors were forced to drop out of the race after officials found traces of banned substances in their blood or urine. He also understood that the French press was frustrated because French riders were not doing well in the race. But he soon grew tired of the accusations and spoke out angrily about the situation.

"I don't take any medication, none whatsoever. I believe it's part of my responsibility to return cycling's good reputation," he stated. "There are journalists in France and there are doctors on French teams who think I've been given something special by my oncologist [a doctor specializing in the treatment of cancer]. They think I was given drugs that boost performance. It's the exact opposite. I was given things that can kill you. That kind of talk, it makes me sick. But when the race is over, that stuff doesn't live. The victory and the people that I touch and the story that I can tell—that lives."

Completing His Miraculous Comeback

Armstrong never looked back, winning the fastest-ever Tour de France by a comfortable margin of 7 minutes, 37 seconds. He completed the total distance of 2,288 miles in 91 hours, 32 minutes, 16 seconds, for an average pace of 24.97 miles per hour.

Armstrong gave credit to his teammates, who often set the pace for him and helped him defend the yellow jersey. "I had a lot of help from my team," he noted. "When we got the jersey and said we would defend it, people thought we were crazy, they said this team isn't strong enough. They proved they're the strongest team in the race." After becoming the second American ever to win the Tour de France, Armstrong claimed that his victory was even more significant than those of Greg LeMond. While LeMond had ridden for French teams, Armstrong won "with an American sponsor and an American team."

Armstrong also gave some of the credit for his miraculous victory to the changes his mind and body underwent during his battle with cancer. "If I never had cancer, I never would have won the Tour de France," he stated. "I'm convinced of that. I wouldn't want to do it all over again, but I wouldn't change a thing."

Soon after his inspirational win in the Tour de France, Armstrong became a huge international celebrity. He received millions of dollars in prize money and endorsements. He also signed contracts to produce a book and a movie about his life. His autobiography, *It's Not about the Bike: My Journey Back to Life* (2000), went on to become a bestseller. Because of all the attention, Armstrong decided to skip the 1999 world championships and take a month off. He returned to the United States and competed in a series of mountain bike races in Colorado for fun. But he soon returned to training for the next Tour de France, as well as for the 2000 Summer Olympics in Sydney, Australia. "I'm going to do my best to try and win the thing again," he said of the Tour de France. "And there's always that Olympic gold medal to shoot for."

Armstrong rides down the Champ Elysees with an American flag after winning his second Tour de France, July 23, 2000.

The 2000 Tour de France

Armstrong was as good as his word. He won the 2000 Tour de France, defeating some of the toughest competition ever in the race, and by a wide margin. Besting 180 other racers, Armstrong rode into Paris on July 23 a full six minutes ahead of the nearest competitor. He had made his big move midway through the race, during the ascent up the Pyrenees mountain range. "It was full-on," he said of that leg of the race. "Full-on aggression." Answering any lingering challenges to his supremacy in the Tour, Armstrong became only the second American, after Greg LeMond, to win back-to-back Tours de France. He finished the 2,774-mile race with a total time of 92 hours, 33 minutes, and 8 seconds.

"Last year he proved a lot to himself," said his wife, Kristin Armstrong. "This year he proved a lot to the people who thought his victory wasn't real."

And on August 1, the United States Olympic Committee chose Armstrong, along with four other U.S cyclists, to represent the United States at

47

*Armstrong hoists his son Luke on the podium after winning his second
Tour de France, July 23, 2000.*

the 2000 Olympics in Sydney, Australia. Armstrong was delighted to have
been chosen. And his team "looks super." He's looking forward to Sydney
and to another chance at Olympic gold. "I'd like to win a gold medal," he

says. "I've been there twice before and been disappointed twice before, so this will be a nice opportunity."

MARRIAGE AND FAMILY

Lance Armstrong met his future wife, Kristin Richard, when she helped publicize one of his cancer fund-raising events. They married in May 1998 and had a son, Luke David Armstrong, on October 12, 1999.

The birth of their son is just one more miracle following Armstrong's illness and recovery. When he learned that he had cancer, Armstrong knew the treatments might make him sterile. Although he was still single at the time, he had some healthy sperm frozen so that he would eventually be able to father a child. Later, his wife Kristin became pregnant through in vitro fertilization. Their son Luke was born shortly after Armstrong won the Tour de France. But the happy father claims that he will not push his son to become a bicycle racer. "He can do whatever he wants to do in his life — whether it's ride a bike, play the trumpet, whatever," he noted. "As long as he does his best." The Armstrong family spends part of the year in a 4,300-square-foot house overlooking Lake Austin in Austin, Texas. They also have a home in Nice, France, where they live when Lance is training and racing in Europe.

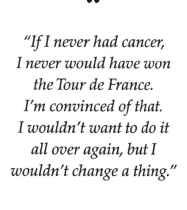

"If I never had cancer, I never would have won the Tour de France. I'm convinced of that. I wouldn't want to do it all over again, but I wouldn't change a thing."

HOBBIES AND OTHER INTERESTS

When Armstrong took a year off from cycling competition in 1997, he had time to enjoy waterskiing, fishing, golf, and gardening. He has always been a music fan, and he also went on tour with the rock band the Wallflowers during this time.

Shortly after being diagnosed with cancer in 1996, Armstrong created the Lance Armstrong Foundation to support cancer research and help victims of cancer. "Had I been more aware of my symptoms, I believe I would have seen a doctor before my condition advanced to this stage," he explained at that time. "I want to take this opportunity to help others who might someday suffer from the same circumstances I face today." To date, the Foundation has raised approximately $3.5 million in donations.

WRITINGS

It's Not about the Bike: My Journey Back to Life, 2000 (with Sally Jenkins)
The Lance Armstrong Performance Program: Seven Weeks to the Perfect Ride—
The Training, Strengthening, and Eating Plan Behind the World's Greatest
Cycling Victory, 2000 (with Chris Carmichael)

HONORS AND AWARDS

U.S. Amateur Champion: 1991
U.S. Olympic Team: 1992, 1996
World Champion: 1993
U.S. National Champion: 1993
Thrifty Drug Triple Crown Winner: 1993
Tour DuPont Winner: 1995, 1996
San Sebastian Classic Winner: 1995, 1996
Cyclist of the Year (*Velonews*): 1995
ARETE Award for Courage in Sports: 1999
Tour de France Winner: 1999, 2000
ESPY Award for Comeback Athlete of the Year: 2000

FURTHER READING

Books

Armstrong, Lance, and Sally Jenkins. *It's Not about the Bike: My Journey Back to Life*, 2000

Periodicals

Bicycling, May 1993, p.59; July 1997, p.86; Jan/Feb. 1998, p.52; May 1998, p.21; Aug. 1998, p.24; Oct. 1999, p.38; Nov. 1999, p.46
Boys' Life, July 1989, p.11; Apr. 1995, p.6
Current Biography Yearbook 1997
Life, Jan. 1, 2000, p.76
New York Times, July 14, 1999, p.C27; July 16, 1999, p.C19; July 25, 1999, sec. Sports, p.23; July 26, 1999, p.D1; July 23, 2000, sec. 8, p.1; July 24, 2000, p.D1; July 25, 2000, p.D4; July 27, 2000, p.D1
Newsweek, July 26, 1999, p.72
Outside, July 1994, p.48; Apr. 1998, p.82
People, Oct. 28, 1996, p.56; Aug. 9, 1999, p.62; Nov. 1, 1999, p.78; Aug. 7, 2000, p.62
Redbook, May 2000, p.119

Sports Illustrated, May 24, 1993, p.50; July 4, 1994, p.52; July 31, 1995, p.34;
   May 20, 1996, p.48; Aug. 9, 1999, p.68; July 24, 2000, p.40
Sports Illustrated for Kids, July 1999, p.54
Time, July 26, 1999, p.66; July 24, 2000, p.60
USA Weekend, Dec. 10, 1999, p.8

ADDRESS

Capital Sports Ventures
1404 West 13th Street
Austin, TX 78703

E-mail: lance@laf.org

WORLD WIDE WEB SITES

http://lancearmstrong.com
http://www.laf.org

BACKSTREET BOYS

Nick Carter 1980-
Howie Dorough 1973-
Brian Littrell 1975-
A.J. McLean 1978-
Kevin Richardson 1972-

American Singers

EARLY YEARS

The popular singing group Backstreet Boys includes five members: Nicholas Gene Carter (Nick), Howard Dwaine Dorough

(Howie D.), Brian Thomas Littrell (Brian or B-Rok), Alexander James McLean (A.J.), and Kevin Scott Richardson (Kev).

Despite how close they are today, the five members of the Backstreet Boys all grew up separately. Most of them didn't know each other until 1993, when they formed the band. Only Brian and Kevin, who are cousins, knew each other before that. Although they couldn't have known it at the time, each of them was preparing for the fame and success that they enjoy today.

Nick

Nick was born on January 28, 1980, in Jamestown, New York. When he was young, his parents, Bob and Jane Carter, helped his grandmother run a restaurant there called the Yankee Rebel. They lived in an apartment upstairs with Nick and his younger sister Bobbie Jean (BJ). When Nick was about five or six, they decided to move to Florida, to get away from the cold and snow. They settled in Ruskin, just outside Tampa Bay, and soon there were three more kids, Lesley and the twins, Aaron and Angel.

Nick grew up to be a real ham. He was always singing, dancing, or acting out parts from movies that he'd seen. At first, his parents assumed it was a phase. But Nick was so determined that his parents signed him up for singing lessons. He was good! He got a part in a school production of *Phantom of the Opera*, then a job singing at the Tampa Bay Buccaneers football games, then some jobs in commercials. Then he started going on all kinds of auditions. By the age of 12, he was working with Nickelodeon and the Disney channel. Nick was only 13 when he joined the Backstreet Boys, so he finished up his high school degree with tutors while he was on the road touring with the band.

Howie

Howie was born on August 22, 1973, in Orlando, Florida. Growing up there, he lived with his parents, Hoke, a police officer of Irish descent, and Paula, a homemaker from Puerto Rico. The baby of the family, Howie has four older siblings—Angela, Caroline, Pollyanna, and Johnny. In fact, Howie is ten years younger than his brother, the sibling to whom he's nearest in age. Despite the big age difference, he is very close to his siblings.

Howie started singing when he was very young. When he was just three, the family was visiting his grandmother when he jumped up on her bed and started belting out the song "Baby Face." Howie was such a natural performer as a young child that his parents wondered if they should help

———— " ————

"We'd go to local labels and sing a capella in their foyers,"Howie recalls. "We'd sing anywhere, for anybody."

———— " ————

him get started as an entertainer, like they had with his older sister Pollyanna, who was an actress and a singer. But they decided to wait a while, to let him have a normal childhood until he was older. Still, Pollyanna took him along when she auditioned for a part in a musical production of *The Wizard of Oz*. She got the role of Glinda the Good Witch—and Howie got a role too, as a munchkin. That was just the first of many such parts. By the age of 12, he had appeared in over 20 productions, including *The Sound of Music, Camelot, Showboat,* and many others. When he was 12, he also began taking lessons in singing and dancing, trying to get the experience he needed.

Howie was trying to break into the entertainment field at a great time. A lot of opportunities for young entertainers in Orlando were created when first Nickelodeon, and then Disney, MGM, and Universal, all opened up studios in the area. Howie did lots of auditions and talents shows, and he won several small parts. But for several years, those small parts didn't really lead to anything. Howie was cast in the pilot of a Nick series called "Welcome Freshmen," but that didn't pan out. He also won small roles in the movies *Parenthood* with Steve Martin and in *Cop and a Half* with Burt Reynolds. By that point he'd finished high school and started taking classes at a local community college. But he always made sure he had enough time to attend all the local auditions, still trying to make his break into the entertainment world. In fact, it was at one of those auditions that the Backstreet Boys first began.

Brian

Brian was born on February 20, 1975, in Lexington, Kentucky, where he lived with his parents and his older brother, Harold III. His father, Harold Jr., worked for IBM, and his mother, Jackie, volunteered for her church. Jackie Littrell is the sister of Ann Richardson, Kevin's mother. His parents didn't know it, but Brian was born with a serious heart condition—he was born with a heart murmur and with a hole in his heart. When he was just five years old, he developed a bacterial infection and started to get very sick. He ended up in the hospital with a temperature of 107 degrees. He was so sick, in fact, that the doctors told his parents to prepare for the worst—they didn't expect him to live through it. But luckily Brian recovered.

One thing that helped them all through their ordeal was their faith. The Littrell family was very active in the Baptist church. They went to services each Sunday, where Brian joined the children's chorus. He sang his first solo before almost 1,500 people when he was just about seven years old. He was certainly nervous, but he also discovered that he liked the attention. He also performed at other churches, at revivals, and at tent meetings. Although he liked to sing, he didn't really think he was that great and he never considered trying to make it his career. But in high school, he performed at one talent show, and the female students screamed so much that he couldn't even hear himself sing. Singing was definitely his favorite activity — except, perhaps, for basketball.

Brian used to see his cousin Kevin often. Their families were close, and they visited a lot. Kevin is a couple of years older than Brian, so Kevin liked to hang out with Brian's older brother, Harold. Still, Brian and Kevin liked to sing together — they liked the way their voices sounded in harmony. So it was no surprise that Kevin thought of him when they were forming BSB. Brian was still in his senior year in high school when he got the call from Kevin.

A.J.

A.J. was born on January 9, 1978, in West Palm Beach, Florida. His parents — Robert, who worked with computers for IBM, and Denise, who worked at a hotel — divorced when he was about four. He was raised by his mother, and he really hasn't maintained contact with his father since then. Although A.J. was an only child, he comes from a large, extended, supportive family.

When A.J. was young, he and his parents lived in West Palm Beach. There, he became involved in entertainment while very young. He was just five when he started modeling for the J.C. Penneys' catalog. Shortly after that he had his first theatrical role, playing Dopey in *Snow White and the Seven Dwarves*. He had a great time in the show, even though he didn't speak a word. He went on to appear in about 20 other local theater productions, including *The King and I*, *Fiddler on the Roof*, and *The Nutcracker*. He liked all sorts of en-

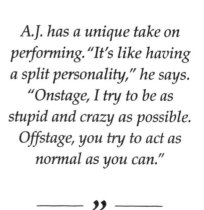

A.J. has a unique take on performing. "It's like having a split personality," he says. "Onstage, I try to be as stupid and crazy as possible. Offstage, you try to act as normal as you can."

tertaining, even puppetry, which he learned after his mother bought him a puppet.

By the time he was 12, his mother felt like they had exhausted the choices in West Palm Beach. There would be so many more opportunities for A.J. in Orlando—the studios at Nickelodeon, Disney, MGM, and Universal, plus a performing arts school where he could take classes in singing, acting, tap, jazz, ballet, and hip-hop dance. So he and his mother moved to Orlando when he was 12. He started making the rounds of auditions, winning small parts on the Nick series "Hi Honey, I'm Home," "Welcome Freshman," and "Fifteen." A.J. hooked up with the other members of Backstreet Boys when he was 15 and still in high school. At the time, he never expected to make it as a singer; he was always much more interested in acting and dance. But he certainly has no regrets about the way things turned out.

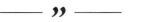

"Everybody is not going to like our music," Kevin recognizes. "Everyone is not going to like us. The main thing for us is we just want people to know that everything they hear on the album is real. It's us. It's our voices singing."

Kevin

Kevin was born on October 3, 1972, in Lexington, Kentucky. He spent his early childhood in a modern log cabin on a 10-acre farm near there. He was the youngest of three kids born to Ann, a homemaker (and the sister of Brian's mother, Jackie), and Jerald, who tried several different jobs, including fireman, pharmaceutical salesman, construction worker, and summer camp director. Kevin's older brothers are Jerald Jr. and Tim. Early on, Kevin developed a love of reading that has continued to this day, and he always takes books with him on tour. Growing up, he was especially close to Tim, and the two of them enjoyed playing football and baseball together. He also spent time helping out around the farm, playing in the woods, and riding horses and dirt bikes. When Kevin was about eight, his family moved to a small town in the Appalachian Mountains where his father ran a summer camp and retreat. During the school year, he and his brothers would ride the bus into town for school. His life would be filled with sports and friends from school. But when summer came, he would hang out with the kids at camp. Each year, he'd fall in love with one of the girls and then get his heart broken when she would leave at the end of the summer. Still, Kevin has said that he had a great childhood.

Backstreet Boys, from left to right—A.J., Nick, Brian, Kevin, and Howie

Music was always part of his family life—on the radio, at church, in the car. His mother was famous locally for her beautiful voice, which she showcased at church each Sunday. Kevin enjoyed singing at church, too, and he also learned to play piano and keyboards. In high school, he was singing in restaurants to provide background music for the diners. He was also a talented dancer—so talented, in fact, that a local dance studio offered him a job as a dance instructor. By the end of high school, it was time to make a decision. He thought about becoming a pilot, and even talked to an Air Force recruiter. But ultimately he decided to stick with music.

There wasn't much he wanted to do musically in Lexington, so Kevin knew he'd have to move to pursue his dream. He settled on Orlando, Florida. Because the theme parks there hire so many young singers and dancers, it's become a great way for young entertainers to break into the business. He got a job at Disney's Epcot Center, and things were going well for a while. Then his father was diagnosed with colon cancer in 1990. Kevin was devastated, and he moved back to Kentucky to be near his family. His father struggled with the illness and died in 1991, at the age of 49. It was very hard on all the family. Later that year, Kevin returned to Orlando and Disney World. He worked as a Teenage Mutant Ninja Turtle for a while, and then switched to performing as Aladdin. Then in 1993, he heard about this group of guys who were looking for another singer — and that's when it all began.

FORMING THE BACKSTREET BOYS

The Backstreet Boys got together in 1993 in Orlando, Florida. It started out like this. Howie and A.J. first met through their singing coach, because they had both taken lessons from the same teacher. After that, Howie, who was 20, and A.J., who was 15, kept noticing each other — they always ended up at the same auditions, trying out for the same jobs. First they started talking, and then they started singing together while they were waiting to audition, just to pass the time. Soon they were joined by another familiar face from the local audition scene, Nick, who was just 13 at the time.

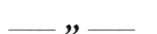

"[There's] a point in the show," Brian says, "it doesn't matter how loud the audience is, but you can hear a pin drop on stage because you're in such a world. You're focused. You don't think about the lyrics or what's going on onstage. You just glance out into the audience and the lights go out and the lighters or those little glow sticks come on. It's just such a sense of fulfillment inside."

The trio went around to local record labels, trying to get someone interested in their sound. "We'd go to local labels and sing a capella in their foyers," Howie recalls. "We'd sing anywhere, for anybody." At first, though, nobody was interested. Then they heard about a new management team called Transcontinental Records that was just getting started. They was looking for new talent, so the guys made an appointment. The owner, Louis J. Pearlman, liked what he heard and thought they had potential. But he also thought they needed a fuller sound — perhaps two more voices to fill it out. From all their time doing auditions in Orlando, they knew plenty of singers. So they picked two guys to join the group. But the group's new lineup lasted just a short time — the two new guys weren't happy with the material, and they quit.

So they were back down to three. But that quickly changed. A friend of Lou's knew of a talented singer who was working at Disney World. It was Kevin, who was then 21. The friend told Kevin about this new vocal group just getting together. He came down and sang with them, and they meshed perfectly. They called themselves the Backstreet Boys, after an outdoor flea market in Orlando called Backstreet Market where kids used to hang out. For a while, they thought about keeping the group at four. But they still thought they needed one more voice to fill out their sound. They auditioned some singers, but no one seemed to mesh with the group. Then Kevin thought of his cousin Brian in Kentucky — he'd heard through his family about Brian's experiences with screaming girls at his school talent show, so he thought Brian might be a great asset to the group. Of course, Brian was just 18 and still in high school, so Kevin talked to his parents first. When they gave the OK, he called Brian at his high school and got him pulled out of his U.S. history class to tell him about the audition. Brian was on a plane to Orlando first thing the next morning. As soon as he sang for the other guys, it was clear—the Backstreet Boys were complete.

CAREER HIGHLIGHTS

Getting Started

The Backstreet Boys started working with Transcontinental Records. The managers there also recruited Donna and Johnny Wright, who had worked with New Kids on the Block. They thought that the fastest route to a record deal was to help them get a lot of experience and exposure. So the group started doing shows wherever they could get booked, at theme parks, parties, and schools. The Backstreet Boys soon began to find their own distinctive sound, with strong harmonies and a blend of pop and R & B. They did a lot of cover tunes, doing new versions of old favorites, and worked on their moves, with A.J. helping out with choreography. And gradually they got more and more live bookings, around the south and then on the east coast, as they built up a strong base of devoted fans.

Within a few months they started thinking about recording. They were having great success as a live act, but the best way to reach a lot of new fans is through records. They put out a single called "Tell me That I'm Dreaming"on their management's independent label, Transcontinental Records, hoping to attract interest from a major label. Mercury Records signed the group, but let the contract lapse without ever bringing the band into the studio to record. Then Donna Wright had a stroke of imagination. Even back then the group was just phenomenal live, and their audiences went absolutely wild for them. She was sure that the group would be signed to a contract immediately if she could just get a recording company executive to come to a show and see and hear the reaction

of the fans. Yet she hadn't been able to get anyone to come to a show. So she did the next best thing. During a concert, when the audience was screaming all around her, she called an executive at Jive records on her cell phone. She let him experience the pandemonium and excitement of a Backstreet Boys concert by recording it on his answering machine. Soon, Jive Records signed them to a recording contract.

International Success

In many ways, it was a tough time in the U.S. for a band like the Backstreet Boys to get started, since the popular music at that time was alternative, grunge, and gangsta rap. The Backstreet Boys just didn't fit those sounds. In 1995 they released a single, "We've Got It Goin' On," but it didn't get much air play in the U.S.

Things were different in Europe, though, where their type of sound was much more popular. In 1995, they were voted Newcomers of the Year by the British music magazine *Smash Hits*. Their success overseas continued in 1996 as their first single was re-released there, soon followed by "I'll Never Break Your Heart," which they performed on British TV's "Top of the Pops." They were voted the No. 1 International Group in Germany, and their singles were hits in Germany, Austria, and soon Canada as well. In the spring they released *Backstreet Boys* (1996), their first full-length CD, in Europe and Canada, and by summer they were headlining a 57-date tour. By fall, Backstreet mania had swept through Australia and Asia as well. By the end of 1996, they had earned the MTV Europe Viewers Choice Award and had sold almost 10 million records world-wide. Not a bad start for the band!

Success in the U.S.

By the end of 1996, the Backstreet Boys were a certified smash through-out Europe. They couldn't walk down a street in Germany or England without being mobbed by fans. But when they returned to Orlando in early 1997, they were virtually un-known in the U.S. "It was weird," Nick said, "because we'd play shows to, like, 10,000 fans in Europe, then we'd come back home and walk down the street and no one would recognize us. It was a very humbling experience." They were determined to change that. They spent the begin-ning of 1997 working on their U.S. debut album, then followed that up by recording their second European album, *Backstreet's Back* (1997). They spent some time during the summer doing concerts in Europe and Can-ada, with occasional appearances on American TV.

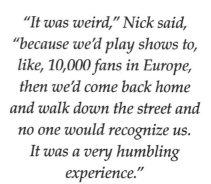

"It was weird," Nick said, "because we'd play shows to, like, 10,000 fans in Europe, then we'd come back home and walk down the street and no one would recognize us. It was a very humbling experience."

By 1997 they were ready to launch their attack on the U.S. Earlier in the year, they'd put out a single, "Quit Playing Games (With My Heart)," with a video that generated a lot of U.S. interest. Their management came up with all kinds of promotional ideas, like distributing the single free with teen romance books and in makeup cases. They also had videos playing in the teen departments of major department stores. And they arranged for a press onslaught, with feature stories about BSB appearing in fan magazines like *16*, *Tiger Beat*, and *Teen Machine*. Their first U.S. release, *Backstreet Boys* (1997), included some of the best tracks from the original European releases, plus several new cuts. The CD quickly produced a bunch of top hits, including "Quit Playing Games (with My Heart)," "As Long As You Love Me," "Everybody (Backstreet's Back)," "I'll Never Break

Your Heart," and "All I Have to Give." It went on to sell 27 million copies — a big success in anybody's book.

But it took a while for that success to build. They toured almost constantly throughout 1997 and 1998 to continue to build their fan base. Some groups make a big splash on the music scene with a hit record and then disappear just as fast. The Backstreet Boys didn't want that to be their fate — they wanted to build a career that would last a long time. "Slowly but surely we're building a nice big fan base," Kevin said. The goal, he explained, is to "build it slowly and create a good foundation and build something that's going to be here for a long time." Their strategy seemed to work. In 1998 they were nominated for a Best New Artist Grammy Award, were named one of the Best Entertainers of 1998 by *Entertainment Weekly*, and were named one of the 25 Most Intriguing People of the Year by *People* magazine.

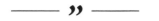

"Personally, we've been through a lot this last year," Howie said about 1998, *"with Brian going through heart surgery and a couple of us having deaths within our families. And even though we've had our most success within this last year, I think that because it has been such a trying year for us, it has helped us grow stronger as a group. We're stronger now than ever and we all have each other's backs."*

Difficulties along the Way

Although 1998 was a year filled with professional highlights, the band endured personal turmoil. Several members dealt with the death of a loved one. And Brian Littrell faced a recurrence of the heart problems from his childhood. He knew that someday he might have to undergo surgery to correct the hole in his heart, and he checked in with his heart doctor each year for a complete examination. But he was always in good physical condition, able to keep up with the band's demanding schedule and difficult choreography and still enjoy pick-up basketball games. That changed in 1998, when he started to feel tired all the time. He went in for his annual checkup, and his doctors discovered that his heart was enlarged — a sign that the problem was getting worse. They recommended that he take time out from his grueling schedule to have surgery and get the problem repaired. Nick, his best friend, tried to stay upbeat, but he was really scared about it. "I couldn't picture life without him," Nick said. "Thank God everything turned out the way it did." Brian had successful open-heart surgery in May 1998. He took eight weeks off to recuperate, and by July he was back on stage and on tour. But he had paramedics standing offstage with oxygen, just in case.

The experience shook up the whole band. "It was just a wake-up call to make you appreciate every day what you have and not take things for granted," said his cousin Kevin. But Howie found a positive side to all this trauma. "Personally, we've been through a lot this last year, with Brian going through heart surgery and a couple of us having deaths within our families. And even though we've had our most success within this last year, I think that because it has been such a trying year for us, it has helped us grow stronger as a group. We're stronger now than ever and we all have each other's backs."

Another difficult issue for the group involved money. In 1998, they filed a lawsuit against Louis J. Pearlman, the founder of Transcontinental Records; Donna and Johnny Wright, the group's managers; and others. In the lawsuit, they called themselves "indentured servants" and accused Pearlman of keeping $10 million while they had received only $300,000 to split among the five of them. Even though they had sold over 27 million records by that point, the money had been split up among their managers and the record label, and the members of the group had received very little of it. They eventually settled their lawsuit with Pearlman, but they no longer work with the Wrights. In late 1999, the Backstreet Boys renegotiated their contract with Jive Records to the tune of about $60 million. They got a five-record deal with "superstar" royalty rates of 20%, among the highest in the music business.

Millennium

The Backstreet Boys continued to build on their success with their next CD, *Millennium*. On the album, according to Kevin, "We were just trying to make good music that not only we loved to sing and perform but that our fans would like. We feel like we've grown on this album; it's deeper lyrically, but it's not over our young fans' heads. We're just trying to evolve with the times, to stay in the pop music scene." They may have also felt that they had something to prove. Not all listeners and music critics took the group seriously. Their success with their first album had led to a resurgence of male pop bands. The Backstreet Boys were constantly compared to these new bands and to other male singing groups. But some of these teen idols were not talented musicians; instead, they were mere fronts who just looked good for the fans. The Backstreet Boys are not that type of group, Kevin is adamant in explaining. "Everybody is not going to like our music. Everyone is not going to like us. The main thing for us is we just want people to know that everything they hear on the album is real. It's us. It's our voices singing." As Steve Dougherty wrote in a *People* magazine review of *Millennium,* "[The Backstreet Boys] possess distinctive voices, and here, as in their concerts, they are adept at vocal interplay, creating harmonic magic as those voices soar and intertwine. They could make a Sears catalog sound sweet."

Released in June 1999, *Millennium* hit No. 1 on the charts and sold over one million copies in its first week out, topping all previous records. By December 1999, it had sold seven million copies in the U.S. alone, and the album was holding its place in the Top 10. Record sales for the album were supported by a nationwide concert tour late in the year. For that tour, tickets went on sale on August 14, 1999, for all 53 shows on the tour. And the whole thing sold out immediately— more than 750,000 tickets were sold for 53 shows in about an hour, for a total box office take of $30 million. The CD has already produced several hit singles, including "I Want It That Way" and "Larger Than Life."

—————— " ——————

As Nick says about the live shows, "All the songs are fun to do. When you do the up-tempo stuff, you get a chance to move around, but with the ballads it's a time to be more intimate with the audience."

—————— " ——————

Live shows account for a big part of the Backstreet Boys' success. The format for the *Millennium* tour is "in the round," with the stage set in the middle of the audience and the fans all around. It allows the fans to get a closer look at the band. In addition to the music, their shows include special effects, lighting, lots of costume changes, and choreography—all the ingredients of an exciting show. Their smoothly blended harmonies keep the girls screaming. Their inventive dance routines are an especially big hit with their fans. Another highlight of each concert is when they bring a member of the audience up on stage to sing just to her. During "The Perfect Fan," they bring up girls with their mothers to sing to them both. Their shows always include solo sets, when each member has a chance to showcase his own singing talents. Their shows also feature a mix of tempos, both slow songs and dance tunes. But the group enjoys them all, as Nick says. "All the songs are fun to do. When you do the up-tempo stuff, you get a chance to move around, but with the ballads it's a time to be more intimate with the audience." Of course, A.J. has a different take on performing. "It's like having a split personality," he says. "Onstage,

I try to be as stupid and crazy as possible. Offstage, you try to act as normal as you can." For Brian, the time spent on stage is what makes it all worthwhile. "I can be on stage in front of thousands of people and there's a point in the show — it doesn't matter how loud the audience is, but you can hear a pin drop on stage because you're in such a world. You're focused. You don't think about the lyrics or what's going on onstage. You just glance out into the audience and the lights go out and the lighters or those little glow sticks come on. It's just such a sense of fulfillment inside."

Support of the Fans

The Backstreet Boys genuinely appreciate their fans, and they are always quick to thank them for their support. They like to meet the fans, sign autographs, and pose for pictures. As A.J. says, "What five guys wouldn't want that kind of attention from girls?"

Many of their parents have become celebrities in their hometowns. A lot of fans have stopped in Kentucky to look for Brian's family home, for example, and Nick's family home in Florida became a stop for tourists also. They were having 30 people a day come by, and fans were picking flowers and even stealing toys and sporting equipment out of the yard until Nick's dad put up a fence. "We were performing, and one girl was holding this big poster," Kevin recalled. "It's a picture of Nick's house and it said, 'I was there!' It's amazing they can track us down like that. There was a fan letter to the whole group with pictures of girls sitting on my car, Brian's car, and standing in front of Nick's house. I found out on the Internet that there's a map to my mother's house in Kentucky!"

"It gets a little crazy out there," Kevin admits. "We're very fortunate. We have a lot of very dedicated fans all over the world, and sometimes they can be a little fanatic, chasing after the bus and being there at the hotels when we pull in." Sometimes it does get a little intense, and some of the fans take things too far. For example, the members of the band often have to move when fans find out where they live. Kevin had spent two years remodeling his home near Orlando, decorating it with deep colors and lots of wood. His favorite spot is a couple of benches out by the pool. He loves it there, but he feels like he has to leave now because he has been discovered. Nick has already had to move once, too, and has had to get his phone number changed numerous times when fans track down his unlisted number and start calling him.

> ——— " ———
>
> *According to Kevin, "We were just trying to make good music that not only we loved to sing and perform but that our fans would like. We feel like we've grown on this album; it's deeper lyrically, but it's not over our young fans' heads. We're just trying to evolve with the times, to stay in the pop music scene."*
>
> ——— " ———

HOME AND FAMILY LIFE

All the members of the Backstreet Boys live in Florida in the Orlando area, and they are all unmarried. At different times members of the group have admitted to having a girlfriend, but none have yet gone public with those relationships.

The members of the Backstreet Boys spend a lot of time together. They've become very close friends over the years, with many similar interests. They all like to play basketball, listen to music, and see movies. But they also have individual hobbies as well. Nick likes to go boating, scuba diving, and fishing; he also likes to draw, collect football cards, and play video games. Howie likes to do weightlifting, water skiing, swimming, surfing, and racquetball, and he also likes to go out dancing at clubs.

Brian enjoys weightlifting, water skiing, golf, and shopping. A.J. enjoys shooting pool, shopping, writing music and poetry, drawing cartoons, playing guitar, bowling, and playing golf, and he likes to go out dancing as well. And Kevin likes playing keyboards, water skiing, swimming, surfing, hockey, and shopping; along with Howie and A.J., Kevin also likes to hit the clubs at night.

RECORDINGS

Backstreet Boys, 1996 (European release)
Backstreet's Back, 1997 (European release)
Backstreet Boys, 1997 (US release)
Millennium, 1999 (US and European release)

FURTHER READING

Books

Alison, Lauren. *Backstreet Boys: Backstage Pass*, 1998
Billboard. *Backstreet Boys: The Unofficial Book*, 1998
Golden, Anna Louise. *Backstreet Boys: They've Got It Goin' On!* 1998
Nichols, Angie. *Backstreet Boys Confidential*, 1998
Rifkin, Sherri. *Given' It Their All: The Backstreet Boys' Rise to the Top*, 1998

Periodicals

Entertainment Weekly, Aug. 15, 1997, p.72; Sep. 4, 1998, p.24
People, Sep. 14, 1998, p.238
Rolling Stone, May 27, 1999, p.42
Teen, Feb. 1998, p.61; Sep. 1998, p.84; July 1999, p.62
Teen People, Aug. 1998, p.58
YM, Dec. 1999/Jan. 2000, p.68

ADDRESS

Jive Records
137-139 West 25th Street
New York, NY 10001

WORLD WIDE WEB SITES

http://www.backstreetboys.com
http://www.bboys.com

OBITUARY

Daisy Bates 1914?-1999

American Civil Rights Leader and Journalist
Led the Fight to Integrate Central High School in
Arkansas

BIRTH

Daisy Bates was born Daisy Lee Gatson in Huttig, Arkansas.
Some of the information about her early life is unavailable or
inconsistent, including the exact date of her birth. Bates herself said that she was born in 1922, but recent sources indicate
that she was probably born on November 10 or November 11,
1914. She grew up with foster parents, Orlee and Susie Smith.

YOUTH

Daisy grew up in a loving and close family. They lived in southern Arkansas, in the small sawmill town of Huttig. The owners of the mill owned pretty much the whole town. Everybody worked at the mill, lived in houses owned by the mill, and shopped at the general store owned by the mill. In fact, mill workers, including Daisy's father, were paid in coupons rather than cash, which they could spend only at the mill's general store. Daisy's family and other African-Americans lived in narrow shotgun houses, so-called because you could stand in the front and look straight through to the back—in theory, you could shoot a gun straight through them.

Daisy grew up in a time and place of deeply entrenched segregation and racial hatred. In 1896, the U.S. Supreme Court had decided in a case called *Plessy* v. *Ferguson* that racial segregation was legal under the Constitution. It paved the way for a series of "Jim Crow"laws, which formed the basis of widespread segregation in the south for over 50 years. (The name "Jim Crow" originally came from an African-American character in a popular song.) *Plessy* v. *Ferguson* established the policy of "separate but equal" public facilities—housing, transportation, schools, restaurants, bathrooms, drinking fountains, and

"[My] life now had a secret goal—to find the men who had done this horrible thing to my mother. So happy once, now I was like a little sapling which, after a violent storm, puts out only gnarled and twisted branches."

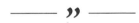

more—for blacks and whites. Although these separate facilities were called equal, in reality those for blacks were miserably inadequate. This was the environment in which Daisy grew up.

Yet when she was very young, Daisy wasn't aware of racial issues. Still, she knew the town was divided. In Huttig, blacks lived in one neighborhood, with rundown houses stained red from the local red dust, and a rundown school made out of wood. Whites lived in another neighborhood, in freshly painted white houses with beautiful green lawns and a new brick school building. As she said, "As I grew up in Huttig, I learned the difference between the races was symbolized by the color of the buildings. Everything in the Negro community was painted a dull, drab red and everything in the white community was white." But that's really all she knew about racial issues, because her parents, like many African-American parents at that time, shielded her from racial abuse and humiliation for as long as they could.

Learning about Racism

Daisy learned the reality of living in a racist society when she was only about seven or eight. Her mother wasn't feeling well one day, so she sent young Daisy to the market to buy meat for dinner. She gave Daisy $1.00 to buy center-cut pork chops, a lean and meaty cut. When Daisy got to the market, there were several white people there. She patiently waited for her turn, until the butcher started waiting on people who came in after her. That's when Daisy spoke up, asking for her turn to be served. The butcher waited until he had served everyone else, wrapped up a package of fatty chops, and pushed the package at her. "Niggers have to wait 'til I wait on the white people. Now take your meat and get out of here!" Daisy ran home crying, sure that her parents would go back to the store to confront the butcher. Her dad had to sit her down and explain that he couldn't go to the market because it would cause trouble for the whole family. As Bates said in her memoir, *The Long Shadow of Little Rock* (1962), her daddy had to explain to young Daisy "that a Negro had no rights that a white man respected." Later, Bates would describe this as a turning point in her life.

> "Hate can destroy you, Daisy," her father said. "You should hate the humiliation, hate the insults, hate the discrimination. But try to do something, try to join with other blacks to change all this. Make your hate count for something."

Not long after, she had to confront an even more intimate and painful fact of life. One day she got in a childish squabble with a neighbor boy who was annoying her by pulling her braids. When she threatened to go home, he said, "You always act so uppity. If you knew what happened to your mother, you wouldn't act so stuck up." Daisy responded by saying that there was nothing wrong with her mother. He said, "I'm talking about your *real* mother, the one the white men took out and killed." Daisy didn't want to believe him, but she started thinking about things that she'd heard that hadn't really made sense.

Finally, she talked to her older cousin. He told her that one night when she was a baby, while her father was working at the mill, a man came to the house and told her mother that her father had been hurt. She immediately

This was the scene at Little Rock's Central High School during the 1957 integration crisis. White students jammed around the front door and lined up at the upper windows to watch the nine black students on their way up the long walk.

left with him to go to the mill to see Daisy's father. She didn't come back. Later, they found her body and eventually concluded that three white men had raped and murdered her, although the sheriff's office never tried to figure out who did it. Daisy's father was so upset about his wife's murder that he left his young child with his best friends, Orlee and Susie Smith. Then he left town. The Smiths dearly loved little Daisy, and they just couldn't find the courage to tell her the painful truth about her parents.

Learning the truth deeply affected her. As she later wrote, "[My] life now had a secret goal—to find the men who had done this horrible thing to my mother. So happy once, now I was like a little sapling which, after a violent storm, puts out only gnarled and twisted branches." She soon learned that one of her mother's killers was the town drunk, who spent much of his time outside the local store. She started going by there every day, taunting him with her resemblance to her dead mother, until he finally said, in a low pleading voice, "In the name of God, leave me alone." He died not long after. For a long time afterward, Bates felt a deep rage to-

Members of the Little Rock Nine at Thansgiving dinner at the Bates home.

ward all whites. Years later, when she was a teenager, Bates was able to overcome her deep hatred of white people. As her father lay dying in the hospital, he warned against letting hate rule her life. "Hate can destroy you, Daisy," her father said. "You should hate the humiliation, hate the insults, hate the discrimination. But try to do something, try to join with other blacks to change all this. Make your hate count for something." After that, she learned that she could be friendly with some white people and work with them to fight against discrimination.

EDUCATION

Growing up, Bates attended the local segregated public schools, graduating from high school. Later, she also took classes at Philander Smith College and Shorter College in Little Rock. She studied public speaking, business administration, accounting, and public relations, although she never completed her college degree.

MARRIAGE AND FAMILY

Daisy first met her future husband, Lucius Christopher (L.C.) Bates, when she was still just a teenager. He was working as an insurance agent at the time, and he stopped by her family's home to talk to her father about insurance. Over the next several years he often stopped by the Gatsons' home, and in time the relationship between Daisy and L.C. deepened into love. They married in 1941 and settled in Little Rock, Arkansas. Daisy and L.C. had no children.

Born in Mississippi, L.C. had attended college in Ohio, majoring in journalism. After college he had worked as a reporter on black newspapers first in Colorado and then in Missouri. But many black papers didn't survive during the Great Depression, and he lost his job. He started to sell insurance, and he proved to be very successful at it. But he always wanted to return to his first love, journalism. Soon after his marriage to Daisy, they decided to use their savings to lease the building and equipment of a struggling church paper. In May 1941, they began a statewide weekly African-American newspaper, the *Arkansas State Press*.

CAREER HIGHLIGHTS

Bates's career had two distinct parts. She worked as a journalist and publisher, which helped her become a leader in her community, and she also worked as a civil rights activist. But the two parts complemented each other perfectly, as she used her position as a journalist and community leader to advance her goals as a civil rights activist.

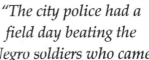

"The city police had a field day beating the Negro soldiers who came into town on weekend passes and who ran afoul of the law."

Speaking Out against Racism

The *Arkansas State Press* got off to a strong start. Circulation numbers grew slowly but steadily, and advertising revenues started to climb as well. Daisy and L.C., along with a small staff, filled the paper with articles on all the daily news in their African-American community, covering the schools, churches, and clubs. But they also used the paper to mount a vocal campaign against racism, injustice, and all acts of discrimination against their people.

The Bateses were not afraid to challenge local authority. In particular, they mounted an ongoing crusade against police brutality toward African-Americans. This became an even greater problem after the start of World War II. The opening of a nearby army processing center, Camp Robinson, brought thousands of soldiers of different races into the area, often with serious results. In Bates's words, "The city police had a field day beating the Negro soldiers who came into town on weekend passes and who ran afoul of the law." When the *Arkansas State Press* printed stories about these incidents, its readers protested against the police brutality. But still, nothing changed.

Then a tragic incident occurred. On a Sunday afternoon in downtown Little Rock in 1942, a black soldier saw one of his buddies being arrested. The soldier went to find out why, and a white city police officer clubbed him with his night stick and then shot him five times. In her newspaper account of the incident, Bates called it "one of the most bestial murders in the annals of Little Rock." The story upset the white community, especially store owners who feared that such publicity would dissuade soldiers from shopping in town, or would even bring about the closing of Camp Robinson. The white community began to put a lot of pressure on the Bateses to back down, and when they refused, all the downtown stores canceled their advertising in the paper. Still, Daisy and L.C. were determined. In order to recoup their loss of income from advertisers, they redoubled their efforts to find new subscribers. Then they launched an intensive campaign against police brutality. Within a few months, they had doubled their number of subscribers. With that, the newspaper expanded the crusade, fighting against slum housing, menial jobs, and legal injustice. It fought for reforms in social and economic conditions throughout black society. Over time, black police officers were added to the force to patrol their community, incidents of police brutality dropped off sharply, and conditions improved overall. "Eventually such a profound change was effected," Bates later wrote, "that Little Rock actually began to gain a reputation as a liberal Southern city."

> "
>
> *In their 1954 decision on* **Brown v. Board of Education,** *the Supreme Court decided that "in the field of public education the doctrine of 'separate but equal' has no place. Separate educational facilities are inherently unequal."*
>
> "

Throughout the rest of the 1940s and the early 1950s, Bates continued to speak out in the *Arkansas State Press* against racism. In particular, she took up the cause of African-American soldiers returning to the U.S. at the end of World War II. Hailed as heroes for serving their country when they returned from the war, they were then treated with hatred and contempt in many parts of the South, including Little Rock. Many of those soldiers became militant in their fight for equal rights, and the *Arkansas State Press*

Six members of the Little Rock Nine, along with Daisy Bates and Thurgood Marshall, sit on the steps outside the Supreme Court in Washington, D.C.

was ready to support them. During this time Bates also became active in many community organizations, forging ties with both blacks and whites throughout Little Rock. She and L.C. had been active in the local branch of the NAACP (National Association for the Advancement of Colored People) since they first moved to Little Rock, and in 1952 she was elected president of the Arkansas State Conference of the NAACP branches.

Brown v. Board of Education

Life in the South, for Bates and other African-Americans, was profoundly changed with the 1954 Supreme Court case *Brown v. Board of Education*. This case pitted the School Board in Topeka, Kansas, against the NAACP and its chief counsel, Thurgood Marshall (see entry on Marshall in *Biography Today*, January 1992, and update in *Biography Today*, 1993 Cumulation).

Arguing before the Supreme Court, Marshall challenged the concept of "separate but equal," arguing that separate education made minority stu-

*Federal paratroopers escort the Little Rock Nine into Central High
on September 25, 1957.*

dents feel inferior. The Court agreed, saying that separate education facilities were not equal and therefore violated the 14th Amendment, which requires that all citizens be treated equally. The Court, therefore, overturned
the concept of separate but equal in the area of education and declared
racial segregation to be unconstitutional. The Court said, "in the field of
public education the doctrine of 'separate but equal' has no place. Separate
educational facilities are inherently unequal." *Brown* v. *Board of Education*
was a pivotal Supreme Court decision that launched the legal movement to
desegregate U.S. society. It also paved the way for the 1957 crisis at Central
High School, which brought Bates to the attention of the world.

Desegregation Plans in Little Rock

Despite the Supreme Court's 1954 ruling, it took a long time for schools to
be integrated. In the South, where outright segregation was widespread,
school districts didn't rush to comply with the Court's decision. Many used
various delaying tactics, including passing segregationist state or local
laws, in an effort to avoid desegregating the schools. The NAACP had to

fight court battles throughout the South to force districts to comply with the Supreme Court's decision. One of the most famous battles took place in Little Rock regarding the integration of Central High School. Central is a huge school—two city blocks long, seven stories high, with acres of playing fields in the back. Considered the best high school in the district, Central had classrooms, science labs, sports facilities, books, and other supplies that were far superior to those at Horace Mann High, the district's high school for blacks.

Soon after the 1954 decision, the Superintendent of the Little Rock schools, Virgil Blossom, drew up a desegregation plan for the city schools, which came to be known as the Blossom plan. It called for a gradual process whereby Central High School would be integrated in September 1957, followed by the other high schools, then the junior highs, then the elementary schools. The whole process would take several years. The plan was accepted by the district school board and then by the federal court. During the period from 1955 through 1957, whites who opposed the plan tried every means to prevent integration of the schools. White extremists denounced the plan at every opportunity, holding public rallies and pushing for legislative action. It was also a period of legal wrangling, as the NAACP tried to force the district to speed up their plan, while the district tried to modify the plan to limit integration. In April 1957, a federal appeals court judge upheld the Blossom plan, decreeing that integration would begin the following September, at the start of the new school year. The legal wrangling continued in August, when a newly formed group called the Mother's League petitioned the court to delay the plan, but Marshall and the NAACP lawyers fought that off as well.

As the Arkansas NAACP president, Bates was involved from the start. She was the liaison among all the different groups—the NAACP, the school board, the reporters, the mayor's office, the police, the children, and the children's families. She was, in effect, the linchpin of the whole effort. Her home became the meeting place for all the planning sessions as NAACP officers and attorneys from out of state came to Little Rock to help plan the attack on segregation. Her home was also where all the national reporters congregated, waiting for news.

The Little Rock Nine

During the spring and summer of 1957, Bates negotiated with the school administration about which African-American students would start at Central. Of the 215 black students who lived within the geographical boundaries for Central High, 17 were selected. Eight students eventually dropped from the group for various reasons, especially because of fear of violence.

By summer 1957, there were nine students prepared to integrate Central High School: Minnijean Brown (later Minnijean Brown Trickey), Elizabeth Eckford, Ernest Green, Thelma Mothershed (later Thelma Mothershed Wair), Melba Pattillo (later Melba Pattillo Beals), Gloria Ray (later Gloria Ray Kalmark), Terrence Roberts, Jefferson Thomas, and Carlotta Walls (later Carlotta Walls LaNier). This group became known as the Little Rock Nine.

The Little Rock Nine was an outstanding group of kids. They all came from homes with strict, hard-working parents who demanded exemplary behavior and superlative school work. All were excellent students who planned to attend college. Many members of the group were already friends, and they quickly became a very close group. If anybody had the moral strength, resolve, and fortitude to face the coming ordeal, it was this group of students. Bates worked closely with them, going along with them to meetings with the school superintendent, the school board, and the NAACP. She supported the students throughout the planning stages to ensure that their rights were protected. They also spent a lot of time at her home, preparing for what might happen at school. They learned how to use nonviolence and passive resistence to deal with hateful incidents like being spit on or shoved or called names.

The Central High School Crisis

Tensions were high in Little Rock as the city prepared for the start of the school year. One hint of the impending violence came in mid-August. One night, Bates was sitting in her living room when something came crashing through the window. Her husband rushed in to find her on the floor, covered in shards of glass but luckily unharmed. They found a large rock in the room with a note attached that said, "Stone this time, dynamite next." The Little Rock Nine and their families also received nonstop death threats.

Despite such tensions, the schools were set to open on September 3, 1957. But the day before, Labor Day, Governor Orval Faubus ordered Arkansas National Guard troops to Central High School. They arrived there in full uniform, with helmets, rifles, and bayonets. They weren't there to keep the peace or to protect the African-American students, though; they were there to prevent the Little Rock Nine from entering Central High. That night, Governor Faubus went on television and said that he had called up the troops because of reports that caravans of cars full of white supremacists were heading to Little Rock. He said that he ordered the troops to surround

Hecklers follow Elizabeth Eckford as she walks in front of the mob outside Central High on September 4, 1957.

Central High "for the protection of life and property." He also said that "blood will run in the streets" if the black students tried to enter Central High.

Plans were made for the children to enter the school on Wednesday, September 4. The night before, Bates stayed up until 3:00 a.m. making arrangements for the following day. She called the parents of the children and arranged for them to meet at her house the next morning. The children would go to school as a group, escorted by black and white ministers from the community. She spoke to all the parents except the Eckfords, because they didn't have a telephone. She meant to go to their home early the next morning, but exhausted from her late night and busy with all the organizational details, she simply forgot.

That next day, September 4, eight of the children arrived at the Bates home. They tried to get to Central, but they turned back because of the mob outside the school. But Elizabeth Eckford arrived alone at school that day. She tried to enter the school, but the National Guard troops kept her out. Throughout her ordeal, she was spit on, taunted, threatened, and accosted by an angry mob of hundreds of white students and adults. The crowd was yelling, "Get her! Lynch her!" Not one member of the National Guard made a move to help her. Eckford managed to escape only because

Elizabeth Eckford is turned away from Central High by the Arkansas National Guard, while a white student is allowed to pass through.

two sympathetic white people — a man and a woman — helped her board a bus. The mob's heinous conduct, and Eckford's dignity, grace, and determination under their assault, were recorded by news photographers. Their coverage brought the situation in Little Rock to the attention of the nation and made Eckford a national heroine.

For the next 16 days, an atmosphere of hysteria and madness gripped Little Rock. Hate-mongers from around the state poured into the city, creating an environment of racial tension and mob violence. Fighting continued in the courts among the various parties — the school district, the NAACP, and the governor. There were talks during this time between Governor Faubus and President Dwight D. Eisenhower. Bates vowed not to let the children return to school until the Guard was removed and demanded that the president guarantee the safety of the students. Her strong stance gained national headlines and made her a national symbol of resistance to injustice. The stalemate came to an end on Friday, September 20, when a federal judge granted an injunction against Governor Faubus, which prevented the National Guard from being used to interfere with public school integration and required the troops at Central High to be withdrawn. With the removal of the National Guard, the city police would be in charge, and the police chief personally assured Bates that the children would be protected.

Integrating Central High

On Monday, September 23, the nine children assembled at the Bates home and drove together to school. The mob outside was frenzied, hysterical, and out of control. The police hurriedly escorted the students into a side entrance, while the mob in front was beating several black reporters; some accounts suggest that the reporters purposely sacrificed themselves to the mob to give the students time to enter the school. The police soon felt that they could no longer protect the students, who were secretly hustled out of the school through a delivery entrance. Mob violence throughout the city quickly became a rampage, as the mob attacked out-of-state reporters, photographers, and any blacks out on the street. Even the Little Rock chief of police called it a "reign of terror."

According to Bates, "Most of the citizens of Little Rock were stunned as they witnessed a savage rebirth of passion and racial hatred that had laid dormant since Reconstruction days. As dusk was falling, tension and fear grew. The mob spread throughout the city, venting its fury on any Negro in sight." That night, Daisy, L.C., several reporters, and others camped out at the Bates home. They stayed up all night in the dark, sitting by the windows, armed with guns, and ready to respond to any attacks. Everybody was expecting trouble, and they figured the Bates home would be the troublemakers' first stop. Sure enough, the police and F.B.I agents intercepted a motorcade of about 100 cars, filled with dynamite, guns, pistols, clubs, and other weapons. The Bateses narrowly escaped death that night.

The Little Rock Nine students considered themselves warriors for integration, as Melba Patillo Beals says here: "I got up every morning, polished my saddle shoes, and went off to war. It was like being a soldier on a battlefield."

The next day, September 24, the students stayed home. That afternoon, President Eisenhower finally acted. He took control of the Arkansas National Guard and ordered the U.S. Secretary of Defense to enforce the integration law. The defense secretary ordered over 1,000 paratroopers from the 101st Airborne Screaming Eagle Division to Little Rock. On September 25, the students again met at the Bateses' home. But this time, they were escorted to school by U.S. soldiers, in an armed convoy. Jeeps rolled up the street, parking at either end of the block. Machine guns were mounted on the tops of the jeeps. Then paratroopers leapt out and charged up to the Bates home. Minnijean Brown spoke for all of them when she said, "It gives you goose bumps to look at them. For the first time in my life, I feel like an American citizen." The students drove to school in an armed convoy. When they arrived at school, they marched up the front steps surrounded by a phalanx of 22 soldiers, all carrying weapons with bayonets. There were U.S. soldiers stationed throughout the school, and a soldier would accompany each black student around the school through-out the day. Once and for all, the Little Rock Nine had integrated Central High School.

> "Most of the citizens of Little Rock were stunned as they witnessed a savage rebirth of passion and racial hatred that had laid dormant since Reconstruction days. As dusk was falling, tension and fear grew. The mob spread throughout the city, venting its fury on any Negro in sight."

Unfortunately, their ordeal wasn't over. There were a few friendly over-tures from white students at the be-ginning of the year, but those quickly stopped. The black students were in the school, the mob outside was dis-persed, but that wasn't the end of the harassment campaign — many white students and their parents were still determined to get the black students out of Central High. The black stu-dents considered themselves warriors for integration, as Melba Patillo Beals says here: "I got up every morning, polished my saddle shoes, and went off to war. It was like being a soldier on a battlefield."

During that first school year, these courageous nine students were beat-en, kicked, spit on, tripped, pushed, and shoved. They were knocked down stairs and shoved into walls. They were the targets of acid, ink, rocks, firecrackers, flaming wads of paper, rot-ten food, raw eggs, scalding water, and urine. They were also burned and lynched in effigy. Even worse was the nonstop stream of hate-filled verbal abuse and psychological terror. And the school administrators did virtually nothing about any of this. They wouldn't take reports from the black stu-dents unless the incident was witnessed by an adult. And even when an adult confirmed their reports, the white students were rarely subjected to any meaningful punishment. The black students practiced peaceful nonvi-olent resistance, and for the most part they didn't respond to their tor-mentors. But occasionally they were provoked beyond tolerance. Minnijean Brown, in particular, was harassed beyond endurance, and she finally responded to several acts of extreme provocation by pouring a bowl

African-American reporter Alex Wilson is kicked by a white segregationist after re-fusing to run from the mob near Central High. He was brutally beaten by the mob that day. Wilson died a few years later from unexplained neurological causes.

of chili over a student's head. Brown was ultimately expelled and spent the remainder of the year attending school in New York City. After that, many of the white students started wearing buttons referring to Brown's departure saying "One Down, Eight to Go." Despite all the harassment, the remainder of the students prevailed and finished the year. And Ernest Green, who was a senior, graduated from Central High in 1958, becoming its first African-American graduate.

But the ordeal still wasn't over. In the words of the *Arkansas Democrat-Gazette*, "The integration of Little Rock's public schools was also under way, but in fact the turmoil here had only begun. It took two more years of intense civic anguish and struggle, fueled by heated emotions over what proponents of segregated schools then called 'race mixing,' before integration on even a token basis took hold here." Before the start of the following school year, Governor Faubus helped pass a state law that gave Little Rock voters the choice of shutting the city's four high schools for the full academic year, or accepting integration of all the Little Rock schools. In September 1958, the residents voted 19,470 to 7,651 in favor of closing the public high schools to prevent integration, and the schools were closed for the 1958-59 school year. That left thousands of students and their families scrambling to find alternatives. Some private all-white schools were set up in the city. But many students, whites and blacks, were forced to leave home, go stay with relatives, and attend school elsewhere in Arkansas or out of state. In August 1959 the federal court intervened and declared the law unconstitutional, and the schools were forced to reopen that fall. Still, intermittent violence continued, things like tear gas bombs and dynamite blasts at several city and school locations, including a dynamite bomb at the Bates home in July 1959. Fortunately, no one was hurt, and their home survived.

> ———— " ————
>
> *President Bill Clinton said that Bates "was a dear friend and a heroine. She was known chiefly as a leader during the crisis of Central High School in 1957 and a mentor to the Little Rock Nine. But she was so much more. . . . Her legacy will live on through the work she did, the friends she made, and the people she touched."*
>
> ———— " ————

Later Years

During and after the Central High School crisis, Daisy and L.C. Bates struggled to continue to publish their newspaper, the *Arkansas State Press*. They lost most of their advertising revenue from local businesses, which refused to buy ads in their paper because of the Bateses' activities in the civil rights struggle. Even advertisers who supported them were forced to pull out after threats from segrega-

tionists. The Bateses had to close the newspaper in 1959. Daisy went to work on her memoir, *The Long Shadow of Little Rock*, published in 1962, while L.C. went to work for the NAACP as a field organizer. In 1963, she was the only woman who spoke at the March on Washington led by Dr. Martin Luther King, where he made his famous "I have a dream" speech. Bates worked in Washington, D.C., for the anti-poverty programs created by Presidents John F. Kennedy and Lyndon B. Johnson. She also worked for the Democratic National Committee, traveling around the country to support voting drives. In 1965 she returned to Little Rock to recover from a stroke.

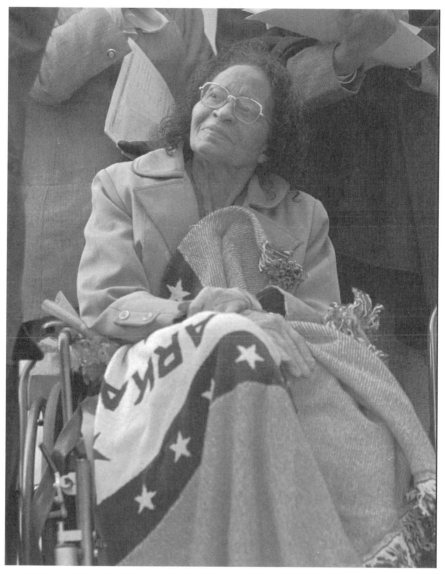

Bates watches the Martin Luther King parade as it makes its way past the Arkansas State Capitol on January 15, 1996.

Back in Arkansas, Bates got involved in voter registration campaigns throughout the state. She also worked as a community development activist in Mitchellville, Arkansas. In 1968 she became the director of the Mitchellville Office of Economic Opportunity (OEO) Self-Help Project. Under her direction, the organization fought for community improvements like new water and sewer systems, paved streets, health care, education, and a community center. According to Bates, "The program gave hope and motivation to people who were on the brink of succumbing to desolation and despair." In 1980, L.C. Bates died at the age of 79. Four years later, Daisy Bates revived the *Arkansas State Press* "as a tribute to my husband, and as a vehicle for positive images and performances for the African-American community in Arkansas." She wanted to revive the paper, she said, to address the pressing political, economic, and social issues in the black community. In 1988, she sold the paper to the managing editor and retired.

Daisy Bates died on November 4, 1999, after suffering a series of strokes and several years of poor health. She was 84. Her body lay in state in the rotunda of the Arkansas State Capitol, just a few feet away from the office where Governor Faubus directed the 1957 conflict. At the time of her death, President Bill Clinton said that Bates "was a dear friend and a heroine. She was known chiefly as a leader during the crisis of Central High School in 1957 and a mentor to the Little Rock Nine. But she was so much more. . . . Her death will leave a vacuum in the civil rights community, the state of Arkansas, and our country. Her legacy will live on through the work she did, the friends she made, and the people she touched."

WRITINGS

The Long Shadow of Little Rock: A Memoir, 1962; reprinted 1988

HONORS AND AWARDS

Springarn Medal (NAACP): 1958
American Black Achievement Award (*Ebony* magazine): 1987
American Book Award: 1988, for *The Long Shadow of Little Rock*

FURTHER READING

Books

African-American Almanac, 8th edition, 2000
Bates, Daisy. *The Long Shadow of Little Rock: A Memoir*, 1962
Beals, Melba Pattillo. *Warriors Don't Cry: A Searing Memoir of the Battle to Integrate Little Rock's Central High*, abridged edition, 1995 (juvenile)
Blossom, Virgil. *It HAS Happened Here*, 1959
Contemporary Authors, Vol. 127, 1989
Huckaby, Elizabeth. *Crisis at Central High: Little Rock, 1957-58*, 1980

Irons, Peter. *The Courage of Their Convictions*, 1988
Levine, Ellen. *Freedom's Children: Young Civil Rights Activists Tell Their Own Stories*, 1993 (juvenile)
Notable Black American Women, 1992
O'Neill, Laurie A. *Little Rock*, 1994 (juvenile)
Who's Who among African-Americans, 1999

Periodicals

Arkansas Democrat-Gazette, Oct. 4, 1997, p.A1; Sep.-Oct. 1997, Special Reprint Section
Crisis, June 1981, p.232
Ebony, Sep. 1958, p.17; Sep. 1984, p.94; Dec. 1997, p.132
Journal of Black Studies, May 1996, p.616
New York Times, Nov. 5, 1999, p.C20; Nov. 10, 1999, p.A16
New York Times Magazine, Jan. 2, 2000, p.44
Washington Post, Mar. 21, 1981, p.C1

WORLD WIDE WEB SITES

http://www.arkstatepress.com/index.htm
http://www.ardemgaz.com/prev/central/index.html
http://www.ardemgaz.com/prev/central/counts.html
http://www.cr.nps.gov/nr/travel/civilrights/
http://www.centralhigh57.org
http://cavern.uark.edu/libinfo/speccoll/bates.html

Harry Blackmun 1908-1999

American Supreme Court Justice
Author of the Controversial Supreme Court Opinion
Roe v. *Wade* That Legalized Abortion

BIRTH

Harry Andrew Blackmun was born on November 12, 1908, in Nashville, Illinois, a small town in the southern part of the state. His parents were Corwin Manning Blackmun, a businessman, and Theo Huegely (Reuter) Blackmun, a homemaker and talented musician who shared her love of music with her two children: Harry and his younger sister Theo, whom they called Betty.

YOUTH

Soon after Harry's birth, the family moved to St. Paul, Minnesota, where he grew up. There, his father held several different jobs over the years: he ran a combination hardware and grocery store, worked as a bank official, and sold insurance. "We lived in a blue-collar neighborhood," Blackmun once recalled. "And we didn't have very much, but nobody complained because everybody was in the same state in our neighborhood. And it didn't do me any harm."

Even as a child, Blackmun was considered diligent, quiet, and hard-working. The members of his family were devout Methodists, and their home was a fairly somber place. Still, his sister once recalled a different side to his personality. "Nothing pleased him more than to make me laugh at church while he sat there looking saintly."

While Blackmun was just in kindergarten, he became close to a neighbor boy, Warren Burger (see entry in *Biography Today*, September 1995). Blackmun and Burger later served together on the Supreme Court. Best friends throughout childhood, they delivered newspapers and played tennis together after school. Years later, Blackmun was the best man at his friend Burger's wedding.

EDUCATION

An exceptional student, Blackmun was considered a bit of a "teacher's pet" during his years in public schools in St. Paul. He excelled in his studies, particularly in math, and won many oratory contests. When he graduated from high school in 1925, he was approached by the Harvard Club of Minnesota, a local group of graduates of the prestigious college. They were looking for a deserving student who might need financial assistance to attend their alma mater. They offered Blackmun a partial scholarship for tuition to attend Harvard College. While a student there, he supplemented that scholarship with his earnings from a variety of odd jobs, working as a janitor, a tutor, a milkman, a painter of handball courts, and an operator of a motor launch for the Harvard crew (rowing team).

At Harvard, Blackmun soon showed an aptitude for logical, rigorous thinking. Elected to Phi Beta Kappa, Blackmun graduated from Harvard summa cum laude (with highest honors), earning a bachelor's degree

———— " ————

> *"If I were to start all over again . . . I would probably study medicine. . . . Medical school was an attraction for me even as late as my last year in law school. But I probably would have failed the basic sciences and would have made a poor physician."*

———— " ————

(A.B.) in mathematics in 1929. Math, Blackmun later said, "is much the same as legal thinking—it teaches you to be precise and logical."

After finishing college, Blackmun decided to continue his studies in graduate school. But he had trouble deciding what to study. He had wanted to be a doctor since childhood, so he hoped to go to medical school. But his father wanted him to go to law school and become a lawyer. His father, in fact, had been so worried about Blackmun's decision to major in math that he had written to the president of Harvard, who had responded that math studies provided a grounding in reason that was ideal for studying law. Ultimately, to keep the family peace, Blackmun enrolled at Harvard Law School. Despite his misgivings about a legal career, Blackmun earned an excellent record there. He graduated from Harvard Law School with his law degree (LL.B.) in 1932.

Blackmun continued to have a strong interest in the field of medicine throughout his career, and he later admitted that he had had second thoughts about that early decision. "If I were to start all over again . . . I would probably study medicine. . . . Medical school was an attraction for me even as late as my last year in law school. But I probably would have failed the basic sciences and would have made a poor physician."

FIRST JOBS

Blackmun finished law school in 1932, during the Great Depression. Jobs were difficult to find, and money was very tight. Yet his successful record at Harvard earned him a coveted spot as a law clerk for Judge John H. Sanborn, who served on the U.S. Court of Appeals, Eighth Circuit. Working as a law clerk, which means serving as an assistant to a judge, is usually a fairly prestigious position. Law clerks write memos to the judge outlining the facts of a case, do research into previous cases whose rulings might apply to the current one, and help work on judicial opinions. Clerking for Judge Sanborn from 1932 to 1933 was Blackmun's first experience working in the federal judicial system, where he would later serve for many years. In fact, about 25 years later, when Sanborn retired, Blackmun was appointed to his seat on the federal bench.

The Role of the Judiciary in the U.S. Government

As set out in the Constitution, the U.S. government is comprised of three branches: the executive branch, the legislative branch, and the judicial branch. Each branch has specific responsibilities. The executive branch includes the president and the vice president. It also includes the Cabinet, a group of presidential advisers who are the heads of federal departments and agencies, including the departments of state, treasury, defense, justice, education, and others. The legislative branch is the Congress, including both the House of Representatives and the Senate. The Congress creates laws, collects taxes, declares war, ratifies treaties, and approves the president's nominations for certain positions, including federal judges. The judicial branch includes the nation's courts.

The federal judicial system, where Blackmun clerked on the appeals court for Judge Sanborn, is comprised of three different levels. The lower courts, the level at which most cases are originally tried, are the 91 District Courts. After a case is tried, if one side disagrees with the decision of the District Court and wants to appeal it, the case would go to the next level, the Court of Appeals. There are 12 Courts of Appeals (also called Circuit Courts) covering the 50 states and the District of Columbia. The appeals (or appellate) court judge reviews the lower court's decision and either sustains it (agrees) or overturns it (disagrees). After that step, the case could be taken to the Supreme Court, the highest court in the land. The decision of the Supreme Court is final. At all three levels in the U.S. judicial system, federal judges are nominated by the president, confirmed by the Senate, and serve for life.

CAREER HIGHLIGHTS

Blackmun spent over 60 years serving in various parts of the U.S. legal system, working all the way up to the Supreme Court. He didn't follow any single judicial or political philosophy, most observers agree, and his views changed a great deal during his lengthy and distinguished career. Though not a great legal scholar, he was widely considered hardworking, meticulous, objective, fair, and intelligent. One of his former clerks, Randall Bezanson, once described him as "a man of moral authority borne of humility; a man of great compassion for the individual; a man who possesses the important qualities of humor and a sense of irony; and, more importantly, a man of true wisdom."

Early Career

After clerking for Judge Sanborn, Blackmun went into private legal practice in Minneapolis. In 1934, he joined the law firm Dorsey, Colman, Barker, Scott & Barber. He worked at the firm, which changed names several times, for a total of 16 years, from 1934 to 1950. He started out there as an associate in 1934, became a junior partner five years later, in 1939, and then became a general partner in 1943. He worked primarily in tax and estate planning, helping people write wills and creating plans to manage their assets after their deaths. In addition, he worked as the firm's representative to one of its clients, the Mayo Clinic, a medical research and treatment center in Rochester, Minnesota. The Mayo Clinic is considered one of the premier medical institutions in the country. While working at the law firm, he also worked as a college instructor, first at the St. Paul College of Law (now known as the William Mitchell College of Law) from 1935 to 1941, and then at the University of Minnesota Law School from 1945 to 1947. It was also during this time that Blackmun was married, to Dorothy (Dottie) Clark; together, they raised three daughters.

In 1950 the Mayo Clinic offered him a position as resident counsel, which he was happy to accept. For Blackmun, this position brought together his two great interests, medicine and law. In fact, he later said, "My ten years at Mayo were the happiest years of my professional experience." Many observers have said that his years at the Mayo Clinic greatly affected his later legal work, making him particularly mindful of medical issues, responsive to the concerns of doctors, and generally strengthening his respect for the medical profession.

Appointment to the Federal Judiciary

In 1959, President Dwight D. Eisenhower appointed Blackmun to the Court of Appeals, Eighth Circuit, to fill the seat vacated by the retiring Judge Sanborn. At the time, Judge Sanborn had this to say about his former clerk: "Harry is the best legal scholar I have ever known. Every opinion . . . is a treatise in itself. He is deliberate, courageous, and moderate. He is the single person who, I believe, would be the ideal appellate judge." Many believe that Blackmun's old friend Warren Burger, who was then an appeals court judge for Washington, D.C., may have suggested Blackmun for the seat.

The Eighth Circuit Court of Appeals covered Arkansas, Iowa, Minnesota, Missouri, Nebraska, North Dakota, and South Dakota. The court met in Saint Louis, Missouri, although Blackmun commuted there from Minnesota, where he and his family continued to live. He served on the court for 11 years, from 1959 until 1970. His opinions there were considered studious, methodical, thoroughly researched, and carefully reasoned. On the circuit court, he developed a reputation as a moderate judge, slightly liberal on civil rights issues but conservative on issues related to civil liberties and defendants' rights. Considered strong on crime, he rejected constitutional challenges to the death penalty and claims by criminal defendants. He was also outspoken in expressing concern about the social turmoil sweeping the country and in criticizing what he considered a growing trend toward permissiveness in American society.

Appointment to the Supreme Court

It was those views that brought Blackmun to the attention of President Richard Nixon in 1970. President Nixon had an opening to fill on the Supreme Court due to the departure of Justice Abe Fortas, who was forced to resign because of reports that he had accepted fees. Nixon then nominated two other judges, both of whom were rejected by the Senate. The president remained determined to appoint a judge with two distinct qualities: he wanted a "law and order" judge who would limit individual liberties and a strict constructionist who would follow a narrow interpretation of the Constitution. For his third candidate, Nixon took the suggestion of Warren Burger, a judicial conservative whom Nixon had recently named Chief Justice to the Supreme Court.

One of his former clerks, Randall Bezanson, once described him as "a man of moral authority borne of humility; a man of great compassion for the individual; a man who possesses the important qualities of humor and a sense of irony; and, more importantly, a man of true wisdom."

Burger suggested his old friend Blackmun. As the president's third choice, Blackmun would from then on wryly refer to himself as "Old No. 3." Reaction to Blackmun's nomination was swift and positive by both conservatives and liberals. He was unanimously confirmed by the Senate on May 12, 1970, and was sworn in on June 9, 1970, as the 98th Justice on the U.S. Supreme Court.

In joining the Supreme Court, Blackmun became one of nine judges — one Chief Justice and eight Associate Justices — on the highest court in the country. The Supreme Court decides whether the laws made by all levels of government — federal, state, and local — follow the Constitution.

Blackman at his confirmation hearing before the Congress, 1970. He is seated between Senators Walter Mondale and Eugene McCarthy of Minnesota.

The Court accomplishes this by interpreting the provisions of the Constitution and applying its rules to specific legal cases. Because the Constitution lays out general rules, the Court tries to determine their meaning and figure out how to apply them to modern situations. After the Justices select a case for review — and they accept fewer than about 100 of the 6,000 cases presented to them each year — they first will hear arguments by the two opposing sides. They begin discussing the case, take a preliminary vote, and then one justice from the majority is assigned to write up the Court's opinion. Drafting an opinion is complex and time-consuming, and the whole process can take over a year. The Court's final opinion has tremendous importance, setting out a precedent that all lower courts and all levels of government throughout the United States are required to follow. The reasoning given in the opinion is also important, because it helps people understand the basis for the decision and how the ruling might apply to other cases in the future.

"The Minnesota Twins"

When Blackmun joined the Court, many observers felt that they knew what to expect. Because of the circumstances of his nomination by President Nixon, and because of his friendship with Burger, they expected him to follow in the footsteps of the Chief Justice. Initially, it seemed that they were right. Blackmun was viewed as a judicial conservative who opposed expanding civil rights or civil liberties and who favored a formal and restrained interpretation of the Constitution. In Blackmun's first term, he voted with Burger in about 90% of the cases, and the next few years saw similar voting patterns. Blackmun and Burger were viewed as ideological twins — in fact, they were called "the Minnesota Twins," and people clearly thought that the junior justice was also the junior twin. Slowly, though, Blackmun began to emerge from his friend's shadow.

In Blackmun's early years on the Court, some of his opinions were considered naive, poorly reasoned, and insensitive. One 1973 case on bankruptcy law, the *United States* v. *Kras*, is often cited to illustrate his early approach. He wrote the majority opinion, which upheld the constitutionality of charging people a fee to declare bankruptcy. He said that a $50 fine for filing bankruptcy was reasonable because poor people could simply save up their weekly movie money to pay for it. Justice Thurgood Marshall wrote a blistering dissent, saying that going to the movies is a luxury for poor people. "It is disgraceful," Marshall wrote, "for an interpretation of the Constitution to be premised upon unfounded assumptions about how people live."

Roe v. Wade

The case that seemed to mark the beginning of an evolution in Blackmun's views was *Roe* v. *Wade*, one of the most pivotal cases ever decided by the Supreme Court. At the center of the case was Norma McCorvey, who was called "Jane Roe" to protect her privacy. McCorvey was a 21-year-old waitress in Texas who was single and pregnant. She wanted to have an abortion, but Texas state law then prohibited abortion except in cases where the woman's life was in danger. At that time, abortion was covered by state laws, rather than federal laws. In most states it was illegal for doctors to perform abortions except in certain limited circumstances, such as rape, incest, or when the woman's life would be endangered by continuing the pregnancy. Some women ended up having illegal "back alley" abortions that often resulted in serious injury or even death. In 1970, McCorvey filed a lawsuit against Henry Wade, who was the District Attorney in Dallas County, Texas, charging that the Texas law was unconstitutional. By spring 1971, the case arrived at the Supreme Court, and it was argued before the Court during the following term. For McCorvey, the decision came too late. The Court took so long to decide the case that, in the meantime, she gave birth and put the baby up for adoption. Years later, McCorvey became an abortion foe.

—— " ——

*The Supreme Court voted
7-2 on* Roe v. Wade, *ruling
that state laws could not
outlaw abortion. Blackmun
was assigned to write the
decision. . . . He determined
that the Constitution
included a "right of privacy
. . . broad enough to encompass a woman's decision
whether or not to terminate
her pregnancy."*

—— " ——

The Supreme Court voted 7-2 on *Roe
v. Wade*, ruling that state laws could
not outlaw abortion. Blackmun was
assigned to write the decision. He la-
bored over it, spending months doing
research into legal and medical history. He even spent two weeks at the library of the Mayo Clinic in Rochester,
Minnesota. Blackmun's written opinion reflected all the research that
went into it. He gave a lengthy dis-
cussion of social, legal, and medical
approaches to abortion, including
those from ancient Greek and Ro-
man times as well as the early
American era when the Constitution
was adopted. He determined that the
Constitution included a "right of privacy . . . broad enough to encompass
a woman's decision whether or not
to terminate her pregnancy." The
"right of privacy" or "zone of privacy,"
where the government had no right to interfere, was the basis on which
he established the right to abortion. States could interfere with this right of
privacy only for compelling reasons, like safeguarding health or maintain-
ing medical standards. He then divided the nine months of pregnancy
into three trimesters, linking a state's right to get involved in the abortion
decision to the progression of the woman's pregnancy. During the first six
months, the first and second trimesters, states could regulate abortions
only to protect the woman's health. But during the final three months,
states had a compelling reason to interfere — to protect the fetus. Since
by that point the fetus is considered "viable" (able to live outside the
womb), Blackmun argued, states had a compelling reason to prohibit
abortion during the final trimester.

Response to the *Roe* Decision

The Supreme Court's decision on *Roe* v. *Wade* was announced on January
22, 1973. It was controversial the day that it was announced, and it's been
controversial ever since. Many legal experts faulted its scholarship, criticizing the opinion because it did not spell out specifically what part of the
Constitution granted the right of privacy and also because it did not spell

out the limits of this right. Some also claimed that it took power that rightly belonged to the lawmakers and gave it to the judges.

Reaction throughout American society was equally strong. The ruling made Blackmun a hero to those who supported a woman's right to choose, who called it a crucial step in women becoming equal in American society. "*Roe* v. *Wade* was a defining moment in our history. It has touched all our lives in one way or another," said Gloria Feldt, the president of Planned Parenthood. Many supporters of the decision felt that it protected a woman's basic right to control her body and to control her reproductive life. It's been seen as the crux of the women's rights movement. "Without it there is no question that progress would have been much longer in coming," said Kim Gandy, a vice-president of the National Organization for Women. "It was the beginning of recognition that women are independent beings who have a legal right to control their destiny in very personal ways. It opened up opportunities for women that they hadn't seen before. It made it possible for women to think of having careers."

But the ruling made Blackmun a villain to abortion opponents, who accused him of being personally responsible for killing unborn babies. "During his confirmation hearings, Blackmun said that he wanted to be remembered for his treatment of the 'little people,'" said Jan Larue of the Family Research Council. "How sad and ironic that he will be remembered for 'finding' a right in the Constitution that has led to the deaths of 35 million 'little people.'" Despite the Court's 7-2 vote, Blackmun was held personally responsible for the decision because he wrote the opinion. He received about 60,000 letters during his years on the Court, more than any other Justice in history, and most of it was hate mail. He was called, in his words, "Butcher of Dachau, Pontius Pilate, King Herod, a child murderer, you name it." One letter promised to "blow your brains out" and "laugh at your funeral." A Christmas card said "this will be your last one." In 1984, he received a

—— *"* ——

"[Roe v. Wade] *was the beginning of recognition that women are independent beings who have a legal right to control their destiny in very personal ways. It opened up opportunities for women that they hadn't seen before. It made it possible for women to think of having careers."*
— Kim Gandy, National Organization for Women

—— *"* ——

97

death threat from an anti-abortion group called "Army of God," after which he received special protection from federal marshals and members of the Supreme Court police force. A year later, a bullet was shot through his apartment window and landed in a chair in his living room. Both he and his wife were in the room, but fortunately neither was injured. It was never determined whether the shot was fired at random or on purpose. Despite all this, Blackmun remained a staunch supporter of a woman's right to abortion.

Protestors express their opposite views during a demonstration outside the Supreme Court in Washington D.C., December 8, 1993.

Challenges to the *Roe* Decision

Over the years, several different cases have been brought to the Supreme Court that challenged the *Roe* ruling. The Court's ideological approach gradually changed as several liberal justices retired and were replaced by more conservative appointees, and soon the Court threatened to limit or overrule *Roe*. Some of the Court's decisions focused on who could be held responsible for paying for abortions, particularly in government-funded health care programs for the poor. In 1977, the Court ruled that government was not obligated to pay for abortions that were not considered necessary for the woman's health; in 1980, the Court decided that government didn't have to pay even for abortions when they were medically necessary; and in 1989, in a famous case called *Webster* v. *Reproductive Health Services*, the Court ruled that government may outlaw abortions in public hospitals, prohibit public employees from assisting in abortions, and require doctors to perform tests for viability after 20 weeks. In his dissenting opinion in that case, Blackmun's concern about the direction of the Court was very clear. "I fear for the future," he wrote. "For today, the women of this nation still retain the liberty to control their destinies. But the signs are evident and very ominous, and a chill wind blows."

Challenges to *Roe* continued in the early 1990s. In 1992, in *Planned Parenthood* v. *Casey*, the Court voted 5-4 to reaffirm the *Roe* decision. But it also set some limits, ruling that states could require women seeking an abortion to receive medical counseling about the procedure and to wait 24 hours between the counseling and the abortion. Even though *Roe* was narrowly upheld, four Justices had called for its overthrow. Blackmun wrote an impassioned opinion that expressed his fears about the future. "I fear for the darkness as four justices anxiously await the single vote necessary to extinguish the light.... I am 83 years old. I cannot remain on this Court forever." Blackmun's fears were probably appeased by several events in 1994.

That year, in the case *National Organization for Women* v. *Scheidler*, the Court decided that protesters who blocked access to clinics could be prosecuted, and Congress passed the Freedom of Access to Clinic Entrances Act, which protects abortions clinics and staff from violence. Also that year, the retirement of Justice Byron R. White and President Clinton's appointment of Ruth Bader Ginsburg changed the balance on the Court to 6-3 in favor of protecting the right to abortion.

Today, over 25 years after *Roe*, the controversy over the decision still continues. "[The] decision ignited one of the most impassioned public debates of the century," Aaron Epstein wrote in the *Detroit Free Press*. "It unleashed a tempest of moral, legal, theological, political, philosophical, and biological conflict that persists to this day." It radically transformed American society and politics, polarizing people on the two sides of this very divisive issue. It also became a key issue for politicians, as voters on each side demanded allegiance to their views on this one crucial issue. It became a rallying point for both supporters and opponents, with both sides organizing rallies to publicize their cause. It has even been a cause for violence, as some pro-life forces became involved in violence at abortion clinics and even in the murder of abortion doctors.

—— " ——

"During his confirmation hearings, Blackmun said that he wanted to be remembered for his treatment of the 'little people.' How sad and ironic that he will be remembered for 'finding' a right in the Constitution that has led to the deaths of 35 million 'little people.'"
— Jan Larue,
Family Research Council

—— " ——

———— " ————

Blackmum strongly backed the idea that government owed an obligation to the poor. In his words, "There is 'another world' out there, the existence of which the Court, I suspect, either chooses to ignore or fears to recognize. And so the cancer of poverty will continue to grow. This is a sad day for those who regard the Constitution as a force that would serve justice to all evenhandedly and, in so doing, would better the lot of the poorest among us."

———— " ————

Evolving Views

Following the *Roe* case, many observers saw a transformation in Justice Blackmun's view of society and his view of the role of the Court. As Linda Greenhouse wrote in the *New York Times*, "A successful middle-aged lawyer and judge when he came to the Court, Justice Blackmun brought with him a certain Midwestern complacency and belief that the Government worked well for most people most of the time without intervention from the Federal judiciary. Over the years, he came to see the Court as an essential voice for the vulnerable and powerless." According to Professor Harold Koh, a former clerk for Blackmun who is now a professor at Yale Law School, joining the Supreme Court forced him to see a different side of American society than he had previously known. "Paradoxically, by donning the robes of high office, Justice Blackmun became less isolated from the everyday world and more aware of the human beings behind the cases," said Koh. "He took his job seriously and did his own work. The Court's sprawling docket exposed him to a broader, more brutal slice of life than he had ever known." The result of all this was his gradual emphasis on supporting the rights of the underdog in society.

There were several areas of law that reflect Blackmun's evolving emphasis on the powerless. One was in his view of the poor. Back in the 1973 *United States* v. *Kras* bankruptcy case, he seemed so ignorant about poverty that he thought that the poor should be able to pay fees when bankrupt. But by the 1977 *Beal* v. *Doe* case on the issue of government payment for abortion, he strongly backed the idea that government owed an obligation to the poor. In his words, "There is 'another world' out there, the existence of which the Court, I suspect, either chooses to ignore or fears to recognize. And so the cancer of poverty will continue to grow. This is a sad day for those who regard the Constitution as a force that would serve justice to all evenhandedly and, in so doing, would better the lot of the poorest among us." His views on affirmative action also reflect this emphasis on the underdog, particularly in the famous case *Regents of the University of California* v. *Bakke*. In that case, a white man brought suit against a university medical school claiming that he had been rejected by the school because of affirmative action policies that favored African-Americans (called reverse discrimination). Beginning in *Bakke* in 1978 and continuing in several later cases, he championed the rights of African-Americans and supported affirmative action programs, saying "in order to get beyond racism, we must first take account of race. There is no other way. And in order to treat some persons equally, we must treat them differently."

Blackmun's views on capital punishment also changed over the years. During his years on the Court, he had been involved in several cases that challenged the constitutionality of the death penalty. Early on he said that he objected to the death penalty personally. But he consistently voted to uphold it, he said, because he felt the issue should be handled by legislation, not by court decree. Yet Blackmun gradually changed his opinion as he began to question whether it was possible for the legal system to be fair, consistent, accurate, and reliable in imposing the death sentence. He was particularly shaken by implications of racism in the death penalty process in the case *McCleskey* v. *Kemp,* in which evidence showed that an African-American accused of killing a white was three times more likely to receive a death penalty sentence than any other racial combination of killer and victim. In 1994 he completely reversed his stance on the issue of the death penalty. In the case *Callins* v. *Collins,* he wrote, "From this day forward, I no longer shall tinker with the machinery of death. . . . I feel morally and intellectually obligated simply to concede that the death penalty experiment has failed."

In 1994 he completely reversed his stance on the issue of the death penalty. In the case **Callins** *v.* **Collins,** *he wrote, "From this day forward, I no longer shall tinker with the machinery of death. . . . I feel morally and intellectually obligated simply to concede that the death penalty experiment has failed."*

The Supreme Court, 1993. Blackman is seated second from the left.

Over his years on the Court, Blackmun abandoned an abstract approach to legal cases and developed, instead, a personal and intimate approach to the law. He focused not just on the legal issues, but also on the people behind the cases, mindful of how the opinions would affect the individuals involved. While some objected to what they considered his overly emotional and sentimental approach, others felt that this concern defines his legacy on the Court. "He brings a sense of caring and compassion that will be missed," said Professor Chai Feldblum of Georgetown University, commenting on Blackmun's decision to retire.

Retirement

Blackmun announced his retirement from the Supreme Court on April 6, 1994. At the time, President Clinton said this: "Justice Blackmun has become part of the rich and evolving story of American justice and Constitutional law. With majesty and reason, with scholarship and grace, he is a good man who has earned the respect and the gratitude of every one of his fellow countrymen and women. When President Nixon nominated Harry Blackmun for service on the Court, his candidacy naturally occasioned a great deal of speculation about what kind of justice he would be. Some labeled him a strict constructionist. But he rejected any attempt to tag him with a label, saying, and I quote, 'I've been called liberal and conservative. Labels are deceiving. I call them as I see them.' Twenty-four years later, we can say that he did exactly what he said he would do 24 years ago. . . . I can only say that every one of us who serves in any capacity in public life would do very well by the people of the United States if we could bring to our work half the integrity, the passion, and the love for this country that Justice Blackmun has given us on the United States Supreme Court for 24 years, and I thank him very much."

Blackmun officially left office on August 3, 1994. After retiring, he continued to go to his office at the Court each day. He was at home on February 22, 1999, when he fell and broke his hip. He had surgery to replace his broken hip, but he never fully recovered. On March 4, 1999, Blackmun died in Arlington, Virginia, of complications from the surgery. He was 90.

Many eulogies followed, including this tribute by David Cole in *The Nation*. "Blackmun's fundamental concern for the disempowered came through in opinion after opinion, as he voted to protect convicted criminals' appeal rights, immigrants' rights to education and public employment, women's rights to abortion, and African-Americans' rights to equal protection and affirmative action. He came to the Court a conservative, but his openness to the pleas of the powerless led to a remarkable transformation; unlike so many, he grew more liberal with each passing year. By the time he stepped down in 1994, he was the only consistently liberal voice on the Court. . . . These days, the Court sorely misses the human touch of Justice Harry Blackmun."

> *"Blackmun's fundamental concern for the disempowered came through in opinion after opinion. . . . He came to the Court a conservative, but his openness to the pleas of the powerless led to a remarkable transformation; unlike so many, he grew more liberal with each passing year. By the time he stepped down in 1994, he was the only consistently liberal voice on the Court. . . . These days, the Court sorely misses the human touch of Justice Harry Blackmun."*
> — *David Cole*, **The Nation**

HOBBIES AND OTHER INTERESTS

Blackmun was known for working very long hours throughout his career. He started each day early, always beginning with an informal breakfast with his law clerks in the cafeteria. He also worked Saturdays and even a few hours on Sundays. So he didn't have a lot of time for hobbies.

Still, Blackmun was a devoted baseball fan. His love of baseball became well known with his opinion in the 1972 case *Flood* v. *Kuhn*. In that case, the Court allowed major league baseball to keep its exemption from antitrust (monopoly) law. Blackmun wrote the Court's opinion, beginning with what's been called an ode to our national pastime. He gave a history of the game, quoted from "Casey at the Bat," and listed 88 of his all-time favorite players, owners, managers, and even umpires. Blackmun especially followed the Minnesota Twins and the Chicago Cubs, although he kept track of statistics for all the teams. One of his former clerks recalled that one summer, he was working at the Supreme Court while Blackmun was on a fishing vacation in Minnesota. Blackmun called the office, which he never did while he was on vacation, so the clerk was sure that he done something terrible and was about to get in serious trouble. Instead, it turned out that Blackmun couldn't get a newspaper — he just wanted his clerk to read him the baseball scores out of the Washington paper.

MARRIAGE AND FAMILY

Blackmun met his future wife, Dorothy (Dottie) Clark, in 1937. He and a friend were at a local tennis court when they agreed to play mixed doubles with two female players. As Dottie later recalled, "I was at the age when I looked the two boys over, and I remember being very much interested in Harry, being struck by his poise and his way of speaking. I didn't look back when I walked to the court, but he followed me." Harry and Dottie dated for four years, attending concerts, plays, and dinner dances. They were married on June 21, 1941, and remained extremely devoted to one another throughout the 50-plus years of their marriage. In fact, Blackmun often lamented the fact that his heavy workload left him little free time to spend with his wife. "It's lonely for her," he once said. The couple had three daughters, Nancy, Sally, and Susan.

HONORS AND AWARDS

Harvard Law School Association Award: 1993
Madison-Jefferson Award (Americans United for Separation of Church and State): 1995

FURTHER READING

Books

The American Bench: Judges of the Nation, 1997-98
Encyclopedia Britannica, 1998
Friedman, Leon, and Fred L. Israel, eds. *The Justices of the United States Supreme Court: Their Lives and Major Opinions,* 1997
Italia, Bob. *Harry Blackmun,* 1992
Who's Who in America, 1999
World Book Encyclopedia, 1998

Periodicals

Current Biography Yearbook 1970
New York Times, Feb. 23, 1994, p.A14; Apr. 7, 1994, p.A1; Mar. 5, 1999, p.A1
New York Times Magazine, Feb. 20, 1983, p.20
Time, Apr. 18, 1994, p.36
Washington Post, Apr. 7, 1994, p.A1; Mar. 5, 1999, p.A1; Mar. 6, 1999, p.A20

Other

"All Things Considered" Transcript, National Public Radio, Dec. 27 and 28, 1993

WORLD WIDE WEB SITES

http://oyez.nwu.edu

George W. Bush 1946-
American Politician
Governor of Texas and Republican Presidential
Candidate

BIRTH

George Walker Bush was born on July 6, 1946, in New Haven,
Connecticut. His father, George Herbert Walker Bush, was a
student at Yale University at the time of his first child's birth,
and would go on to become the 41st President of the United
States. His mother, Barbara Bush, was a homemaker who,
after her children were raised, devoted much of her time to

improving literacy in the U.S. The oldest child in the family, George had five siblings: two sisters, Robin and Dorothy, and three brothers, Jeb (nickname of John Ellis Bush), Neil, and Marvin. Because of the confusion caused by the father and son's similar names, the son and current presidential candidate is often called George W.

YOUTH

George lived in New Haven until he was two, when the family moved to the area near Midland, Texas. His father had decided to try the oil business, and George spent most of the next 12 years living in what would become a boomtown where his family and many others would make their fortunes. But when the young Bush family started out in Texas, they could only afford a small apartment in nearby Odessa. Then George Bush took a job selling drill-bits in California for one year, with his wife and son living in motels wherever his oil job took him. Finally, in 1950, they bought a small house in Midland, where George spent his time playing with friends and exploring the neighborhood.

Barbara Bush remembers her eldest son as "a wonderful, incorrigible child who spent many afternoons sitting in his room, waiting for his father to come home and speak to him about his latest transgression."

Bush and his friends from that time remember Midland with great fondness. "It was an idyllic place to grow up, a real Ozzie-and-Harriet sort of town," remembers one friend. It was a safe neighborhood, where kids could ride their bikes around and the parents weren't afraid. It made a big impression on young Bush. "I don't know what percentage of me is Midland, but I would say people, if they want to understand me, need to understand Midland and the attitude of Midland." The families were all struggling together, and they would spend the evenings at barbeques in each other's backyards, while the parents talked and the kids played. Bush's friends from that time remain close friends today. In the summers, Bush and his siblings would travel to Maine, where they would spend time with their grandparents, Dorothy Walker Bush and Prescott Bush. Prescott Bush had been a successful financier and later a U.S. Senator.

Future President George Bush remembers his son as a spirited kid. In a letter to a friend he wrote, "Georgie has grown to be a near-man, talks dirty once in a while and occasionally swears, aged four and a half."

George W. Bush with his mother, Barbara Bush, father, George Bush, and grandparents, Dorothy and Prescott Bush, Midland, Texas, 1950.

Barbara Bush remembers "a wonderful, incorrigible child who spent many afternoons sitting in his room, waiting for his father to come home and speak to him about his latest transgression." For his part, George W. Bush remembers his childhood with great warmth: "I can't exaggerate to you what wonderful parents George and Barbara Bush were," he says. "They were liberating people. There was never that oppressiveness you see with other parents, never the idea that their way was the only way." Of the father to whom he would be compared throughout his business and political career, he says, "My dad went out of his way to make sure that I felt accepted by him."

Bush remembers endless games of baseball and a passion for collecting baseball cards. He would send his cards to the great players of the day, along with return postage, and ask the players to sign and return his cards, which they did.

A Tragic Death

But a cloud appeared over this happy family scenario when George was seven. His sister Robin, just three years old, died of leukemia. George knew she was sick, but he really had no idea that she would die. His parents were nearly inconsolable in their grief. "We awakened night after night in great physical pain—it hurt that much," Barbara Bush would write later. Its effect made her cling to George and to Jeb, who was just a baby at the time. One day she heard George on the phone with a friend, refusing an invitation to play, because his mom needed him. "That started my cure," Barbara Bush remembers. "I realized I was too much of a burden for a little seven-year-old boy."

Friends and family members remember that George's characteristic humor—wise-cracking and irreverent—emerged at this point, perhaps as a way to help his parents' get over their grief. Shortly after Robin's death, his dad took him to a football game. When he couldn't see over the taller people in front of him, George declared that he wished he was his sister. His father, embarrassed, asked him what he meant. "I bet she can see the game better from up there than we can here," he said.

EDUCATION

Midland and the Public Schools

Part of the experience that molded Bush into the man he is today was his schooling in Midland, Texas. As a student at Sam Houston Elementary School, he was known as a good student and athlete—especially at baseball—but he could be a cut-up, too. Once, he was sent to the principal's office for drawing a beard on his face during music class. The punishment at the time in many public schools

> *"I can't exaggerate to you what wonderful parents George and Barbara Bush were," he says. "They were liberating people. There was never that oppressiveness you see with other parents, never the idea that their way was the only way."*

was spanking with a wooden paddle. The principal, John Bizilo, gave George three "licks," and the young child let out a wail. "When I hit him, he cried," remembers Bizilo. "Oh, did he cry! He yelled as if he'd been shot. But he learned his lesson." While this kind of physical punishment seems terribly harsh by today's standards, it was part of life in Texas back in George Bush's youth.

His friends and teachers from that time don't remember that Bush expressed any political aspirations. He claims that as a young kid he "wanted to grow up to be Willie Mays," not President of the United States. He did, however, run for class president at San Jacinto Junior High in Midland, and he won, too.

Bush at Yale, mid 1960s.

When Bush was in eighth grade, his parents moved to Houston. His father had done very well in the oil business, and the family moved into a big house with a pool. Bush attended an elite prep school, Kinkaid, and felt like an outsider. Once, while he waited for the bus to go home, one of his classmates offered him a ride. "This was an eighth grader, who might have been 14 at the time," recalls Bush, "and he was driving a GTO—in the eighth grade! I remember saying, 'No thanks, man.' It was just a different world."

Andover

After two years at Kinkaid, Bush was accepted to Phillips Academy in Andover, Massachusetts. Commonly known as "Andover," it is one of the most exclusive, all-male, prep schools in the country. His dad had gone to Andover, where he was an outstanding student and athlete. Now George would try to make a name for himself at one of the most elite—and difficult—schools in the country.

As Bush's classmate and fellow Texan Clay Johnson remembers it, "We were in way over our heads in a foreign land" at Andover. "We found we had to struggle just to catch up with everybody else." Bush got a "0" on his first English assignment, an essay on his sister Robin's death. His teacher had written "disgraceful" on the essay. He didn't distinguish himself academically at Andover, but Bush made friends easily and got along with all kinds of boys. He played varsity baseball and basketball, and, in his senior year, was made head cheerleader. He is remembered as a wisecracking, likeable slob, who wore wrinkled clothes and sat with the jocks at meals. He was also the self-appointed "high commissioner of stickball," a variation of the game played by city kids everywhere. Bush organized a stickball tournament, which was enjoyed by students, athletic and nonathletic, throughout the school. While he didn't make a name for himself in student government at Andover, Bush recently joked that his "job" as stickball commissioner "makes me perfectly suitable to become the president." He graduated from Andover in 1964.

Yale

Bush applied to Yale University, a prestigious Ivy League college that his father and grandfather had attended. The head of Andover didn't think Bush had a very good chance of getting into Yale because of his mediocre grades and suggested that he also apply to other schools. But Yale accepted him, and he started college in the fall of 1964. Once again, Bush didn't distinguish himself academically—his grades were recently leaked to the press, and they indicate a "C" average in most classes—but he is remembered for being very social and getting along with a wide variety of students. He joined Delta Kappa Epsilon, a fraternity known for its parties, and he eventually became its president. His old roommates remember that he continued his slovenly ways from Andover. "He would grab a T-shirt off the floor and put it on," remembers one. And although he wasn't an intellectual, he "spent a lot of time learning from other people," according to a college friend. "Those who were book-oriented would think he wasn't a serious student, but he was a serious student of people."

During his college years, Bush remained removed from any political activity, and he also began to feel alienated from the smug intellectualism he sometimes found around him. In 1964, his father ran for, and lost, a race for the U.S. Senate. Walking across campus soon after, Bush encountered the famous campus chaplain, William Sloane Coffin. After Bush introduced himself, Coffin told him, "Oh yes, I know your father. Frankly, he was beaten by a better man." The cruelty and condescending attitude stung Bush, and he never forgot it. "What angered me was the way such people at Yale felt so intellectually superior and so righteous," he said. "They thought they had all the answers."

By the time Bush graduated with a degree in history in 1968, the nation was going through a period of political and social turmoil. During the late 1960s, many college campuses, including Yale, were places of political un-

Although Bush wasn't an intellectual, he "spent a lot of time learning from other people," according to a college friend. "Those who were book-oriented would think he wasn't a serious student, but he was a serious student of people."

Bush in the Texas Air National Guard, late 1960s.

rest, as students became involved with protesting U.S. involvement in the escalating war in Vietnam. Racial protests turned violent in many urban areas, and riots rocked cities like Detroit and Los Angeles. Two political assassinations, those of Martin Luther King Jr. and Bobby Kennedy, took place in the spring of his senior year. Bush remembers feeling that "something was fundamentally, frighteningly wrong. It was a confusing and disturbing time."

At that time, all young men had to register with the armed services — the "draft" — when they reached 18. The draft was a system of mandatory military service that had been in place since World War II. The destination for many draftees was Vietnam. Many young American men didn't believe in the Vietnam War, and they considered what they would do if they were drafted, including leaving the country or serving jail time for avoiding service. The decision wasn't difficult for Bush. "I knew I would serve," he says in his autobiography, *A Charge to Keep.* "Leaving the country to avoid the draft was not an option for me; I was too conservative and traditional." He decided instead to fulfill his military service by joining the Texas Air National Guard.

FIRST JOBS

Bush spent one year on active duty, then was assigned to Ellington Air Force Base in Houston. He learned to fly the F-102, a single-seat jet fighter. As part of his National Guard service, Bush continued to fly on the weekends, and also took a series of jobs during the week, none of which really worked out for him. He worked for awhile for an agribusiness, which he found boring, and then helped out as a mentor in a program for disadvantaged African-American boys.

Bush now refers to this period of his life, from about 1969 to 1973, as "rootless. I had no responsibilities whatsoever." He and his friends would party a lot, and recent media pieces focusing on his behavior at this time suggest that he may have taken drugs and drank too much. Bush declines to discuss this period in his life, except to say that the "question is: have you learned from your behavior? The answer is, yes." In 1973, he decided to go back to school and get an M.B.A., a Master's of Business Administration, at Harvard University. In 1975, M.B.A. in hand, he returned to his old hometown of Midland, Texas, to try to make it as an independent businessman.

CAREER HIGHLIGHTS

Oil Man

With no experience but with a lot of desire, Bush decided to learn what he could about the oil business. On the advice of family friends still in the area, he took classes at Permian Basin Graduate Center to learn about drilling, leasing, and other aspects of the business. Then he looked up deeds to see who had mineral rights to certain areas so he could investigate leasing property and drilling for oil. He called his first company Arbusto—Spanish for "Bush." He lived in a small cramped apartment that a friend describes as "looking like a toxic waste dump." He found several investors among family and friends, and he started to drill.

Two events happened in the late 1970s that were watersheds for Bush. In 1977, he met Laura Welch, a school librarian in Midland who had actually gone to junior high with him, though they had never met. He says it was "love at first sight." They had a whirlwind courtship and were married three months later. That same year, Bush decided to run for a seat in the Texas House of Representatives. It was his first burst of political ambition, and it surprised his family and friends. During that first race, he also encountered the kinds of accusations that have dogged him to the present day: that he was trading on his family's money and political connections, and that he was an Eastern-educated snob who didn't know or understand Texas. He lost the race, 53% to 47%, but it was a good showing for a political novice.

Bush returned to his fledgling oil business. The first wells—and the first years—were dry ones for the company. By the early 1980s, the company was in financial decline, and the oil business in general wasn't doing well, either. He merged with another company, Spectrum 7, but even with the infusion of cash that brought, the company continued to lose money. Spectrum then merged with another company, Harken Energy, in a deal in which Bush received 200,000 shares of stock and an annual salary of $120,000 as a member of the company's board of directors.

Personal Changes

In 1986, after a wild party to celebrate his 40th birthday and a raging hangover the next morning, Bush decided to stop drinking. He had had a reputation for a hard-partying lifestyle, and his wife says that she had spoken to him about his drinking. For Bush, the decision was simple. He quit and hasn't had an alcoholic drink since. "I'm not sophisticated enough to figure out if I had a clinical problem," he says. "And I can't say there was something significant that happened to make me change my life. All I know is that I was a high-energy person, and alcohol began competing with my ability to keep up my energy level. I wish I could say there was some more profound reason. But I just stopped." He also became recommitted to his Christian faith.

> "I'm not sophisticated enough to figure out if I had a clinical problem," Bush says about his drinking. "And I can't say there was something significant that happened to make me change my life. All I know is that I was a high-energy person, and alcohol began competing with my ability to keep up my energy level. I wish I could say there was some more profound reason. But I just stopped."

Father's Presidential Campaign

In 1988, Bush moved his family to Washington, where his father, then-Vice President George Bush, was running for President. The two men became very close, as George W. took on the role of one his father's most trusted advisors. With his father's victory in November 1988, the younger Bush returned to Texas and to the world of business.

Part Owner of the Texas Rangers

Bush, who always loved baseball, now became the central figure in a deal to buy the Texas Rangers baseball team. Bush liquidated his Harken stock, worth approximately $850,000, and used part of the proceeds to buy into the team.

Later, when he entered politics, this stock sale would generate a series of investigations and allegations of insider trading on Bush's part. Within a short time after he sold his stock, the value of Harken stock tumbled, leading some to allege that Bush had known the stock's value was about to fall, and that he used that insider knowledge to sell while the stock was

Bush family portrait, 1992. George W. is in the back row, fourth from left.

worth more. It would have been illegal for Bush, as a member of the company's board, to use inside information in a stock sale. However, investigations into the deal by federal authorities and the *Wall Street Journal* didn't show any wrongdoing on Bush's part.

Bush became managing partner for the Rangers. He went to most games, chatting with Ranger great Nolan Ryan, talking with fans, and always sitting in the general section—not up in a special owners box. Through his job with the Rangers, Bush became a well-known and popular Texan.

In 1992, George Bush ran for re-election as president and lost to newcomer Bill Clinton. The Bush camp, including George W., was stunned. Now he says he learned some major lessons from his father's loss. "People don't care what you did for them last year," he says. "They want to know what next year is like." His father had not been as concerned with the state of the national economy as had his challenger, and that proved to be a crucial factor in his defeat. When George W. Bush announced his intention to enter politics in 1994, he took that wisdom with him.

Getting into Politics

In what seemed to be an impossible race to win, George W. Bush took on popular Governor Ann Richards in the 1994 Texas governor's race. Richards had already gained fame for a phrase she used to mock Bush's father at the 1988 Democratic convention. "Poor George," she said of the then-Vice President, "He was born with a silver foot in his mouth." She took on her opponent in her race for re-election in a similar vein. She derided Bush as inexperienced and reliant on his name and connections, calling him "Shrub" or "Junior," and once saying he was a "jerk." Bush kept his temper under control and never responded in kind. Instead, he claimed, "The last time I was called a jerk was at Sam Houston Elementary School in Midland, Texas. I'm not going to call the governor names. I'm going to elevate this debate to a level where Texans want it." He focused on four key issues: reforming education, welfare, personal property law, and juvenile crime. He beat Richards in a close contest that November, becoming only the second Republican elected governor of Texas since the 1860s.

Governor of Texas

Bush says he learned some major lessons from his father's 1992 loss to Bill Clinton. "People don't care what you did for them last year," he says. "They want to know what next year is like."

Bush proved to be a popular and effective governor, and a different sort of Republican leader. The year 1994 was the year that Newt Gingrich and other conservative Republicans won the majority of seats in the U.S. House of Representatives. Gingrich and several of the other Republican conservatives were known for their hostile, combative political stance. Unlike them, Bush was a consensus builder. He worked with the Democrats in the Texas Congress to pass the legislative initiatives he wanted, in all the key areas he had promised. He enjoyed some of the highest approval ratings in the nation, and in 1998 he cruised to an easy re-election with 69% of the vote, becoming the only Texas governor ever re-elected to a four-year term. That same year his brother Jeb was elected governor of Florida.

As his success in Texas became known around the nation, Bush began to be touted as a possible presidential candidate for the 2000 election. In 1998, the country was in the throes of the Monica Lewinsky scandal and the resulting impeachment proceedings against President Clinton. For his part, Bush was unsure if he wanted to put his family through what he called the "meat grinder" of the media glare. Even before he announced his intentions to run, his finances came under scrutiny. He sold his interest in the Texas Rangers in 1998 for $14.9 million, prompting investigations into how he had built such a large fortune. This led to re-examinations of the Harken stock deal and a spate of articles closely examining his financial history.

The Race for the Republican Nomination

Despite qualms about his background and qualifications, Bush emerged as the frontrunner in the race for the Republican nomination. In March 1999 he announced that he was forming an "exploratory committee" to look into running for president. At that time, his fellow contenders for the nomination included former Vice President Dan Quayle, former Secretary of Labor Elizabeth Dole (see *Biography Today*, July 1992), author and radio talk show host Alan Keyes, and millionaire publisher Steve Forbes. But his strongest competition emerged in the unlikely person of Senator John McCain (see *Biography Today*, April 2000). McCain, a relative unknown with little support within his own party, declared his candidacy in April 1999. Bush, by then the favorite, had raised some $63 million, more than any presidential candidate in history.

In the American political process, the presidential candidates are selected for both the Republican and Democratic parties through primaries. In the primaries, voters cast ballots for delegates pledged to vote for a particular candidate at the party's convention, held in the summer of an election year. The earliest primary of the election year occurs in February in New Hampshire. The candidates spent a good part of late 1999 and early 2000 in New Hampshire, talking to voters and taking part in debates. Bush looked invincible, but McCain came from behind and pulled out a stunning victory in the New Hampshire primary. For the first time, Bush's lock on the nomination seemed questionable. McCain's popularity surged, but Bush rallied and beat him in the South Carolina primary.

But Bush's win in South Carolina came at a cost. He had begun his South Carolina bid with a speech at Bob Jones University, a college that forbade interracial dating and was known as a bastion of ultra-conservative politics. The Bush campaign pulled out all the stops in South Carolina, engaging in some nasty political activity. At one point, an anti-McCain ad came out that questioned the paternity of two of McCain's children and ridiculed the racial background of his adopted daughter, who is from Bangladesh. Bush tried to deny he'd had any involvement in the ad, but it was obviously created and aired by people who were trying to defeat McCain.

McCain was furious and lashed out at the Bush campaign and the tactics of supporters of the religious right, whom he blamed for the mean-spiritedness of the South Carolina campaign. Many Americans were also ap-

*Bush and his wife Laura wave to the crowd during the
Republican National Convention, August 3, 2000.*

palled at the campaign tactics. McCain came back and bested Bush in the
Michigan and Arizona primaries, doing particularly well with independent
voters as well as with Democrats.

"Super Tuesday," March 7, 2000, was the decisive day for the campaign.
Super Tuesday was the single largest primary in the nation's history. The
delegates were up for grabs in 16 states, including two of the largest states,
California and New York. Bush won decisively there, as well as in 10 other
states. The nomination was his in all but name. McCain withdrew, and
Bush focused on November. By this point, it was clear that his opponent
would be Vice President Al Gore, who had won the Democratic Party's
contest against Senator Bill Bradley.

Running for President

Since his big win on Super Tuesday, Bush has made several major an-
nouncements about key areas he would focus on if elected president. They
include education, foreign policy, and reform of Medicare and Social Security. In mid-summer, Bush was leading Gore in the polls by approximately 10 percentage points. In July 2000, Bush chose his vice presidential

running mate, Dick Cheney. Cheney, from the conservative wing of the party, had served as secretary of defense in his father's administration and as chief of staff in President Gerald Ford's administration.

On August 3, 2000, the Republican Party nominated George W. Bush for president at the Republican Convention in Philadelphia. On August 4, 2000, Bush accepted his party's nomination for President. He gave his acceptance speech at the Republican Convention, outlining the focus for his campaign. He pledged to "renew America's purpose," and he chided the Clinton and Gore administration for "wasting the moment of promise" in America's current prosperity. He claimed that America is "daring, decent, and ready for change," and that Clinton and Gore "have not led; we will." He reiterated the central tenets of his campaign: to strengthen education, Social Security, health care, and defense. In an obvious swipe at the scandal-ridden Clinton White House, he pledged to bring "civility and respect to Washington, D.C."

In his acceptance speech at the Republican Convention, Bush pledged to "renew America's purpose." He claimed that America is "daring, decent, and ready for change," and pledged to bring "civility and respect to Washington, D.C."

Bush and Cheney have started on a train tour of the Midwest. They are concentrating on states like Ohio, Michigan, and Pennsylvania, states with many independent voters who they're hoping will vote Republican in November. Whether his lead against Gore will continue up to the November election, and whether he will become the first son of a president since John Quincy Adams to be elected to the highest office in the land, remains to be seen.

MARRIAGE AND FAMILY

Bush married Laura Welch, who at the time of their marriage was a public school librarian, in 1977. Five years later, they had twin girls, Jenna and Barbara, who are now 18. The Bushes have kept their girls out of the political limelight, and the media has respected their wishes that Barbara and Jenna not be subjected to the kind of scrutiny and loss of personal privacy their father has experienced. Both girls recently graduated from a public high school in Austin and start college in the fall of 2000.

HOBBIES AND OTHER INTERESTS

Bush is an avid runner and has completed several marathons. He also loves to fish, both on his property in Texas and at the Bush family home in Kennebunkport, Maine.

WRITINGS

A Charge to Keep, 1999

FURTHER READING

Books

Bush, George W. *A Charge to Keep*, 1999
Who's Who in America, 2000

Periodicals

American Spectator, June 1999, p.20
Current Biography Yearbook 1997
Fortune, Mar. 29, 1999, p.72
GQ, Oct. 1998, p.252
Los Angeles Times, Mar. 8, 2000, p.A1
National Review, Dec. 22, 1997, p.52; Dec. 31, 1999, p.28
New Republic, Apr. 3, 1989, p.19; Mar. 16, 1998, p.21
New York Times, Aug. 22, 1994, p.A8; May 8, 1999, p.A1; May 21, 2000, p.A1;
    June 10, 2000, p.A1; July 29, 2000, p.A1; Aug. 1, 2000, p.A1; Aug. 4, 2000,
    p.A1
New York Times Magazine, Sep. 13, 1998, p.52
New Yorker, Oct. 19, 1998, p.30
Newsweek, July 4, 1994, p.38; Apr. 21, 1997, p.26; Nov. 2, 1998, p.30; June
    21, 1999, p.31; Feb. 28, 2000, p.22; Aug. 7, 2000, p.21
People, Nov. 8, 1993, p.56; Aug. 7, 2000, p.56
Rolling Stone, Aug. 5, 1999, p.36
Texas Monthly, Apr. 1989, p.126; May 1994, p.112; Nov. 1996, p.120; June
    1999, p.105
Time, July 31, 1989, p.60; Oct. 28, 1991, p.78; Sep. 26, 1994, p.39; Mar. 15,
    1999, p.42; June 21, 1999, p.34; Oct. 18, 1999, p.50; Jan. 17, 2000, p.47
U.S. News and World, Mar. 16, 1992, p.57; Dec. 25, 1995, p.89; Nov. 1, 1999,
    p.28; Feb. 7, 2000, p.64
Vogue, Feb. 1999, p.232

ADDRESS

Office of the Governor
P.O. Box 12428
Austin, TX 78711

WORLD WIDE WEB SITE

http://www.georgebush.com

Carson Daly 1973-

American TV Personality
Host of MTV's Hit Show "Total Request Live"

BIRTH

Carson Jones Daly was born on June 22, 1973. His parents
were J.D. and Pattie Daly (now Pattie Daly Caruso). His father
died of cancer when Carson was about six, and his mother
later married Richard Caruso, who became Carson's stepfather. Currently, Pattie hosts a local TV talk show in Palm
Springs, and Richard owns a golf shop. Carson has one sister
named Quinn.

YOUTH AND EDUCATION

Growing up in Santa Monica, a beach town in southern California, Daly had a good relationship with his mother. She once said, "He was the greatest kid—never a problem. I'm his first and biggest fan." Daly had to agree. "Of course I was a perfect kid. I was a geek! I got up early every morning to play golf. My mom's motto was, 'Nothing good happens after midnight,' and for a long time I actually believed it."

Daly attended Santa Monica High School, where he became one of the top high school golfers in the state. In his words, "I was a four-year varsity letterman in golf, which is like the lamest sport ever. And I went to a really cool high school, where Rob Lowe and Chad Lowe went, so everybody thought I was a complete geek." He has admitted that he didn't have a lot of girlfriends during high school. "I was the one girls would sit down with and say, 'Carson, you're a great listener . . . like an older brother.' It was a dry four years."

After graduating from Santa Monica High School, Daly won a golf scholarship to Loyola Marymount University in Los Angeles. There, he studied theology; he has said that he considered becoming a priest. "I seriously considered [religion as a vocation] when I was about 18," he says. "I thought, I'm the sort of person who could very easily be a priest or a deacon or work in an old-persons' home. I would have been willing to take an oath of poverty, of celibacy, and do good in a religious capacity." After his first semester at Loyola Marymount, though, he dropped out of school and moved to Palm Springs, hoping to join the amateur golf circuit and eventually become a pro golfer. All those plans changed, though, when a friend of the family helped him get a job as an intern at KCMJ, a radio station in Palm Springs. In just a short time, Daly was promoted to producer of the morning show at KCMJ. And that's how his career as a music host got started.

Daly didn't have a lot of girlfriends during high school. "I was the one girls would sit down with and say, 'Carson, you're a great listener . . . like an older brother.' It was a dry four years."

FIRST JOBS

During the next few years, Daly moved around from city to city, taking on new and better jobs at ever-bigger radio stations. After KCMJ he worked in San Diego and San Francisco before moving to KOME in San Jose to cover the afternoon drive time. His first job there was to cover the 1995 MTV Video Music Awards in New York City. The following year, he moved to Los Angeles to take the 6 to 10 p.m. shift at KROQ, a trendsetting alternative rock station that's considered the height of cool. "I had the total KROQ attitude," he recalls. "I had my nose pierced, I wore punk rock T-shirts, I painted my nails, and I was like, 'That's cool, that's not cool.'" For Daly, all that moving around was leading up to an even better opportunity. "Once I'd been somewhere for a year," he recalls, "I'd get this feeling that something was going to happen. Sure enough, I'd get a job at a bigger radio station or in a bigger market. I ended up at KROQ in Los Angeles, and after a year, I got that feeling that something else was going to pop. That turned out to be MTV."

> *"['TRL' is] a very simple show. It's gone beyond our wildest expectations. It's turned into this pop culture phenomenon. Kids come home from school and have to watch 'TRL.' They get a chance to see Britney Spears in person, see all the cool videos, call in, write in, and they even come down to the studio. It's just superseded anything that we ever imagined. Now it's just like this little teen-age hangout."*

CAREER HIGHLIGHTS

Since starting with MTV in 1997, Daly has worked on a variety of assignments. He was recruited that summer to work on "Motel California," a beach party show. He went on in 1997 and 1998 to host "MTV Live," an unsuccessful live show; "The Carson Daly Show," his own talk show; and "Total Request," a pre-taped countdown show. He also hosted several MTV specials, including "Wannabe a VJ Search," "Say What? Karaoke," "MTV Spring Break," and "MTV New Year's Eve."

"Total Request Live"

Daly's current show is "Total Request Live," which airs on weekday afternoons at 3:30 p.m. (Eastern time). The show was created in 1998 when the network combined "Total Request" with the short-lived "MTV Live" and selected Daly as the new show's host. "TRL" is a countdown show, in which the Top 10 music videos are aired each day. But the difference is that fans determine the Top 10 by direct vote, by calling the network or e-mailing their requests on MTV's web site. The show also features guest artists who drop in to chat with Daly and to premier their newest videos.

"TRL" is filmed live in front of a studio audience, and the studio itself has become a major draw in New York City. MTV is located right on Times Square, and the studio is surrounded by glass. Each day, hundreds of fans camp out outside the studio, hoping to become part of the studio audience and to catch a glimpse of their favorite stars. Sometimes the crowd gets a little big — for example, 8,000 fans congested the streets around the studio when the Backstreet Boys appeared on "TRL." "It's a very simple show. It's gone beyond our wildest expectations," Daly said. "It's turned into this pop culture phenomenon. Kids come home from school and have to watch 'TRL.' They get a chance to see Britney Spears in person, see all the cool videos, call in, write in, and they even come down to the studio. It's just superseded anything that we ever imagined. Now it's just like this little teen-age hangout."

One highlight of the show is the eclectic and diverse mix of music. Until recently, music was pretty stratified, with many people sticking to just one type of music. For example, fans who listened to rap usually didn't like rock, so most music shows — on TV or radio — couldn't mix different types of music together on the same program without alienating their audience. But that's not true on "TRL." Because fans decide which music videos will be played, each show includes an eclectic mix of hard rock, rap, pop, alternative, and any other current style. "Music's at a time now where you can get away with playing Jay-Z, a rapper, and have the very next video be Limp Bizkit. It all sounds similar. Rock bands are using drum loops. Rappers are using guitar riffs. This show could not have been pulled off in the early '90s. You couldn't play Nirvana and then go into LL Cool J. It wouldn't have worked. But the audience, the kids like all this stuff," Daly says. "Nowadays, it's safe to say if kids have Limp Bizkit or Kid Rock, they might also have Jay-Z or even 'N Sync or Backstreet Boys CDs. There's a

Daly with Christina Aguilera on the set of "TRL."

lot more crossover now, whether it's rock bands using dance beats or rappers sampling guitars." As Daly says about the mix of musical genres, "I like to call 'TRL' the United Nations of music-video shows. Everybody gets represented."

But an equally important highlight of "TRL" is its host. "I hired Carson because he knew music, and that's the No. 1 thing," said MTV executive Bob Kusbit. "He eats, sleeps, and breathes music. He's grown at being very good television. It's something that he's just naturally good at. Things don't throw him very much. As he's grown more comfortable, I think people are comfortable watching the show. I think they trust his music credibility." On "TRL," viewers say, Daly is knowledgeable, easygoing, funny, smart, charismatic, and good-looking. The show owes a lot of its success, in fact, to its heartthrob host—Daly is considered as much of a hunk as his celebrity guests. He shares the fans' enthusiasm for music and for meeting the musicians, even when the style of music is clearly not his favorite. While he admits to preferring rock over pop music, he still treats all his guests—as well as his fans—with respect. "This is a place for teens to have respect," he says. "They run the show, they pick the videos. I don't make fun of them. If they've written something on their face, like 'N Sync or Backstreet Boys, I'll tell them they look cool, 'cause I did stuff like that too."

Since its debut, "Total Request Live" has become a powerful and influential force in the music industry. "'TRL' is currently the undisputed epicenter of the pop world," according to *Rolling Stone* magazine writer Gavin Edwards, "essential viewing for teens and preteens." The show, which is credited with helping to unify the fragmented world of popular music, has become a pop culture sensation, launching the careers of new singers and groups. With a daily viewership of one million fans, each video played on the show is seen by a huge group of potential buyers—the teen audience is renowned for its phenomenal spending power. And many videos stay in the Top 10 for an extended period, so the "TRL" Top 10 videos are practically guaranteed a huge increase in sales. For example, Britney Spears was a virtual unknown when her video "Baby One More Time" first appeared on "TRL" on December 11, 1998; the album and the single hit No. 1 just a short time later, on January 30, 1999. Record companies recognize the power of "TRL," and their agents

"This is a place for teens to have respect. They run the show, they pick the videos. I don't make fun of them. If they've written something on their face, like 'N Sync or Backstreet Boys, I'll tell them they look cool, 'cause I did stuff like that too."

work frantically to get their artists' videos on the show. According to Columbia Records executive Gary Fisher, "It's one of the most important vehicles right now for getting new music to the right people." And the right people, of course, are the show's large audience of teen viewers—sophisticated, media savvy teens, who control a tremendous amount of spending money and who spend much of it on new music.

Other Plans

For the time being, Daly seems to relish his role as spokesperson for today's teens. But TV is a fickle business, and he has acknowledged that the popularity of his show, or his own role as its host, could end at any time. So he has branched off into other areas as well. He recently hosted both the 1999 Miss Teen USA and the 2000 Miss USA pageants. He appeared in the MTV made-for-TV movie *2gether*, a send up of boy bands in which he played himself. And he has set up a record company called Spunout Records with Steve Harwell, lead singer of Smash Mouth. But he's not ready to give up as a TV host, not just yet. "In a perfect world," Daly once said, "I could see myself in 10 years with my own late-night show, like Conan O'Brien or David Letterman."

HOME AND FAMILY

Daly, who is unmarried, lives in New York City. Until recently he was dating actress Jennifer Love Hewitt, with whom he was seriously involved for two years. Since they broke up, he hasn't been involved in a steady relationship.

HOBBIES AND OTHER INTERESTS

Daly's hobbies are golf, basketball, and music, of course. Some of his favorite musicians are Rage against the Machine, Beastie Boys, and Kid Rock.

FURTHER READING

Periodicals

Entertainment Weekly, Oct. 22, 1999, p.25
People, Nov. 16, 1998, p.93
Rolling Stone, July 8, 1999, p.27; Feb. 17, 2000, p.13
Teen, Jan. 1999, p.48

ADDRESS

MTV Viewer Services
1515 Broadway
New York, NY 10036

WORLD WIDE WEB SITES

http://www.mtv.com
http://www.mtv.com/mtv/tubescan/vj
http://www.us.imdb.com/Bio?Daly,+Carson

Ron Dayne 1977-

American Football Player
Winner of the 1999 Heisman Trophy

EARLY LIFE

Ron Dayne was born March 14, 1977, in Blacksburg, Virginia. His parents are Brenda and Ron Dayne. Ron has one sister, Onya. The family moved from Virginia to New Jersey when Dayne was small. Ron showed an early interest in sports, playing football, soccer, and running track while he was growing up.

Dayne poses with his daughter Jada Dayne, two, and her mother Alia Lester, in front of the 1999 Heisman Trophy following the awards ceremony.

Dayne's early life was full of turmoil. His parents divorced when he was a young teenager, and his mother became addicted to crack cocaine. She couldn't care for her children, and Ron and Onya went to live with an aunt and uncle, Rob and Debbie Reid, in Woodbury, New Jersey. Ron grew extremely close to his relatives, who gave him lots of love and stability.

Dayne was an outstanding football player at Overbeck High School in Berlin, New Jersey. When he graduated from high school in 1995, he was recruited by colleges all over the country. He chose the University of Wisconsin, where coach Barry Alvarez promised he could play tailback. "Coach Alvy gave me a chance to go out and show what I could do," recalled Dayne. "As a player, that's all you want. Just give me an opportunity and I'll take care of the rest."

College Years

In his four years at Wisconsin, Dayne proved to be a powerhouse. He's big—5'10" and 250 pounds—and he can plough through a defensive line. "Ron came onto the scene so strong as a freshman," remembers Coach Alvarez. "He basically carried our football team, carried our offense, from the fifth game on."

Dayne was such a strong player that he considered leaving college after his third year and going pro. Several factors went into his decision to stay in school. First, Alvarez called several NFL teams to see if there was interest in Dayne, and they told him that Dayne would not be their choice as a first-round pick in the NFL draft. But, more importantly for Dayne, he wanted to stay in Wisconsin for family reasons. During college, he and his girlfriend, Alia Lester, had had a child, Jada, who was born in 1997. "If I was away for a year, when I came back she wouldn't even notice me," said Dayne. He decided to stay, and to complete his undergraduate degree in African-American Studies.

In his senior year, Dayne entered the record books and won nearly every award available to a college player. He ended the season with a record-breaking 6,397 yards rushing, also winning the Doak Walker Award as best running back, the Maxwell Award as best all-around player, and was named player of the year by the Associated Press, *Football News*, *The Sporting News*, and the Walter Camp Foundation.

——— " ———

The usually shy and soft-spoken Dayne gave an emotional acceptance speech. "I'd like to thank my daughter, Jada, for being the biggest inspiration in my life. . . . I'd like to thank the real Heisman winner, for me, Uncle Rob, who is always there for me."

——— " ———

MAJOR ACCOMPLISHMENT

The Heisman Trophy

Dayne's greatest prize of all came in December 1999, when he was awarded the Heisman Trophy, the most prestigious honor in college football. The Heisman is awarded by the Downtown Athletic Club in New York City to the most outstanding player of the year. The honor usually goes to a quarterback or running back, and has been given to some of the finest football players in history, including Barry Sanders, Doug Flutie, Archie Griffin, Tony Dorsett, and Marcus Allen. Dayne won the 1999 Heisman in a landslide, with more than 2,000 points.

The usually shy and soft-spoken Dayne gave an emotional acceptance speech. He thanked his teammates and coach, then said, "I'd like to thank my daughter, Jada, for being the biggest inspiration in my life." His family, including Jada, his girlfriend, aunt and uncle, and his mother were in the audience, as Dayne went on to say, "I'd like to thank the real Heisman winner, for me, Uncle Rob, who is always there for me."

FUTURE PLANS

Dayne will be chosen by an NFL team in the April 2000 draft. It is expected that he will go in the first round. So after graduating from the University of Wisconsin in May, he will begin training for his first professional season. He and his girlfriend plan on getting married sometime in the future.

HONORS AND AWARDS

Most Valuable Player (Rose Bowl): 1999, 2000
Heisman Trophy (Downtown Athletic Club): 1999
Doak Walker Award (Southwestern Bell/SMU Athletic Forum): 1999
Maxwell Award (Maxwell Memorial Football Club): 1999
College Player of the Year (Associated Press): 1999
College Player of the Year (*Sporting News*): 1999
College Player of the Year (*Football News*): 1999
Walter Camp Foundation Award: 1999

FURTHER READING

Periodicals

Los Angeles Times, Dec. 27, 1999, p.D1
New York Times, Dec. 12, 1999, Sunday Sports, p.1
Sport, Jan. 2000, p.40
Sports Illustrated, Nov. 15, 1999, p.50

ADDRESS

Sports Marketing and Management
111 E. Kilbourn
Suite 2800
Milwaukee, WI 53202

Henry Louis Gates, Jr. 1950-

American Scholar, Author, Educator, and Activist
Director of the Afro-American Studies Department
at Harvard University
Editor of *Encarta Africana* and Host of the PBS Series
"Wonders of the African World"

BIRTH

Henry Louis Gates, Jr., was born Louis Smith Gates on September 16, 1950, in Keyser, West Virginia. As a young adult, he changed his name to Henry Louis Gates, Jr., to honor his father, Henry Louis Gates, Sr.; his mother was Pauline Augusta

(Coleman) Gates. Skip, as Gates Jr. is widely known, has one older brother, Paul (called Rocky).

YOUTH

In many ways, race has been a defining factor for Gates throughout his life. During the years that he grew from child to man, life for African-Americans changed radically in the United States. Growing up in the 1950s and 1960s, he lived through a period of momentous social change that touched him in many ways. In the mid-1950s school segregation was outlawed; in the late 1950s and early 1960s the civil rights movement flourished; in the mid-1960s federal legislation was passed that prohibited discrimination in employment, public accommodations, transportation, housing, and voting; and in the late 1960s the black power movement came to fruition. In the 1970s and beyond, when Gates was first a college student and later a college professor, the subject of race became critical to many of his intellectual interests. All of these experiences inform his work today, as a scholar widely renowned for promoting knowledge of the African-American experience throughout American society.

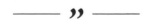

"As a child, I was secure in [my mother's] knowledge of things, of how to do things and function in the world, of how to be in the world and command respect. In her courage I was safe. . . . But more important of all, for Piedmont and for me, she did not seem to fear white people. She simply hated them, hated them with a passion she seldom disclosed. . . . The revelation was both terrifying and thrilling."

Gates grew up in the small village of Piedmont, West Virginia, in the Allegheny Mountains, two hours west of Washington, D.C. Piedmont was a predominantly white, working-class town with a small black population. A mill town, its fortunes were determined by those of the Westvaco Paper Mill, where the majority of the townspeople worked. Like most African-American men in Piedmont, his father worked on the loading platform at the mill. He worked there from 6:30 a.m. until 3:30 p.m., using forklifts to move huge wooden crates of paper, each weighing as much as seven tons, from the loading docks to the waiting trucks. So many Piedmont residents worked at the mill that at 3:30, when the mill whistle blew, school would let out, too. Gates's family would eat dinner right at 4:00, because his father had a second job. At night, he worked from 4:30 to 7:30 as a janitor at the telephone company.

When Gates was young, he never felt close to his father. His father and his brother were both big sports fans, and Rocky, six years older, was a gifted athlete. Gates was uncoordinated and heavy, and he felt excluded from the camaraderie that his father and his brother shared. One summer he joined Little League baseball, feeling pressured because all the kids his age played Little League. He played in just one game, as catcher. He says he closed his eyes each time the ball came near him, and caught it just by luck. He closed his eyes while at bat, too, and got on base on a walk. After the game, his father confessed that he hadn't been a very good player. Gates quit the team, became the league scorekeeper, and started developing a closer relationship with his father.

Gates was especially close to his mother, who worked cleaning houses for white people in town. She also became the secretary of the school P.T.A., the first black woman to hold that job. "As a child," Gates later wrote in his 1994 memoir, *Colored People*, "I was secure in her knowledge of things, of how to do things and function in the world, of how to *be* in the world and command respect. In her courage I was safe. . . . But more important of all, for Piedmont and for me, she did not seem to fear white people. She simply hated them, hated them with a passion she seldom disclosed." Gates first figured that out in 1959 while watching a TV documentary called "The Hate that Hate Produced." The show was about Black Muslims, including Malcolm X, who believed then that white people were evil. "While I sat cowering in our living room, I happened to glance over at my mother. A certain radiance was slowly transforming her soft brown face, as she listened to Malcolm X naming the white man the Devil. 'Amen,' she said quietly at first. 'All right now,' she continued, much more heatedly. All this time, and I hadn't known how deeply my mother despised white people. It was like watching the Wicked Witch of the West emerge out of the transforming features of Dorothy. The revelation was both terrifying and thrilling."

Race Relations in Piedmont

When Gates was young, Piedmont was still a segregated community, which he described in rich detail in *Colored People*. Despite the social upheaval of the civil rights years, many of those changes were slow to reach Piedmont. But when they did, they brought both good and bad repercussions to the town's African-American residents. Certainly, they welcomed improved employment opportunities and the end of outright discrimination, like local restaurants where blacks hadn't been allowed to sit down. But some of the changes were less welcome. The African-American residents of Piedmont had built up a strong and resilient community with vigorous institutions, like its schools and churches. Their community was filled with impressive role models of hard work, family stability, and academic achievement. But the end of segregation in some ways changed the nature of that community. "[For] many of the colored people in Piedmont," Gates wrote, "integration was experienced as a loss. The warmth and nurturance of the womblike colored world was slowly and inevitably disappearing."

—— *"* ——

"[For] many of the colored people in Piedmont, integration was experienced as a loss. The warmth and nurturance of the womblike colored world was slowly and inevitably disappearing."

—— *"* ——

Gates gives as an example the mill's annual employee picnics, one white and one colored. For the African-American community, the mill picnic was the most enjoyable social event of the year and one that helped unify and strengthen the community. In the 1960s, those segregated picnics were combined into one. "Some colored people," Gates wrote, "claimed that they welcomed the change, that it was progress, that it was what we had been working for for so very long, our own version of the civil rights movement and Dr. King. But nobody really believed that, I don't think. For who in their right mind wanted to attend the mill picnic with the white people, when it meant shutting the colored one down? . . . So the last wave of the civil rights era finally came to the Potomac Valley, crashing down upon the colored world of Piedmont. When it did, its most beloved, and cementing ritual was doomed to give way. Nobody wanted segregation, you understand; but nobody thought of this as segregation."

EDUCATION

One place that integration did work in Piedmont was in the local schools. In 1954 the Supreme Court ruled in *Brown* v. *Board of Education* that segregated schools were unconstitutional, and Davis Free Elementary School in Piedmont was integrated the following year. Gates started there one year later, in 1956. He was an outstanding student, and his academic talents were soon recognized; as he later wrote, "there was no discrimination in the classroom." By first grade, he was marked to excel. Gates was one of the top students throughout his school years in Piedmont.

Despite his good grades, though, Gates wasn't interested in reading until about seventh grade — and then only because of a girl. There was a white girl named Linda who also excelled in school, and he liked her from afar throughout his school years. Despite the smooth integration at the school, blacks and whites really couldn't date each other. Linda was an avid reader, so Gates started reading more, to give them something in common. His teacher gave him a little push too, giving him books by Charles Dickens, Victor Hugo,

President Bill Clinton poses with Gates during a presentation of the 1998 National Humanities Medal Awards.

Bertrand Russell, William Shakespeare, and biographies of Albert Einstein and Albert Schweitzer. Gates would look in the back of the books for lists of other authors, and he'd start reading his way through their books, too. Pretty soon he was hooked on literature. But at the same time he had a strong interest in science, and he was sure that he was going to become a doctor.

A Serious Injury

When Gates was 13, he injured his leg playing touch football during the summer. He tried everything he knew to treat it — heat, ice, elastic wraps. Then he went to see two different doctors, and each gave him different advice. By September, when school started, he was on crutches. After lunch one day, he was heading back into school when he was suddenly overcome by intense pain. "I ran into a wall of pain. It seemed to rise up out of the earth, surrounding me on all sides. . . . This kind of pain lived in its own dimension, and I could hardly see because of it. To move was only to make it worse, left or right, up or down. I was frozen in midstep." Some students came by and essentially carried him into the school, with Gates screaming in agony the whole way.

They rushed him to the hospital, where a surgeon diagnosed a torn ligament in the knee—wholly missing the fact that his hip joint was disconnected. The surgeon then started to put on a walking cast for the torn ligament. At the same time, he began asking Gates questions about school. When the doctor learned that Gates was good at science and wanted to be a doctor, he started quizzing him on the subject. Then he told Gates to get up and walk. He tried, but he just fell to the floor in pain. The doctor took his mother out to the hall and said, "Pauline, there's not a thing wrong with that child. The problem's psychosomatic. Because I know the type, and the thing is, your son's an overachiever." That white doctor was saying that the pain was completely imaginary, that Gates was making it up because he was an overachiever—because any African-American who thought he could be a doctor was clearly delusional and headed for a breakdown.

Gates's mother knew better. Appalled by the doctor's bigotry, she packed her son up and took him to another hospital 60 miles away. She had made the right decision. His injury was serious, and he had to have three operations over the next year. In the first, the joint was pinned together with metal pins. He had to use crutches for six weeks after that. Then the doctors decided that the pins had failed and scheduled surgery to remove them. Finally, they did a third operation to insert a metal ball on his hip. After that he was confined to bed for six weeks in traction, with a system of weights and pulleys attached to his legs. "It was six weeks of bondage—and bedpans. It was also my first glimpse of eternity. Eternity is a 14-year-old boy strapped down to a bed, held rigidly in place by traction and a system of pulleys and weights, unable to move to the left or to the right, to lift up his body beyond 45 degrees, unable to turn over, unable to use the bathroom . . . for six weeks." For that whole time, his mom stayed in a motel nearby and spent each day at the hospital with him. Gates says they fought all the time, argued all day long, so he didn't have to think about being in traction. After six weeks in bed, he had to retrain his muscles to walk. When he left the hospital, he spent the next six months on crutches, then switched to a cane. He also had to wear special corrective shoes with a lift in the heel. The injury and subsequent medical mistreatment caused him serious trouble for much of his life, including a pronounced limp. Years later, as an adult, he had hip replacement surgery.

By the time Gates was in high school, it was the mid to late 1960s, a time of tremendous change for African-Americans. His eyes were opened when he read *Notes of a Native Son* by James Baldwin. "It was the first time I had heard a voice capturing the terrible exhilaration and anxiety of being a person of African descent in this country," Gates recalled. After that, he and three of his friends read books by Claude Brown, Eldridge Cleaver, Ralph Ellison, and Malcolm X. They listened to jazz and soul and rhythm and blues. They heard Stokely Carmichael call for black power. They watched TV together, seeing scenes from the Vietnam War, the assassination of Martin Luther King, the assassination of Robert F. Kennedy, and the riots in major American cities. Gates was an excellent student throughout these years of social turmoil, and in 1968 he graduated first in his class from Piedmont High School.

College Years

After high school, Gates spent one year at Potomac State College of West Virginia University. Potomac State was located in Keyser, just five miles from Piedmont. Gates never really decided to go there; everybody from Piedmont who went on to college went to Potomac State. He planned to study medicine and become a doctor. But along the way, he was sidetracked by an English professor. His cousin Greg had suggested that he take a class from Duke Anthony Whitmore, saying "This guy Whitmore is *crazy*, just like you." As Gates recalls, "It was love at first sight, at least for me. And that, in retrospect, was the beginning of the end of my 12-year-old dream of becoming a doctor." It was in Whitmore's classroom that Gates fell in love with the study of literature. "It was a glorious experience. Words and thoughts, ideas and visions, came alive for me in his classroom. It was he who showed me, by his example, that ideas had a life of their own and that there were other professions as stimulating and as rewarding as being a doctor." After that first year at Potomac State, Whitmore encouraged Gates to transfer to an elite Ivy League college, so Gates applied to Harvard, Princeton, and Yale. On the essay for his application to Yale, he wrote, "My grandfather was colored, my father was Negro, and I am black. . . . As always, whitey now sits in judgment of me, preparing to cast my

> "
> *"[Studying literature with Duke Whitmore] was a glorious experience. Words and thoughts, ideas and visions, came alive for me in his classroom. It was he who showed me, by his example, that ideas had a life of their own and that there were other professions as stimulating and as rewarding as being a doctor."*
> "

Henry Louis Gates, Jr.

fate. It is your decision either to let me blow with the wind as a non-entity, or to encourage the development of self. Allow me to prove myself."

They did. In 1969, Gates entered Yale University in New Haven, Connecticut, along with 95 other black students. For Gates, who had grown up in a small town where many of the other African-Americans were related to him, it was a revelation. "When I came [to Yale] in 1969, I encountered the most black people I had come across in one place in my life. It's ironic that one would go to Yale to learn about blackness." As one friend said, he longed to "immerse himself in blackness." He became active in many of the campus groups, attending rallies and meetings. He also became deeply interested in Africa. The continent of his ancestors had fascinated him since fifth grade, when he first studied it in school. He spent years reading about Africa's leaders, its geography, and its history. He was enthralled by "the idea that black people — Africans — could actually run a whole country or fly airplanes or do electronic technology without some white colonial looking over their shoulder."

At Yale, Gates continued to study African issues. The university at that time had a program where students could spent a year working in a Third World country following their sophomore year. Gates won a Carnegie Foundation Fellowship for Africa and a Phelps Fellowship from Yale to join the program. He spent six months living in a small village in Tanzania, which is in southern Africa on the eastern coast, on the Indian Ocean. During 1970 to 1971 he worked at the Anglican Mission Hospital, where he was trained to administer general anesthesia for surgery. Afterwards, he and another student hitchhiked across the equator. In Africa, he says, "I learned, inevitably, how very American I was." After that experience, Gates returned to Yale and completed his undergraduate degree. In 1973, he earned his Bachelor of Arts (B.A.) degree in history, graduating summa cum laude (with highest honors).

Graduate Studies

Gates then earned a Mellon Fellowship to attend Clare College, part of Cambridge University in England. He was the first black to win this prestigious fellowship. By that time he had decided not to become a doctor and planned, instead, to study and publicize the accomplishments of African-Americans. "It is somewhat embarrassing to admit this today," he said in 1988, "but I felt as if I were embarked upon a mission for all black people, especially for that group of scholars whom our people have traditionally called 'race men' or 'race women,' the intellectuals who collect, preserve, and analyze the most sublime artifacts of the black imagination."

Gates soon discovered that Cambridge University did not share his enthusiasm. At that time the black Nigerian dramatist Wole Soyinka was about to become a lecturer in the English department. But they made him take an appointment in the department of social anthropology instead, apparently because African literature didn't rank highly enough to be grouped with English literature. Soyinka went on to win the Nobel Prize for Literature in 1986. Soyinka had a huge influence on Gates, and they became close friends. The dramatist urged Gates to study literature and introduced him to the mythology of the Yoruba, Soyinka's tribe from West Africa. Gates earned a Master of Arts (M.A.) degree in English Language and Literature from Cambridge University in 1974.

"In the past, each generation of black intellectuals has had to reinvent the wheel because we didn't have a set of definitive reference books to build on," says Gates. The Africana *encyclopedia "will give us a base of knowledge about black people around the world so strong no one can ever say we have no culture, no civilization, no history."*

Gates soon went to work on his doctoral degree, working on a dissertation in literature for his Ph.D. But he soon felt discouraged by what he felt was a lack of support from Cambridge University. Gates returned to the U.S. and to Yale, and briefly entered the law school. But he also went to talk to

Charles T. Davis. A Yale professor who chaired the Afro-American Studies department, Davis agreed to oversee his dissertation. So Gates continued to write his dissertation for Cambridge while living in the U.S. and consulting with Davis. "Now I knew what I was doing," he says. "Charles had vision. He told me I should be an academic, that I should stick with it, that one day I would be chair of Afro-American Studies at Yale." Over the next few years Gates worked in several other jobs. He worked as a correspondent for *Time* magazine, which sent him, among other assignments, to Paris to interview James Baldwin and Josephine Baker; he worked as a public relations representative for American Cyanamid Company in New Jersey; and he worked as a lecturer at Yale. But throughout all this, he also continued the study of literature. In 1979, he finished his dissertation and earned his Ph.D. in English Language and Literature from Cambridge University. He was the first African-American to earn a Ph.D. at Cambridge.

"I'd never been anywhere, and here was this young man who'd trekked across Africa," his wife Sharon recalls. *"[He] was so funny. There was a lightheartedness about him. He was absolutely brilliant. I just found him irresistible."*

MARRIAGE AND FAMILY

Gates met his future wife, Sharon Lynn Adams, while he was still a student at Yale. After returning from Africa, he went back to West Virginia for a while to work on Jay Rockefeller's 1972 campaign to become governor. Through his work as historian of the campaign, he met Adams, a white woman who had dropped out of college. At that time interracial dating was uncommon, and Gates was the first black man that she had ever dated. "I'd never been anywhere, and here was this young man who'd trekked across Africa," she recalls. "[He] was so funny. There was a lightheartedness about him. He was absolutely brilliant. I just found him irresistible."

After the campaign, Adams moved up to Connecticut with Gates. They became deeply committed to each other, but the only problem was her parents. When her mother found out about their relationship she made her daughter promise not to tell her father she was in love with a black man. The news would kill Adams's father, an avowed racist, according to her mother. So for a long time her father knew that Adams was involved with Gates, but he didn't know that Gates was black. They continued the deception in England, where Adams stayed with Gates while he was in school in Cambridge. In the meantime, Gates developed a good relationship with her father over the phone. "It never occurred to Dad that Skip might be black," she says. "Every time I called home, Skip would get on the phone voluntarily. And it was really awful for us, because neither of us likes to be dishonest. But there I had my mother saying, 'He's going to have a heart attack, and if he does, it's on your head, damn it to hell.' And she meant it."

After they returned to the U.S. from England, they finally confronted the situation and told Sharon's father the truth. "He was an avowed, explicit racist," Gates says, "and I thought the mother made the right decision not to tell him. But Sharon decided one day she was going to tell her father and until he accepted me, she wasn't going to go home again. And her mother was absolutely correct — the man flipped out." Later, though, her father accepted Gates.

Gates and Adams were married on September 1, 1979. They now have two daughters, Maggie and Liza. An artist, Adams worked for many years as a potter, until medical problems forced her to give it up. She now works as a landscape designer.

CAREER HIGHLIGHTS

Gates began his professional career in 1979, when he earned his Ph.D. from Cambridge. Since then, he has been active in a variety of academic areas; in fact, fellow scholars often marvel at the amount he is able to accomplish. He has worked at several different universities over the years, both as a professor and as a department head in the area of African-American Studies. He has also done extensive research, writing, and editing in the fields of literary criticism, literary history, and cultural criticism. Many of these activities have brought him to the attention of the public, and in the process Gates has become one of the best known academics in the country.

As a University Professor

As a university professor, Gates started out at Yale, where he worked as a lecturer while finishing his doctorate. After that, he continued teaching at Yale from 1979 to 1985, first as an assistant professor and then as an associate professor of English and Afro-American Studies. In 1985 he left Yale for Cornell University in New York. At Cornell, he was a professor of English, comparative literature, and African Studies from 1985 to 1990.

He then left Cornell and spent just one year, from 1990 to 1991, at Duke University in North Carolina as a professor of English and literature. He left Duke in 1991 for Harvard University in Massachusetts, where he continues to the present time. At Harvard he works now as a professor of English and the humanities, as head of the department of Afro-American Studies, and as the director of the W.E.B. DuBois Institute for Afro-American Research.

Most university professors, no matter how brilliant or talented, are pretty much unknown outside their schools. But that hasn't been true for Gates. Back in the early 1980s, two different events brought him national attention. In 1981, he won a MacArthur Prize Fellowship totaling $164,000 from the MacArthur Foundation. The MacArthur Prizes are the so-called "genius grants." The foundation gives them out to talented individuals so they can pursue their areas of interest, with no strings attached. Recipients don't have to produce anything in particular as a result of winning the grant. Instead, the five-year stipend is intended to give recipients time to devote to their own intellectual or artistic pursuits. Gates won the prize in the first year that it existed. He has said that the award meant feeling the "financial and psychological freedom" to study literary theory.

> "We were raised to think that Africans were just savages waiting on Europeans to discover them and educate them in the University of Slavery." But that's wrong, according to Gates: "Africans have been creating civilizations for 5,000 years."

Just a short time later, Gates was in New York when he came across a discovery in a rare-book store: *Our Nig; or, Sketches from the Life of a Free Black,* written in 1859 by Harriet E. Wilson. Scholars had long assumed that Wilson was the pseudonym for a Northern white man. But Gates investigated the novel and its author. He and several of his students did research into copyright information, census data, birth and death records, and old newspaper and magazine articles. Eventually they were able to confirm that Harriet E. Wilson was in fact an African-American woman, making *Our Nig* the earliest known novel by a black woman. *Our Nig* was a monumental find for a literary historian, and it contributed to his growing fame. He was profiled in *People* magazine, with a lovely photo of Gates, his wife, and their two daughters. Because of his marriage to a white woman, the family received hate mail afterward.

Since then, Gates has studied a wide range of interests in his academic life. But taken together, these interests promote knowledge of African-American literature, history, and culture as part of the "canon." That's the group of intellectual and artistic works that are generally agreed to represent the best of our society. As he says, "What we're trying to do is establish the canon of African-American literature in the larger American society, in the larger American curriculum. . . . I am trying to establish a black presence in the canon of American culture."

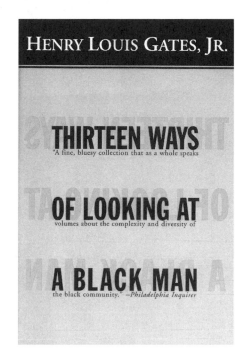

As an Editor and Writer

One way that Gates has done this is by finding, editing, and publishing many works by and about African-Americans. Beginning with *Our Nig*, he has earned a reputation as a literary archeologist. He's been co-director of the Black Periodical Literature Project (originally called the Black Periodical Fiction Project), which has unearthed tens of thousands of short stories, poems, and reviews from the years 1829 to 1940. He has also compiled and edited other reference books on African-Americans, including *The Oxford-Schomburg Library of Nineteenth-Century Black Women Writers* (1998 and 1991), *The Dictionary of Global Culture* (1995), and *The Norton Anthology of African-American Literature* (1996). The books in the *Norton Anthology* series are widely used in classrooms in both high school and college, making the selection of reprinted texts very influential. He recently edited *Africana* (1999), an encyclopedia of the African world that was first envisioned by W.E.B. DuBois 100 years ago. Gates's version was published in two formats: as *Encarta Africana*, in CD-ROM form, and as *Africana*, in book form.

Another area where Gates has promoted the study of African-Americans is in the field of literary criticism. He has written and edited criticism on African-American literature, analyzing African myths, early African-American slave narratives, and modern African-American literature. He explained many of his ideas in what's considered his most important book, *The Signifying Monkey: A Theory of African-American Literary Criticism* (1988). In this and other works, Gates reinterprets African-American culture and literature, relating it to the culture and literature of West Africa. He links current African-American writings to a distinct literary tradition from West Africa that derives from spoken language. Throughout his career, Gates has rejected the idea that only European literature is great. Instead, he shows how literature from all different cultures should be studied and valued. In fact, he even testified at the trial of the rap group 2 Live Crew. They had been charged with obscenity after a concert in Florida, and Gates testified that their writings derived from African-American literary tradition. The group was later acquitted.

Gates has also written books for general readers. He often writes articles in the *New York Times* newspaper, the *New Yorker* magazine, and other contemporary publications, and he has developed a reputation as a cultural critic with outspoken views on many social issues. Some of these essays appeared in *Thirteen Ways of Looking at a Black Man* (1997), a collection of his writings on 13 black Americans, including James Baldwin, Harry Belafonte, Louis Farrakhan, Colin Powell, and O.J. Simpson. Gates has also published a memoir, *Colored People* (1994), a captivating account that brings to life his experiences as a child and young man in Piedmont.

As a Director of African-American Studies

In addition, Gates has helped several universities develop their African-American Studies departments. In fact, he moved in 1991 to his current position at Harvard University because he was offered the opportunity to rebuild the department. Gates has brought several respected scholars to Harvard, including those working in philosophy, literature, women's studies, theology, art, political science, history, sociology, and anthropology. These scholars bring their special area of research to the study of African and African-American life, and then also try to show how black culture has affected American society. Today Harvard's Afro-American Studies department is considered one of the best, if not the best, in the nation, and Gates is one of the most visible and respected scholars working in the field.

At the university level, African-American Studies departments have several purposes. One is the scholarly analysis of African-American life and culture. But another purpose is related to education reform. Many feel that the current educational system in the United States stresses the Western tradition. They say that it over-emphasizes the contributions of people of European descent, especially white men, and that it under-emphasizes the contributions of African-Americans and other non-white people. University programs in African-American Studies help to identify and categorize the important contributions made by blacks, so those can be added to the curriculum for younger students as well. This is called a multicultural curriculum, in which many different cultures are considered equally valid. Gates has been one of the leaders in the fight for a greater representation of non-European cultures in the curriculum. This has been an extremely controversial position. When asked by *Time* magazine about multicultural curriculum in American education, here is how Gates explained his views.

"What I advocate is a more truly diverse notion of excellence. What [our society has] done is exclude the best that's been thought by everybody but this slender sliver of people who happen in the main to be white males. Now I wouldn't want to get rid of anything in that tradition. I think the Western tradition has been a marvelous, wonderful tradition. But it's not the only tradition full of great ideas. And I'm not talking about any diminishment of standards. Even by the most conservative notion of what is good and bad, we will find excellence in other cultures, like the great Indian cultures, the great Chinese cultures, the great African cultures."

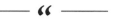

"In Timbuktu, there's this great university, one of the oldest in the world, founded in 1391, which had 25,000 students and scholars. We met a man who was a protector of this library that had been owned by 12 families in Timbuktu, passed down from generation to generation since 1600 . . . 50,000 volumes! Uncatalogued! Written by black men, in Arabic, between the 14th and 17th centuries! . . . It's the mind of the black world, hidden away. Isn't that great!"

Recent Activities

One of Gates's most recent projects is *Wonders of the African World*, a six-part TV documentary that aired on PBS in November 1999. "Part travelogue and part ancient history," according to *The Economist*, "it is the story of a singular African-American confronting his roots from Zanzibar to Timbuktu." The documentary presents Gates's very personal encounters with the continent. But as he wanders through ancient ruins and explains recent archeological findings, the documentary also showcases his efforts

Gates in Ethiopia in a shot from his PBS series, "Wonders of the African World."

to debunk the common charge, dating back to the Enlightenment, that Africans, unlike Europeans, had no culture and no ability to create great civilizations. As he explains, "We were raised to think that Africans were just savages waiting on Europeans to discover them and educate them in the University of Slavery." But that's wrong, according to Gates: "Africans have been creating civilizations for 5,000 years."

Gates and crew made one amazing find during the filming of the documentary. "In Timbuktu, there's this great university, one of the oldest in the world, founded in 1391, which had 25,000 students and scholars. We met a man who was a protector of this library that had been owned by 12 families in Timbuktu, passed down from generation to generation since 1600 . . . 50,000 volumes! Uncatalogued! Written by black men, in Arabic, between the 14th and 17th centuries! I got a grant from the Mellon Foundation, and [now] we're cataloguing them. . . . It's the mind of the black world, hidden away. Isn't that great!" Such enthusiasm for these experiences, coupled with knowledge of his subject, animated the TV documentary *Wonders of the African World*.

For Gates, then, race has been a defining factor throughout his life, and one in which he continues to take great pride. Yet Gates does not let that limit him in any way. "I want to be able to take special pride in a Jessye Norman aria, a Muhammad Ali shuffle, a Michael Jordan slam dunk, a Spike Lee movie, a Thurgood Marshall opinion, a Toni Morrison novel. . . . Even so, I rebel at the notion that I can't be part of other groups, that I can't construct identities through elective affinity, that race must be the most important thing about me. Is that what I want on my gravestone: Here lies an African-American? So I'm divided. I want to be black, to know black, to luxuriate in whatever I might be calling blackness at any particular time — but to do so in order to come out the other side, to experience a humanity that is neither colorless nor reducible to color."

SELECTED WRITINGS

As Author

Figures in Black: Words, Signs, and the Racial Self, 1987
The Signifying Monkey: Towards a Theory of Afro-American Literary Criticism, 1988
Loose Cannons: Notes on the Culture Wars, 1992
Colored People: A Memoir, 1994
Speaking of Race: Hate Speech, Civil Rights, and Civil Liberties, 1995
The Future of the Race, 1996 (with Cornel West)
Thirteen Ways of Looking at a Black Man, 1997
Wonders of the African World, 1999

As Editor

Black Is the Color of the Cosmos: Charles T. Davis's Essays, 1942-1981, 1982
Our Nig; Or, Sketches from the Life of a Free Black, by Harriet E. Wilson, 1983
Black Literature and Literary Theory, 1984
The Schomburg Library of Nineteenth-Century Black Women Writers, 30 volumes, 1988; 10 volume supplement, 1991
The Dictionary of Global Culture, 1995 (with Kwame Anthony Appiah)
The Norton Anthology of African-American Literature, 1996
Africana, 1999 (with Kwame Anthony Appiah)

SELECTED HONORS AND AWARDS

MacArthur Prize Fellowship (MacArthur Foundation): 1981-86
Award for Creative Scholarship (Zora Neale Hurston Society): 1986
Woodrow Wilson National Fellow: 1988-89 and 1989-90
Candle Award (Morehouse College): 1989
American Book Award: 1989, for *The Signifying Monkey*
Anisfield-Wolf Book Award for Race Relations: 1989, for *The Signifying Monkey*
Elected to the American Academy of Arts and Sciences: 1993
George Polk Award for Social Commentary: 1993
National Humanities Medal: 1998

FURTHER READING

Books

Contemporary Authors New Revision Series, Vol. 75, 1999
Contemporary Black Biography, Vol. 3, 1992
Gates, Henry Louis, Jr. *Colored People: A Memoir,* 1994
Who's Who among African-Americans, 1999
Who's Who in America, 1999

Periodicals

Booklist, Feb. 15, 1997, p.972
Boston Globe, Apr. 29, 1993, Living section, p.53
Boston Globe Magazine, May 12, 1991, p.12
Boston Magazine, Apr. 1998, p.64
Christian Science Monitor, Apr. 10, 1992, Books section, p.11
Current Biography 1992
Ebony, Dec. 1981, p.77
New Republic, June 16, 1997, p.19
New York Times Book Review, June 19, 1994, p.10
New York Times Magazine, Apr. 1, 1990, p.24
People, Sep. 12, 1983, p.115
Publishers Weekly, June 20, 1994, p.80
Time, May 23, 1994, p.73
Washington Post, Aug. 10, 1983, p.B1

ADDRESS

Department of Afro-American Studies
Harvard University
1430 Massachusetts Avenue
Cambridge, MA 02138-3810

WORLD WIDE WEB SITES

http://www.harvard.edu
http://www.pbs.org/wonders/BehindSc/behind.htm
http://www.booknotes.org/authors/10279.htm
http://prelectur.stanford.edu/lecturers/gates/

Doris Haddock (Granny D) 1910-

American Political Activist
Walked over 3,000 Miles across the United States to
Promote Campaign Finance Reform

EARLY YEARS

Doris Haddock, who is affectionately known as "Granny D," was born on January 24, 1910. She lived in Dunbar, New Hampshire, with her husband, Jim, who worked for a utility company. They were married for 62 years before his death in 1993. They had two children (a son, Jim, and a daughter, Betty), eight grandchildren, and 12 great-grandchildren (at last count).

152

As a young woman Haddock spent several years at Emerson College in Boston, Massachusetts, planning to become an actress. But she left school in her junior year, when she decided to elope with her husband. That's also when she became interested in politics and activism. "My husband was always very politically minded," she recalls. "We both found politics fascinating."

Doris Haddock has never been reluctant to speak up for what she feels is important. In the 1930s, during the Great Depression, she toured throughout New England as a one-woman theater troupe, presenting feminist plays supporting a woman's right to have a career and work outside the home. In her own community, she lobbied local churches to hold dances for teenagers and worked to stop construction of a major highway in her town. In the 1960s, she and her husband led a successful effort to stop nuclear blasting in Alaska. They learned about U.S. government plans to detonate a thermonuclear bomb in an indigenous Inuit village, to demonstrate how a canal could be created by using nuclear bombs. Haddock, her husband, and their local Episcopal priest drove up to Alaska in an old Volkswagen bus. They discovered that the government planned to uproot a village of Native Alaskans in order to carry out the underground nuclear bomb test. They returned to New Hampshire and publicized the government's plans, recruiting other New Englanders to fight against test bombing. The plan was stopped.

> "
>
> *"I didn't have an upbringing like other kids," her son Jim recalled. "My mother hated housekeeping. The house was always a mess — never dirty, but always a mess. She didn't like to cook, so we had peanut butter sandwiches under a blanket. She'd call it a tent and we'd be going on a picnic. . . . [She] always had a cause. . . . These battles have always been there. She never went looking for them, but when she sees something that's really wrong, she will address it. She always has."*
>
> "

"I didn't have an upbringing like other kids," her son Jim recalled. "My mother hated housekeeping. The house was always a mess—never dirty, but always a mess. She didn't like to cook, so we had peanut butter sandwiches under a blanket. She'd call it a tent and we'd be going on a picnic. . . . [She] always had a cause. . . . These battles have always been there. She never went looking for them, but when she sees something that's really wrong, she will address it. She always has."

Her daughter Betty concurs. "My mother has always been an adventurer," Betty says. "She just is. . . . If there's a cause she wanted to be a part of, she'll do it. [But] she wasn't doing it all her life. She was making a living." Before she retired, Haddock also worked as a secretary in a shoe company.

MAJOR ACCOMPLISHMENTS

Her Inspiration

Several different events came together to inspire Haddock to begin her walk across America. She and a group of her friends in New Hampshire, who called themselves the Tuesday Morning Academy, would get together each week for exercise and stimulating conversation. They discussed the issue of campaign financing, did some research, and even sent off petitions in protest. During that time a law that would reform campaign financing came up in Congress, but Congress failed to pass it. "I didn't like the idea that elections were being taken over by corporations and unions," she said. "I want my great-grandchildren to be brought up in a democracy, not an oligarchy. When the congressmen didn't pass campaign-finance reform last year, they said the people back home don't care about it. I said, 'I don't think that's true, and I'm going to see if it is.'"

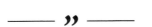

"My mother has always been an adventurer," her daughter Betty says. "She just is. . . . If there's a cause she wanted to be a part of, she'll do it. [But] she wasn't doing it all her life. She was making a living."

Then while traveling in Florida a few years ago with her son, Haddock saw an older man walking along the side of the road. That got her thinking about a walking campaign. Her decision was further inspired by the deaths over the last few years of her husband and her best friend. She wanted to honor their memory by bringing attention to an important cause. "I looked at my life and my lifelong beliefs and said to myself, how can I turn my pain into something beautiful or at least useful to the world? What work can I do as a memorial to those I miss?" She decided to work toward campaign finance reform.

Campaign Financing

Haddock decided to try to reform the way American political campaigns are financed. It costs a lot of money to run for political office, and politi-

Haddock makes her way along Pike St. in downtown Clarksburg, West Virginia, January 3, 2000.

cians are constantly raising money for reelection. Currently, individuals and businesses can only contribute up to $1,000 to a politician's campaign. What concerns Haddock and many other observers is what is called "soft money." This is unregulated, undocumented contributions that are given to a political party, not to an individual. There are no limits on soft money. For the year 2000 presidential campaign, the advocacy group Common Cause has estimated that the election will include as much as $760 million in soft money, mostly from big business and labor unions.

According to those who want to reform the campaign finance process, powerful companies and individuals use soft money to "buy" access to politicians, influencing the outcome of legislation to their benefit. For example, large, powerful companies, in industries ranging from tobacco to telecommunications, can send unlimited amounts of money to political parties to try to influence various politicians. And these politicians are

155

Haddock continues her journey from Cumberland, Md., to Washington, D.C., on January 27, 2000, on cross-country skis.

then responsible for writing the laws that govern key aspects of the business activities of those large, powerful corporations. According to many political observers, that gives these special interests a tremendous amount of power in the political process—and diminishes the amount of power that ordinary Americans have over their own government.

Haddock decided that the best way for her to address the campaign finance issue would be to walk across America. "I'm a poor woman. I live on Social Security. I've got [12] great-grandchildren, and I want them to live in a great democracy. I asked, 'What can one person do?' Well, I can walk." She said that she hoped to accomplish several things. She wanted to awaken Americans to the dangers of big campaign contributions, which corrupt our electoral system and threaten to destroy our democracy. She also wanted to send a message to politicians that the high cost of campaigns gives wealthy special interests the only voice in Washington and shuts out the public. In addition, she hoped to convince members of Congress to pass meaningful campaign finance reform legislation.

"Why am I doing this? Because our democracy is in peril, and the corporations have taken over the government," Haddock said. "I do not think that it is a democracy in a country where a poor man has to sell his soul or his votes in order to become elected, or he has to be a multimillionaire."

"Why am I doing this? Because our democracy is in peril, and the corporations have taken over the government. I have 12 great-grandchildren, and I want them to be brought up in a democracy. And I do not think that it is a democracy in a country where a poor man has to sell his soul or his votes in order to become elected, or he has to be a multimillionaire."

Walking across America

When Haddock told her children about her plans, they were ambivalent. She was about 88 years old at that point, and they were concerned about her health. Her son set up an arduous training program, certain that she would quit. During 1998 Haddock started training, gradually building up her strength and stamina until she was able to hike 10 miles each day, carry a 25-pound backpack, and sleep outdoors. She successfully managed the training program, determined to prove that one person could make a difference.

On January 1, 1999, Doris Haddock set out to walk across America. She started in Pasadena, California, at the end of the Rose Bowl parade, and then just kept going. Her route took her all the way across the continent, from the Pacific to the Atlantic, through 11 states—California, Arizona, New Mexico, Texas, Arkansas, Tennessee, Kentucky, Ohio, West Virginia, Maryland, and Virginia—plus Washington, D.C. For most of the route, she hiked on smaller state highways, with a van traveling alongside. She made the trip despite having arthritis, emphysema, poor hearing, and a sore back from a damaged nerve. She wore a steel corset to provide support for her sore back.

Haddock started using the name Granny D—the nickname used by her grandchildren—because she thought it would sound more appealing. And she soon started to become well known. Journalists wrote articles about her in just about every town she passed through, and she ended up appearing on local and national TV and radio programs as well. As Americans learned of her crusade, they were captivated by her story. Many people would join her to walk for part of the route, some for just a few miles and some for hundreds of miles. Haddock didn't have any financing for her cross-country trip; instead, she relied on the people she met along the way to help her with food and shelter. She stayed in more than 200 houses and told her life story every day for over a year. "I travel as a pilgrim seeking food and shelter," she said. "I haven't gone without a meal or slept on the ground yet. I am prepared to do that, but so far the people of this country have been kind and good and have supported me." Six days each week, she would get up early in the morning and walk ten miles, then mark the pavement with spray paint so she'd know where to start the next day. After that, she'd go out and meet people to discuss campaign finance issues. She talked to people in truck stops, restaurants, bars, and university classrooms. Everywhere she went, people were eager to talk to her about politics and concerned about campaign financing. Over and over, they reinforced her belief that the American people care deeply about these issues.

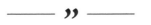

> *One anonymous participant, who marched on the final day, summarized the experience like this. "There was the excitement of being connected, of understanding how our forefathers began this country, with just an idea and the courage to make it happen. I began to understand exactly how important Doris's walk is. I began to understand what campaign reform means. It is giving people back their personal power. . . ."*

Overall, she ended up covering more than 3,200 miles over the course of 14 months. She spent five months just walking across Texas. She wore out two pairs of hiking boots, four pairs of sneakers, and five wide-brimmed hats. Along the way she had a range of adventures. The high point of the

Haddock leads a walk to Capitol Hill on February 29, 2000, to complete her 3,200-mile trek to call for campaign finance reform.

trip, she says, came while crossing a bridge over the Colorado River in Arizona on January 24, 1999, her 89th birthday. "I was feeling rather sorry for myself, thinking nobody knew it was my birthday. The mayor of Harper, Arizona, came out to mid-bridge, handed me the keys to the city, and then a Marine band began playing 'Happy Birthday.'" The low point of the trip came in the southwestern deserts. In the Mojave Desert, she faced such blistering heat that she was hospitalized for four days with dehydration and pneumonia. After that, she had to wear a special backpack filled with water. Later, she faced a foot of snow in the east, where she pulled on her cross-country skis and covered 85 miles on skis. She hoped to arrive in Washington on January 24, 2000, her 90th birthday. But she attracted so much attention that she ended up making many unexpected special appearances along the way, which delayed her. Sometimes she would leave the route and travel to another city to make a special appearance at an event for campaign finance reform, and then return to the exact same spot on her route to continue her trek. Hiking all the way across the United States is an amazing achievement for anyone to accomplish. But it's even more amazing for someone Haddock's age. Granny D was 88 when she started her trek; she celebrated two birthdays along the way, finishing her great trek when she was 90 years old.

Arriving in Washington

Haddock arrived in Washington, D.C., on February 29, 2000. She was accompanied on that final leg of her march by about 2,000 supporters, young and old, on foot and in wheelchairs, carrying banners and signs, chanting "Go Granny Go," and playing drums, horns, and bagpipes. She finished her cross-country march by arriving on the steps of the U.S. Capitol building to address a cheering crowd.

In her speech there, Haddock attacked U.S. senators who have repeatedly blocked legislation that would reform campaign financing. "The people I met along my way have given me messages to deliver here. The messages are many, written with old and young hands of every color, and yet the messages are the same. They are this: Shame on . . . those of you who raise untold millions of dollars in exchange for public policy. Shame on you, senators and congressmen, who have turned this headquarters of a great and self-governing people into a bawdy house. . . . If I have offended you speaking this way on your front steps, that is as it should be. You have offended America and you have dishonored the best things it stands for. Take your wounded pride, get off your backs and onto your feet, and go across the street to clean your rooms. You have somewhere on your desks . . . a modest bill against soft money. Pass it. Then show that you are clever lads by devising new ways for a great people to talk to one another again without the necessity of great wealth. If you cannot do that, then get out of the way — go home to some other corruption, less harmful to a great nation. We have millions of people more worthy of these fine offices." She also said, "The time has come, senators, for reform, or for some new senators. Tell us which it will be and then we will go and vote."

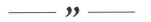

> *"Doris is a beacon, someone who shows us that you can be passionately interested in ideas, that 90-year-olds do not sit in rocking chairs, that an idea has power and strength to move the hearts of many people. More than anyone, she has lifted the idea of campaign reform before the American people."*

Haddock's courageous act has inspired many people, especially those who accompanied her along the way. One anonymous participant, who marched on the final day, summarized the experience like this. "There was the excitement of being connected, of understanding how our forefathers began this country, with just an idea and the courage to make it happen. I began to understand exactly how important Doris's walk is. I began to understand what campaign reform means. It is giving people back their personal power. . . . Doris is a beacon, someone who shows us that you can be passionately interested in ideas, that 90-year-olds do not sit in rocking chairs, that an idea has power and strength to move the hearts of many people. More than anyone, she has lifted the idea of campaign reform before the American people."

Future Plans

Haddock has finished her cross-country adventure, but she hasn't finished working on the issue of campaign finance reform. She plans to continue the fight by going state-to-state to discuss the issue and to work to unseat Congressional representatives who oppose reform. She will remain active in the fight for campaign finance reform throughout the year 2000 presidential election. She plans to continue to work on other issues as well, with civic groups like Common Cause, the League of Women Voters, Public Campaign, the National Civic League, and the Rainforest Action Network. She has also expressed interest in writing a book about her experiences. While glad the trek is over, she has also said that she'll miss the excitement of meeting so many supporters. "Of course I'll miss it," Haddock said. "But I'm very happy. The idea of not having to walk 10 miles a day sounds pretty good to me right now."

FURTHER READING

Periodicals

Boston Globe, June 28, 1999, p.A1; Mar. 19, 2000, New Hampshire Weekly section, p.1
Christian Science Monitor, June 30, 1999, p.3
Nation, May 15, 2000, p.7
New York Times, Apr. 27, 1999, p.A16
People, May 10, 1999, p.25

WORLD WIDE WEB SITES

http://www.grannyd.com
http://www.commoncause.org

Jennifer Love Hewitt 1979-

American Actress
Appeared in the Hit TV Series "Party of Five" and the
Teen Horror Films *I Know What You Did Last Summer*
and *I Still Know What You Did Last Summer*

BIRTH

Jennifer Love Hewitt was born on February 21, 1979, in Waco,
Texas. She was the daughter of Danny Hewitt, a medical tech-
nician, and his wife Pat Hewitt, a speech pathologist. Her parents divorced when she was six months old and her brother,
Todd, was eight.

It was Pat who named her daughter after her best friend in college, a beautiful young woman named Love. But Todd worried that his little sister would be teased for having such an unusual name. He insisted that she have a "real" first name as well, and chose Jennifer because it was the name of a girl he had a crush on, who lived down the street. But everyone called his sister Love. She didn't start using the name Jennifer until she was a teenager and had a career in Hollywood.

YOUTH

After Hewitt's parents divorced, her mother moved her two young children to the nearby town of Killeen, where her daughter showed an early interest in singing and dancing. By the time she turned five, she was taking tap, jazz, and ballet lessons and was convinced that she wanted to be a performer when she grew up. "I was inspired by the TV series 'Punky Brewster' and the actress Soleil Moon Frye," she recalls. "I saw this little girl my age on television and thought, 'I could do that, too.'" At age six she sang Whitney Houston's hit song, "The Greatest Love of All," at a Texas talent show held in a pig barn. The audience gave her a standing ovation, and a local talent scout encouraged Pat to take her daughter to Hollywood. But her mother felt that Love was too young at the time for such a big change.

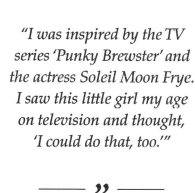

"I was inspired by the TV series 'Punky Brewster' and the actress Soleil Moon Frye. I saw this little girl my age on television and thought, 'I could do that, too.'"

After winning a beauty pageant in Texas, Hewitt was invited to join The Texas Show Team, a song-and-dance youth group, which was preparing to tour Russia and Denmark for several weeks. Her mother accompanied her on the tour, and the thunderous applause that greeted her performances made a huge impression on both of them.

EARLY MEMORIES

When Hewitt was only three years old, she managed to slip away from her mother at a local supper club in Killeen. When she discovered that her daughter was missing, Pat Hewitt began to panic. Then she heard a familiar little voice and found her daughter on top of the grand piano in an adjoining room, singing "Help Me Make It Through the Night" to a surprised and appreciative audience.

EDUCATION AND FIRST JOBS

Hewitt spent kindergarten and first grade at the Belair Elementary School in Killeen, where she was a bright, outgoing child who made friends easily. Shortly after she turned seven, she switched to the Nolanville Elementary School, where she could often be seen in the center of a group of children, and by third grade she was entertaining them with performances of country-and-western songs. Although she was a good student who never caused any problems, Hewitt was already beginning to feel frustrated. She would host, direct, and star in plays that she'd put together, but none of her friends were all that interested in participating.

Although Hewitt never had the everyday life of a high school student, she didn't really miss it. "I'm not missing out on high school," she said. "I played a cheerleader on 'Byrds of Paradise.' I went to a prom on 'McKenna.' I went to a high school on all the shows I've done. I cannot comprehend just going to school, riding my bike, doing homework and going to bed. I need more in a day than that."

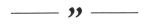

While still in elementary school, Hewitt was ready to make the move to Los Angeles. The same talent scout who had been impressed by her performance at the livestock show a few years earlier put her in touch with a Hollywood agent. On February 19, 1989, the Hewitts left Killeen for Los Angeles, arriving on Hewitt's tenth birthday.

Within a few weeks of arriving in Los Angeles, Love made her professional debut on the Disney Channel series, "Kids Incorporated." Because the show was set in a kids' musical club, Hewitt had plenty of opportunities to sing and dance as well as act. In fact, when she sang "Please Save Us the World" in a skit about cleaning up the environment, the pop ballad was such a big hit that it became the show's theme song. During her three years with "Kids Incorporated," Hewitt attended a child actors' professional school. At the same time, she began appearing in commercials and print ads, including several with basketball champion Michael Jordan. L.A. Gear, the sneaker manufacturer, hired her as a dancer for trade shows in Japan and Paris, and she started making brief appearances on television.

It was while she was playing the role of Robin in "Kids Incorporated" that Hewitt attempted to lead a more "normal" life by enrolling in a regular junior high school in the San Fernando Valley. But she felt out of place with her less experienced classmates, and the teachers added to her unhappiness by warning her that she would grow up to be stupid if she continued in show business instead of getting an education.

Once her career as an actress and singer took off, Hewitt completed high school with the help of tutors. She graduated as a correspondence student with straight A's in June 1997 from the Laurel Springs High School in Ojai, California. Although she had never had the everyday life of a high school student, she didn't really miss it. "I'm not missing out on high school," she said. "I played a cheerleader on 'Byrds of Paradise.' I went to a prom on 'McKenna.' I went to a high school on all the shows I've done. I cannot comprehend just going to school, riding my bike, doing homework and going to bed. I need more in a day than that." Her education is on hold right now, but she plans to go to college in a few years, perhaps to Stanford, where she would like to major in creative writing.

CAREER HIGHLIGHTS

Hewitt's career started with a series of small parts. After finishing with the "Kids Incorporated" show, she was invited to dance and sing for the *Dance! Workout with Barbie* video in 1991. The following year she had a role in a children's movie called *Munchie,* starring Loni Anderson and Dom DeLuise. It wasn't long before she landed her first role in a prime time television series called "Shaky Ground," in which she played the precocious daughter, Bernadette Moody. Although the show was canceled after only 17 episodes, it brought in dozens of job offers for Hewitt. That same year (1993) she landed parts in *Sister Act 2: Back in the Habit,* the sequel to Whoopi Goldberg's hit movie, and the USA Network movie *Little Miss Millions,* about the adventures of a wealthy nine-year-old who tries to locate her real mother while hiding from her money-grubbing stepmother.

Hewitt was cast in two ABC television series in 1994. She played Franny Byrd in "The Byrds of Paradise," a family drama about a Yale professor whose wife is killed and who moves his family to Hawaii to escape his painful memories. She also played Cassie McKenna in "McKenna," a dramatic series filmed in Oregon about a family whose wilderness adventure business begins to fall apart after one of the sons is killed. Another son, who has been estranged from the family for years, returns home to help get the business back on track and to reconcile with his father. Both shows were canceled before the season was over, but Hewitt managed to bounce back from these disappointments and not to take their failure personally.

Sarah (Jennifer Love Hewitt) and Bailey (Scott Wolf), "Party of Five."

The cancellation of "The Byrds of Paradise" and "McKenna" gave Hewitt a chance to spend more time in the recording studio. Her singing talent had already caught the attention of Japan's Medlac Records, which groomed pop stars for European and Asian audiences. In 1992 she released her first CD, *Love Songs,* in Japan, where she became an overnight sensation and embarked on a promotional tour of the country. She went on to record two other CDs in the U.S., consisting mostly of pop and rhythm-and-blues ballads: *Let's Go Bang* in 1995 and *Jennifer Love Hewitt* in 1996.

"Party of Five"

At 16, Hewitt won her breakthrough role on the Fox network drama "Party of Five," about a group of five siblings who are left in the oldest brother's care after their parents die in a car accident. Hewitt joined the cast during the show's second season, playing the role of girl-next-door Sarah Reeves, who becomes romantically involved with Bailey (Scott Wolf). "She was not the character we had envisioned Sarah to be," one of the producers recalls. "We completely changed the character to fit with who [Hewitt] was when she walked in." Although she was only hired to appear in nine episodes, Hewitt was such a popular addition to the cast that she was asked to stay on for another 13 episodes, and eventually she became a regular.

As the long-suffering girlfriend of Bailey, Hewitt played a character who was sweet and wholesome, and the show's many fans identified with her. Hewitt herself loved the character. "Really, truly, I would have been a different teenager without Sarah in my life," she said. "It sounds weird, but she has been my best friend growing up. I learned a lot of valuable things from her when I really needed them, being a teenager, being on TV, going through all the things that teenagers go through."

"Time of Your Life"

Hewitt stayed with "Party of Five" for four years, at which time she was offered a spin-off series of her own called "Time of Your Life." Premiering in November 1999, the new series followed Sarah, who found out she was adopted, as she went off to New York to track down her birth father. Although the new series developed a loyal following, the critics panned it and network executives decided to cancel it in June 2000.

I Know What You Did Last Summer and Other Films

In 1997 Hewitt played the role of Julie James in the teen horror film *I Know What You Did Last Summer*. The film had been written by the popular writer Kevin Williamson, who had rejuvenated the teen horror genre with his 1996 hit movie *Scream* (see entry on Williamson in *Biography Today Authors,* Vol. 6). Teenagers loved *Scream* because it cleverly made fun of some of the slasher movies that had come before it. Thanks to Williamson's fresh, hip approach, *Scream* ended up revitalizing the horror movie genre. For his next hit, *I Know What You Did Last Summer*, Williamson chose the popular Lois Duncan novel of the same name. It's about a group of four teens at the end of their high school years who accidentally run over and kill a stranger after a night of wild partying. Rather than go to the police, they decide to get rid of the body and try to forget the whole incident. A year later, they return to the town where the crime occurred, only to discover that they're being stalked by a mysterious stranger.

Starring Sarah Michelle Gellar, Ryan Phillippe, and Freddie Prinze, Jr., the movie gave Hewitt a chance to work with some of the industry's best young actors and to perform her own stunts, for which she trained by studying kickboxing and ballet. The cast members became great friends, in fact. Sarah Michelle Gellar recalls that it was "like a sleep away camp because the guys have rooms in one building and Love and I have rooms in another. And we all have *I Know What You Did Last Summer* matching luggage." The film was a tremendous success, and Hewitt began to emerge as a major young actress.

———— **"** ————

"Really, truly, I would have been a different teenager without Sarah in my life," Hewitt reveals. *"It sounds weird, but she has been my best friend growing up. I learned a lot of valuable things from her when I really needed them, being a teenager, being on TV, going through all the things that teenagers go through."*

———— **"** ————

Hewitt revisited the role of Julie in the 1998 sequel, *I Still Know What You Did Last Summer*. Julie, who has become increasingly paranoid, is a student at Boston University when her best friend (played by pop star Brandy) talks her into taking a trip to the Bahamas. Once there, Julie discovers she is still being stalked and ends up fighting off the repeated and bloody attacks of a slasher. This time Hewitt trained with weights and aerobics to prepare for the filming, much of which took place in the bug-infested mango orchards of Mexico. "At any given time, you'd have 15 of them crawling on all different parts of your body—up your pants, in your shirt, on your head," she says. "I even got one on my tongue in the middle of a scream." She did so much screaming for this movie, in fact, that she lost her voice twice and had to take special care of her vocal cords before she could record the single, "How Do I Deal," for the movie's soundtrack.

In between *I Know What You Did Last Summer* and its sequel, Hewitt played Amanda Beckette in *Can't Hardly Wait*, a romantic comedy about a prom queen who gets dumped by her boyfriend. Ethan Embry played the loser who has worshiped Amanda from afar and is trying to get up the courage to tell her how he feels. Hewitt had always been a fan of classic

Hewitt with the cast of I Know What You Did Last Summer.

teen movies like *Sixteen Candles* and *The Breakfast Club,* and *Can't Hardly Wait* was the same type of film.

Not long after she appeared in *I Still Know What You Did,* Hewitt co-starred with Ben Stiller in *The Suburbans,* a comedy about a band from the 1980s that recorded one hit song before falling apart. Eighteen years later, the band members have settled into boring suburban lives. When they get together to perform their old hit at a wedding, it attracts the attention of Cate Phillips (Hewitt), a record executive who wants them to make a comeback. In addition to giving Hewitt a chance to play a more mature character, her role in *The Suburbans* also provided her with an opportunity to "pay homage to all the people I've worked with in the music industry."

The Audrey Hepburn Story

Hewitt's career reached a turning point when she won the lead role in a made-for-TV movie about screen legend Audrey Hepburn, who died in 1993. It was a far more challenging role because Hepburn's elegance, grace, and style made her unique among the actors of her generation. In addition, Hepburn had been Hewitt's role model since she was seven years old and saw *Breakfast at Tiffany's* for the first time. "She was the kind of woman I wanted to grow up to be like," Hewitt explains.

The movie told the story of Hepburn's life, from her birth in Belgium to her teenage years during the Nazi occupation of Holland and her two unhappy marriages. The screenplay was written by Pulitzer-Prize-winning playwright Marsha Norman, and it required Hewitt to sing Hepburn's most famous song, "Moon River." She also had to lose 11 pounds to make her look more like Hepburn, who was known for her slim figure and her 20-inch waist, and she had to practice walking around with a book on her head to reproduce Hepburn's graceful way of moving. Imitating Hepburn's accent, the result of her growing up in both Holland and England, was another challenge. Two weeks before production started, Hewitt seriously considered dropping out of the project because she thought she wasn't beautiful or talented enough. Her mother reminded her that Audrey Hepburn had expressed similar self-doubts, and Hewitt decided to face up to the challenge and do her best. When *The Audrey Hepburn Story* aired in March 2000, the critics were not uniformly enthusiastic. But even those who panned the movie gave Hewitt high marks for her efforts.

Recent Projects

At this point, Hewitt's singing career is temporarily on hold, although she intends to get back to it, she says, "when I know I can give it more time and heart." Instead, she continues to focus on acting. She recently completed work on a film originally called *Cupid's Love* and retitled *Marry Me Jane*. Hewitt pitched a script idea of her own to New Line Cinema, which bought it for $500,000 and made her the film's executive producer and star. It's a romantic comedy about a wedding planner who falls in love with a client—the groom whose wedding she's planning. The film has been shot, but hasn't yet been released.

At the moment Hewitt is busy working on *Breakers,* in which she and Sigourney Weaver play mother-daughter con artists who trick wealthy, lonely men out of their fortunes at a Palm Beach resort hotel. She has also started her own production company, Love Spell Entertainment, which has optioned five films.

Hewitt with Johnathon Search in "Time of Your Life."

In addition to doing print and TV ads for Neutrogena cosmetics, Hewitt recently signed a deal with Nokia, the world's largest mobile phone manufacturer. She was chosen to increase the company's brand awareness among young adult wireless phone users in the U.S. She will also support Nokia's charitable efforts with the Big Brothers Big Sisters of America organization. Hewitt is also known for her involvement in Tuesday's Child, a pediatric AIDS organization. She contributed a story about a child with AIDS for the best-selling *Chicken Soup for the Teenage Soul,* a collection of stories from celebrities and ordinary teens on such topics as dating, eating disorders, and drunk driving. Her clean-cut, girl-next-door image is something she takes seriously, avoiding cigarettes and alcohol and trying to serve as a role model for young people. "I know how terrible it is to look up to somebody and then meet them and have them not be everything you want them to be," she adds.

Hewitt is "an absolute powerhouse," according to Amy Pascal, the president of Columbia Pictures. "She's always so together, so organized." She has earned the respect of far more experienced performers for acknowledging that she has a lot to prove, and for taking the time to listen and learn from those around her. And she has earned their respect for being willing to go out on a limb and take a chance. "I'm terrified of not doing a good job. I'm terrified of them laughing in my face. But I'd rather have that than not doing it at all. My only mission in life is when I do leave the planet, when I'm like, 120 and I'm doing the 85th *I Can't Recall What You Did Last Summer*, I want to be able to say that everything I wanted to do on the planet I at least did once."

—— " ——

"I'm terrified of not doing a good job. I'm terrified of them laughing in my face. But I'd rather have that than not doing it at all. My only mission in life is when I do leave the planet, when I'm like, 120 and I'm doing the 85th I Can't Recall What You Did Last Summer, *I want to be able to say that everything I wanted to do on the planet I at least did once."*

—— " ——

HOME AND FAMILY

Hewitt lives in Toluca Lake, a Los Angeles suburb, with her mother, who has given up her work as a speech pathologist to manage her daughter's career and make sure she doesn't push herself too hard. Unlike the stereotypical "stage mother," Pat Hewitt worries constantly about whether her daughter is taking enough time to enjoy life. "She has always tried to get me to stop working so much and relax and have fun," Hewitt says. "She taught me that you are never doing anything wrong in your life if you stay completely true to who you are." Hewitt lives near her older brother Todd, a chiropractor, and she sees him and his wife regularly. She also has two cats named Haylie and Don Juan DeMarco.

And even though she loves being a Hollywood star, she likes to kick back, too. "I love that whole princess mentality," she says. "But I also like throwing my hair in a ponytail and just wearing jeans, going on a hike and then eating a big chili cheeseburger."

Hewitt had a long-term relationship with MTV veejay and "Total Request Live" host Carson Daly that was widely discussed in the press. Since that ended in 1999, Hewitt has kept her social life out of the public eye.

FAVORITE MOVIES

Hewitt's favorite movies are *Splendor in the Grass, Don Juan DeMarco,* and above all, *Sixteen Candles.* "I can't tell you how many times I would stare out the window and dream about seeing the guy in the red Porsche waiting for me," she recalls.

HOBBIES AND OTHER INTERESTS

Hewitt collects celebrity autographs and porcelain angels because "they make you feel safe." She likes to rollerblade around her neighborhood and eat junk food, especially McDonald's cheeseburgers.

CREDITS

Television

"Kids Incorporated," 1989-91
"Shaky Ground," 1992-1993
"The Byrds of Paradise," 1994
"McKenna," 1994-1995
"Party of Five," 1995-1999
"Time of Your Life," 1999-2000
The Audrey Hepburn Story, 2000

Film

Munchie, 1992
Little Miss Millions, 1993
Sister Act 2: Back in the Habit, 1993
House Arrest, 1996
Trojan War, 1997
I Know What You Did Last Summer, 1997
Telling You, 1998
Can't Hardly Wait, 1998
I Still Know What You Did Last Summer, 1998
The Suburbans, 1999

Recordings

Love Songs, 1992
Let's Go Bang, 1995
Jennifer Love Hewitt, 1996

Video

Dance! Workout with Barbie, 1991

FURTHER READING

Books

Aronson, Virginia. *Jennifer Love Hewitt,* 2000
Contemporary Theatre, Film, and Television, Vol. 20, 1998
Golden, Anna Louise. *Jennifer Love Hewitt,* 1999
Shapiro, Mark. *Love Story: The Unauthorized Biography of Jennifer Love Hewitt,* 1998

Periodicals

Biography, Sep. 1999, p.108
Cosmopolitan, Nov. 1998, p.228
Entertainment Weekly, Nov. 13, 1998, p. 28; Sep. 10, 1999, p.40
Mademoiselle, Oct. 1999, p.127
Newsweek, Apr. 3, 2000, p.82
Rolling Stone, May 27, 1999, p.39
Teen, May 1998, p.52; Sep. 1999, p.70
TV Guide, Mar. 25, 2000, p.52
USA Today, Oct. 26, 1999, p.D3

ADDRESS

William Morris Agency
151 S. El Camino Drive
Beverly Hills, CA 90212-2775

WORLD WIDE WEB SITE

http://www.jennifer-love.com

Chamique Holdsclaw 1977-

American Professional Basketball Player with the
Washington Mystics
1999 WNBA Rookie of the Year
Winner of Three NCAA Championships with the
Tennessee Lady Volunteers

BIRTH

Chamique (pronounced sha-MEE-kwah) Holdsclaw was born
on August 9, 1977, in Queens, a borough of New York City.
Her mother, Bonita Holdsclaw, was a data-entry worker, and
her father, Willie Johnson, was a car mechanic. Chamique has
a younger brother, Davon.

—— " ——

"I just thank God for my grandmother because she definitely implemented structure in my life. I thought that was key, because I could have been out there running every which direction, but it's like she set a path for me and I followed that path."

—— " ——

YOUTH

When Holdsclaw was a girl, her young, unmarried parents struggled to make a good home for her and her brother. As a result, Chamique took on a great deal of responsibility around the house. "I had to make sure things didn't fall too much out of order," she recalled. "If they did, I'd call my grandmother or my aunts and uncles." When Holdsclaw was 11, her parents separated. Her mother could not care for the children alone, so Chamique and her brother went to live with their maternal grandmother, June Holdsclaw.

June Holdsclaw, who worked as a records clerk in a hospital, lived in a federal housing project called Astoria House in Queens. Although the housing complex was located in a tough neighborhood—there were bullet holes in the front door and graffiti in the hallways—she managed to provide her grandchildren with a stable home environment. She made sure they did their homework immediately after school, for example, and took them to church with her every Sunday. "I just thank God for my grandmother because she definitely implemented structure in my life," Chamique stated. "I thought that was key, because I could have been out there running every which direction, but it's like she set a path for me and I followed that path." Davon eventually returned to live with their mother, but by this time Chamique had grown so close to her grandmother that she decided to stay at Astoria House.

Holdsclaw was shy as a girl, but also very active. She took ballet lessons for several years and danced in a recital at Lincoln Center in New York City. Her grandmother dreamed that she would become a ballerina, but instead was drawn to basketball. Holdsclaw started out playing basketball indoors against her brother. They would rig a wire clothes hanger as a basket and use balled-up socks as balls. "She went through so many hangers," her grandmother remembered. "All I would hear is bump, bump, bump, that sweat sock hitting the wall."

Before long, June Holdsclaw sent her grandchildren outside to play basketball on the asphalt court at the housing project. At first, the neighborhood boys did not want Chamique on their team. But she gradually improved her skills by shooting baskets before school and playing one-on-one every chance she got. Sometimes she would even shovel snow off the court in order to practice. Before long, she was accepted as a regular player among the boys. "I was just out there every day playing with the guys," she said. "When I got pushed down, it was kind of like I had to get right back up. I couldn't complain and I couldn't cry, because if I did, they wouldn't let me play the next day."

Playing street ball with the local boys—most of whom were older and bigger than she was—helped Holdsclaw develop her skills very quickly. "I had to figure out how to get around them," she remembered. "For me to go out there and keep my face, I had to be quick to the ball. I learned how to tip in offensive rebounds rather than bringing them down and how to put an arc on my shot so they couldn't block it." Holdsclaw joined her first organized team, in a boys' recreation league, a short time later. She chose jersey number 23, which she has worn throughout her career, to honor her grandmother. "Everybody thinks I wear the number for [former Chicago Bulls star Michael] Jordan," she noted. "But my grandmother instilled in me that I should never forget the 23rd Psalm, that it would carry me through whatever happens in life."

EDUCATION

Holdsclaw was a good student and maintained a solid B average throughout her years at Queens Lutheran Grammar School and Christ the King High School, also in Queens. Her favorite subjects were history and Spanish, and she thought about becoming a lawyer someday. She also continued playing basketball in school. As it turned out, Christ the King had one of the top high school basketball programs in the country. The women's team had won two straight Class A state titles before she arrived in 1991.

Holdsclaw made the varsity squad as a freshman and quickly emerged as a star. In fact, she led her team to an amazing 106-4 record and four more state titles before she graduated in 1995. She averaged 24.8 points and

> *Playing street ball with the local boys helped Holdsclaw develop her skills very quickly. "I had to figure out how to get around them. For me to go out there and keep my face, I had to be quick to the ball. I learned how to tip in offensive rebounds rather than bringing them down and how to put an arc on my shot so they couldn't block it."*

15.9 rebounds per game during her senior season, and she left Christ the King as the school's all-time leader in scoring (with 2,118 points) and re-bounding (with 1,523 boards). Her impressive career earned her New York's Miss Basketball title three times, as well as the prestigious Naismith Award as the best female high school player in the country in 1995.

By the time she left Christ the King, Holdsclaw was the most highly recruited female basketball player in the country. After consulting with her grandmother, who was born in the South, she finally decided to attend the University of Tennessee in Nashville. She attended the school for four years, playing for their basketball team, the Lady Volunteers, and studying political science. Holdsclaw graduated from the University of Tennessee in 1999 with a bachelor's degree in political science.

CAREER HIGHLIGHTS

College — University of Tennessee Lady Volunteers

By deciding to attend the University of Tennessee, Holdsclaw had selected a basketball powerhouse coached by Pat Summitt (see profile in *Biography Today Sports*, Vol. 3). Under Coach Summitt, the Lady Volunteers basketball team had won National Collegiate Athletic Association (NCAA) national championships in 1987, 1989, and 1991. The program had also produced 12 players who appeared in the Olympics. But more importantly to Holdsclaw, she liked her prospective teammates at Tennessee and felt that she would fit in with them.

——— *"* ———

"There have been few players who take the power and quickness and combine it with the grace so that almost everything looks like a ballet dance out there," said her high school coach, Vincent Cannizzaro. *"When you watch her play, it's almost like someone floating out there."*

——— *"* ———

Holdsclaw adjusted quickly to the college game and made the starting team as a freshman during the 1995-96 season. Although she played well, she was hesitant to take charge when the game was on the line. In a game against the University of Connecticut, for example, Holdsclaw failed to score in the final nine minutes of play. As a result, the Lady Vols suffered their first home loss since 1991. "My nature is not to be a pushy person," she explained. "And I kind of just watched there when we fell behind, thinking the upperclassmen [juniors and seniors] would help us come back, instead of getting in there myself." Afterward, Holdsclaw discussed the situation with her teammates and coach and began to feel more comfortable about being a leader on the floor. "After that I didn't really care what anybody else thought," she stated. "I knew [taking charge] was what the coach wanted me to do."

By the end of her first year with the Lady Vols, Holdsclaw led the team in scoring with 16.2 points per game, and in rebounding with 9.1 boards per game. She became the only freshman player named to the All-American first team. As the annual 64-team NCAA championship tournament approached, however, Holdsclaw sprained her right knee. For a while it looked like she might miss some or all of the NCAA tournament. But her teammates banded together and became determined to work harder. "Her injury was the key to the championship," Coach Summitt stated. "When she went down, all the others realized they had to do more. It made us a better team."

Holdsclaw came back 12 days later to play in the opening round of the tournament. Her team progressed all the way to the semifinal round known as the Final Four, where they beat defending champion Connecticut in overtime. In the finals, the Lady Vols dominated the University of Georgia, 83-65, to win the national championship. Holdsclaw contributed 16 points and 14 rebounds in the final game.

A Tough Sophomore Season

As Holdsclaw entered her sophomore year at Tennessee, she was already recognized as one of the top college players in the country. But most experts doubted that she could lead the Lady Vols to another national championship. Two key players had graduated the previous season, and the team had slipped out of the top 10 in many national polls. As expected, the team struggled throughout the 1996-97 season and ended up losing 10 games — more than any Tennessee team had lost in recent years. "We were setting so many bad records, we were wondering if anything positive would come out of the season," Holdsclaw stated. But Holdsclaw had a good year individually, leading the team with 20.2 points and 9.4 rebounds per game.

Despite their regular-season struggles, the Lady Vols managed to pull together during the NCAA tournament. They upset top-ranked Connecticut, 91-81, to make it to the Final Four. Then, on the strength of 31 points by Holdsclaw, they beat Notre Dame in the semifinals to earn a spot in the championship game. They capped their surprising run by defeating Old Dominion, 68-59, to become only the second women's team to win two consecutive NCAA titles. "Only one other team has done what we've done — win championships back-to-back," Holdsclaw noted. "We have our place in history now." Holdsclaw dominated once again in the championship game, with 24 points and seven rebounds. Her performance earned her Final Four Most Valuable Player honors.

Toward the end of Holdsclaw's sophomore year, National Basketball Association (NBA) officials announced the formation of a new women's professional basketball league called the WNBA. Before this time, female bas-

ketball stars had few options for playing after college. The only professional leagues for women were in Europe. The WNBA — which would feature eight teams in its first year of competition — was intended to fill this void. The WNBA would play its season in the summer, while the men's league, the NBA, was on summer break.

As soon as the WNBA was formed, people began speculating about whether Holdsclaw would leave Tennessee in order to play professionally. The new league had a rule prohibiting college players from leaving school early, but many felt that Holdsclaw had a high enough profile to challenge the rule successfully. But Holdsclaw repeatedly stated that she wanted to stay at Tennessee in order to earn her degree. "I think what the league needs is mature young ladies who have their degrees and who want to go farther than playing basketball as a career," she noted. "And I think also by playing college basketball, you develop your name. Then by your graduation or going pro, it does a greater good for the sport of women's basketball."

———— " ————

"When I used to play basketball, people would call me names and make fun of me. It's cool young girls have someone to look up to. Athletics can open a lot of doors and I want them to experience the same thing I did."

———— " ————

Continued Success as a Junior and Senior

Holdsclaw spent the summer of 1997 as the only college player on the U.S. National Women's Basketball Team. This team, which consisted mostly of professionals and former Olympians, represented the United States in competitions against top teams from around the world. Despite being the youngest member, Holdsclaw led the team in scoring and rebounding and was named USA Basketball's Female Athlete of the Year. When she returned to Tennessee in the fall for her junior season, she possessed a new confidence and maturity.

The Lady Vols added several strong young players for the 1997-98 season, including guards Tamika Catchings and Semeka Randall. These players joined the starting lineup along with Chamique to form the "Three Meeks." They led Tennessee to a perfect 33-0 record that year. Holdsclaw once again led the team in two areas: in scoring, with 23.5 points per game, and in rebounding, with 8.4 boards per game.

The Lady Vols entered the NCAA tournament as heavy favorites, and they did not disappoint their fans. They rolled through the competition and defeated Louisiana Tech in the finals, 93-75, to claim their third consecutive national championship. Their final season record of 39-0 was the best ever in college basketball, in either the women's or men's divisions. Holdsclaw was named the Final Four MVP and the Associated Press National Women's Player of the Year. She also received the Honda-Broderick Cup as the nation's outstanding female collegiate athlete. "I guess I'm used to winning right now," she stated afterward. "I want to come back as a better player, win another championship and go out in style."

During the summer of 1998, Holdsclaw once again joined the U.S. National Team and helped them win the World Championship. When she returned to Tennessee for her senior season, she found herself in the middle of a whirlwind of public attention. She was constantly asked to give interviews, and fans hounded her for autographs everywhere she went. Once again, Holdsclaw lived up to the high expectations with an outstanding season. As a senior, she became the Lady Volunteers' all-time leading scorer, with 3,025 career points. She also became the leading rebounder in the school's history, with 1,295 career boards.

Holdsclaw hoped to complete her college basketball career by leading Tennessee to a fourth consecutive NCAA title in the 1998-99 season. Unfortunately, the Lady Vols were upset by Duke University, 69-63, in the East Regional final, one step short of the Final Four. Holdsclaw's last college game was a disappointing one. She missed her first 10 shots, scored only eight points, and fouled out of the game. Afterward, she broke down in tears. It was the first time she had failed to win a season championship since junior high school.

Although she did not claim a fourth national championship, Holdsclaw still posted one of the most successful college careers ever by a female basketball player. She led the Lady Vols to a 131-17 record and three NCAA titles. She set NCAA tournament records for scoring and rebounding, and she became the third-leading scorer in NCAA history. In recognition of her achievements, she became the first female basketball player to receive the James E. Sullivan Memorial Award as the nation's top amateur athlete. But as she finished her years at Tennessee, Holdsclaw wasn't concerned only with her athletic experiences; she was equally proud of her academic success. "When I graduated, it was the greatest day of my life just to see the excitement on my grandma's face," she recalled.

WNBA—Washington Mystics

As Holdsclaw completed her college career in 1999, basketball fans across the country waited to see where she would begin her professional career. Many people thought that she would be an immediate star in the WNBA and completely transform whatever team she joined. Some experts predicted that she would become the first female athlete to break the million-dollar barrier for endorsement contracts. Holdsclaw responded calmly to all the hype. "People have expectations, but in my case, I have higher expectations for myself than some people can point at me," she stated. "This isn't new for me. I'm used to being in the spotlight. I just go out and play my game."

When the 1999 WNBA draft finally took place, Holdsclaw was selected with the first overall pick by the Washington Mystics. She received only the maximum WNBA rookie salary of $50,000, but she also signed a special deal to promote the league for another $250,000. As expected, she also signed major endorsement deals with Nike and Gatorade. Holdsclaw was very excited about playing professionally and was determined to help the Mystics improve on their 3-27 record from the 1998 season. She scored 18 points and grabbed six rebounds in her first game with her new team, but the Mystics lost.

As the team continued to struggle throughout the season, Holdsclaw sometimes found it difficult to play on a losing team. "At first it was hard, but I realized I'm going to have to go through some growing pains," she noted. "I've been spoiled. I guess I've always enjoyed a lot of success, but losing that championship in college was probably the best thing for me. Right now I'm disappointed, but I know it's going to get better and I know that this team is going to be a championship-caliber team."

"I've been spoiled. I guess I've always enjoyed a lot of success, but losing that championship in college was probably the best thing for me. Right now I'm disappointed, but I know it's going to get better and I know that this team is going to be a championship-caliber team."

At mid-season, Holdsclaw became the only rookie to be voted onto the WNBA All-Star team. She led the Mystics to six straight victories at the end of the season, but they fell just short of making the playoffs with a 12-18 record. Holdsclaw received Rookie of the Year honors for her performance, and she looked forward to helping her team continue to improve the following season. "This team is the youngest team in the WNBA. We have a lot of talent, we're only going to get better," she stated. "In two years, this team is going to be one to be reckoned with because we have all the elements. I think, once you believe what you can do, the sky's the limit."

The Mystics picked up several promising players during the off-season, including All-Star center Vicky Bullett. Early in the 2000 season, Holdsclaw felt so confident about her team's chances that she promised the Mystics would make the playoffs. "We've got to make the playoffs," she said. "If we can't make it with these people in this room, I don't know. Get rid of me, get rid of the coach. It's not going to happen."

Holdsclaw continued her strong play during the 2000 season, leading her team with 17.5 points and 7.4 rebounds per game, but the Mystics continued to struggle. One problem was that Coach Nancy Darsch favored a structured offense that was not well-suited to Holdsclaw's playmaking skills. In early July, the coach kept Holdsclaw on the bench during the last several minutes of a loss to the Sacramento Monarchs. The star player resented being benched and criticized Darsch in the media. A few weeks later, Darsch resigned as coach of the Mystics and was replaced by Darrell Walker.

—— " ——

"I want to be able to say I helped the women's game become more competitive and exciting," she noted. *"I want to bring a flair to the game. I want people to say, 'That Holdsclaw kid, she really could play.'"*

—— " ——

By the end of the regular season in early August, Holdsclaw's team had a 14-18 record, yet had snagged the last playoff spot in the WNBA eastern conference by a narrow margin. That brought the Mystics up against the New York Liberty in the first round of the eastern conference playoffs, a best-of-three-game series played in mid-August 2000. Holdsclaw scored 18 points with eight rebounds and four turnovers in the first game, and 12 points with three rebounds and two turnovers in the second game. But that wasn't enough to stop New York. Unfortunately the Mystics lost both games to the Liberty, 72-63 and 78-57. That brought an abrupt and disappointing end to the series and to the season. "It is definitely a missed opportunity," Holdsclaw said. "We just made some stupid plays down the stretch. We couldn't make the plays when we needed to."

Holdsclaw's Style of Play

The most prominent feature of Holdsclaw's game is her versatility. She can handle the ball as well as any point guard, using fancy moves like crossover dribbles and behind-the-back passes. Yet she also possesses the outstanding jump shot and strong rebounding ability of a forward. At the same time, her size and quickness allow her to score near the basket against taller defenders like a center. In fact, she was listed as a forward/guard/center in the Tennessee Lady Volunteers media guide. "There have been few players who take the power and quickness and combine it with the grace so that almost everything looks like a ballet dance out there," said her high school coach, Vincent Cannizzaro. "When you watch her play, it's almost like someone floating out there."

Holdsclaw is also known for her quiet determination and leadership on the court. She claims that she never becomes angry or "talks trash" during games because her grandmother would not stand for it. "Oooh, she'd tell me to shape up, that I don't need to be doing that because it's rude and doesn't look good," she admitted. Holdsclaw fires herself up by writing inspirational messages on her size 13 sneakers before games. "They're personal motivational quotes that I need to help pump myself up, that I feel I need to be wrapped up in, and the easiest way is by my feet," she explained.

With her unique combination of skills and ability to dominate a game, Holdsclaw is often compared to former NBA star Michael Jordan. She is pleased to serve as a role model for young girls, the way Jordan did for many young boys. "When I used to play basketball, people would call me names and make fun of me," she recalled. "It's cool young girls have someone to look up to. Athletics can open a lot of doors and I want them to experience the same thing I did." These days, there are many girls playing on the basketball courts outside Astoria House. They all wear number 23, but they aspire to "Be like 'Mique" instead of "Be like Mike."

Once the 2000 WNBA season concludes, Holdsclaw will represent the United States as a member of the U.S. National Women's Basketball Team at the Olympic Games in Sydney, Australia. She hopes her appearance in the Olympics will expose more young people to the game of women's basketball. "I want to be able to say I helped the women's game become more competitive and exciting," she noted. "I want to bring a flair to the game. I want people to say, 'That Holdsclaw kid, she really could play.'"

HOME AND FAMILY

Holdsclaw lives in Alexandria, Virginia, a suburb of Washington, D.C. She shares a large townhouse with her boyfriend, Larry Williams. The two met during Holdsclaw's freshman year at Tennessee, and they were friends for a long time before they started dating. Holdsclaw keeps in touch with her parents and her brother, but she remains closest to her grandmother, who is listed as her parent in team media guides.

HOBBIES AND OTHER INTERESTS

In her spare time, Holdsclaw enjoys shopping, visiting amusement parks, and going to the movies.

SELECTED HONORS AND AWARDS

Miss Basketball (State of New York): 1993, 1994, 1995
Basketball Player of the Year (New York City): 1993, 1994, 1995
Naismith Award: 1995, Best Female High School Basketball Player in the
    Nation; 2000, Best College Basketball Players of the 20th Century
NCAA National Championship in Women's Basketball: 1996, 1997, 1998,
    with University of Tennessee Lady Volunteers
NCAA All-American: 1996, 1997, 1998, 1999
Female Athlete of the Year (USA Basketball): 1997
Gold Medal, Women's Basketball World Championship: 1998, with Team
    USA
Women's Basketball Player of the Year (Associated Press): 1998, 1999
Honda-Broderick Cup (NCAA): 1998, as Most Outstanding Female
    Athlete
ESPY Award: 1998, 1999, Women's Basketball Player of the Year; 1999,
    Female Athlete of the Year
National Women's Basketball Player of the Year (*Sports Illustrated*): 1999
National Women's Basketball Player of the Year (*Sporting News*): 1999
James E. Sullivan Memorial Award: 1999, as the Nation's Best Amateur
    Athlete
WNBA Rookie of the Year: 1999
WNBA All-Star: 1999, 2000

FURTHER READING

Books

Fisher, David. *Chamique Holdsclaw,* 2000 (juvenile)
Nelson, Kristi. *The Chamique Holdsclaw Story,* 2000 (juvenile)
Sports Stars, 1998 (juvenile)
Stewart, Mark. *Chamique Holdsclaw: Driving Force,* 2000 (juvenile)
Who's Who among African Americans, 1999

Periodicals

Baltimore Sun, Mar. 26, 1998, p.E1; May 31, 2000, p.D2
Boston Globe, Apr. 1, 1997, p.E7
Life, Apr. 1, 1999, p.108
Newsday, Nov. 6, 1994, Sports Section, p.20; Dec. 30, 1996, p.A42; Nov. 16, 1997, p.C17; Mar. 14, 1999, p.C8
Newsweek, Mar. 15, 1999, p.63
Philadelphia Inquirer, Mar. 27, 1998, p.C1
Sacramento Bee, July 8, 2000, p.C1
San Francisco Chronicle, Mar. 20, 1999, p.E1; July 29, 1999, p.D1
Sport, Apr. 1998, p.90
Sporting News, Apr. 7, 1997, p.17
Sports Illustrated, Dec. 2, 1996, p.100; Apr. 7, 1997, p.42; Apr. 6, 1998, p.54
Sports Illustrated for Kids, Dec. 1998, p.66
St. Louis Post-Dispatch, Mar. 30, 1997, p.F9
Time, Mar. 22, 1999, p.95
TV Guide, Mar. 13, 1999, p.34
USA Today, Mar. 13, 1998, p.C1; June 10, 1999, p.C7; July 17, 2000, p.C13
Washington Post, June 10, 1999, p.H4; July 7, 1999, p.C1; May 27, 2000, p.D8; July 16, 2000, p.D1

ADDRESS

Washington Mystics
MCI Center
601 F Street NW
Washington, DC 20001

WORLD WIDE WEB SITES

http://www.wnba.com/playerindex.html
http://www.usabasketball.com/usa_bios/bioindex.htm

Katie Holmes   1978-

American Actress
Star of the Hit Television Series "Dawson's Creek"

BIRTH

Kate Noelle Holmes was born December 18, 1978, in Toledo, Ohio. Her father, Martin Holmes, is a well-respected Toledo lawyer, and her mother, Kathy Holmes, is a homemaker who has recently gone back to school to study nursing. Katie has three older sisters and an older brother. When asked what it was like to grow up as the youngest of five children, she responded, "I loved being the baby."

YOUTH

The Holmes children were known for being tall and athletic, and Katie spent much of her childhood attending her older siblings' sporting events. "She was very content; she'd just bring her coloring books and do her thing," recalls her brother, Martin Holmes, Jr. With no athletic ability herself, Katie was much more interested in playing with her Barbie doll collection. "I have about 20 [Barbie] dolls," she recalled recently, plus "the huge house, the hot dog stand, game room, workout center, Corvette, and water slide park." Katie was very family-oriented, and it was always hard for her when one of her older siblings went off to college.

Katie's mother enrolled her in a local modeling school when she was in her early teens so that she could learn more about grace and good manners. Students from the school attended the International Modeling and Talent Association convention in New York City every year, where agents got a chance to look them over. When she was 14, Katie went to the convention for the first time, as a model. Two years later, after she'd studied drama at school and had some acting lessons, she returned there to compete as an actress. She performed a monologue from *To Kill a Mockingbird,* and she received 30 calls from interested agents. But her father was against the idea of her getting involved in show business because he wanted her to be a doctor. Eventually he gave in, and both her parents flew with her to Los Angeles to meet with potential agents. She ended up signing with a California-based agency, and her life changed almost immediately.

"I feel sad when I see kids who have experienced too much too young. I'm just learning myself what the real world is like. I'm glad I could wait this long before I had to deal with reality."

Holmes describes her childhood as "very happy." She was so carefree, in fact, that she was in no hurry to grow up. "I feel sad when I see kids who have experienced too much too young. I'm just learning myself what the real world is like. I'm glad I could wait this long before I had to deal with reality."

EARLY MEMORIES

As the youngest of five children, Holmes remembers watching her older brother and sisters very closely. When they had friends over, she would sneak into the room and listen without saying a word. She wanted to find out what they did to get in trouble—so she could avoid doing the same thing. "I was observant," she says. "I think that helped with acting."

EDUCATION AND FIRST JOBS

Holmes attended Notre Dame, a "very strict" Catholic high school for girls in Toledo. She thrived there, but she remembers that "there was a lot of pressure about grades." Going to an all-girls school and wearing a uniform freed her from worrying about how she looked or how boys perceived her. Instead, she was able to concentrate on her studies.

During her junior year at Notre Dame, Holmes auditioned for a part in *The Ice Storm,* Taiwanese director Ang Lee's film about the disintegration of two upper middle class Connecticut families in the early 1970s. She was standing out in the hallway waiting for her turn when someone called her in to read some lines with another actor. She read for a few minutes and after she left, the film's screenwriter turned to the director and said, "This is it; this is a movie star." She was given the role of Libbets Casey, the rich prep school girlfriend of the Hood family's teenage son, Paul. *The Ice Storm,* which starred veteran actors Kevin Kline and Sigourney Weaver, went on to win the "Best Screenplay" award at the 1997 Cannes Film Festival.

Most young actresses would have followed up their success in *The Ice Storm* by immediately looking for a part in another film. But Holmes surprised everyone—including her agent—by returning to Toledo to finish high school and try out for roles in the school plays. When the producers of "Dawson's Creek" asked her to fly out to Los Angeles for a screen test during her senior year, Holmes said she couldn't because the date coincided with opening night of *Damn Yankees,* and she was playing the lead role. She refused to let her classmates down, even if it meant throwing away the opportunity of a lifetime. So she and her mom made a video. She took the part of Joey, her mom took Dawson's part, and they taped a scene in the Holmes's basement. As "Dawson's Creek" creator Kevin Williamson later recalled, "I'll never forget the day when, after weeks of searching for the right actor to play the virtuoso role of Joey, we got her tape. After viewing it, everyone in the room was speechless. My first response was, how fast can we get her here? Unfortunately, she wasn't available. . . . She refused to ditch her classmates to run off to Hollywood to audition. My response? I wanted her even more." (See the entry on Williamson in *Biography Today Authors,* Vol. 6.) Williamson and the producers were willing to reschedule her audition, and she won the part of Joey.

The cast of "Dawson's Creek"

Holmes maintained a 3.8 average at Notre Dame and graduated in 1997. She has already been accepted at Columbia University in New York City, where she hopes to major in English some day. But for now, she has put her college plans on hold until things calm down in her acting career. "College is not something I look upon lightly. I want to give it my entire attention, and that's not possible right now," she explains. But she often points to Jodie Foster—a successful child actress who took time out to attend Yale University before resuming her acting career—as one of her role models.

CAREER HIGHLIGHTS

"Dawson's Creek"

In the WB's top-rated teen drama "Dawson's Creek," Holmes plays the role of Joey Potter, the sensitive, intelligent tomboy-next-door. Joey is a life-long friend of Dawson Leery, played by James Van Der Beek. The show is the creation of screenwriter Kevin Williamson, best known for his teenage horror movies *Scream, Scream 2,* and *I Know What You Did Last Summer.* But "Dawson's Creek" is different. Based on Williamson's own experiences growing up in rural North Carolina, the series follows the coming-of-age adventures of four teenagers in the fictional town of Capeside.

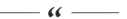

> "Only a few girls get to be prom queen and get all the guys," Holmes comments. "Joey isn't the girl who gets all the guys."

Joey's life is far from perfect: Her mother has already died of breast cancer, and her father is in jail for drug trafficking. She lives with her sister and her sister's child. Joey's life-long friendship with Dawson is her salvation. His family takes her under their wing, and, as a young girl, she sleeps over whenever she wants—usually by climbing up a ladder and into Dawson's window. But as she matures, she begins to wonder whether her relationship with Dawson couldn't be something more than friendship. The attraction between Dawson and other girls forces Joey to confront her feelings for him. Joey's relationship with Dawson has changed over the course of the first few seasons, as they have developed romantic interests in each other, and in other characters. "Only a few girls get to be prom queen and get all the guys," Holmes comments. "Joey isn't the girl who gets all the guys."

Holmes admits that she has a lot in common with the character she plays, including Joey's tomboy image, small-town upbringing, and lack of sophistication when it comes to boys. Just as Joey's first love turns out to be her closest friend and neighbor, Holmes's first real romance was with Joshua Jackson, the actor who plays Pacey Witter on "Dawson's Creek." She refuses to comment on the relationship, which has ended. "I guess you could say that Joey and I are learning about life together," she says.

Helen Mirren and Katie Holmes from Teaching Mrs. Tingle

The Big Screen

Through her portrayal of Joey in "Dawson's Creek" was only her second professional acting job, it made Holmes a star who was soon in demand for feature-length films. In the horror movie *Disturbing Behavior* (1998), she played a sexually precocious girl from the wrong side of the tracks, a role that made her father cringe. "It was terrible," he recalls. "All I was thinking about is, 'If the nuns [from Notre Dame] see her now—oh, my gosh!'" Her next movie was the independent film *Go!* (1999), in which she played a

195

checkout girl at a Los Angeles supermarket who reluctantly gets caught up in a co-worker's drug deal. Although she didn't have a leading role in either film, she gained valuable experience.

Her first major film role was in *Teaching Mrs. Tingle* (1999), written and directed by Kevin Williamson, whom Holmes already knew from "Dawson's Creek." Also appearing in the film was Helen Mirren, the well-known British stage actress and star of PBS's "Prime Suspect." Mirren played Eve Tingle, a spiteful hag of a high school history teacher who wants her students to fail because she herself never managed to achieve anything beyond the narrow confines of her job. Holmes played Leigh Ann Watson, an honor student and working-class girl who is desperate to win the school's only college scholarship, awarded to the top student in the senior class. Her hopes are dashed when Luke, a rebellious classmate (played by Barry Watson) gets his hands on a copy of Tingle's final exam and hides it in Leigh Ann's backpack, where Mrs. Tingle finds it. When Luke, Leigh Ann, and her best friend Jo Lynn go over to Mrs. Tingle's house to explain, the situation gets out of hand and the three teens end up holding their teacher hostage.

> **"**
>
> *"Dawson's Creek" creator Kevin Williamson is full of praise for the actress he discovered a few years ago: "To meet her is to instantly fall under her spell. She is that rare jewel, the real deal. In one word: hypnotic, smart, funny, sweet, shy, boisterous, sneaky, talented, pretty, soulful, sleek, sophisticated, innocent, naive, comical, womanly, childish, caring, gracious, dependable, nurturing, protective, generous. . . I could go on."*
>
> **"**

Like "Dawson's Creek," *Teaching Mrs. Tingle* is based on Williamson's own experience with a teacher who repeatedly humiliated him in class and told him that he had no hope of becoming a successful writer. His original title for the script was *Killing Mrs. Tingle,* but he changed it after the April 1999 massacre at Columbine High School in Littleton, Colorado, in which a teacher was among the 13 victims.

Holmes's next film is *Wonder Boys*, due for release in 2000. In it she plays a college freshman—a role she hopes to fill in real life some day—who has a big crush on one of her professors, played by Michael Douglas.

196

HOBBIES AND OTHER INTERESTS

One of Holmes's favorite pastimes is running. Although she admits she'll never be as athletic as her older siblings, she has discovered that running at her own pace while listening to her favorite music is a good way to ease the tensions of her busy life. "Running really helps clear my head and makes me feel good, especially when I'm stressed," she says. "Lately I've been doing it several times a week. Nothing long-distance or anything, just three or four miles each time."

HOME AND FAMILY

For ten months a year Holmes lives in Wilmington, North Carolina, where "Dawson's Creek" is filmed. She owns her own condo there and lives near the other cast members, who serve as a surrogate family. They shop, eat, and hang out together, and Holmes feels that their closeness has helped them portray their friendships more realistically on the show. But, she confides, sometimes "the four of us get pretty sick of each other."

When the pressures of filming a weekly television show get to be too much for her, Holmes heads back to Ohio to spend time with her family. She considers her mom one of her best friends, and she's equally close to her dad and her siblings.

Holmes also has a very close relationship with Kevin Williamson. Although he recently left the show because he has too many other commitments, he still talks to Holmes on the phone as often as three times a day. Williamson is full of praise for the actress he discovered a few years ago: "To meet her is to instantly fall under her spell. She is that rare jewel, the real deal. In one word: hypnotic, smart, funny, sweet, shy, boisterous, sneaky, talented, pretty, soulful, sleek, sophisticated, innocent, naive, comical, womanly, childish, caring, gracious, dependable, nurturing, protective, generous... I could go on."

One of the things that annoys Holmes most about Hollywood is that it seems to be fashionable for young actors and actresses to say they never want to get married. "I don't want to get married now," she says. "But I want to grow old with somebody!"

CREDITS

The Ice Storm, 1997
"Dawson's Creek," 1998 – (TV series)
Disturbing Behavior, 1998

Go! 1999
Teaching Mrs. Tingle, 1999

FURTHER READING

Books

Catalano, Grace. *Meet the Stars of Dawson's Creek,* 1998
Zier, Nina. *Scene: Katie Holmes,* 1999

Periodicals

Life, Mar. 1, 1999, p.50
Mademoiselle, Apr. 1999, p.125
Rolling Stone, Sep. 7, 1998, p.44
Seventeen, Mar. 1998, p.159; Aug. 1999, p.176
TV Guide, Jan. 16, 1999, p.32
USA Today, Oct. 7, 1998, p.3D
YM, Sep. 1998, p.114

ADDRESS

"Dawson's Creek"
4000 Warner Blvd.
Burbank, CA 91522

WORLD WIDE WEB SITES

www.dawsons-creek.com
www.dawsonscreek.com

Charlayne Hunter-Gault 1942-

American Print and Broadcast Journalist
First Black Woman to Attend the University of
Georgia

BIRTH

Charlayne Hunter-Gault was born Charlayne Alberta Hunter
on February 27, 1942, in Due West, South Carolina. Her parents were Charles Hunter, Jr., who served as an Army chaplain for his entire career, and Althea Hunter, who ran a real
estate office for blacks in Atlanta while Charlayne was growing up. Her parents thought their first born would be a boy,

so her name was created by her mother based on the name of her father, Charles. The eldest of three children, she had two younger brothers, Franklyn and Henry.

YOUTH

Because her father was an Army chaplain, and because she was born during World War II, Charlayne Hunter moved often as a young child. Charles Hunter was sent wherever there were troops, so sometimes Althea Hunter moved the family to be with him, and sometimes they settled near relatives during Charlayne's early years. When she was an infant, her father was stationed in California, so she and her mother lived with him briefly there. They also lived for a short time in Cleveland, Ohio, then moved back to Due West, where she had been born.

World War II ended in 1945, when Charlayne was three years old. Her dad came home and the family lived together in Covington, Georgia, where she spent most of her first 10 years. When the civil war in Korea began in the early 1950s, her father again left the family to minister to the U.S. troops serving in that conflict. By that point, she and her mother and her grandmother were living together in a house in Covington. They were very close, and Charlayne and her brothers were raised surrounded by a loving, extended family.

The South and "Jim Crow" Laws

As a college student, Hunter-Gault would become a symbol of the civil rights movement, which fought for equal rights for African-Americans in the 1950s and 1960s in the U.S. But when she was growing up, the South was still dominated by the Jim Crow laws that legally separated the races and deprived black Americans of their rights for years.

Jim Crow laws came about as the result of a Supreme Court case called *Plessy* v. *Ferguson*. This 1896 decision said that racial segregation was legal according to the Constitution. It paved the way for a series of laws that formed the basis of widespread segregation in the South. (The name "Jim Crow" originally came from an African-American character in a popular song.) *Plessy* v. *Ferguson* established the policy of "separate but equal" public facilities for blacks and whites — separate housing, transportation, schools, restaurants, bathrooms, drinking fountains, and more. Although these separate facilities were called equal, in reality those for blacks were miserably inadequate.

EDUCATION

Charlayne experienced the inequality and inadequacy of facilities for blacks when she first went to school. She attended Washington Street School in Covington, the only school for blacks in the area. Classes were large and books and supplies were scarce. As Hunter-Gault recalls in her memoir *In My Place*, "There was no science or laboratory equipment, in fact barely a playground, other than the gravelly expanse of red clay in front of our school. . . . The school didn't have money for other things like crayons, art materials, even books for the library." Despite the deprivations, Charlayne did well in school. She had actually started school a year earlier than most children, and she skipped the first grade.

The inequality of services Charlayne faced extended beyond education to all areas of life, including medical care. When she was growing up in Covington, there was no dentist in the area to take care of black patients. Instead, a white dentist treated blacks only on certain days, in a small, dirty lab at the back of his office. Charlayne's mother took her in for a toothache. The dentist didn't take care of her minor tooth decay by drilling and filling her cavities, the standard procedure. Instead, he pulled all four of her permanent molars. Charlayne was unable to chew properly for years. Later, as a teenager, she had to have a partial denture made to replace the lost teeth.

"Brenda Starr was one of my favorite characters," Hunter-Gault recalled of her youth. *"I loved her sense of adventure, and the adventures she was always having as the star reporter on the* New York Daily Flash. *. . . The fact that Brenda Starr was a redheaded, blue-eyed white woman who worked in an all-white newsroom did not even register with me. . . ."*

Hunter's educational opportunities improved in the early 1950s, when her family moved to Atlanta, Georgia. There, she lived in a predominantly black middle-class neighborhood and attended the local public school, which was named for a prominent black religious leader, E.R. Carter. The students were taught to revere their African-American heritage. "We learned black history routinely," Hunter-Gault wrote in her memoir, "taught by people who understood that while it was not within their power to confer first-class citizenship legally, they could prepare us through the power they knew no one could deny them: the transmission of a heritage that we could be proud of and inspired by."

Another important aspect of Charlayne Hunter's education was her religious training, centered around the A.M.E. (African Methodist Episcopal) Baptist church. Her father was an A.M.E. minister, as was her grandfather. She attended church regularly and took an active part in youth groups and services throughout her early years. At this point, many of the leaders of the civil rights movement were ministers, including the Reverend Dr. Martin Luther King, Jr., and the black churches played a major part in supporting the drive for equality for African-Americans. Hunter later became a Catholic, and she has often stated that her faith sustained her as she took part in the struggle for racial equality.

Brown v. Board of Education

A defining moment in the fight for equal rights occurred in 1954. In a major decision, *Brown v. Board of Education*, the Supreme Court changed the landscape of public education in the United States, for Charlayne Hunter and generations of Americans, black and white. The court ruled that segregation in the public schools was unconstitutional. That ruling overturned the Jim Crow laws, which had relegated blacks to second-class status. The Court ruled that schools should be integrated, with blacks and whites attending the same schools, with the same educational opportunities. Yet the implementation of the ruling would take years, and would require a fundamental change in the attitude of whites.

Hunter-Gault remembers that her teachers talked about the ruling, but that changes were indeed slow in coming to her area of the country. Also, in the same year that she started high school, her father moved the family to Alaska. She was crushed. Having just started Turner High School, she was looking forward to getting involved in all aspects of student life. Instead, she flew with her mother and brothers to Alaska, for a life unlike any she'd ever encountered. The landscape was cold and forbidding; she was the only black person in her entire school. Her father encouraged her to study and do well, and she did. But there were problems at home. Her parents were living together for the first time in many years, yet they weren't happy. Although Charlayne was young, she knew that something was wrong. Just nine months after they had arrived, she and her mother and brothers moved back to Atlanta; her parents' relationship continued to disintegrate over the years and they eventually divorced.

Charlayne was delighted to be back in Atlanta, and she threw herself into all kinds of activities at Turner High. In addition to doing well academi-

Hunter-Gault registering at the University of Georgia, January, 1961. In the foreground is journalist Calvin Trillin; to Hunter-Gault's right is Vernon Jordan.

cally, she acted in plays, took part in student government, edited the school paper, was elected homecoming queen, and showed such strong skills in English that her teacher asked her to help correct papers. Hunter knew by this time that she wanted to be a journalist. She claims that one of her sources of inspiration was Brenda Starr, the comic strip newspaper glamour girl. "Brenda Starr was one of my favorite characters," Hunter-Gault recalled later. "I loved her sense of adventure, and the adventures she was always having as the star reporter on the New York *Daily Flash*. . . . The fact that Brenda Starr was a redheaded, blue-eyed white woman who worked in an all-white newsroom did not even register with me until, one day during my senior year, I had a conversation with my counselor

203

about what I wanted to do after I graduated. 'I'm going to go to college to study journalism,' I said confidently. 'I want to be a reporter.'"

What her counselor said shocked her: "You better hand up those pipe dreams and go on over there to Spelman [a black women's college in Atlanta] and become a teacher," she said. Her counselor's warning made Charlayne even more adamant: she would study journalism and become a journalist. When it came time to apply to colleges, she chose universities that had journalism schools within them, or that had good undergraduate programs in journalism. This led her to choose Wayne State University, a college in the heart of downtown Detroit. Charlayne Hunter graduated from Turner High School in 1959.

INTEGRATING THE UNIVERSITY OF GEORGIA

Before she left Georgia for Michigan, she and a fellow Turner High graduate, Hamilton ("Hamp") Holmes, were approached by the Atlanta Committee for Cooperative Action, a group of black professionals who wanted to try to integrate the Georgia colleges. They were looking for "two squeaky-clean students who couldn't be challenged on moral, intellectual, or educational grounds," according to Hunter-Gault. Although she and Hamp had already decided to attend other colleges, they were willing to be part of the process of integrating the Georgia university system.

The group's first attempt was at Georgia State University, but neither Charlayne nor Hamp were interested. Georgia State didn't offer the kinds of career-track classes they wanted. Charalyne wanted to be a journalist, and Hamp wanted to be a doctor. They wanted to go to the best state university, the University of Georgia in Athens, a school that had a good academic reputation, but was also staunchly segregated. They were in for a long fight, and they knew it. With the courage and grace that marked the next four years of their lives, Charlayne Hunter and Hamp Holmes began the battle that would make them famous, and that would end segregation at the University of Georgia.

The two students were aided throughout their battle by the NAACP Education Committee, which offered legal and economic support. The first step was to apply to the university. Charlayne and Hemp had graduated from Turner High in June 1959, she third and he first in their class. By July, their applications to UGA had been declined; the university claimed the school was full. So Hunter and Holmes spent their first year of college at other schools, Charlayne going to Wayne and Hamp going to Morehouse, a prestigious black college in Atlanta.

Hunter found the campus of Wayne State University to be another world. It wasn't like the beautiful, leafy campuses of Atlanta that she was used to; it was gritty, urban, and stark, not attractive at all. The school was full of serious students, most of whom worked part-time to finance their educations. It took her awhile, but she grew to like it. She remembers that it was at Wayne that she "fell in love with ideas and art."

Meanwhile, in Georgia, the NAACP was continuing its legal battle against the University of Georgia. Atlanta at this time was a hotbed of civil rights activity, and many of Hunter's former schoolmates were taking part in it. When she returned to Atlanta after her freshman year of college, she began to write for a local black newspaper that covered the story of the emerging civil rights movement, which had been ignored in the mainstream, white press.

Hunter returned to Wayne for her sophomore year, but she left Detroit in December 1960, when the integration case finally went to court in Georgia. The team of lawyers arguing the case included a recent law school graduate named Vernon Jordan, who would later become a major figure in the civil rights movement and the Democratic Party. The legal team felt they had a good chance of winning, and the case drew national media attention. They had uncovered a lie at the heart of the University of Georgia's case. A white female student had been admitted after UGA claimed it

> **——— " ———**
>
> *The true temperament of the university and the state of Georgia was described by Calvin Trillin, then a reporter for* **Time** *magazine, who would go on to write a book about Hunter and Holmes's case and become a well-known and respected journalist. He wrote that Georgia was "a state whose highest officials were declaring daily that there would be no integration, a state that had a law on the books establishing that funds would be cut off from any school that was integrated, a state whose governor had promised in his campaign that 'not one, no, not one' Negro would ever attend classes with whites in Georgia."*
>
> **——— " ———**

had no room for Hunter and Holmes. UGA officials also claimed that they couldn't transfer Hunter's college credits from Wayne because of a different semester system, which was also untrue. The true temperament of the university and the state of Georgia was described by Calvin Trillin, then a reporter for *Time* magazine, who would go on to write a book about Hunter and Holmes's case and become a well-known and respected journalist. He wrote that Georgia was "a state whose highest officials were declaring daily that there would be no integration, a state that had a law on the books establishing that funds would be cut off from any school that was integrated, a state whose governor had promised in his campaign that 'not one, no, not one' Negro would ever attend classes with whites in Georgia."

───── *"* ─────

She heard firecrackers, and all of a sudden a brick was thrown through her window, sending shards of glass all over her bedroom. She recalls in her memoir: "Strangely, I was not at all afraid at this moment. Instead, I found myself thinking, as I stood there in the midst of the wreckage, 'So this is how it is'."

───── *"* ─────

The Integration Ruling

It was in this atmosphere that the judge ruled, on January 6, 1961, that the University of Georgia had to admit Hunter and Holmes. Within days, Hamp tried to register, amid burning crosses and effigies designed to frighten him and reinforce the atmosphere of racial hatred. Then Hunter, accompanied by her mother and Vernon Jordan, tried to register, to the racist taunts of students. They were not successful in that first attempt: the university had been granted a request to halt their registration. Wearily, they went home to Atlanta, but only temporarily: a judge in an appeals court reversed the ruling. Yet the university continued to fight, taking their claim all the way to the Supreme Court, which refused to hear the case.

Hunter and Holmes finally were allowed to register and begin attending classes, though subject to the racist taunts of fellow students and other agitators who had come to the campus to disrupt activities and to threaten the new black students. Hunter felt a certain distance from the rabid emotions. Instead, she remembered her family and her community, and how they had given her "a strong sense of myself, based on my history. So the first time I was called a 'nigger,' it didn't faze me. I thought of myself as a queen. Mere words couldn't touch me inside, and inside is where I was strongest."

Things took an ugly, violent turn their first evening at UGA. Hunter was living in a dorm on campus and had the only room on the first floor. A mob appeared outside and began to chant. She heard firecrackers, and all of a sudden a brick was thrown through her window, sending shards of glass all over her bedroom. She recalls in her memoir: "Strangely, I was not at all afraid at this moment. Instead, I found myself thinking, as I stood there in the midst of the wreckage, 'So this is how it is'." The dean of the school appeared at her door and told her she had to leave the university, "for your safety." Later, she learned that the riot had been planned, and that the state police, who had been called in to stop the violence, took hours to appear.

Hunter and Holmes returned to Atlanta that night, and once again became the center of a court battle and a media frenzy. The future reporter remained an observer even during this trying time. She remembers that she would interview those reporters who were sent to interview her, her passion for journalism enveloping her own story. The NAACP lawyers once again argued for the students' reinstatement, and once again Hunter and Holmes returned to UGA, this time to stay.

For the next two and a half years, Hunter endured the stares and taunts of fellow students, which subsided occasionally. It was a lonely time for her, but she was able to study journalism, which was for her both a vocation and a dream. She spent most weekends at home, and her mother continued to be a source of love and support. Hunter was a good student, getting mostly A's and B's in her classes. By the time she was a senior, there were a total of five black students at UGA. She still faced on-going discrimination: she had to live in the freshman dorm, with several other African-American freshman. When she tried to find a job working on the school paper, she was ignored. Yet she found friends among some of the faculty, which gave her a respite from the often hostile treatment she received from most of her fellow students. During her senior year, Hunter began dating a white student, Walter Stovall. They endured a good deal of discrimination, but it didn't do anything to hurt their relationship. They fell in love and married secretly, not telling anyone until after Charlayne had graduated, in the spring of 1963.

Later that year, after the university found out about the marriage, they threatened to take away her degree. At that time, there were still laws on the books in Georgia that forbade intermarriage between the races, and if the couple had returned to the state they could have been prosecuted. But by then, they had moved to New York City, where Charlayne Hunter had her first job in journalism.

Hunter-Gault with Hamilton Holmes,
November 2, 1992

FIRST JOBS

Hunter's first job out of college was with the *New Yorker* magazine, where she started in 1963. She was personally picked by then-editor William Shawn. The first black ever to be hired by the magazine, she started out as an editorial assistant, then rose through the ranks to become a feature writer. Her marriage to Walter Stovall ended in divorce around this time. In 1967, Hunter-Gault left the *New Yorker* to attend Washington University in St. Louis as a Russell Sage fellow in journalism. That same year, she worked in television for the first time, serving as an anchor for a news station in Washington, D.C. Next, Hunter-Gault joined the staff of the *New York Times*, where she worked from 1968 to 1978. While working for the *Times*, she met and married her second husband, Ronald Gault.

CAREER HIGHLIGHTS

New York Times

Hunter-Gault started out at the *New York Times* in 1968, a time of continuing change for African-Americans in major urban areas like New York City, as well as around the country. She wrote on issues affecting urban blacks, ranging from the meetings of the radical political group the Black Panthers to health care. In 1970 the *Times* sent her back to the University of Georgia to report on the progress of integration. She wrote about the continuing division of the student body by race, noting that many black students still felt intimidated by the racist atmosphere of the school.

In 1970 Hunter-Gault also won the first of three *New York Times* Publishers Awards. She shared the honor with fellow reporter Joseph Lelyveld for a heart-wrenching series on the youngest person ever to die of a heroin overdose in Harlem. Their profile of the tragic life and senseless death of 12-year-old Walter Vandermeer moved readers all over the country and established her reputation as a reporter with instincts for the human aspects of a story.

In 1972 Hunter-Gault was named the first Harlem bureau chief for the *Times*. She described it as "almost like a foreign bureau, only I call it a community outpost." Once again focusing on the human, community aspects of stories, she wrote about "something no one else on staff was— blacks, Harlem, the Bedford-Stuyvesant riots." She won praise throughout the city and within the reporting community for her work as the Harlem bureau chief. Arthur Gelb, then metro editor of the *Times*, described her as "a reporter with wit, grace, style, and a character of steel." Her reporting garnered her two more *New York Times* Publishers Awards, one in 1974 for coverage of then-mayor Abraham Beame's appointment of the first black deputy mayor in the city's history, and one in 1976, for her story about the renaming of a Harlem mosque for Malcolm X.

Hunter-Gault left her mark on the *Times* in other ways, too. Once, after a story she had written was returned to her with all references to "blacks" changed to "Negroes," she wrote a lengthy memo to management explaining how and why the African-American community objected to the term "Negro." Her memo resulted in the change of *New York Times* policy. From that time forward, the editorial directive was to use the term "black" in reference to people of African-American descent.

"The MacNeil-Lehrer NewsHour"

In 1978 Hunter-Gault left the *New York Times* to join the respected team of Robin MacNeil and Jim Lehrer as a reporter on the long-running "MacNeil-Lehrer Report" on PBS. When Hunter-Gault joined the show, it was a half-hour news program that focused on only one topic each day. In 1983, the show expanded to a full hour as the "MacNeil-Lehrer NewsHour." Unlike most network television news, which give only one to two minutes to each news story, "MacNeil-Lehrer" gave depth and breadth to coverage and won the respect of viewers and media around the world. Hunter-Gault covered a broad range of topics for the show, including the continuing struggle for integration across the U.S., the health care crisis for poor Americans, and, increasingly, international news.

She traveled to the Mideast to report on the continuing conflict between the Arab and Israelis, with special reports on the plight of the Palestinian peoples displaced during the years of war. In 1983, she won an Emmy for her reporting on the American invasion of the Caribbean island of Grenada. In 1985, she won a second Emmy, this time for a moving piece entitled "Zumwalt: Agent Orange." In deeply felt, human terms, Hunter-Gault told the tragic story of Elmo Zumwalt III, the son of Admiral Elmo Zumwalt Jr. Elmo III had developed cancer after being exposed to the defoliant Agent Orange while serving in Vietnam. It was Admiral Zumwalt who had given the order for the defoliant to be sprayed.

In 1986, Hunter-Gault received a Peabody Award, one of the most prestigious honors in journalism. She received the award for her series "Apartheid's People," an investigation into the lives of black and white South Africans under the racial separatist policies that ruled that nation until the early 1990s. Of the series, Hunter-Gault said, "American TV viewers are now used to seeing the unfolding events and the violence in South Africa on the nightly news, but events ultimately are about people. I think we got at some of the reasons *behind* the events. We talked to people on both sides who, like most of us, normally are not violent. We wanted to see from their perspective how their rage could become so extreme and lead to violent actions."

—— " ——

"American TV viewers are now used to seeing the unfolding events and the violence in South Africa on the nightly news, but events ultimately are about people. I think we got at some of the reasons behind the events. We talked to people on both sides who, like most of us, normally are not violent. We wanted to see from their perspective how their rage could become so extreme and lead to violent actions."

—— " ——

The Peabody honor was touched with both irony and justice for Hunter-Gault. The awarding body is the University of Georgia H.W. Grady School of Journalism, the school that had fought so doggedly to keep her out. The school later endowed a scholarship in her name, and in 1988 invited her to give the commencement address; she was the first African-American to give the speech.

As senior reporter for MacNeil-Lehrer, Hunter-Gault continued to file stories from around the world, interviewing heads of state from King Hussein of Jordan to Nelson Mandela on his release from prison in South Africa. She covered the Gulf War in 1990 as a correspondent in the field, bringing her knowledge of Mideast affairs to bear on her reporting. "She was always prepared," said her fellow newsman Steve Futterman of NBC, "always seemed to know the answers to the questions she was asking. The generals were very impressed with her. And her reports from Iraq were brilliant, very thorough. She cared more about the story than the sizzle."

While she continued to work for MacNeil-Lehrer, Hunter-Gault took on the role of anchor for an independent television show on human rights around the world, "Rights and Wrongs." The show was produced on an extremely tight budget, but it garnered viewers and awards from around the world. Still, even with Hunter-Gault at the helm, the show suffered because it couldn't find a permanent network willing to pick it up for national distribution, which would have given it a much wider viewership. Even though it aired on PBS, the home network for "MacNeil-Lehrer," PBS wasn't interested in being the national distributor. This dismayed Hunter-Gault, who was very open in a 1994 interview in the *Los Angeles Times* about her frustration with the network in general. She complained of a "glass ceiling" at PBS that wouldn't allow her to advance. "Where do I go? I mean, where does someone like me now

*Hunter-Gault on the
"MacNeil-Lehrer NewsHour"*

go? At a certain point, with this much time invested, I should have a series of my own where I make the decisions, where I decide what goes on the air." Later in the interview she remarked, "Why is it that others who are not white and male can't find some place in this universe of public television?"

Partly in response to her outspoken interview, many more stations decided to air the program. "I think that one of the problems was that a lot of the stations weren't aware of the program because PBS did not embrace it, but now that people are more aware of it, there's more interest in it," she said in 1995. Hunter-Gault felt that while she had made her point, she still had more to offer, and that PBS and the networks in general still "have a ways to go yet." "I think that when people speak out, things happen. I'm not sure that left to its own devices, there would be significant change. I think that we have to protect the gains that we have made and at the same time not be complacent if we feel that we're not where we ought to be."

National Public Radio

In 1997, after twenty years with PBS, Hunter-Gault decided to leave the network and move to South Africa, where she became a reporter for

———— " ————

In the press release that accompanied news of her second Peabody Award in 1999, Hunter-Gault was praised for her "talent for ennobling her subjects and revealing a depth of under-standing of the African experience that was unrivaled in the Western media. More-over, her reports illustrated the power of radio. Described and introduced with intelligence and passionate eloquence, her subjects were given voice, and their personal stories moved from our ears into our hearts."

———— " ————

National Public Radio (NPR), the network that is heard on public radio stations around the country. Her reports were heard on the pro-grams "All Things Considered," "Morning Edition," and "Weekend Edition." Her husband, Ron Gault, had been transferred to South Africa a year earlier by his employer, J.P. Morgan. And Hunter-Gault thought she was ready for a change. "The news business was in a rut," she said. She sensed that there was a "kind of malaise worldwide, be-cause the guideposts of the past have disappeared with the end of the Cold War. Everyone was strug-gling to figure out 'What is news now?' and I've always felt that change was what news was about."

Soon, Hunter-Gault was sending back stories on the transition of South Africa from apartheid to black rule. She also covered the hearings of the Truth and Reconciliation Com-mittee, a group convened to judge those accused of atrocities during the years of apartheid. These often harrowing tales of torture and oppres-sion she rendered with characteristic grace and insight. She also covered news stories coming out of other African nations, including Senegal, Congo, Rwanda, and the Sudan. For her work, she and NPR shared a Peabody Award, her second. In the press release that accompanied news of the award, Hunter-Gault was praised for her "talent for ennobling her sub-jects and revealing a depth of understanding of the African experience that was unrivaled in the Western media. Moreover, her reports illustrated the power of radio. Described and introduced with intelligence and passionate eloquence, her subjects were given voice, and their personal stories moved from our ears into our hearts."

CNN

In March 1999, Hunter-Gault announced that she would be leaving NPR and joining CNN (Cable News Network) to become the Johannesburg bureau chief for the cable news channel. She was excited about the move, because of the importance of CNN's presence in Africa. "Just about anywhere you go in Africa, people are able to see CNN," she said. "Even in cases where people can't access CNN because they don't have TVs or they don't have electricity, [CNN's] stories get told." She is reporting stories from all over Africa, and she's trying to bring greater depth and breadth to coverage of the continent. "Coverage of Africa has usually been about who the bad guys were, or the end product of the action of the bad guys. So you get starvation and massacres, you get Somalia. But I think we have to look at even those stories in a different way. We have to do the coverage of the breaking news, and we also have an opportunity, if not an obligation, to report those things that go on between crises. . . . You'll see more of the people on the ground, the people who are impacted by the leaders, as well as the people who make the policy."

After more than 35 years in journalism, Hunter-Gault remains true to her original focus: "If you look to the people to tell the stories, how people survive, people's aspirations, I think that's where the new news is."

MARRIAGE AND FAMILY

Hunter-Gault has been married twice. She met her first husband, Walter Stovall, while they were both students at the University of Georgia. They married in 1963 and divorced several years later. They have one daughter, Susan. In 1971, Hunter-Gault married Ronald Gault, an executive with J.P. Morgan, a multinational global finance company. They have one son, Chuma. Both her children are grown now and live and work in the United States. Hunter-Gault lives in Johannesburg with her husband and her mother, Althea Hunter.

HONORS AND AWARDS

Publishers Awards (*New York Times*): 1970, 1974, 1976
Emmy Award: 1983, 1985, both for reporting on "The MacNeil-Lehrer NewsHour"
Peabody Award (University of Georgia): 1986, for reporting on "The MacNeil-Lehrer NewsHour"; 1999, for reporting on NPR
Journalist of the Year (National Association of Black Journalists): 1986

WRITINGS

In My Place, 1992

FURTHER READING

Books

Hunter-Gault, Charlayne. *In My Place*, 1992
Streitmatter, Rodger. *Raising Her Voice: African-American Women Journalists Who Changed History*, 1994
Trillin, Calvin. *An Education in Georgia: The Integration of Charlayne Hunter and Hamilton Holmes*, 1963

Periodicals

Atlanta Constitution, Mar. 10, 1999, p.B1
Boston Globe, Dec. 13, 1993, Living Section, p.27; June 12, 1997, p.F1
Chicago Tribune, July 30, 1995, Womanews, p.8
Current Biography Yearbook 1987
Essence, Mar. 1987, p.42
Jet, Mar. 1, 1993, p.30
Los Angeles Times, July 31, 1994, p.A5
New Choices, Oct. 1997, p.62
New York Times, Dec. 16, 1992, p.C3
New York Times Magazine, Jan. 25, 1970, p.24
New Yorker, July 13, 1963, p.30; July 20, 1963, p.32; July 27, 1963, p.34
Newsday, July 10, 1995, p.B25
Los Angeles Times, Dec. 17, 1987, Part 6, p.1; July 31, 1994, p.A5
People, Dec. 7, 1992, p.73
Philadelphia Inquirer, Jan. 23, 1994, Features Section, p.7
Fort Lauderdale Sun-Sentinel, June 20, 1997, p.E4

OTHER

"Weekly Edition" Transcript, National Public Radio, Sep. 27, 1997

ADDRESS

CNN
100 International Blvd.
1 CNN Center
Atlanta, GA 30303

WORLD WIDE WEB SITE

http://cnn.com/CNN/anchors_reporters/huntergault.charlayne.html

BRIEF ENTRY

Johanna Johnson 1983-

American Student
Played with the New York Philharmonic as a
Make-A-Wish Recipient

EARLY LIFE

Johanna Johnson was born on July 12, 1983, in California. Her parents are Richard Johnson, a Lutheran minister, and Lois Johnson, an elementary school teacher. Johanna and her family, including a brother, Luke, live in Grass Valley, California, near Sacramento.

Johnson currently attends Nevada Union High School, where she plays in the band. She has loved music from a very young age. She started playing the piano and clarinet in grade school, and when she got to high school, she started playing the oboe. The oboe is an incredibly hard instrument to play. It has a double reed, and it takes a lot of practice to develop the breath control and technique necessary to make a good sound.

———— `` ————

When Johanna told the Make-A-Wish people that she wanted to sit with an orchestra, they didn't believe her. Most kids want to go to Disney World or meet a celebrity. "They thought it was my parents' wish, but it was definitely mine," says Johnson.

———— `` ————

Diagnosed with Cancer

In May 1999, Johnson was diagnosed with Hodgkin's disease, which is cancer of the lymph nodes. Hodgkin's disease has a 90 per cent cure rate, but Johanna needed to undergo an aggressive therapy that included several months of chemotherapy and radiation. As a result of the chemo, Johanna's hair began to come out in clumps. She decided to have her head shaved, and when her hair came back after her treatment was over, it grew back curly. Even though the treatments made her weak and exhausted, Johanna continued to practice while still undergoing chemotherapy. An avid soccer player, Johanna continued to go to soccer practice, too.

Make-A-Wish Foundation

One of the social workers at the cancer treatment center where Johanna received her therapy referred her to the Make-A-Wish Foundation. The Make-A-Wish Foundation is a national organization that grants the wishes of children with life-threatening illnesses. At first, Johanna didn't know what to ask for. Then, she remembered that her mom had said that "the first time she sat in an orchestra, it was an amazing experience. And so she brought it up again, and I said, 'That's what I want to do. I want to sit with an orchestra'." When she told the Make-A-Wish people, they didn't believe her. Most kids want to go to Disney World or meet a celebrity. "They thought it was my parents' wish, but it was definitely mine," says Johnson.

Next, Johnson had to choose an orchestra and a musician to play with. She wanted to choose from the top orchestras in the U.S., and she nar-

Johnson looks toward her instructor, Joseph Robinson, at a performance of the New York Philharmonic at New York's Avery Fisher Hall on December 11, 1999.

rowed it down to Chicago, Boston, and New York. Then, she went on-line and checked the Internet Web pages of principal oboists for those orchestras. She chose Joseph Robinson of the New York Philharmonic, because she thought "he sounded like a wonderful person." Robinson has three daughters and had started an oboe camp for young players.

Robinson was delighted to have been chosen. He arranged for Johnson to come to New York and play with the Philharmonic in December 1999. He sent her the music they would play—Aaron Copland's *Third Symphony*—and she got a recording so she would be prepared.

MAJOR ACCOMPLISHMENT

But nothing could prepare Johnson for the thrill of playing with the New York Philharmonic. When she attended a rehearsal the day before the performance, the orchestra members greeted her warmly. She received a number of gifts, including an autographed trombone mute, timpani mallets, and a teddy bear. But the most incredible gift came from Robinson. He had arranged for Johnson to receive a Loree oboe, the finest oboe made. Robinson had called the French manufacturer, who had agreed to sell him one of the hard-to-find Lorees at half the usual $5,000 price. Robinson, two board members of the Philharmonic, and a friend who is an amateur oboist chipped in and presented her with the instrument. Johnson was overcome. "I wasn't expecting this at all," she said. She used to flip through music magazines and gaze at ads for Loree oboes. "No, never going to have it," she used to say to herself. "Maybe someday when I'm rich and famous, I'll get one of those, but not before then."

> **Robinson claimed that he and the orchestra were the ones who'd received a special gift. "She just made every member of the New York Philharmonic feel that what we do is so important that this wonderful, radiant all-American girl from California would rather come sit in the New York Philharmonic than do anything else."**

Johnson spent several hours with Robinson, practicing and making reeds. Then, it was time for the performance. She was nervous. "I was about to walk into a New York Philharmonic concert and I couldn't move," she recalled. But, "I knew I had to go on." She loved every minute of it. Robinson claimed that he and the orchestra were the ones who'd received a special gift. "She just made every member of the New York Philharmonic feel that what we do is so important that this wonderful, radiant all-American girl from California would rather come sit in the New York Philharmonic than do anything else. And, as one horn player told me yesterday, you know, Johanna reminds me that

I felt exactly the same way when I was her age, that I would have done anything to be in the New York Philharmonic."

FUTURE PLANS

At this point, Johnson's cancer is in remission. She will undergo tests every three months for the next year to make sure the cancer hasn't come back, then every six months for the year after that. If she remains clear of cancer for two years, she's considered cured.

Now finishing her junior year of high school, Johnson thinks she might like to become a professional musician. She thinks she might like to conduct junior high school bands. And, as Joseph Robinson said, there might be something else in her future. Robinson recalled that "after hours of working away, being interviewed and what not, she looked at me quite earnestly and she said, 'You know, I want to be somebody's wish someday.' I'm sure she will be."

FURTHER READING

Periodicals

Daily News of Los Angeles, Dec. 13, 1999, p.N2
New York Times, Dec. 11, 1999, p.B1
Sacramento Bee, Dec. 12, 1999, p.A1

Other

"Weekend All Things Considered" Transcript, National Public Radio, Dec. 12, 1999

ADDRESS

Richard O. Johnson
P.O. Box 235
Grass Valley, CA 95945

WORLD WIDE WEB SITE

http://www.wish.org

Craig Kielburger 1982-

Canadian Activist against Child Labor
Founder of Free the Children

BIRTH

Craig Kielburger (pronounced KEEL-burger) was born on December 17, 1982, in Toronto, Ontario, a province of Canada. His parents are Fred and Theresa Kielburger, who are both teachers. Craig has one older brother, Marc, an environmental activist since his childhood.

EARLY YEARS

Until he was 12, Craig had a pretty typical childhood. He lived in a well-off neighborhood in Thornhill, a prosperous suburb outside Toronto, with his parents and brother. They have a spacious house there with a swimming pool and tennis courts. He attended Bishop Scalabrini, a local Catholic school, and spent time with his friends rollerblading, shooting hoops, or playing floor hockey. A member of a Boy Scout troop, he also liked swimming, skiing, tae kwan do, pizza, and computer games. He also followed his brother around while Marc worked on environmental issues. Early on, Craig learned how to pass out leaflets, circulate petitions, and speak in front of groups.

READING ABOUT IQBAL MASIH

Kielburger's life changed when he read about a young Pakistani boy named Iqbal Masih. (For more information, please see the entry on Masih in *Biography Today*, January 1996.) Iqbal lived with his family in Pakistan. When he was four, his parents needed a loan to pay for his older brother's wedding. (Expensive weddings are traditional in Pakistani families, even poor ones.) The family made arrangements with a local carpet factory owner, who gave them a loan of about 600 rupees with the agreement that Iqbal would work there in order to pay it off. Iqbal was paid one rupee a day (about 3 cents), but his family's debt grew from 600 rupees to a much greater amount—13,000 rupees—because of the high interest rate tied to the loan. The carpet industry employed many children, because their small hands were ideal for tying the carpets' tiny tight knots. But many other industries in poor countries around the world benefit from child labor as well, reaping greater profits for their owners by exploiting young children.

Iqbal worked for six years, essentially as a child slave, along with many other children. The conditions were terrible—he and others were chained to the looms and forced to tie tiny knots for 12 hours each day. They were constantly pressured to work faster and faster, and they were beaten if they were injured or if they slowed down. Many were physically stunted from being forced to work in a hunched-over position without adequate food or fresh air. By the time he was about 12, Iqbal weighed 50 pounds and was the size of a six-year-old.

When he was about 10, Iqbal escaped from the factory. He attended a rally organized by a group trying to fight child labor. With that group's help, he left the factory for good, attended school, and soon became one of its speakers. He became an international activist against child labor, traveling around the world giving speeches criticizing child labor practices. He wanted to end the practice of forcing children to work and to free all the children. Because his efforts inspired people not to buy Pakistani carpets, he was considered the Pakistani carpet industry's most powerful and damaging critic. He began to receive death threats. Iqbal Masih was murdered on April 16, 1995, at the age of 12, while riding a bicycle with two cousins on a deserted road. The investigation into his death was never resolved, but many believe he was killed by someone working for the carpet industry.

———— " ————

After reading about the life and death of Iqbal Masih, Kielburger was deeply touched. "I just compared my life to his. I saw the differences and I saw how truly lucky I was. . . . [I saw] that there was a need for action on the part of Canadians and I was in a position to take action."

———— " ————

Kielburger learned about Iqbal Masih in April 1995, just after he died. Kielburger was having a normal morning getting ready for school, eating his breakfast cereal and reading the comics section of the newspaper. Then he came across the headline, "Boy, 12, murdered for speaking out against child labor." After reading the story about Iqbal's life and death, Kielburger was deeply touched, particularly because they were both 12 at the time. "I just compared my life to his. I saw the differences and I saw how truly lucky I was," Kielburger said. "[I saw] that there was a need for action on the part of Canadians and I was in a position to take action."

Later, questions about Iqbal's age were raised, and he may have been a few years older than was first believed. But no one has questioned his dedication to freeing other imprisoned children.

LEARNING ABOUT CHILD LABOR

Moved by Iqbal's story, Kielburger started doing research into the issue of child labor. So he pulled together articles and contacted nonprofit organizations that monitor child labor around the world. He learned that an estimated 200 to 250 million children worldwide work as virtual slaves. In many cases, parents desperately need money—perhaps because of unemployment, medical problems, natural disaster, or war. They take out a loan, using the child as collateral. Because the parents can't afford to pay off the loan, the child ends up working to pay off the debt. Factory own-

*Craig with children living and working on a garage dump
in Manila, Philippines, 1998*

ers prefer to hire children because they are easily intimidatcd, thcy don't organize into labor unions, and they are cheap labor—which means greater profits for the factory owners. In many cases, children are working because a parent is unemployed; for example, India has about 50 million child laborers and 55 million unemployed adults. And the reality of child labor is that it reinforces the cycle of poverty—the children can't go to school, so they don't get an education, they remain illiterate, and they are thus unable to break out of their impoverished circumstances.

Here's just a small part of the horrifying material Kielburger uncovered. In India, perhaps 50 million children are working in bondage in factories making rugs, glass, and matches; they earn as little as 40 cents a week. In Pakistan, very young children are chained to the ground making bricks. In Bangladesh, more than 80,000 children under the age of 14 work more than 60 hours a week in clothing factories. In Haiti, about 50,000 girls work as domestics, sleeping on the floor and eating at most only meager scraps. In Brazil, malnourished young children load charcoal. In Thailand, about half the child labor force is involved in prostitution. Around the world, children are beaten and starved in agricultural environments and in factories and plants making stone, carpets, brassware, bricks, fireworks, silk, clothing, blue jeans, and sports equipment. And many of these products are destined for the insatiable consumers living in North America—the United States and Canada.

FOUNDING FREE THE CHILDREN

Kielburger pulled together his research and asked his teacher if he could talk to his seventh grade class. "I think the teacher thought I wanted to make an announcement about having a softball game or something," he said. Instead, he talked to his classmates about Iqbal, about the problem of child labor, and about his desire to form an organization that would fight it. "Basically, I said, 'This is a problem. This is what I know at this point, and this is how you can help.'" About 18 kids first joined him in forming a new volunteer organization, Free the Children. They would meet on Saturdays in Craig's den to plan out letter-writing campaigns, fundraising, petitions drives, and public speaking engagements at schools and community groups. Their initial fundraising consisted of things like bake sales and selling their old toys and clothes at garage sales. Their first speaking engagements came before fifth and sixth grade students. But the group gradually expanded.

———— " ————

"Meeting these children, I learn from them, you know — that's their gift to me — and then in turn going to the media and taking their voices and repeating what they say, acting as a funnel for what they say — that's my gift to them. I want to be able to give them something."

———— " ————

The group's first big break came in November 1995 when Kielburger was asked to speak to a convention of the Ontario Federation of Labor, a trade union group. The poised young speaker quickly surprised and impressed the audience. He proved to be a polished, articulate, confident, and impassioned speaker, ready with statistics and stories about exploited children. His speech closed to a standing ovation, and the audience was visibly moved. One union member rushed up to the microphone and said, "My local is so moved by the dedication of this young brother, we pledge $5,000 to his campaign." Others quickly followed, and by the end of the night the Ontario Federation of Labor had pledged $150,000 to Free the Children. They also offered to set up a trust fund to administer the money.

TRAVELING TO ASIA

The next big break came when Craig took a trip to Asia. By late 1995, he strongly felt that he should travel to Asia to do research into the problem—to meet the children, hear their opinions, and see the conditions in which they worked. His parents initially opposed the idea because they felt he was too young. "The idea was utterly ridiculous at the time," his mother said. "I wouldn't even let him take the subway downtown." But his parents eventually agreed because, according to Kielburger, "They knew I would be a complete pain for the rest of the year if they didn't let me go." They made arrangements for him to miss seven weeks of school and to make up his homework. Craig's mother says she doesn't know where he gets his courage and audacity. And neither she nor her husband have been activists. "Craig has had a real conscience about right and wrong since he was very little," she says.

> *Craig's mother says she doesn't know where he gets his courage and audacity. And neither she nor her husband have been activists. "Craig has had a real conscience about right and wrong since he was very little."*

Kielburger made plans to travel through Asia with Alam Rahman, a college-age student from the Youth Action Network, a Toronto youth activist group. Rahman was going to Asia to do volunteer work, and he agreed to organize the trip and to accompany Craig. Beginning in December 1995, Kielburger went on a seven-week fact-finding trip to five Asian countries, Bangladesh, Thailand, India, Nepal, and Pakistan, financed by his parents. Local human rights groups helped out with housing and transportation along the way. In Asia, he saw abused young domestic workers in Bangladesh. He watched ten-year-old children packing explosives into fireworks in southern India. He met four-year-olds making bricks in Pakistan. He observed boys and girls as young as eight years old forced into prostitution in Thailand. After a raid on a carpet factory in northern India that freed young workers ages eight to twelve, he helped several children return to their families.

During Kielburger's trip, the Canadian Prime Minister, Jean Chretien, also visited Asia. He arrived there with a group of 300 business leaders, trying to drum up business for Canadian companies and to sign import-export

Craig with street children in Morocco, 1998

deals worth billions of dollars. Kielburger asked Chretien for a meeting to discuss the issue of child labor. When Chretien said no, Kielburger did what any 13-year-old kid would do—he held a press conference. He introduced reporters to two children who had been set free from a fireworks factory in India. It became a big story in Canada, followed by newspapers and TV stations all over the country, and Chretien suddenly found time to meet the young activist. That led to an appearance on the U.S. news show "60 Minutes," and even more coverage by the press. By his actions, Kielburger was able to focus the attention of his government and his nation on the issue of child labor.

While traveling in Asia, Kielburger and Rahman were also accompanied by a documentary film crew that took film footage of their encounters overseas. The documentary, *It Takes a Child: Craig Kielburger's Story (A Journey into Child Labour)*, was shown on Canadian TV in 1998. Telling the story of Kielburger's life through the age of 15, it intersperses scenes from home videos of his own childhood with footage from his trip to Asia and his later trips as well. It effectively highlights the horrendous experiences of children living in poverty around the world. On the video, Kielburger explained some of what continues to motivate him. "Meeting these children, I learn from them, you know—that's their gift to me—and then in turn going to the media and taking their voices and repeating what they say, acting as a funnel for what they say—that's my gift to them. I want to be able to give them something."

RECENT ACTIVITIES

Since then, Free the Children has continued to grow. The group works to create a greater awareness of child labor; to pressure world leaders to protect and educate children; to create programs to free children from exploitation and abuse; and to work in cooperation with children around the world. Their mission is to free children from poverty and exploitation and to empower young people to become leaders in their communities.

But Free the Children is different from other child advocacy organizations: it was created by kids and it's run by kids. The group's members are 8 to 18 years old, although there are some adult "associate members" who help with research, accounting, and administrative tasks (like answering the phones when kids are in school). The group now has more than 5,000 kid members, with chapters in 20 countries. They collect about $300,000 in donations each year, with about half from foundations, unions, and government. The other half comes from kids, often

"The most important thing I've learned is that kids can make a difference. Knowledge is the key, knowledge is the power. Take that power and bring about change."

from walk-a-thons, bake sales, raffles, pop bottle collections, and donations of their own money. And Kielburger donates the money he raises back to the group, including royalties from a book he wrote, *Free the Children* (1998), about his odyssey. The money raised by Free the Children goes to build schools for children in poor countries and to fund leadership training courses for kids, to help them develop the leadership skills to take on important issues. Members of the group do a lot of public speaking to educate people about child exploitation. They have spoken to small-scale groups, like local schools, and to larger groups, like a committee of the U.S. Congress studying human rights in Washington, D.C., a UNESCO conference in France, a conference of business executives in India, and meetings of the World Council of Churches in Switzerland and Zimbabwe, among many others.

Currently, Kielburger attends an alternative high school that allows him a more flexible schedule, so he can travel and speak on behalf of Free the Children. In fact, since his trip to Asia he has traveled to over 30 countries to meet with government officials and with children, and to speak with the media on their behalf. For the future, he has talked about working overseas for a non-governmental organization. He has also expressed interest in the French humanitarian group Medecins sans frontieres (Doctors without Borders), the independent and respected medical relief agency that won the 1999 Nobel Peace Prize. "They provide relief in Third World countries, regardless of the politics involved," Kielburger says. "They will go anywhere to help. That's the work I want to do."

But for the time being, Kielburger will continue to work with kids. "The most important thing I've learned is that kids can make a difference," he said. "Knowledge is the key, knowledge is the power. Take that power and bring about change."

WRITINGS

Free the Children, 1998 (with Kevin Major)

HONORS AND AWARDS

Ontario Medal for Good Citizenship: 1996, 1998
Congressional Leadership Award (U.S. Congress): 1996
Reebok Youth in Action Award: 1996
James Keller Youth Award (Christopher Award): 1997
Franklin D. Roosevelt Four Freedoms Medal (Franklin Institute, Holland): 1998
Global Leader of Tomorrow Award (Economic Forum, Switzerland): 1998
Governor General's Award for Meritorious Service: 1998

FURTHER READING

Books

Kielburger, Craig, and Kevin Major. *Free the Children*, 1998
Who's Who, 1999

Periodicals

Biography Magazine, Nov. 1999, p.70
Christian Science Monitor, Apr. 26, 1996, p.1

Los Angeles Times, Dec. 17, 1996, p.E1
Maclean's, Dec. 23, 1996, p.46
New York Times, Apr. 17, 1999, p.B1
Ottawa Citizen, Feb. 4, 1996, p.A1
People, May 10, 1999, p.235
Saturday Night, Nov. 1996, p.40
Seventeen, Sep. 1997, p.130
Time for Kids, Mar. 15, 1996, p.7; Feb. 26, 1999, p.7
Toronto Star, June 23, 1995, p.B1
Washington Post, Feb. 23, 1996, p.A22

Other

It Takes a Child: Craig Kielburger's Story (A Journey into Child Labour),
    video, 1998

ADDRESS

Free the Children USA
12 East 48th Street
New York, NY 10017

Free the Children International
1750 Steeles Avenue West, Suite 218
Concord, Ontario
Canada L4K 2L7

WORLD WIDE WEB SITES

http://www.freethechildren.org

John Lasseter 1957-

American Movie Animator and Director
Creator of *Toy Story*, *A Bug's Life*, and *Toy Story 2*

BIRTH

John Lasseter was born in Hollywood, California, probably on January 12, 1957. Other than that, he hasn't revealed many specific details about his early family life.

YOUTH

Lasseter grew up in Whittier, California, where he learned to love many of the same things that he still enjoys today: toys,

230

art, and animation. Toys have always held a deep fascination for Lasseter. Even today he has an office filled with toys, and he still has one of his first childhood companions, a stuffed Casper the Friendly Ghost doll. Lasseter recalls fondly, "He's got a plastic head, a pull string, and a scratchy little disc which recites 'I'm Casper the Friendly Ghost.' My mother always used to say she knew when I was asleep when Casper stopped talking."

Art has always been one of Lasseter's major interests as well, thanks in part to his mother, who was a high school art teacher for almost 40 years. His first recognition as an artist came in 1962. When he was about five, he won a $15 prize for a crayon drawing of the "Headless Horseman." Throughout his years in school, he was always considered the best artist of his class.

According to Lasseter, learning about animation was one of the major turning points in his life. "I remember thinking, 'Hey, you can do this and you can make money? . . . I realized people made cartoons for a living!"

Animation was one of Lasseter's passions by the time he was a teenager. "In high school, I always, always loved cartoons. I would get up every Saturday morning and watch cartoons until the bowling or golf matches came on. And then, it was in high school that I read this book on the art of animation that talked about the way Disney did its films. And it dawned on me — people do this for a living. I was a freshman in high school and I said, 'That's what I want to do.' I was very much caught up in the art of animation as opposed to the technology of animation." According to Lasseter, finding that book on animation was one of the major turning points in his life. As he says, "I remember thinking, 'Hey, you can do this and you can make money? . . . I realized people made cartoons for a living!"

EDUCATION

Throughout high school, Lasseter studied drawing and painting and the art of animation. He even wrote to the Walt Disney Company to ask for advice about how to develop his interest in animation. Lasseter's timing was perfect. When he was finishing high school, Disney was just creating a new program for animators at the California Institute for the Arts, a school for art, design, and photography in Valencia, California. Lasseter was the second student accepted into the new program at Cal Arts, in what would become a class of just eight students that first year. One of his classmates was the filmmaker Tim Burton, who went on to make the movies *Beetlejuice, Batman* and *Batman Returns, Edward Scissorhands,* and *The Nightmare Before Christmas,* among others. While he was at Cal Arts, Lasseter won two Student Academy Awards for his short films, "Lady and the Lamp" and "Nightmare." He graduated from the California Institute for the Arts in 1979 with a B.A. degree in fine arts in film.

FIRST JOBS

While he was still at Cal Arts, Lasseter worked as an apprentice animator at Disney studios during his summer vacations from school. After graduation, he immediately landed a job in Disney's feature animation division. He worked there for five years, contributing to the films *The Fox and the Hound* and *Mickey's Christmas Carol.* When Lasseter was starting out, traditional animation was done by hand. He worked in cel animation, then the most common technique for making animated cartoons. "Cel" comes from the word celluloid, a type of transparent acetate on which the drawings were made. Movies using cel animation are made by creating thousands of separate drawings, and then photographing each of the drawings as an individual frame in the movie. In the sequence of drawings, the position of a character or an object changes very slightly from one drawing to the next. Thus, action is shown by creating very subtle changes in the drawings so that when the film is shown, the objects or characters appear to move. Cel animation can be very specialized, and often several animators will work on the same drawing, with one doing the backgrounds, one doing the characters, and another painting in the colors. It's a very labor-intensive process.

At that point in his career, it would seem that Lasseter should have been content with his work. He had achieved his lifelong dream of working in the feature film division at Disney, the top company for animated films. And he was content—for a while. But Disney was in a bit of a slump at that point. Most people consider the Disney releases from that era, the early and mid-1980s, to be pretty uninspired—this was before the release of several recent successes, including *The Little Mermaid* in 1989, *Beauty and the Beast* in 1991, and *The Lion King* in 1994—and Lasseter wasn't working on anything that really excited him. Then he happened to see some work being done on *Tron* (1982), about a computer whiz who is sucked into a giant computer and must fight for his life in a video game sequence. He was fascinated by this live action feature film that used computer graphic imagery (CGI) for its special effects. "I wasn't working on the movie, but what I saw fascinated me. I had never before encountered computer animation, and being exposed to it caused me to begin thinking of ways to combine it with traditional animation."

Intrigued by this new approach, Lasseter was eager to try it himself. "They worked with outside computer animation studios to do all of the effects," he recalls. "I remember seeing some early dailies from one of the sequences they produced, and it absolutely amazed me. I felt that Disney was, at the time, doing the same old thing. They had reached a certain plateau technically and artistically with, I think, *101 Dalmatians*, and then everything had been kind of the same ever since then, with a glimmer of characters or sequences that were special. But it hadn't advanced anywhere.

"When I saw the very last bits of *Tron*, my gut said, 'This is it. This is the future.' I already was making the leap to character animation and what we were working on. So I got very excited and started talking about this. I thought it was obvious, and no one else was seeing it." Over and over, in interviews, Lasseter comes back to this same point. "It was amazing. I saw right away that this was the future. I couldn't believe that nobody else could see it."

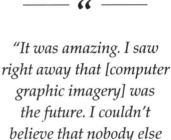

"It was amazing. I saw right away that [computer graphic imagery] was the future. I couldn't believe that nobody else could see it."

First Attempt at Computer Animation

Lasseter and a colleague at Disney made a 30-second test piece called "The Wild Things," based on the Maurice Sendak book *Where the Wild Things Are*. In this piece, they showed how traditional hand-drawn characters could be combined with computer-generated backgrounds. But nobody at Disney was interested in the artistic possibilities of CGI. "Disney at the time was only looking at the computer as a cost savings. They immediately thought, 'Maybe a computer can make what we do cheaper.' But I was looking at it as an artistic advance. This is something that is going to change the way movies look and the way that we make movies. I didn't know if it was going to be a cost saving or not. That is not what excited me."

While Disney wasn't interested in "The Wild Things," other companies were. Soon afterward, the piece was seen by Ed Catmull, who was developing a new computer graphics division for LucasFilm, owned by George Lucas, the creator of *Star Wars*. "At the time we had the best people in the world who were working in the field of computer graphics," Catmull recalls. "I met John for the first time on the Queen Mary [the ship was docked near the site of a computer convention they were attending]. We talked about his coming up to join us. He was the first traditional animator to join our team."

CAREER HIGHLIGHTS

In 1984, Lasseter left Disney to work for a division of LucasFilm, which later turned into Pixar Animation Studios. Since that time, Lasseter has become a renowned creator of animated films using computer graphic imagery, or CGI. Computer animation is a team pursuit, and it takes a lot of people to put together Pixar's films. Yet people are quick to credit Lasseter with much of the company's success. They especially point to his clever, playful, and fiendish sense of humor. According to Andrew Stanton, his co-director on *A Bug's Life*, it's Lasseter's sensibility that pervades these films. "He truly gets it. He has both the kid's perspective and the filmmaker's perspective. The childlike charm and the maturity, that's John." "To see a Pixar film," Kenneth Turan wrote in the *Los Angeles Times*, "is to know that the comedy will be as smart as the visuals are impressive."

"We're storytellers who happen to use computers. You can dazzle an audience with new technology, but in the end people walk away from a movie remembering the characters."

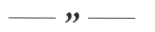

Lasseter is credited with being the first to make full-length, computer-animated, all-digital films. But it's not the process but the content of his films that has grabbed everyone's attention. Despite all that technology has added to his films, he and others at Pixar are quick to stress that computers are not the cause of their success. Instead, they say that the secret is good storytelling and strong characters, and Lasseter is considered by many to be a brilliant storyteller and a creative genius. He has won acclaim for bringing together several influences, using technologically sophisticated graphics created by top computer scientists, plus meticulously crafted screenplays created by top creative artists, all featuring emotional, likable characters that capture the audiences' hearts. "We're storytellers who happen to use computers," Lasseter says. "You can dazzle an audience with new technology, but in the end people walk away from a movie remembering the characters."

From Toy Story.

Early Years

"My story is in a sense what's happening now in computer animation," says Lasseter. "When I first started in this medium, the tools were in the hands of computer scientists. The people using the tools were the people who developed the tools. It's similar to paintings being done by the chemists who mixed and created the paint. But gradually, people from artistic disciplines moved in, someone like myself from traditional animation and other artists and filmmakers who began to get excited about computer animation once exposed to the tools. Then more collaborative efforts evolved."

These collaborative efforts started in 1984, when Lasseter left Disney to work for LucasFilm in the computer research group, which then consisted primarily of hardware and software designers. There he worked on special effects for the film *Young Sherlock Holmes* (1985). For that film he animated the stained glass knight sequence, in which a stained glass figure comes to life and terrorizes another character. The film was nominated for an Academy Award for its special effects. In 1986, Lucas sold part of the company to Steven P. Jobs, the founder of Apple Computer, who had been ousted from that company the previous year. The group from Lucasfilm was reborn as Pixar. Located in northern California, Pixar was then a team of computer scientists, plus a few filmmakers who wanted to make computer-animated films. The company developed the Pixar computer workstation and software that could be used to enhance digital images; the software could be used in many applications, ranging from satellite photographs taken by intelligence agencies to X-ray images taken in hospitals. Eventually Pixar quit making computers and devoted its efforts to software instead. But these activities still weren't very profitable, and Jobs ended up having to prop up the company with $50 million of his own money.

At the same time Jobs also funded Pixar's small group of computer specialists and animators, including Lasseter, which was creating short animated films. Although the animation department constantly lost money, it was useful for showing off interesting applications of the company's products. "I was very fortunate to continue doing the research by doing an animated short film every year," he admits. "I worked with a small group [of technical directors], and we worked together as a team and made these little short films." For Lasseter, the situation was ideal. "I had the best job for an animator. I could sit with the best minds in computer animation and just think up films." But in his mind, he kept expecting the job to end. "This couldn't last. We were a computer company, for goodness' sake. I thought I'd just keep doing this as long as I could, then go somewhere with a lot of knowledge."

Pixar's Animated Short Films

During the late 1980s, Lasseter completed several short films that won widespread acclaim in the animation world for both Lasseter and Pixar. First up in 1986 was *Luxo Jr.*, which features a couple of desk lamps, clearly a father and son, playing with a ball. What was so remarkable about that short piece was the way in which Lasseter was able to animate these inanimate objects. In other words, these lamps seemed to have thoughts and feelings, including sadness, remorse, and compassion. They seemed almost alive—a quality that has characterized his other films as well. The first computer animated film to be nominated for an Oscar, *Luxo Jr.* was recently re-released for current audiences to enjoy, as an accompaniment to the 1999 theatrical release of *Toy Story 2*. *Luxo Jr.* was followed in 1987 by *Red's Dream*, about a unicycle's dream to join the circus. Next up in 1988 was *Tin Toy*, which won the 1988 Academy Award for Best Short Animated Film, the first computer animated film ever to win an Academy Award. *Tin Toy* tells the story of a wind-up toy's first encounter with a rambunctious baby. Then came *Knickknack*, released in 1989, which tells the story of a snowman on a shelf full of knickknacks, who is lured outside of his snow globe by a bunch of partying vacation souvenirs.

———— **"** ————

According to Ralph Guggenheim, a Pixar executive and a producer of *Toy Story*, "We'd spend six months out of the year developing new software to help us make films and six months of the year making the film, then we'd go back and take the ideas that we gained for that and pour it back into researching next year's movie. But what had always united us and the reason why we kept an animation group going at all was that we always thought one day we'd want to do a feature-length animated film." But they didn't have the money for such an ambitious project, so they started producing animation sequences for TV commercials as a way to eventually fund their film project. Then

"To get great acting out of characters, you need traditional animators. That's the only place where you're trained to think in terms of acting with your characters. When we started hiring people, the most important criterion, no matter what the medium, was whether they made the characters look as though they were thinking."

———— **"** ————

Disney became interested in CGI. They repeatedly tried to lure Lasseter away from Pixar, but he wasn't interested. So instead, the two companies agreed to work jointly to produce what would become Pixar's first full-length animated feature film.

To do that, Pixar needed to expand its animation department. But Lasseter couldn't just go out and hire experienced computer animators; at that point, he was basically the only one. So he looked at the process to determine what type of background the animators would need. And he decided that he needed people who understood acting and how to bring char-

*Lasseter after receiving his 1995 Special Achievement Oscar
for his work in animation.*

acters to life, who knew how to make a character in a drawing "act" in the same way that actors "act" in a film. "To get great acting out of characters, you need traditional animators," Lasseter concluded. "That's the only place where you're trained to think in terms of acting with your characters. When we started hiring people, the most important criterion, no matter what the medium, was whether they made the characters look as though they were thinking. I didn't care if they knew computers or not, and would say the vast majority of the animators had no computer backgrounds."

"When I was looking for animators," Lasseter explains, "I looked at guys who worked with clay, cel, sand, and pencils; no matter what the medium, I wanted to see if they were able to take a character and make us feel that it was breathing and thinking. You need to have an innate sense of time and motion to do that, which is sometimes harder to come by than drafts-manship. I think there are gifted animators out there who can't draw worth beans. The computer made me a better animator because even though I wasn't a great draftsman, it enabled me to deal with pure motion."

Here, Lasseter reveals how the animators develop the characters. "As the animators work at Pixar, we really talk in terms of character motivations. Our animators are really the actors of the films. At the beginning we really analyze the characters and try to come up with the traits and ways that they move that are unique to that character, so that not all the characters in the film move the same way or have the same kind of gestures. Part of the goal is to make all the movement that the characters make in the film appear to the audience that they're generated by that character's own thought process, as opposed to just moving from point A to point B. Once it's really alive and thinking, that's when people suspend belief and it be-comes compelling. Those characters then become alive to us as well."

Making a Computer Animated Film

Pixar has developed a defined process for animation with CGI. Of course, any film—with live action, traditional animation, or computer anima-tion—has to start with an idea, and then a script. When the script is com-pleted, actors record the characters' voices and the composer goes to work on the movie's score. At Pixar, they constantly stress that the story is more important than the special effects. "Sooner or later, all this stuff is going to seem antiquated," admits Andrew Stanton, the co-director and screen-writer of *A Bug's Life*, about all of the fancy computer graphics. "The script is the only thing that isn't going to deteriorate over time."

The animation process starts with *storyboards*—over 4,000 storyboards make up the blueprint for the movie's action and dialogue and essentially serve as the film's script. These consist of rough sketches that portray the action of the story, along with the accompanying dialogue. The hand-drawn storyboards, which look like a giant comic strip, are often revised during the creative development process. The next step is *modeling*. They use Pixar's own animation software to create three-dimensional computer models of characters, props, and sets. These models describe the shape of the object and include motion controls that the animators use to control movement and facial expressions. That step is followed by *animation*, for which they use Pixar-created animation software. For each scene, the ani-mators do the layout by choreographing the motion in key sequences, and the computer automatically creates the "in-between" frames, which the animator can adjust. They start with just geometric shapes for the characters, then gradually fill in the rest. After animation, it's time to add the details. The following step is *shading*. Again, computer programs are used to give the objects surface characteristics — like textures, colors, and finishes. Shading programs can replicate many different surfaces, like plastic, wood, metal, fabric, and hair. Next is *lighting*, in which lighting is added to each scene to enhance the mood, emotion, and action. That's followed by *rendering*. Pixar created its own software for this, RenderMan, which "draws" the finished image by computing all the information from the previous steps in modeling, animation, shading, and lighting. Each final rendered image takes anywhere from one to 20 hours of computer time to produce. Then these final images are transferred to film or video.

Some of the statistics from the creation of *Toy Story* put this process in perspective. During rendering, 110 computers were running 24 hours a day for a total of more than 800,000 machine hours. The movie included 114,240 frames, and each frame of *Toy Story* took anywhere from 45 minutes to 20 hours to render. The total film equaled 600 billion bytes, and it took 1,000 CD-ROMs to hold the film's data.

All these technical processes work together to create a totally different look than that created by other types of animation. Traditional animation relies on hand-drawn and painted pictures, and the look of these films is flat and two-dimensional. Part of the appeal of computer animation is that it gives a sense of depth: characters appear to be fully formed, three-dimensional objects in space. In fact, when it's done well, CGI makes it look as if real 3-D objects were filmed by a camera. "Computers are a completely different animation medium," says Peter Docter, a supervising animator at Pixar. "You're always conscious of three dimensions." He has also said that it's hard to get used to doing all the work on the computer rather than on paper. "The first time I saw dailies, even though I had animated a certain shot, I swore I was looking at a real set that had been built somewhere. But it just doesn't exist, anywhere. It's kind of baffling to me, too."

Toy Story

The first full-length animated feature created by Pixar was *Toy Story*. Despite the lighthearted tone of the film, it wasn't an easy movie to make. Pixar and Disney had agreed to jointly produce three films, of which *Toy Story* would be the first. Lasseter and his colleagues had been pondering an idea for the film for a while. They wanted to make a contemporary buddy picture, but the buddies would be toys that come to life. They wanted the two buddies to be opposites. One would be new, a space super-

Slinky Dog, Bo Beep, Mr. Potato Head, Woody, Hamm the Piggy Bank, and Rex the Dinosaur in Toy Story.

hero, which they gave a cool astronaut name: Buzz Lightyear. And one toy would be more old-fashioned, something like the old Howdy Doody character. Lasseter thought back to his own stuffed Casper the Friendly Ghost doll and created Woody, the talking cowboy with a pull string. And of course there would be other toys, lots of old favorites that parents would remember fondly, like Mr. Potato Head, Slinky Dog, Etch-a-Sketch, Barrel of Monkeys, and the bucket of little green army men.

When they first began working on the movie they had trouble with the tone: Woody and Buzz were too sarcastic, the whole attitude was unpleasant, and it just wasn't fun. When they showed an early rough version of some scenes to the head of the Disney animation department, he told them it wasn't working. They went back and retooled it, trying to make it warm and funny and appealing. This time they succeeded. They started with the idea that toys come to life when there's no one around and then created a story about the rivalry in a group of toys in a child's bedroom. Woody, the head of the gang, feels threatened when the boy Andy receives the new Buzz Lightyear toy for his birthday, a flashy new action figure. Woody has always been Andy's favorite, but not anymore. Soon Woody and Buzz are off on a round of adventures together, as they follow Andy to a pizza restaurant, get caught in evil Sid's bedroom, and learn how to help each other as friends. In the process, they both learn what it means to be a toy.

Toy Story was an immediate smash when it was released in 1995, as box office receipts soon climbed to infinity and beyond. People of all ages loved the film, and it proved to be a box-office blockbuster as well as a critical triumph. Lasseter's vision was rewarded when he won a Special Achievement Oscar for the development and inspired application of techniques for *Toy Story*. The movie was also nominated for Best Original Screenplay, the first animated film ever nominated for that award. The success of *Toy Story* ultimately allowed Pixar to renegotiate its contract with Disney, so that profits from future films would be split evenly between the two companies.

—— " ——

> "As the animators work at Pixar, we really talk in terms of character motivations. Our animators are really the actors of the films. At the beginning we really analyze the characters and try to come up with the traits and ways that they move that are unique to that character, so that not all the characters in the film move the same way or have the same kind of gestures."

—— " ——

While all were awed by the film's great technological advances and eye-catching scenes, it was unquestionably the story and the characters that kept people's interest. "*Toy Story* pops off the screen with a vibrancy that's totally unlike traditional hand-painted animation," David Ansen wrote in *Newsweek*. "Harder edged, with a superrealist sheen, the images have such a tactile, three-dimensional presence that you have to keep reminding yourself they're not models photographed in space—that indeed none of the movie's images has been touched by human hands. . . . This first flight into feature-film making—a glimpse of animation's future—is remarkably seamless. Lasseter and his team have resisted the temptation to merely show off the computer's limitless spatial freedom. *Toy Story* is a marvel because it harnesses its flashy technology to a very human wit, rich characters, and a perception no computer could think of: that toys, indeed, are us."

"The moment when I realized what these movies are about was five or six days after *Toy Story* came out," says Lasseter. "I was in the Dallas/Fort Worth airport and this little boy, three or four years old, was clutching a Woody doll. It really touched me to see the joy and excitement of that boy. Woody meant a lot to him. I realized that these characters didn't belong to me anymore."

Geri's Game

After *Toy Story*, the folks at Pixar were hard at work on several projects. One was the movie *A Bug's Life*. But before that reached the screen they completed another film. *Geri's Game* is an animated short, about five minutes in length, about an older man playing a game of chess against himself in the park. The goal in that film was to make a realistic-looking human. In making *Toy Story*, they'd learned a lot about how to make things look real. The most realistic looking stuff was the inanimate objects, like the toys and furniture. Living things were much more difficult, and humans were probably the hardest of all. In fact, some critics thought the humans in *Toy Story* looked creepy.

Pixar addressed those problems in *Geri's Game* with great success. Many were impressed with the way the man's face moved when he laughed, the way he walked in a stooped-over fashion, and the way his clothes wrinkled when he moved. Making this short helped the people at Pixar create more lifelike, believable characters in their later films. Released as a short along with *A Bug's Life*, *Geri's Game* won the 1998 Academy Award for Best Animated Short Film.

A Bug's Life

Lasseter and Pixar went on to their next great success with *A Bug's Life* (1998). This story is about a colony of ants terrorized by a team of bullying grasshoppers, and the usually unlucky and unsuccessful member of the colony, Flik, who sets out to defeat them. He teams up with a ragtag group of bugs from a circus troupe. Together, they pull off some silly and courageous adventures that provide the soul of this movie.

Early on, when the Pixar team decided to do a movie about bugs, they went outside their own office building in northern California to do research. The animators would lay down in the grass, trying to look under the plants and see things from a bug's view. "I love working for a company full of geeks," Lasseter later joked. "Our techie colleagues said, 'Y'know, we can help you with this.' They invented this tiny, tiny video camera—we called it the Bugcam—that they put on a stick with little wheels, and we could roll it along in the grass and look up underneath plants from half an inch above the ground. You can't even get your eye that low." Ultimately, their experience with a bug's-eye view of the world provided the inspiration for the whole look of the film. "What you suddenly realized was that to insects, the world seemed to be made of stained glass, with sunlight coming through the grass blades and leaves."

In making the film, Lasseter and his team were faced with a whole new set of problems, because natural shapes, textures, and movements are difficult for computers to copy. "Geometric is easy to do on computers, and that's what *Toy Story* mostly was," Lasseter says. "But organic is hard. Computers like things neat, orderly, rational. We knew the minute we ventured into nature that it was going to be very challenging because shapes, shadings, movement—there's very little that is simple or geometric in the organic realm."But the story added other animation difficulties as well. For example, they needed to create crowd scenes, which required animating large groups of ants all moving in similar yet distinctly different ways. And whereas *Toy Story* was set indoors, with static background objects, *A Bug's Life* is set primarily outdoors. These exterior backgrounds meant new challenges, including grasses swaying in the breeze, leaves rustling on the trees, and clouds floating overhead. And while Woody and Buzz each had about 750 control points on their bodies, Flik had 3,000 movable parts with 320 facial controls. Still, as Bob Strauss pointed out in the *Daily News of Los Angeles*, they were able to overcome these technical difficulties. "Composed almost entirely of natural shapes (which are much harder for geometrically minded computers to copy), busy with 12 main characters and a background throng of hundreds, and shot through with never-before-seen qualities of light, color, translucence, and scale, it's a quantum leap forward, technically and artistically, from the adventures of Buzz and Woody."

—————— " ——————

"I love working for a company full of geeks,"Lasseter once said about the making of A Bug's Life. "[Our techie colleagues] invented this tiny, tiny video camera—we called it the Bugcam—that they put on a stick with little wheels, and we could roll it along in the grass and look up underneath plants from half an inch above the ground. You can't even get your eye that low."

—————— " ——————

When it was released in 1998, *A Bug's Life* was an audience and critical delight. Reviewers were quick to note the clever comedy, especially the sight gags, and the gorgeous visuals, especially the vivid colors and details. "The animation, from its opening frames, is miraculous," Owen Gleiberman wrote in *Entertainment Weekly*. "We're near a tree trunk in the glorious sun, where a friendly army of ants is placing seeds atop a giant, rickety pile, all

From A Bug's Life.

as a ritual offering to a tribe of grasshopper bullies. Everything is gleaming yet tactile, from the swaying grass blades to the insects' faces and bodies, which cast the subtlest of shadows and reflect slivers of light. The images have an eerie, sculpted vitality that literally seduces your eye into forgetting it's watching animation." Many reviewers also commented on the Pixar team's creative skill with the computer, as Michael Sragow wrote in the *New Times*. "Lasseter and [co-director Andrew Stanton] and the rest of the animators and gagsmiths use the computer with staggering imaginative freedom. It's as if their collective unconscious were the hard drive."

With the success of *A Bug's Life*, Lasseter and Pixar started to receive a lot of attention. While some may have wondered if the previous success of *Toy Story* was a fluke, *A Bug's Life* proved otherwise. And people were quick to credit Lasseter with that success. Steve Jobs, the boss at Pixar, said with great pride, "John Lasseter is the closest thing we have to Walt Disney today." And Peter Schneider, president of Disney Animation, said, "Look at Walt Disney's legacy: he told great stories, with great characters, and he pushed the boundaries of animation. With *Toy Story* and *A Bug's Life*, Lasseter has astounded us twice." Lasseter seems to have the same goal in mind. "Building great character is the most important thing in the movies. We know someday the technology will be far beyond *Toy Story* and *Bug's*

Life. But three years after *Toy Story*, Buzz and Woody live on in people's minds. And that's what we want—movies that live on."

Toy Story 2

Luckily for viewers, Lasseter and his group decided to bring back Woody, Buzz, and all the gang in *Toy Story 2*. The film was originally intended to be released in a direct-to-video format—most Disney animated sequels are never shown in theaters but instead go directly to video stores. But when Lasseter and Jobs showed the executives at Disney some early scenes from the movie, they agreed on a theatrical release. The Disney execs liked the inventive humor and sophisticated story line that would have emotional appeal for both kids and adults.

Lasseter gives his own children credit for helping with the idea for *Toy Story 2*. His office at Pixar is filled with hundreds of toys, some of which are valuable one-of-a-kind collectibles. His own sons would show up at the office and head straight for the toys. But of course they couldn't tell and didn't care which were valuable—they wanted to play with them all. "There I was," he says, "trying to tell them that maybe they're not all meant to be played with. But toys are put on this earth to be played with by a child. Suddenly, because they're old, they're considered collectible and they have to sit on a shelf for the rest of their life. What kind of life is that for a toy?"

From that inspiration, Lasseter and others fashioned another story about Woody, Buzz, and friends. "As in *Toy Story*," Lisa Schwarzbaum wrote in *Entertainment Weekly*, "serious issues of love, friendship, and faithfulness beat in the deep heart of a light adventure." Andy is headed off to cowboy camp for a few days, when at the last minute Woody gets ripped. Woody gets left behind when Andy tosses him aside and goes off to camp without him. Shortly after that, Andy's mom puts one of the toys out in a garage sale, and Woody tries a daring rescue mission. But in the process he's picked up by a toy collector named Al McWhiggin, who's been looking for a Woody doll to complete a valuable set. At Al's, Woody finds out about his past and looks ahead to his future—would it be better to remain part of a collection and live out his life under glass in a museum, or would it be better to return to Andy's room, to be loved and cherished but eventually discarded when Andy grows up? As Lasseter explained, "The worst, most tragic thing that can happen to a toy is to be outgrown by a child who loves you. When you think about what happens to every single toy, like each of us, it's going to die some day. [*Toy Story 2* is] Woody coming to grips with his mortality."

Many reviewers, including Roger Ebert in the *Chicago Sun Times,* found that *Toy Story 2* made them think back to their own childhoods and their own favorite toys. "I forgot something about toys a long time ago, and *Toy Story 2* reminded me," Ebert wrote. "It involves the love, pity, and guilt that a child feels for a favorite toy. A doll or an action figure (or a Pokemon) is yours in the same way a pet is. It depends on you. It misses you. It can't do anything by itself. It needs you and is troubled when you're not there.

"*Toy Story 2* knows this," Ebert continued, "and for smaller viewers that knowledge may be the most important thing about the film—more important than the story or the skill of the animation. This is a movie about what you hope your toys do when you're not around—and what you fear. They have lives of their own, but you are the sun in the sky of their universe, and when you treat them badly, their feelings are wounded."

Current Projects

Lasseter recently served as executive producer of a new Pixar short film called *For the Birds* (2000), about a group of birds who are bullied by a larger bird. For that short, he and the Pixar team developed techniques that will be used in his next feature-length film, *Monsters, Inc.,* which is scheduled to be released in 2001. This comedy about things that go bump in the night reveals what happens when a boy accidentally gets sucked into the monsters' secret world. As he explains, "It's about two monsters, who live in an alternative universe that's similar to our own. The only way that they get back and forth to our world is through the closet doors of kids' bedrooms." While Lasseter has served as director of all previous Pixar feature films, he will oversee production as executive producer on this next release. At the same time, he is said to be working on a later animated film that he will direct. At this point, information about that film is still secret, and no word has yet been given out on the film's title or story.

Working at Pixar

Under Lasseter, Pixar has created a very singular environment in which its employees thrive. "There's an atmosphere of building something," says Sarah McArthur, a vice president of production. "There's energy, camaraderie, creativity." According to Karen Jackson, the producer of *Toy Story 2*, "[Lasseter] says it is one of the happiest places on Earth—and everyone agrees. He allows [the employees] the freedom to do whatever it takes to bring their creativity to work." And people have taken full advantage of that freedom.

> *"Lasseter and [co-director Andrew Stanton] and the rest of the animators and gagsmiths use the computer with staggering imaginative freedom. It's as if their collective unconscious were the hard drive."*
> —*Michael Sragow, New Times*

For a visitor arriving at Pixar's offices in northern California, the first impression is of toys—the entrance area is filled with shelves of toys, from the company's films and from other movies and comics. Many Pixar employees display interesting collections of playthings also. But employee work spaces feature more than that. Each person has a cubicle, and they have the freedom to decorate them wildly—one decorated it like a Tiki Hut from the South Seas, complete with a bamboo frame and native masks; another used palm trees and other plants to create a jungle, complete with toy soldiers from *Toy Story*; still another built a bunk bed into her work space so she would have someplace to sleep when she works all night. Employees don't really wear standard business attire; instead, they can wear whatever clothing they want—Lasseter is known for his colorful Hawaiian shirt collection. Several pets accompany their owners to work each day, including some dogs, a parrot, and even a few snakes. Employees are well paid and they have a creative voice in the work that they do. The company offers classes to its employees to keep them happy, including sculpting, writing, and painting, and also provides an allowance so they can go to movies and film festivals.

It's no wonder, then, that the company has a very low employee turnover rate and that artists and computer experts are eager to work there. "We have the lowest [employee] turnover rate in Hollywood history," Lasseter says. "People just don't leave. That's one of the things I'm most proud of.

We created this studio we want to work in. We have an environment that's really open, a culture that's wacky. It's a creative brain trust. It's not a place where I make my movies — it's where a group of people make movies."

MARRIAGE AND FAMILY

Lasseter and his wife Nancy live in Sonoma, California, a rustic town in northern California. They have five sons, whose ages range from 20 down to three. The boys serve as Lasseter's first and best audience.

FILMS

Luxo Jr., 1986 (short film)
Red's Dream, 1987 (short film)
Tin Toy, 1988 (short film)
Knickknack, 1989 (short film)
Toy Story, 1995
A Bug's Life, 1998
Toy Story 2, 1999
For the Birds, 2000 (short film)

HONORS AND AWARDS

Academy Awards (Academy of Motion Picture Arts and Sciences): 1988, Best Animated Short Film, for *Tin Toy*; 1995, Special Achievement Oscar, for the development and inspired application of techniques for *Toy Story*

Gold Award of Excellence (Broadcast Designers Association): 1989, for *Tin Toy*

Clio Award: 1993, Gold Medal Winner, for "GummiSavers Conga" commercial

Annie Awards (International Society for Animated Films): 1996 (2 awards), Best Animated Feature and Directing, both for *Toy Story*; 1998, Outstanding Achievement in an Animated Short Subject, for *Geri's Game*

Golden Globe Award (Hollywood Foreign Press Association): 1999, Best Picture — Musical or Comedy, for *Toy Story 2*

Christopher Award: 2000, for *Toy Story 2*

Broadcast Film Critics Association Award: 2000, Best Animated Feature, for *Toy Story 2*

FURTHER READING

Books

Who's Who in America, 2000

Periodicals

Business Week, Nov. 23, 1998, p.154
Entertainment Weekly, Dec. 8, 1995, p.26
Los Angeles Times, Nov. 19, 1995, Calendar section, p.4; Nov. 18, 1999,
    Calendar section, p.6; Dec. 3, 1999, p.C1
New York Times, Aug. 4, 1991, section 3, p.4; Nov. 19, 1995, section 2, p.17;
    Feb. 24, 1997, p.D1; Apr. 3, 2000, p.E1
Newsweek, Dec. 4, 1995, p.54; Nov. 16, 1998, p.78
Time, Nov. 30, 1998, p.108; Dec. 14, 1998, p.100
Time for Kids, Nov. 17, 1995, p.6
USA Today, Nov. 10, 1995, p.D1
Wall Street Journal, Mar. 19, 1998, p.R17

ADDRESS

Pixar Animation Studios
1001 West Cutting Blvd.
Point Richmond, CA 94804

WORLD WIDE WEB SITE

http://www.pixar.com

Peyton Manning 1976-

American Professional Football Player
Record-Setting Quarterback for the Indianapolis Colts

BIRTH

Peyton Manning was born on March 24, 1976, in New Orleans, Louisiana. His parents were Archie Manning, a former All-Pro quarterback in the National Football League (NFL), and Olivia Manning, a homemaker. They met at the University of Mississippi, where Archie was the football team's star quarterback and Olivia was the homecoming queen.

Peyton grew up in New Orleans, where his father played professional football for the New Orleans Saints. He is the sec-

———— " ————

"I didn't push [Peyton] into football," remembered his father. "I didn't try to mold him into a quarterback in my own image. I felt very strongly about not interfering. . . . I'll be his father, and that's it."

———— " ————

ond of three sons, all of whom have made their mark on the football gridiron. Manning's older brother, Cooper, was a high school star who also played for the University of Mississippi. But he was forced to give up the rough sport when doctors discovered that he had a spinal condition called spinal stenosis. Peyton's younger brother, Eli, recently accepted a scholarship to play quarterback for the University of Mississippi.

YOUTH

Peyton Manning's early life was greatly influenced by his father's fame. During the 1970s and early 1980s, Archie Manning was regarded as one of the best quarterbacks in the NFL. The Saints team never emerged as a powerhouse during this time, but no one blamed Manning for their losing seasons. In fact, his exciting, scrambling style of play, combined with his Southern charm and good looks, made him a near-legend in New Orleans and throughout the American South.

Peyton spent much of his youth hanging out with his dad in the Saints' locker room, practice field, and stadium. He even got to sit in on quarterback meetings with his father, where he gained an early understanding of many of the sport's basic strategies. This early exposure to his father's world convinced Peyton that he wanted to be a quarterback himself someday.

Even as a youngster, Manning showed promising athletic ability and an understanding of football fundamentals. By the time he was four years old, he could copy the seven-step drop that quarterbacks commonly make when throwing a pass, and he could throw a Nerf football in a tight spiral across the family's living room. Still, his father did not permit him to play organized football until the seventh grade. "I didn't push [Peyton] into football," remembered his father. "I didn't try to mold him into a quarterback in my own image. I felt very strongly about not interfering. . . . I'll be his father, and that's it."

Once he got the green light to play organized ball, however, Manning quickly showed that he had very advanced skills for his age. "He always wanted to play quarterback," recalled his father. "Usually, on those seventh and eighth grade teams, it's mostly just turn around and pitch it, hand it off, to the biggest, fastest kids. But they [his school team] had a little passing game. They threw to tight ends and ran bootlegs. . . . He got experience there."

Manning also showed his strong competitive instincts in these youth football leagues and other athletic competitions. "Peyton, without a doubt, [was] the most intense athlete I've ever been around," recalled M.K. Phillips, his youth baseball coach. "He always wanted to be successful, and he knew what it took."

EDUCATION

Peyton attended elementary and high school at the Isidore Newman School, a prestigious private school in the New Orleans area with an excellent academic reputation. Manning did well in his studies, but he made his biggest splash on the school's football field. He took over as the varsity team's starting quarterback as a sophomore. This development delighted young Peyton, for it gave him an opportunity to play with his older brother, Cooper, a wide receiver. Throughout the 1992 season, the Manning brothers hooked up for long gains and touchdowns, just as if they were playing catch in their own backyard. In fact, they led their team to a 12-2 record and a run deep into the state football playoffs. "That year made us buddies," Cooper recalled fondly.

After Cooper graduated and moved on to Ole Miss, the college their dad had attended, Peyton became a nationally known high school star. During his junior year, he passed for 2,345 yards and 30 touchdowns while throwing only four interceptions. As a senior, his statistics — and his fame — were even greater. He threw for 2,703 yards and 39 touchdowns and was named the Gatorade National High School Player of the Year. These amazing numbers boosted his high school career totals to 7,207 yards and 92 touchdowns passes.

In middle school, recalled his father, "He always wanted to play quarterback. Usually, on those seventh and eighth grade teams, it's mostly just turn around and pitch it, hand it off, to the biggest, fastest kids. But [his school team] had a little passing game. They threw to tight ends and ran bootlegs. . . . He got experience there."

Manning (16) drops back to throw a pass during a game between Tennessee and UNLV, August 31, 1996.

When Manning graduated from Newman in 1994, every top college team recruited him. These schools knew that Manning's incredible talent, combined with his football upbringing, made him a special player. Needless to say, he was under tremendous pressure to follow in his father's and brother's footsteps and attend the University of Mississippi, commonly known as "Ole Miss." Even Peyton's father got a taste of this pressure. Archie Manning recalls with distaste that some of his old friends and associates called and told him, "You make him go to Ole Miss."

In the end, of course, Peyton's family urged him to choose the college that would be best for him. After giving the matter a great deal of thought, Manning decided not to go to Mississippi. "I kind of had the feeling if I went to Ole Miss, I'd be an instant celebrity without doing anything," he said at the time. "Mississippi people think I'm a good quarterback, but I could never live up to how good they think I am." Instead, Manning decided to join the powerhouse football program at the University of Tennessee. While continuing with football, he completed his bachelor's degree in speech communication in just three years, graduating in 1997 with a 3.6 grade point average. During his final year of eligibility on the playing field —what would have been his senior year of college—he went on to do a year of graduate work in the master's degree program at Tennessee in sports management.

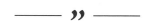

"Peyton, without a doubt, [was] the most intense athlete I've ever been around," recalled M.K. Phillips, his youth baseball coach. "He always wanted to be successful, and he knew what it took."

CAREER HIGHLIGHTS

College—Tennessee Volunteers

When Manning joined the Tennessee Volunteers, he expected to spend his freshman season on the bench, learning from the team's more experienced quarterbacks. Just four games into the 1995 season, however, the team's top two quarterbacks went down with injuries, and Manning became the starting quarterback. Many Tennessee fans worried that the inexperienced freshman would struggle, but instead he led the team to seven victories in their last eight games. In recognition of his poised performance, he was named Southeastern Conference (SEC) Freshman of the Year.

During his sophomore season, Manning attracted national attention with his performance. He set a National Collegiate Athletic Association (NCAA) record for lowest interception percentage (just over 1 percent) for a season when he threw just four interceptions in 380 passes. Sparked by Manning's pinpoint passing, the Volunteers marched to an 11-1 record for the year and a victory over Ohio State in the Citrus Bowl. At the end of the season, Manning was named one of the finalists for the Davey O'Brien Quarterback Award, awarded each year to the nation's top college quarterback.

By the end of his sophomore year, Manning was a near-legend on the Tennessee campus. But his popularity was not due exclusively to his on-the-field exploits. In fact, he garnered considerable attention for the way he conducted himself off the field. At a time when many college and professional athletes engage in rude or boorish behavior, Manning became known for his polite and personable manner, his willingness to sign autographs (it's estimated that he signed more than 250,000 while at Tennessee), and his involvement in local charities. In Manning, Tennessee fans had a shining star they could hold up to the rest of the country as a perfect example of what a UT (University of Tennessee) student-athlete should be.

> *In deciding whether to stay at Tennessee for his final year of eligibility or turn pro, Manning said that "staying was strongest in my heart. I knew that's what I wanted to do. I want pro football, believe me. But I want college football one more year, also, and it kind of came down to that."*

By the time Manning was a junior, he was recognized around the country as one of the best quarterbacks in all of college football. As the 1996 season unfolded, he continued to rip up opposing defenses. He led the Vols to a 10-2 record and another win in the Citrus Bowl, this time over Northwestern University. More impressively, by the end of his junior year, Manning had accumulated enough class credits to graduate from Tennessee with a degree in speech communication.

Weighing His Choices

Manning's upcoming early graduation convinced most fans and sports journalists that the young quarterback would bypass his senior season of college eligibility and make himself available for the National Football League draft in April 1997. After all, he already held most of the school's career and single-season passing records, and he had guided the Volunteers to three straight great seasons. And many experts believed if Manning left Tennessee for the NFL, he would be the first player selected in the draft. As the first selection, he would be able to command a contract that would make him a very wealthy young man.

Before Manning made his decision, though, he talked to several other pro and college athletes about the advantages and disadvantages of turning pro. He also discussed his options with his father, who counseled him on football and life in general throughout his first three years at UT.

In the end, Manning decided that he "didn't have enough memories yet" and that he would return to school "to create some more memories." He admitted that the prospect of an NFL salary was tempting. But he added that "staying was strongest in my heart. I knew that's what I wanted to do. I want pro football, believe me. But I want college football one more year, also, and it kind of came down to that." He then announced his intention to continue his education at Tennessee by working toward a master's degree in sports management.

Tennessee fans had come to love and respect Manning so much—both as a player and as a person—that the press conference at which he announced his decision was carried live on closed-circuit television inside the school's basketball arena. Fans watching the broadcast cheered wildly when his decision came out in their favor.

Manning's surprise decision also attracted considerable attention outside of Tennessee. Fans, educators, and journalists from around the country praised his decision. They referred to him as a symbol of "old-fashioned" values and a role model for young children about the importance of staying in school. The Tennessee House of Representatives even passed a resolution honoring Peyton for staying in school. For their part, Manning's parents were thrilled with his decision, as well as the outpouring of affection he received from Tennessee fans. "I am so proud of him," said Olivia Manning. "As a mother, it's a great feeling to know he's this well-thought of. And, I definitely did want him to stay. He's just 20 years old, a baby. If he'd given up this chance to play one more year in college and this part of his youth, he could never have it back."

The Final Year

Once Manning decided to play one final year with the Volunteers, he set some clear goals for the upcoming season. On a team level, he wanted to beat the arch-rival University of Florida Gators (which he had never beaten), win the SEC championship, and claim the school's first national championship. On a personal level, he hoped to win the Heisman Trophy, which is awarded to the best player in college football. By the end of the season, however, Manning had achieved only one of those goals—winning the SEC championship.

*Manning drops back in the pocket to make a pass during a Colts' game,
November 8, 1998.*

Manning was brilliant for much of the 1997 season. He finished with
nearly 4,000 yards passing and threw for 39 touchdowns and only 11 interceptions. Unfortunately, two of those interceptions came against Florida, which pasted the Volunteers by a 33-20 score. This defeat deeply disap-

pointed Manning, for it gave him an 0-3 record as a starter against the Gators. But he dismissed any suggestions that his losses to Florida meant that he could not win big games. "It bothers me that we never beat Florida in my career," he says. "But I can't worry about how people around the country see Tennessee and how they view my career. . . . I'm disappointed for our fans, our coaches, our seniors, and all the people who wanted to win so badly."

Manning and his teammates rebounded from the tough loss to Florida and qualified for the SEC championship game, where they faced the Auburn Tigers (Florida lost other SEC games and failed to qualify for the title game). Manning was at his best against Auburn, throwing for 373 yards and four touchdowns to earn the game's Most Valuable Player award as Tennessee held on for an exciting 30-29 win. The win gave the Vols an 11-1 record for the year and left them ranked third in the country, behind the University of Michigan Wolverines and the University of Nebraska Cornhuskers. As the regular season ended, Tennessee prepared to face the second-ranked Cornhuskers in the Orange Bowl.

In one of his first NFL games, a 29-6 pounding at the hands of the New England Patriots, Manning threw three interceptions and lost a fumble. "There were times in that game when you just wanted to say, 'Look, get me out of there. Please take me out. Just get me to the locker room alive.'"

The Heisman Trophy

Before the bowl season began, however, Manning and a handful of other college stars were invited to New York City for the Downtown Athletic Club's Heisman Trophy Award presentation. Ever since he announced he was returning for his senior year, Manning had been the front-runner to win this prestigious award, and his spectacular senior season helped him keep his place as the favorite. But as the season progressed, Michigan's Charles Woodson — a star cornerback and receiver for the University of Michigan Wolverines — made a stunning late run at the award. At first, no one believed that Woodson had a legitimate shot at winning. He was known primarily as a defensive player, and a defensive star had never won the Heisman. But Tennessee's loss to Florida hurt Manning's chances, especially after Woodson led Michigan to a victory over *its* arch-rival, Ohio State, on the same Saturday afternoon.

Tennesseans refused to believe that Woodson could win the award over their beloved Manning, but he did just that. The response to Manning's second-place finish was angry and swift in Tennessee. Newspaper editorials denounced the Heisman voters, and seemingly every person in the state — including Governor Don Sundquist — joined in the public outcry. The general feeling was that Manning represented everything that was good about college sports, that he was a winner, and that he had done the right thing by returning for his senior year — yet he still lost to a player that many felt was not as talented.

> ""
>
> *As the 1998 season progressed, Manning got high marks for his humility, charm, and thoughtful manner. "I've tried to keep myself out of bad situations, and if that means I'm a Goody Two-Shoes, so be it. I see myself as very normal. Growing up in New Orleans as Archie Manning's son, I felt like a target, and I've always known that whatever I'd do, people would hear about it. So I've had my guard up, and maybe that's molded my personality."*
>
> ""

For his part, Manning remained classy in defeat. While photographers captured the look of disappointment on his face as the winner's name was read, he was gracious and complimentary to Woodson in interviews after the ceremony. "I'd be less than honest if I said I didn't want to win this award for the people back home in Tennessee," Manning told reporters after the announcement. "In a lot of ways, I wanted to win it for them because they've been so supportive throughout my four years. I apologize to them. . . . But, like me, they'll be ok. When you start out on top there is nowhere to go but down, and I guess I fell. . . . I'm happy for Charles. I congratulate him on a great year."

With the Heisman over and the focus back on the Orange Bowl, Manning had to contend with a nagging knee injury that briefly landed him in the hospital. Although he was cleared to play in the bowl game, it was obvious he was not 100 percent. Manning struggled throughout the game, and Nebraska rolled to an easy 42-17 victory.

Manning hated ending his Tennessee career on a losing note. But the loss to Nebraska did not change his standing among Volunteer fans. In fact, he concluded his senior season as the most popular athlete in school history.

In recognition of his standing, Tennessee honored Manning's career by re-tiring his jersey number in 1998. This marked the first time in the school's history that a football player's number was retired. Around the same time, Manning received the 1998 Sullivan Award, which is bestowed upon the top amateur athlete in the United States.

Turning Pro — Indianapolis Colts

As the 1998 NFL draft approached, many observers thought that the Indianapolis Colts, which had the first pick that year, would make Manning the first selection of the entire draft. But the Colts actually con-sidered picking another quarterback who was available. Their choice came down to Manning or Washington State's Ryan Leaf, a big, strong quarter-back with a rifle arm. Some scouts said Leaf deserved to be the top pick, while others gave the nod to Manning.

Indianapolis finally decided to take the Tennessee quarterback after an early April breakfast between Manning and Colts owner Jim Irsay. At that meeting, Manning looked Irsay in the eye and told him "I'll win for you," a gutsy move that greatly impressed the owner. In April 1998, the Colts made him their number one choice. "Peyton Manning very much wanted to be a Colt," said Indy's head coach Jim Mora on the day of the draft. "We must now surround Peyton with the right people. But we feel he is going to be one of our pillars for the next decade."

A Record-Setting Rookie Quarterback

When Manning joined the Colts, Indianapolis was one of the worst teams in the entire league. But the Indianapolis coaching staff chose to give their young star experience right away, so they made him the club's starting quarterback. Even though the Colts won only three out of 16 games that season, the team's fans could see that the Colts and their new quarterback improved as the season progressed.

Those first few games were a struggle for Manning. He threw 12 intercep-tions and only five touchdowns in his first four games. In one of those games, a 29-6 pounding at the hands of the New England Patriots, Manning threw three interceptions and lost a fumble. "There were times in that game when you just wanted to say, 'Look, get me out of there. Please take me out. Just get me to the locker room alive,'" he recalled. But Manning gained more confidence as the season went on, and when the Colts played the Patriots again, their young quarterback nearly produced a big upset victory. "The second time, he just had tremendous poise," said New England defensive back Ty Law after the season. "It was like he was a different person out there. He's going to be one of the special ones. He's going to be a problem [for us] for a long time."

As the 1998 season progressed, Manning also got high marks for his humility, charm, and thoughtful manner. "I've tried to keep myself out of bad situations," he explained, "and if that means I'm a Goody Two-Shoes, so be it. I see myself as very normal. Growing up in New Orleans as Archie Manning's son, I felt like a target, and I've always known that whatever I'd do, people would hear about it. So I've had my guard up, and maybe that's molded my personality."

Manning finished his rookie campaign with a number of NFL records. He had the most pass completions (326) and attempts (575) ever for a rookie. He also registered new rookie records for touchdown passes (26) and yards passing (3,739). And he showed that he was tough and durable, becoming only the eighth quarterback in league history to take every one of his team's snaps for the year. All the records did not make losing any easier, however. "I don't think you ever learn how to lose," Manning said. "It gets tougher and tougher. You play closer and closer and feel like you deserve to win."

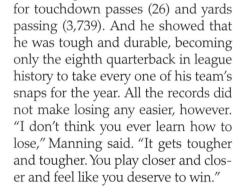

"It's incredible how far advanced he is for his experience," said Coach Jim Mora. "Peyton is a dream player to have. He's got it all. He's got talent. He's got leadership. He's got determination. He's got class. I can't think of a more enjoyable player to work with, and I think he's got a chance to be something very special."

The 1999 Season

At the start of Manning's second season in the league, many NFL fans were predicting that the Colts would make the playoffs for the first time in years. They believed that Manning, rookie running back Edgerrin James, and explosive wide receiver Marvin Harrison were all on the verge of breakout seasons. As it turned out, the experts were right. The Colts unleashed one of the most potent offenses in the NFL and marched to their first playoff appearance in years. Manning led the way, tallying 26 touchdowns, 4,135 yards passing, and an excellent quarterback rating of 90.7 during the season.

Unfortunately, the Colts' dreams of a Super Bowl appearance were crushed in the playoffs, when the team suffered a heartbreaking 19-16 loss to the Tennessee Titans. Manning scored a rushing touchdown with less than

Manning gives throwing instruction to Aaron Nagasawa during a Pro Bowl Special Olympics event, February 5, 2000.

two minutes left in the game to draw the Colts close, but time ran out before he could guide the team to a winning score. The loss disappointed Indianapolis players and fans, but it did not detract from Manning's amazing season. "It's incredible how far advanced he is for his experience," said Mora. "Peyton is a dream player to have. He's got it all. He's got talent. He's got leadership. He's got determination. He's got class. I can't think of a more enjoyable player to work with, and I think he's got a chance to be something very special."

After nearly reaching the Super Bowl in 1999, the Colts feel they are positioned to be one of football's elite teams for years to come. In Manning, James, and Harrison, the Colts have three of the top young offensive stars in the entire NFL. Armed with that kind of leadership, the Colts could certainly have a Super Bowl in their future.

HOME AND FAMILY

Manning divides his time between Indianapolis and Louisiana. He is unmarried but has been dating girlfriend Ashley Thompson since his college days. He also continues to spend a lot of his free time with his parents and his brothers. He enjoys a particularly close bond with his older brother, Cooper, and served as best man at his wedding.

HOBBIES AND OTHER INTERESTS

Peyton is a huge country music fan. In fact, he once joined singer Kenny Chesney on stage in front of a packed stadium to act as a backup singer. He also devotes a lot of time and energy to church activities. While at Tennessee, for example, he never missed the pregame chapel service, even though he often had to take creative steps to avoid fans and not create an unintended scene. He was even the guest speaker at chapel services.

Manning has always been actively involved in charity work. While at UT, he spoke regularly at local churches and in front of children's groups such as the Boys and Girls Clubs. Since joining the Colts, he has been involved with several groups that help underprivileged children, including a foundation that he formed called PeyBack that helps needy kids.

HONORS AND AWARDS

Gatorade Circle of Champions National High School Player of the Year: 1993
All SEC First Team: 1995, 1997
Academic All-SEC Team: 1996
All SEC Second Team: 1996
Citation for Extraordinary Campus Leadership and Service (from the chancellor of the University of Tennessee): 1996
Citrus Bowl Most Valuable Player: 1996
College Football Hall of Fame Scholar-Athlete Award: 1997
NCAA All-American Team: 1997
Davey O'Brien National Quarterback Award: 1997
ESPY Award (ESPN): 1997, College Player of the Year
Johnny Unitas Golden Arm Award: 1997, best senior college quarterback
Maxwell College Football Player of the Year: 1997
National Football Foundation Scholar-Athlete Award: 1997
SEC Player of the Year: 1997
James E. Sullivan Memorial Award: 1998, top amateur athlete in the United States
NFL All-Pro: 1999

FURTHER READING

Books

Frisaro, Joe. *Peyton Manning: Passing Legacy,* 1999 (juvenile)
Hyams, Jimmy. *Peyton Manning: Primed and Ready,* 1998 (juvenile)

Periodicals

Boy's Life, Aug. 1998, p.24
Chicago Tribune, Dec. 5, 1999, p.1
Current Biography Yearbook, 1998
Denver Rocky Mountain News, Apr. 19, 1998, p.C1; June 7, 1998, p.C30
Esquire, Sep. 1999, p.92
GQ, Sep. 1996, p.122
Houston Chronicle, Oct. 4, 1998, p.22
Newsday, Aug. 25, 1996, p.B6; Nov. 14, 1999, p.C12
People, Dec. 11, 1995, p.133
San Francisco Chronicle, Feb. 12, 1998, p.D7
Sport, May 1999, p.38
Sporting News, Aug. 21, 1995, p.S14; Aug. 23, 1999, p.78
Sports Illustrated, Oct. 10, 1994, p.86; Aug. 26, 1996, p.108; Apr. 13, 1998,
    p.30; Nov. 12, 1999, p.42
USA Today, Aug. 7, 2000, p.C11

ADDRESS

Indianapolis Colts
7001 W. 56th Street
Indianapolis, IN 46254

WORLD WIDE WEB SITES

http://www.nflplayers.com/players
http://www.nfl.com/colts
http://www.peytonmanning.com

Ricky Martin 1971-
Puerto Rican Singer

BIRTH

Ricky Martin was born Enrique Jose Martin Morales on December 24, 1971, in Santurce, Puerto Rico. His father is Enrique Martin, a psychologist who now works as a regional supervisor for a Puerto Rican mental-health agency, and his mother is Nereida Morales, an accountant who currently manages her son's financial affairs. His mother had been married before, and Martin has two older half-brothers, Fernando and Angel Fernandez, from her first marriage. Martin's parents divorced when he was young, and his father

266

later remarried. Ricky also has two half-brothers and a half-sister from his father's second marriage, Eric, Vanessa, and Daniel Martin.

Martin's birth name is a product of his culture. In Spanish-speaking cultures, the traditional custom is to use a double surname, a combination of part of the father's and the mother's names. The father's name goes first and the mother's name goes second, creating a double last name.

YOUTH

Martin grew up in San Juan, the capital and the largest city of Puerto Rico, an island that is about 1,000 miles southeast of Florida. There are two official languages there: while Spanish is the main language, many Puerto Ricans also speak English. Puerto Rico is a commonwealth of the United States. As a commonwealth, the island is overseen by the U.S. government. But the Puerto Rican government, which is democratically elected, has authority in local issues. People in Puerto Rico are U.S. citizens, and they can move to the mainland without any immigration restrictions. The nation's political status has been the subject of vigorous debate for years. At various times the people of Puerto Rico have voted on their country's status: should it continue as a commonwealth, become a U.S. state, or become an independent country. Each time the majority of people have voted that Puerto Rico should remain a U.S. commonwealth.

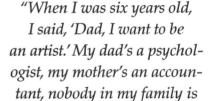

"When I was six years old, I said, 'Dad, I want to be an artist.' My dad's a psychologist, my mother's an accountant, nobody in my family is in show business. He said, 'What did you say, Kiki?' Because he calls me Kiki. 'How can I help you?' he asked. He was not the typical father."

Martin's parents separated when he was just two. Martin lived primarily with his mother, who never remarried, but he also spent plenty of time with his father, who remarried after several years. After the divorce his parents continued to get along well, and Martin was able to move freely between their homes. "I never had to make decisions about who I loved more," he now says. "I was always happy."

Martin was raised a Catholic, and religion was a big part of his life when he was growing up. He was an altar boy at his church, and he attended elementary school at Colegio Sagrado Corazon, a bilingual (Spanish and English) Catholic grade school. Martin was considered a serious, responsible student. He also had some of his first performances there, acting in school plays and singing in the choir.

One rather odd experience he had as a child was visiting his father at work—at a prison. "I always say I grew up in a jail," Martin jokes. "My father was a penal psychologist who worked in jails, giving therapy to drug-addicted convicts. . . . I wouldn't go into the cells with him; I stayed in his office. And I'd go to the prison Christmas parties."

CHOOSING A CAREER

Martin was pretty young when he first started thinking about a career. "When I was six years old, I said, 'Dad, I want to be an artist.' My dad's a psychologist, my mother's an accountant, nobody in my family is in show business. He said, 'What did you say, Kiki?' Because he calls me Kiki. 'How can I help you?' he asked. He was not the typical father." After that, both his parents supported his dream to become an entertainer. They helped him take acting and singing lessons, find an agent, and attend auditions. His first commercial, when he was just seven, was for the soft drink Orange Crush. It paid $1,600 that day, plus residuals every six months— payments based on the number of times the commercial aired on TV. Martin was hooked. He went on to appear in 30 commercials over the next three years. "He was cast each time he went to an audition," his father recalls. "They told him, 'Do this,' and he would do it. He had an incredible ability."

CAREER HIGHLIGHTS

Joining Menudo

Martin started working toward a singing career before he was even a teenager. He was just 11 when he first unsuccessfully auditioned to join Menudo, a Latin pop band. The group was first formed in 1977 by Edgardo Diaz, who had a new idea for a band. He would select five good-looking teenage boys to be in band that would feature pop songs, stylish outfits, and choreographed stage moves. As the kids got older they would be forced to drop out, always by the time they turned 16 or 17. The band would continue, though, adding new, younger members. "Menudo is a formula and we take care not to break it," Diaz once said. "Each member is selected very carefully, because it is a hard life, with rehearsals, shows, recording sessions, and so much traveling." Menudo was based in Florida,

Martin, far right, with Menudo, circa 1986

where they learned new songs and worked on their dance routines, but the group spent lots of time on the road touring.

When Martin first tried out for the group he was turned down, told he was too short. He was rejected a couple more times before being selected in 1984. At the time, they told him, "You are the new Menudo. Tomorrow you're on a plane for Orlando. Maybe you're not the best singer or dancer, but you wanted it so bad. That's why you became a Menudo." Even though joining Menudo meant that Martin was leaving his family and Puerto Rico at just 12, his parents supported him completely. "[They] knew if they didn't let me, I'd be the most frustrated guy in the world. I'd see Menudo and get this sparkle, like I couldn't live without being in the band."

For Martin, passing the Menudo audition started a whirlwind of activity. "Everything moved so fast," he recalls. "The next morning at six, I was on a plane to Orlando. When I got there, I did six interviews, fittings, hairstyle. In 24 hours my life completely changed. It was dramatic. . . . I was having fun. I learned 18 [dance] routines in 10 days. I have to brag about it. There were guys who took four days on one routine. . . . My debut was at Radio City Music Hall [in New York City], where we played for 10 days. I went from riding my bike to learning my steps to Radio City."

—— " ——

"Two things can happen when you join a group like a Menudo," says his friend Robi Rosa, another former Menudo member. "You can get all messed up, or you can pay attention and learn from it. We learned a lot. For Ricky and me, the studio is like home now."

——  ——

Life with Menudo

Martin spent five years with Menudo, from 1984 to 1989, and from age 12 to 17. He was lucky enough to join the band at the height of its fame. The members of Menudo sang primarily in Spanish, and at first most of their fans were Spanish speakers living in Latin America. With time, though, they developed a fan base in the United States, first among Hispanics and then among Anglos, too. Menudo became a huge pop sensation during the 1980s, and its members became teen idols—in Puerto Rico, in the U.S., and around the world. They sold out concerts at huge stadiums, they were besieged by the press, and they were constantly followed by hordes of screaming girls. Their fans snapped up Menudo T-shirts and posters, fueling the craze. Menudo eventually sold more than 26 million albums worldwide, becoming one of the first Latin groups to cross over to the world market.

Martin has talked about both good and bad aspects of this life. They had very little free time, and it was difficult to get away because of the fans. They often worked 16 hours a day, between traveling, rehearsing the music, learning new dance routines, giving interviews, filming TV appearances, recording in the studio, and signing autographs. On top of that, they had to devote time to their schoolwork, studying with tutors in their hotel rooms three hours each day. All that intense training unquestionably taught Martin the showmanship and flamboyant style that have made him famous today. "Two things can happen when you join a group like a Menudo," says his friend Robi Rosa, another former Menudo member who co-wrote Martin's current album. "You can get all messed up, or you can pay attention and learn from it. We learned a lot. For Ricky and me, the studio is like home now."

One frequent complaint was the intense discipline, which Martin sometimes seems to praise and sometimes seems to condemn. "Menudo was my school," he once said. "I'm very proud of those beginnings. Menudo taught me the true meaning of the word discipline." But he has also described the experience as regimented and militaristic. When he was 15, his grandfather became sick and he asked for time off. His request was denied, and Martin was on tour when his grandfather died. He grew to hate that type of regimentation. "You were part of a concept. You weren't allowed to express yourself," he once said "My personality was sabotaged in the band. We were told what to sing and wear, what haircut to have. I didn't know who I was. When I left the band in '89, I had to think, 'Do I like this haircut? Do I like these jeans?'"

His years in Menudo also had some serious consequences on Martin's family life. His parents had always managed to maintain a good relationship after their divorce. But the stresses of Menudo frayed that relationship. Because Ricky had so little free time, his father and mother began fighting over who would get to spend time with him when he returned home on vacation to Puerto Rico. "It was all about love," Martin says. "My parents both wanted me with them so badly." They argued about where he should stay, and dumped it on to Ricky. "They kept asking me, 'Who do you want to be with?' It's a terrible thing to say to a child." Ultimately, his father forced him to choose between the parents. Ricky's decision to stay with his mother made his father very angry and precipitated a huge fight between them. Martin was so angry about the ultimatum that he rarely spoke to his father for the next 10 years. Soon tensions arose between Martin and his mother, too. They fought so much that he grew to hate being at home and started staying away. Martin blamed himself for the conflict with his mother and the estrangement from his father, and they have since resolved these issues and reconciled. "One day I called up my father and said, 'Enough is enough,'" Martin says. "He was always there for me. It was up to me. Today our relationship is amazing."

"You were part of a concept [in Menudo]. You weren't allowed to express yourself. My personality was sabotaged in the band. We were told what to sing and wear, what haircut to have. I didn't know who I was. When I left the band in '89, I had to think, 'Do I like this haircut? Do I like these jeans?'"

After Menudo

In 1989, when Martin was 17, it was time to leave Menudo. Emotionally and physically exhausted, he had no clear idea of what he wanted to do next. "I was tired and confused," he later explained. "I didn't know if I wanted to be a

singer or a carpenter." He returned to Puerto Rico, where he decided to return to high school and complete his education there.

After finishing his studies, Martin decided to take a vacation in New York City. "One day I said, 'Mom, I'm going to New York for a vacation. I'll be back in 10 days.' Never came back. I found an apartment and did nothing. I needed some anonymity, to get to know myself, because, for the last five years, it had been about, 'You wear *these* clothes, get *this* haircut, sing *this* song.' I needed my personality back, to find out what I liked and hated." He spent his time visiting museums, working out, seeing movies and concerts, and cleaning his apartment. He also took acting and dancing lessons. He lived off his earnings from Menudo, and added to his savings by occasionally signing autographs at stores that sold Menudo merchandise.

Restarting His Career

In 1990 Martin flew down to Mexico, planning to take a vacation with some friends. Although he didn't know it at the time, that trip would mark his return to the entertainment world. It turned out to be the first of many small steps Martin would take to build his solo career as an actor and a singer, first in Spanish and later in English.

While visiting Mexico City Martin went to see a play, *Mama Ama el Rock (Mom Loves Rock and Roll)*. Within a week he was appearing in the long-running musical, starting a new acting career. As he recalled, "Menudo was a big theatrical play on the road, but that night I saw the acting and said, 'I can do that.' I went to see the producer, a friend of mine, and she said, 'You're not going back to New York; I want you here because an actor is leaving—and if he's not, I'll kick him out.'" Martin became a big hit on the stage. His Mexican fans remembered him from Menudo, and they would show up at the theater chanting "Queremos a Ricky rockero, lo queremos entero" ("We love Ricky the rocker, we love him completely"). Martin's success on stage led to a role as Pablo on "Alcanzar Una Estrella II" ("To Reach a Star"), an extremely popular Mexican TV soap opera. On the show, Pablo was a member of a rock band. The band on the show was such a big hit that they did some concerts as their TV characters, and the concerts drew audiences of 65,000 fans. The TV soap opera became so popular that it was spun off into a feature film, *Mas que Alcanzar Una Estrella* (1991), that Martin starred in as well. For that film he won a Heraldo Award, the Mexican equivalent of an Oscar.

Martin's success as a performer in Mexico led to an offer to record an album, so soon he was combining his new career as an actor with a re-

Ricky Martin kissing his 1999 Grammy Award for Best Latin Pop Performance for Vuelve

turn to the recording studio. His first solo album of original songs was *Ricky Martin* (1991). This album of pop ballads sung in Spanish went gold, selling over half-a-million copies. That success was followed up with his second Spanish-language pop record, *Me Amaras* (1993), which earned him the Billboard Music Video Award for Best New Latin Artist. Although neither of these first releases were huge sellers, they allowed Martin to go back on tour and return to performing live music. With these concerts, he started to build up his fan base, primarily in Latin America.

Returning to the U.S.

In late 1993 or early 1994 Martin moved to Los Angeles, California. There, he won a role on the popular TV soap opera "General Hospital." From 1994 to 1996 he played Miguel Morez, a sexy bartender with a mysterious past. Miguel had been a pop star back home in Puerto Rico, but had left to recover from a broken heart. The role gave Martin an opportunity to sing and to connect with new American fans.

At the same time, Martin was working on his third solo Spanish-language album, *A Medio Vivir* (1995). That recording, according to many, marked a turning point for Martin. Here, he explains how he was searching for a new style and started mixing the two musical influences from his childhood: rock and roll and Latin music. "[That's] when I stared having fun with my background, with the Latin sounds, with the percussive, when I started working with Robi [Rosa]. . . . I was looking and looking and suddenly I said, 'Wait a minute. Keep it simple. You were born in Puerto Rico, and you're a Latin — even though the first stuff you listened to was Journey, Foreigner, Cheap Trick, Boston — so let's play with it a little, not be stereotypical.'" The CD became a huge hit in Latin America and opened the door to Europe, too — the song "Maria," in particular, became a huge hit in Spain and then throughout Europe.

> "You're at the Grammys, you've already seen Madonna and a couple of other acts perform, and it's the same-old, same-old. Then Martin comes up with 30 people, and goes cha-cha-cha. He's the epitome of timing is everything. He's at the right place at the right time with the right sound."
> — John Lannert,
> **Billboard Magazine**

In the midst of this musical success, Martin landed a prestigious role as the French revolutionary Marius in the Broadway production of *Les Miserables* in 1996. He also made time to provide the voice of the main character for the Spanish-language version of *Hercules* (1997), the popular Disney animated movie.

Success as a Solo Artist

Martin soon went on to greater success as a solo artist. It all started because of the song "Maria" on his previous CD, *A Medio Vivir*. "Maria" became such a huge hit in Europe that the organizers of the 1998 World Cup men's soccer tournament came to Martin and said that they wanted something similar as the official anthem for their event. For that, he and Rosa created "La Copa de la Vida" ("The Cup of Life"), which became Martin's first big musical breakthrough and cemented his international

Martin, after winning two awards for his album Vuelve *at the 1999 Billboard Latin Music Awards, April 22, 1999*

reputation. His thrilling performance at the 1998 World Cup was broadcast to two billion people, and the song soon became a No. 1 single in 30 countries worldwide. "La Copa de la Vida" was included on his next solo recording, *Vuelve* (1998), his fourth and most recent Spanish-language CD.

By 1999, Martin was a worldwide superstar. His four solo recordings had sold over 16 million copies. He had given concerts around the world, filling huge stadiums with sell-out crowds of ecstatic fans in South America,

Australia, Europe, India, China, and the rest of Asia. But despite his phenomenal success, he still wasn't known to most Americans.

That was about to change. In February 1999, Martin appeared on the 1999 Grammy Awards ceremony. He gave an electrifying performance of his World Cup hit "La Copa de la Vida," bringing the audience to its feet. A complete entertainer, a talented singer and dancer, he put on a show filled with charisma, energy, warmth, fun, and sex appeal. His joyous dancing combined his trademark swiveling hips with sensational choreography. Martin looked like he was having a blast, and the crowd responded. According to Leila Cobo in the *Miami Herald*, "Martin turned just another award ceremony into a sizzling nightclub act that got the staid industry crowd dancing in the aisles." That view was echoed by John Lannert, the Latin America editor for *Billboard Magazine*. "You're at the Grammys, you've already seen Madonna and a couple of other acts perform, and it's the same-old, same-old," said Lannert. "Then Martin comes up with 30 people, and goes cha-cha-cha. He's the epitome of timing is everything. He's at the right place at the right time with the right sound." In addition, his show-stopping performance was broadcast to more than a billion viewers worldwide. To further heighten his profile that night, his recording *Vuelve* won the Grammy Award for Best Latin Pop Performance.

"People ask me what I'll be doing 30 years from now and I tell them I'll be in the entertainment business; singing, acting, maybe even producing. I was born for this. I enjoy what I do."

After the Grammy Awards

After the Grammy Awards, suddenly everyone wanted to know more about Ricky Martin. New fans wanted to hear more of his music and the press wanted to cover his roots, both wondering where he had come from. Even Madonna got into the act, offering to record a song with him, "Be Careful/ Cuidado Con Mi Corazon." For Martin, the timing of all that attention was perfect. In April 1999 he released the first single from what would be his first English-language album, *Ricky Martin* (1999). That single, "Livin' La Vida Loca," along with the rest of the album, was filled with what has become his trademark approach: upbeat Latin beats, pulsing rhythms, and blaring brass, all combined with a pop sound. According to

Martin performing on NBC's "Today" show in New York's Rockefeller Center, June 11, 1999

Martin, he picked "Livin' La Vida Loca" as the first single "because I want to say, 'Hey! Boom! I'm here! Check this out!' The song has a little bit of Latin, a little bit of ska, a little bit of rock, there's even a little bit of the '60s, sort of a James Bond sound." He had outstanding help on the album from his producers, including Robi Rosa, his friend from Menudo and one of the writers of "Livin' La Vida Loca"; Desmond Child, one of the writers of "Livin' La Vida Loca"; and Emilio Estefan, the husband of Gloria Estefan and the creator of the Miami Sound Machine.

It's ironic that "Livin' La Vida Loca" became Martin's first big U.S. hit, because that certainly describes his life right now in the spotlight. Suddenly, he became an overnight sensation in the U.S. — even though it took him 15 years of hard work to get here. Many see him, along with Marc Anthony, Enrique Iglesias, Jennifer Lopez, Jon Secada, and Shakira, as part of a wave of Latin performers who are crossing over, finding success in the U.S./English language market as well as overseas. In part that reflects an ongoing change in the population of the U.S., because the Latino population is currently growing six times faster than the population of the U.S. as a whole. But some say that also reflects a growing acceptance within the U.S. of Latin rhythms and Latin music— not to mention an appreciation for Martin's good looks and phenomenal dancing. Martin, for one, is happy to be an ambassador for Latin-flavored music. "I don't have any problem with that. I like talking about my little island, to let people know about the poetry, the literature, the sounds."

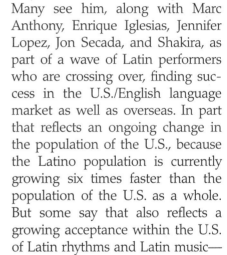

"I've always been searching for spirituality," Martin says. "I'm looking for stillness, serenity, peace of mind, God — whatever word describes the ultimate."

For the future, Martin plans to have a long career as an entertainer. "I'd like to do it all," he says. "People ask me what I'll be doing 30 years from now and I tell them I'll be in the entertainment business; singing, acting, maybe even producing. I was born for this. I enjoy what I do." Down the road, he says, "I'd like to be remembered as someone who taught others about Latin cultures. Someone who worked a lot. Someone to trust. And at the same time, someone who was always grounded. In this business it could get crazy because you are constantly looking for acceptance, and the acceptance of an audience is applause, and the applause is people telling you how good you are. But at the same time, when a lot of people are telling you you're great, it can get you a little messed up if you aren't in control or in touch with yourself. If you're not spiritually solid. I want to stay the same and in 20 years go back [and ask myself] . . . 'Hey, are you proud of who you've become?'"

HOME AND FAMILY

Martin owns a five-bedroom, Mediterranean style home on the water in Miami Beach, Florida. But he has been on the road touring so much that he has been able to spend little time at home with his two dogs, Icaro, a golden retriever, and Titan, a Chihuahua. Martin is unmarried, but he has been involved in a long-term, on-again, off-again relationship with Rebecca de Alba, a TV presenter now working in Spain.

HOBBIES AND OTHER INTERESTS

Martin leads a very fast-paced and busy lifestyle, which has left him longing for peace and quiet. So each day, he eats breakfast in silence, meditates, and spends 20 to 40 minutes doing yoga. "I've always been searching for spirituality," he says. "I'm looking for stillness, serenity, peace of mind, God—whatever word describes the ultimate."

In addition, Martin likes reading, writing poetry, relaxing in a bubble bath. He owns a restaurant in the trendy South Beach section of Miami. Called Casa Salsa, it serves gourmet Puerto Rican food. Customers there can take salsa lessons between courses!

CREDITS

Solo Recordings

Ricky Martin, 1991 (in Spanish)
Me Amaras, 1993 (in Spanish)
A Medio Vivir, 1995 (in Spanish)
Vuelve, 1998 (in Spanish)
Ricky Martin, 1999 (in English)

Menudo Recordings with Martin

Reaching Out, 1984
Evolucion, 1984
Mania, 1984
16 Greatest Hits, 1984
Menudo: 1985, 1985

Ayer y Hoy, 1985
Refrescante, 1986
Festa Vai Comecar, 1986
Menudo: 1986, 1986
Can't Get Enough, 1986
Viva Bravo, 1986
Somos Los Hijos del Rock, 1987
Menudo in Action, 1988
The Best of Menudo, 1988
Sons of Rock, 1988
Sombras Y Figuras, 1989

TV, Theater, and Film

Mama Ama el Rock, 1990? (theater)
"Alcanzar Una Estrella II," 1991? (TV)
Mas que Alcanzar Una Estrella, 1991? (movie)
"General Hospital," 1994-96 (TV)
Les Miserables, 1996 (theater)
Hercules, 1997 (voice-over for animated film)

HONORS AND AWARDS

Heraldo Award: 1992, for *Mas que Alcanzar Una Estrella*
Grammy Award: 1999, for Best Latin Pop Performance, for *Vuelve*

FURTHER READING

Books

Furman, Elina. *Ricky Martin,* 1999
Marrero, Letisha. *Ricky Martin: Livin' La Vida Loca,* 1999 (bilingual
    edition — English and Spanish)
Tracy, Kathleen. *Ricky Martin: Red-Hot and on the Rise!* 1999
Walsh, Kimberly. *Ricky Martin: Backstage Pass,* 1999

Periodicals

Entertainment Weekly, Apr. 23, 1999, p.32
Interview, June 1999, p.98
Miami Herald, May 9, 1999, Arts section, p.51
Newsweek, May 31, 1999, p.72
People, May 15, 1995, p.109; May 31, 1999, p.58; June 26, 1999, p.52

Rolling Stone, Aug. 5, 1999, p.48
Time, May 10, 1999, p.84
TV Guide, June 5, 1999, p.14
USA Weekend, Nov. 5-7, 1999, p.6

ADDRESS

Sony Records
550 Madison Avenue
New York, NY 10022

WORLD WIDE WEB SITES

http://www.rickymartin.com

John McCain 1936-

American Politician
U.S. Senator Who Ran for the Republican Presidential
Nomination

BIRTH

John Sidney McCain III was born August 29, 1936, in the
Panama Canal Zone. His father, John McCain, Jr., was a career
Navy officer stationed in Panama at the time of his son's birth.
McCain's mother, Roberta, was a homemaker who raised
John, his older sister, Sandy, and his younger brother, Joseph,
at Navy installations around the world.

YOUTH

John McCain is from a military family with a long history of distinguished service. He claims that one ancestor served George Washington in the Revolutionary War. Both his father and grandfather were Navy admirals, and his life was shaped by their ideals of honor, patriotism, and service. In his new memoir, *Faith of My Fathers* (1999), McCain explains the effect of this background on him when he was young:

"As a boy and young man, I may have pretended not to be affected by the family history, but my studied indifference was a transparent mask to those who knew me well. As it was for my forebears, my family's history was my pride. When I heard my father or one of my uncles refer to an honored ancestor or a notable event from our family's past, my boy's imagination would conjure up some future glory when I would add my own paragraph to the family's legend."

But he would have to do a lot of growing up before then. McCain's legendary temper, noted in most media coverage of his presidential bid, first showed up when he was a toddler. At the age of two, he threw such violent temper tantrums that his parents didn't know what to do. When he got mad, he would hold his breath, turn blue, and pass out. In desperation, his parents started putting him in a tub of cold water when he'd go into a tantrum. It did the trick.

Growing Up in the Navy

McCain grew up on Navy bases all over the country, and sometimes abroad. This meant that the family was constantly on the move. McCain remembers getting used to a new school, making friends, then having to move again. His father was at sea most of the time. When McCain was young, he resented his father's absence from his life. He was taught to honor his father and his father's calling, yet couldn't help sometimes missing his dad and challenging the circumstances of his life.

EDUCATION

McCain attended school at the various Naval bases where he grew up. He was a rebellious kid who got into trouble often, usually for fighting. He says that at the time he "foolishly believed that fighting, as well as challenging school authorities and ignoring school regulations, was indispensable to my self-esteem and helped me to form new friendships." Moving from school to school, he kept the same attitude. "At each new school I became a more unrepentant pain in the neck."

When he was 15, his parents decided to send him to a boy's boarding school, the Episcopal High School in Alexandria, Virginia. It was an exclusive school for the sons of wealthy, white Southerners. He was the only one whose father was in the military. McCain continued his bad boy ways, breaking curfew and wearing rumpled shirts with jeans to class, even though the dress code required students to wear ties and jackets. He accumulated more than his share of demerits for breaking rules, showing up late to class and sneaking off campus at night to go to bars. He was an indifferent student and did well in classes he liked, like English and history, and poorly in math and science. He enjoyed sports and was a decent athlete, joining the football, tennis, and wrestling teams during his years at Episcopal.

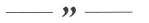

> *It had been assumed that he would go to the Academy since he was a boy, an attitude that McCain resented. "My father never asked me once, 'Do you want to go to the Naval Academy?' It was always, 'He's going to the Academy'."*

When McCain graduated from high school in 1954, he went on to the Naval Academy at Annapolis, as had his father and grandfather before him. It had been assumed that he would go to the Academy since he was a boy, an attitude that McCain resented. "My father never asked me once, 'Do you want to go to the Naval Academy?' It was always, 'He's going to the Academy'."

Naval Academy

McCain responded to the harsh discipline of the Naval Academy with the same kind of cocky rebellion he'd shown in his high school days. One aspect of life at the Academy McCain particularly hated was the tradition of hazing. At the Academy, upper classmen mistreated the freshman "plebes," as they were called. McCain describes their "campaign to humiliate, degrade, and make miserable me and every other plebe they encountered." He says that "arrogant nonconformists" like him "encountered open hostility." He recalls the atmosphere as "excruciating," with the sadistic physical and mental hazing "mindless and unrelenting." His response: "I reverted to form and embarked on a four-year course of insubordination and rebellion."

Yet although McCain "hated every minute of it," he says he now understands the purpose of hazing. For him, "It rests in memory, paradoxically, with my appreciation, gratitude really, for the privilege of surviving it, and

McCain family portrait, approximately 1944. From left to right: Roberta (John's mother), Joe (about two years old), John III (about eight years old), Admiral John S. McCain, Sandy, John S. McCain, Jr. (John's father)

for the honor of that accomplishment." He sees it as a preparation for combat, and the purpose of the Academy is to train officers to lead men in battle. As he himself later experienced, "At moments of great stress, your senses are at their most acute; your mind works at a greatly accelerated pace. That's the purpose, I take it, of plebe year—not simply to test your endurance, but to show that you can function exceptionally well, as a leader must function, in concentrated misery."

In McCain's four years at the Academy, he proved to be, in his own words, "an arrogant, undisciplined, insolent midshipman." He didn't do well in classes, and he was constantly in trouble. He was the leader of a group of party boys known as the Bad Bunch. Once again, he was known for breaking rules and partying hard.

"I spent the bulk of my free time being made an example of, marching many miles of extra duty for poor grades, tardiness, messy quarters, slovenly appearance, sarcasm, and multiple other violations of Academy standards," he says. When he finally graduated in 1958, he was fifth from the bottom in his class rankings.

STARTING HIS NAVY CAREER

McCain graduated from the Academy with the rank of ensign and moved to Pensacola, Florida, to begin training to become a Navy pilot. True to form, McCain continued his rowdy ways. "I liked to fly," he admits, "but not much more than I liked to have a good time." For the next several years, he flew Navy planes, but partied during his time off. Once, he crashed his plane in Corpus Christi Bay off the coast of Texas. He was unconscious when he hit the water, came to when the plane hit the bottom, then struggled out of the cockpit and swam to the surface. Once, while flying in southern Spain, he flew too low and knocked down power lines.

Eventually, McCain's attitude began to change. He had gotten married in 1965 and adopted his wife's sons from her first marriage. Soon, he started to settle down and think about his future. He began to see himself differently. He wanted to be a leader and to lead men in combat. That meant getting involved in the major armed conflict of the era, the Vietnam War. He saw his military service as part of the honor and pride he took in his family heritage. "More than professional considerations lay beneath my desire to go to war," says McCain in his memoir. "Nearly all the men in my family had made their reputations at war. It was my family's pride. And the Naval Academy, with its celebration of martial valor, had penetrated enough of my defenses to recall me to that honor. I wanted to go to Vietnam, and to keep faith with the family creed."

THE VIETNAM WAR

When the U.S. got involved in Vietnam in the late 1950s, it was essentially a civil war between North Vietnam and South Vietnam. The political makeup of these two countries contributed to the decision by the U.S. to get involved there. It was the Cold War at that time, a period of extreme distrust, suspicion, and hostility between, on the one side, Communist countries like the Soviet Union, China, and their allies, and, on the other side, the United States and its allies. North Vietnam was controlled by Communists, who wanted to bring their political system to South Vietnam also. Many people in the U.S. felt that it was important to support South Vietnam in order to stop the spread of Communism to other nations. In the late 1950s, the U.S. began sending in military advisers to help South Vietnam; by the early 1960s, the U.S. began sending in military troops to fight in the war.

By the time McCain was called up to serve in Vietnam in late 1966, there were strong voices of dissent in the U.S. against American involvement. Under President Lyndon Johnson, the war had escalated. Hundreds of thousands of soldiers had been sent to Vietnam to fight a ground war against the North Vietnamese. Thousands of tons of bombs were being dropped daily on targets in the North.

When John McCain went to Vietnam in 1967, he went as a bomber pilot, attached to a unit that flew off aircraft carriers in the waters off Vietnam. On board one of those carriers, the U.S.S. Forrestal, he was witness to one of the greatest tragedies in modern Navy warfare. On July 29, 1967, McCain was in the cockpit of his plane when a stray missile from the ship's own arsenal struck the fuel tank of his plane, starting a fire. The fuel poured onto the deck and ignited bombs. McCain crawled into the nose of his plane, then leapt onto the deck to try to save his shipmates from the explosion and fire that consumed the ship. The fire raged for 24 hours. When it was over, 134 men were dead. The story of the Forrestal disaster, and McCain's part in it, made the front page of the *New York Times*.

McCain was to make the front page of the *Times* again, just three months later. He had signed up for another tour of combat duty, this time aboard the carrier Oriskany. During his days as a pilot, he completed 22 bombing raids over North Vietnam. Of his experience as a bomber pilot, McCain says, "I did not take a perverse pleasure in the terror and destruction of war. I did not delight in the brief, intense thrill of flying combat missions. I was gratified when my bombs hit their target, but I did not particularly

Of his experience as a bomber pilot, McCain says, "I did not take a perverse pleasure in the terror and destruction of war. I did not delight in the brief, intense thrill of flying combat missions. I was gratified when my bombs hit their target, but I did not particularly enjoy the excitement of the experience."

enjoy the excitement of the experience." Still, he and his fellow pilots felt the American cause was just, and that they should be there fighting the North Vietnamese.

On the morning of October 26, 1967, McCain's target was a power plant in Hanoi, the major city of North Vietnam. He flew his plane as part of a squadron to drop bombs on the plant, facing enemy fire and SAMs— strategic air missiles designed to intercept planes. McCain describes the SAMs as looking like "flying telephone poles." After he'd dropped his bombs, his plane was hit by a SAM that sheared off one wing. The plane

*John S. McCain III in 1956 in his yearbook photo from the
U.S. Naval Academy, Annapolis, Maryland.*

began to spiral toward the ground. Ejecting from his plane, McCain broke both arms and one knee. He landed in a small lake near his target.

He was soon surrounded by a group of North Vietnamese who began to beat him. One broke his shoulder with a rifle butt and another bayoneted him in the groin and ankle. Soon, a truck appeared to take John McCain to what would become his home for the next five years: the Hoa Lo prison, called the "Hanoi Hilton" by the American prisoners of war (POWs) who were incarcerated there during the Vietnam War.

PRISONER OF WAR

Over the next several days, McCain was in and out of consciousness. He was not treated for his injuries; instead, the prison officials interrogated him about his mission. He was told that he would receive treatment only if he gave information. When he refused, he was beaten. Throughout the war, the North Vietnamese tried to break the will of their American prisoners. Over the course of their imprisonment, McCain and the other POWs were subjected to torture to make them reveal secret military information. They were also expected to show their shame for what they had done by praising their captors and denigrating the U.S. In prison, McCain's physical condition deteriorated to the point that his captors thought he would die. Then they discovered that his father was an admiral. This made him more valuable to the North Vietnamese as a bargaining tool. He was transferred to a hospital and left in a room with rats and cockroaches for two weeks. Back in the States, his parents and wife were told that he had been shot down and was presumed dead.

After he'd been in the hospital for two weeks, a doctor tried to set one of McCain's broken arms, without anesthesia. During the procedure, McCain passed out from the pain. The attempt to set his arm didn't work. The doctor didn't try to set the other broken arm or the knee. The North Vietnamese officials then put McCain in a room with a French television newsman. If he said he was "grateful to the Vietnamese people and sorry for his crimes," he would be given medical treatment. McCain wouldn't do it. The segment, which aired on U.S. television, showed McCain in conversation with the French correspondent. He refused to say what the North Vietnamese wanted him to say. But he was able to get a message to his family. He told them he loved them and was getting well.

For refusing to recant, McCain was returned to the hospital but not treated. He was repeatedly beaten, fed starvation rations, and was never bathed. At one point, his captors cut all the ligaments and cartilage in his knee, making him unable to bend his leg. McCain's physical condition continued to deteriorate. The North Vietnamese again thought he would die, so they returned him to the prison. His cell mate was another POW named Bud Day. He remembers the day they brought McCain back to the prison.

"I've see some dead that looked at least as good as John," said Day. His hair had turned white, he was filthy, and he had lost about 50 pounds.

"His eyes, I'll never forget, were just burning bright. They were bug-eyed like you see in those pictures of the guys from the Jewish concentration camps." Day didn't think McCain would live another 24 hours. But McCain hadn't seen another American in months, and he talked to Day and his cellmate, Norris Overly, for as long as he could. The other POWs cleaned McCain up and tried to nurse him back to health.

During those early months of McCain's imprisonment, his father had been named commander of the entire Pacific, an area that included Vietnam. The North Vietnamese, realizing the enhanced value of their prisoner, made McCain a new offer. If he would recant, they would release him. McCain refused. He steadfastly stood by the Code of Conduct for American Fighting Men, developed by the military after the Korean War in the 1950s. It states that prisoners of war cannot accept any special favors from their captors and that they can be released only in the order in which they were captured. By the time of McCain's capture, there were more than 300 American POWs in Vietnam.

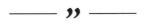

"I had learned what we all learned over there: every man has a breaking point." He wrote a forced confession, rewritten by an interrogator, in which he said, "I am a black criminal, and I have performed deeds of an air pirate. I almost died, and the Vietnamese people saved my life, thanks to the doctors."

For his refusal, McCain was placed in solitary confinement. For the next two years, he was alone in his cell. He desperately tried to make contact with other prisoners, through a tapping code in which the prisoners would communicate, using a morse-code like alphabet. He was interrogated regularly, and when he continued to refuse, he was tortured. McCain's broken arms, never properly set and healed, were tied behind his back and he was hung by ropes for hours at a time. After a while, McCain couldn't take it. "I had learned what we all learned over there: every man has a breaking point." He wrote a forced confession, rewritten by an interrogator, in which he said, "I am a black criminal, and I have performed deeds of an air pirate. I almost died, and the Vietnamese people saved my life, thanks to the doctors."

McCain couldn't live with himself for making his forced confession. He tried to hang himself, but was stopped by a guard, who beat him. Years later, McCain said he had no idea if he could really have committed suicide. "But I still believe I failed," he said. After two-and-a-half years in solitary, McCain was finally united with other American POWs. The men kept their minds active by sharing as much information as they could. They kept running lists of other POWs, memorized in alphabetical order. They would entertain one another recounting plots and dialogue from movies, even if they hadn't seen them and had to make them up. McCain even taught a makeshift course in American Literature, lectures that, according to Robert Timberg's account of McCain in his *The Nightingale's Song*, was more like "Classic Comics" than serious teaching.

McCain and his fellow POWs held common views about the Vietnam War. They felt that President Johnson had abandoned them. They felt that the president's military advisers had been wrong about how to fight the war, and they thought that Johnson's decision to cease bombing North Vietnam in 1969 had been dead wrong. When President Richard Nixon began bombing the North again in 1972, they were delighted. "We knew that unless something very forceful was done that we were never going to get out of there," said McCain later. The bombs were often dropped close enough to their prison that the walls shook. They cheered anyway. In early 1973, an agreement to end the war was signed by the U.S. and the North Vietnamese. It was time to go home.

RETURNING TO THE U.S.

John McCain returned to the U.S. in March 1973. He had been in captivity for more than five years. When he was finally reunited with his family he faced a great shock. In 1970 his wife, Carol, a former fashion model, had been in a terrible car accident that had nearly killed her. After 23 operations, she was permanently disabled. She had not wanted him to know about her accident. When they saw each other again, they were both on crutches, unable to walk.

McCain wanted to fly again. He began intensive physical therapy and slowly regained some range of motion in his arms and leg. But to this day, he can't raise his arms over his head, and he walks with a limp. He was able to return to pilot status, and he became an instructor, serving for several years. From 1974 to 1977 he served as the executive officer, then as commanding officer of a Navy attack squadron in Florida.

In 1977, McCain moved to Washington, D.C., to become the Liaison Officer between the Navy and the U.S. Senate. Living at the heart of national politics, McCain began to think about a political career. When he had returned from Vietnam, he had been welcomed by President Nixon. Future President Ronald Reagan also got to know the former P.O.W. By

1977, the Republican Party was assessing his political viability. Yet McCain's personal life was in turmoil, and he appeared unable to control the chaos. In a period of his life he says he is ashamed of today, he was openly unfaithful to his wife, and his marriage disintegrated. As Michael Lewis wrote in a profile in the *New York Times Magazine*, "Just when others, including the Reagans, hoped he was grooming himself for political office, McCain ejected from his first marriage in a semipublic blaze of womanizing."

John and Carol McCain divorced in 1980. That same year, he married a woman he had been dating, Cindy Hensley, whose father was a wealthy Arizona beer distributor and conservative Republican. McCain retired from the Navy and moved to Arizona.

POLITICAL CAREER

U.S. House of Representatives

In 1982, McCain decided to run for the U.S. House of Representatives from a district in Arizona. He'd only lived in Arizona for two years, and he had to confront the accusation that he was a "carpetbagger," a political opportunist who runs out of greed rather than out of desire to serve. He told his detractors that as a Navy brat, he'd never spent much time in one place. The only place he'd lived for very long was Hanoi. The crowds loved it. Reporters eagerly dug into the dirty aspects of McCain's divorce. Yet Carol McCain refused to say anything against her former husband, and she supported him in his first and all his subsequent elections. In November 1982, McCain won election to the U.S. House.

As a member of the House of Representatives, McCain proved to be a consistent conservative, voting with the right-wing Republican block during the early years of Ronald Reagan's presidency. He supported such conservative initiatives as prayer in the schools, the 1986 tax revision, and subsidies to the tobacco industry. Yet he also voiced independent opinions, especially on foreign policy matters. He thought it was wrong for Reagan to veto the bill creating economic sanctions against the racist regime in South Africa, and he also exposed a Reagan initiative to transfer millions of dollars from a food program for the poor to give pay raises to people in the Department of Agriculture.

In 1985, McCain returned to Vietnam for the first time since his release from prison in 1973. He wanted to talk to Vietnamese officials about U.S. serviceman who had been listed as "missing in action" in the Vietnam War. The U.S. didn't know what had happened to almost 2,500 men who had fought in the war and had never been accounted for. This is a painful issue for the families of those missing in action. Some never feel sure if their

McCain is greeted by President Richard Nixon, left, in Washington on September 14, 1973, after returning from prisoner of war camp.

loved one was killed in action or was imprisoned as a POW and might still be alive somewhere. McCain said the trip was difficult for him, but that he held "no animosity toward the Vietnamese people." It was a grim tour, but there was a moment of humor. One of the people on the trip was the famous CBS newsman Walter Cronkite. He and McCain made a visit to the site of McCain's plane crash, where the Vietnamese had built a monument. As McCain describes it, "Walter Cronkite and I and a film crew went down there one day to the statue. A very large crowd of Vietnamese had gathered, all pointing to me and repeating my name—'Mahcain, Mahcain.' It was perhaps the first time that someone was more recognized than Walter Cronkite."

U.S. Senate

McCain served two terms in the House, then, in 1986, he ran for and won the seat of retiring Arizona Senator Barry Goldwater. McCain was a big supporter of Goldwater and followed in his conservative Republican footsteps. He served on the Commerce and the Science and Transportation committees of the Senate. He kept the subject of Vietnam in the political agenda, calling for an end to hostile relations with the country. He also spoke at the 1988 Republican convention, where George Bush was chosen as the Republican nominee. McCain was so well thought of within the party that Bush considered him as a possible running mate. McCain still felt free to speak his mind about what was wrong with the party, however. He knew that many voters felt excluded by the Republicans. He said he was concerned with "the future of the Republican Party, and its ability to attract good candidates who can win. We need to reach out. We don't have the right to shut out a constituency just because they didn't vote for us."

The Keating Five

McCain's rising star dimmed in 1989, when he was linked to a campaign finance scandal. From 1982 to 1986, he had accepted over $100,000 in campaign contributions from a man named Charles Keating. Unbeknownst to McCain, Keating was under investigation by federal officials for allegedly stealing millions of dollars from his own bank, Lincoln Savings and Loan, and leaving the bank $2.5 billion in debt. Keating approached McCain to ask him to use his influence to get Keating off. McCain refused, and Keating began to insult McCain behind his back, calling him a "wimp." Keating was a powerful, money-wielding force inside Washington, and he made similar requests of Senators John Glenn, Don Riegel, Dennis DeConcini, and Alan Cranston, all of whom had received campaign contributions from him. Even though he had personally refused Keating's request to intervene on his behalf, McCain, along with Glenn, Riegel, DeConcini and Cranston, met with the head of the Federal Home Loan Bank Board, Edwin Gray, in 1987. They urged Gray to cease his investigation of Keating and Lincoln S & L. Gray later claimed that he found the senators' request "tantamount to an attempt to subvert the regulatory process."

The five senators, who became known as the "Keating Five," were investigated by the Senate Ethics committee. After a 14-month investigation, the committee found that McCain and Glenn had been guilty of "poor judgment." The other senators were reprimanded more harshly, especially Alan Cranston, who was charged with "impermissible conduct" and whose case was turned over to the full Senate.

McCain was humiliated by the Keating affair. Almost half of his constituents in Arizona called for his resignation, and his reputation for integrity and patriotism was compromised. He had also learned a lesson in the temporary nature of political power. "One thing I learned from the Keating affair," he said years later, "was that this could all end *tomorrow*. Just like *that*."

From that point forward, McCain became devoted to the cause of campaign finance reform. It has become as much a part of his personal history as his Vietnam experience. "My honor and integrity were at stake in Vietnam when the Vietnamese offered me freedom," he says. "I was very tempted to take it. But when I didn't, it was over—at least when the beatings stopped it was over. In the Keating scandal, my honor and integrity were at stake again: I was accused of betraying my oath of office. I've never been able to explain very clearly how I felt. How painful it was. And, by the way, I did wrong. I shouldn't have attended that meeting. But I don't think I'll ever be absolved. I'll always be known as one of the Keating Five."

"My honor and integrity were at stake in Vietnam when the Vietnamese offered me freedom. I was very tempted to take it. But when I didn't, it was over — at least when the beatings stopped it was over. In the Keating scandal, my honor and integrity were at stake again: I was accused of betraying my oath of office. I've never been able to explain very clearly how I felt. How painful it was. And, by the way, I did wrong. I shouldn't have attended that meeting. But I don't think I'll ever be absolved. I'll always be known as one of the Keating Five."

Campaign Finance Reform and "Soft Money"

With the zeal of a crusader, McCain has spent the last 10 years trying to reform the way political campaigns are financed. It costs a lot of money to

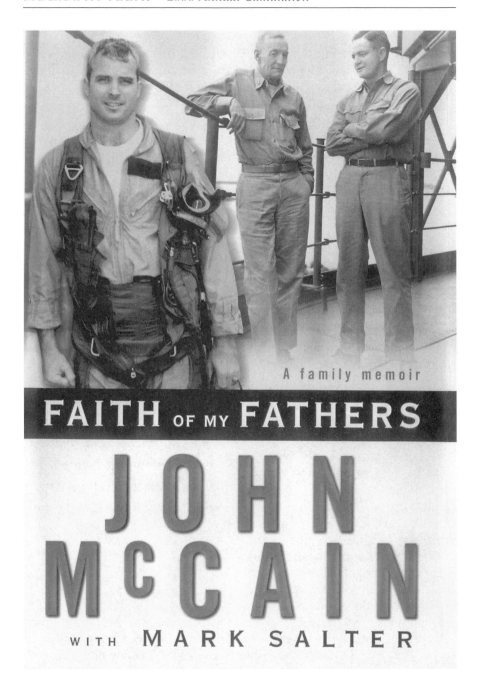

A family memoir

FAITH OF MY FATHERS

JOHN McCAIN

WITH MARK SALTER

run for political office, and politicians are constantly raising money for re-election. Currently, individuals and businesses can only contribute up to $1,000 to a politician's campaign. What concerns McCain is what is called "soft money." This is money that is given to a political party, not to an individual. There are no limits on soft money. In the eyes of McCain and others who want to reform the campaign finance process, powerful companies and individuals can "buy" access to politicians, influencing the outcome of legislation to their benefit. For example, large, powerful companies, in industries ranging from tobacco to telecommunications, can send unlimited amounts of money to political parties to try to influence various politicians. And these politicians are responsible for writing the laws that govern certain key aspects of the business activities of those large, powerful corporations.

McCain's stance on campaign finance reform has made him famously unpopular in both parties, and he has many enemies among Republicans. Many have long-standing relationships with large, powerful companies that have contributed millions of dollars over the years, and they aren't interested in changing the system. As such, McCain and his calls for reform have made him something of a pariah in politics.

Political Alliances Outside the Republican Party

Because of his independent stance, McCain has formed an unusual number of close political partnerships with Democrats over the years. When McCain first arrived in Washington, he was taken under the wing of Mo Udall, a legendary liberal Democrat from his home state of Arizona. McCain remembers it was Udall, rather than his party's own Goldwater, who guided McCain through his early years. When he won his Senate seat, it was Udall, not Goldwater, he thanked. "There's no way Mo could have been more wonderful," McCain remembers. "And there was no reason for him to be that way."

In 1993, McCain formed another close alliance with a Democrat, this time over the issue of Vietnam. Senator John Kerry, Democrat of Massachusetts, had been a high-profile member of a group of Vietnam veterans against the war. In the early 1990s, these two men worked together to resolve the issue of Vietnam soldiers still missing in action, which McCain had been concerned with for years. As part of the process, they went to Vietnam to meet with officials. They returned with almost 5,000 photographs of U.S. servicemen taken by the Vietnamese during the war, as well as other artifacts, like clothes and other personal items. One of the retrieved items was McCain's flight helmet.

McCain, Kerry, and their committee sifted through the evidence to try to get to the truth. They also got the Defense Department to declassify a million pages of documents relevant to the case. The families of the men missing in action had suffered for years, wondering what had happened to them. The final report concluded that "while the Committee has some evidence suggesting the possibility a POW may have survived to the present, and while some information remains yet to be investigated, there is, at this time, no compelling evidence that proves that any American remains alive in captivity in Southeast Asia." McCain and Kerry's work also led to the normalization of relations with Vietnam, which occurred in 1995.

The McCain-Feingold Reform Bill

In his continuing quest to do something about campaign finance reform, McCain formed an alliance with Democrat Russell Feingold. He and Feingold shared a passion for reforming the way that money works in Washington. In addition to trying to curb the "soft money" that finances political campaigns, the two were devoted to cutting federal spending drastically. One of their main target was "pork-barrel legislation." That's money that members of Congress try to tack onto other bills that benefit their own district. McCain has a staff member, called the "Ferret," whose job it is to find the "pork" in pending legislation, and to forward the information to McCain, so that he can expose this kind of wasteful spending.

> *McCain's views on lowering taxes came with a clear message about money in politics: "You're never going to get a simpler, flatter tax code unless you reform the way we finance our campaigns," he said. "And you're never going to get rid of pork-barrel spending and make government smaller until you remove the special interests that dominate our political process."*

But it was ending the unlimited flow of money into politics that truly brought McCain and Feingold together. They drafted a bill, the McCain-Feingold reform bill, in 1995, and placed it before Congress every year since then. It has been voted down each time.

McCain's crusade for reform has continued to garner him enemies. He drafted anti-tobacco legislation economically harmful to the tobacco industry, which has been a major contributor to Republican and Democrat campaign funds. Once again, he ran afoul of his party. In 1996, he was the only Republican to vote against the Telecommunications Act, which he felt was drafted to ensure the economic power of the telephone companies, to the detriment of individual Americans.

Running for President

On April 14, 1999, John McCain announced that he would run for the Republican nomination for president. From the beginning, he knew it would be an uphill battle: he didn't have the endorsement of a single major Republican, and he had only a handful of loyal supporters. George W. Bush, son of former President George Bush, was the clear favorite, and he had already raised millions of dollars for his campaign. Bush stood for—and had benefitted from—politics as usual within the Republican Party. McCain's positions on most issues were clearly from the conservative side of the Party: anti-abortion, anti-gun control, lower taxes. But his lower tax stance came with a clear message about money in politics: "You're never going to get a simpler, flatter tax code unless you reform the way we finance our campaigns," he said. "And you're never going to get rid of pork-barrel spending and make government smaller until you remove the special interests that dominate our political process."

McCain's appeal was broadly based—outside of the Republican Party. The Party faithful much preferred George W. Bush, whose fund-raising abilities made him the early front runner. Yet McCain continued to appeal to independent voters, and even some Democrats. Some commentators thought he was popular because he was the "anti-Clinton," especially after the Lewinsky scandal. The nature of McCain's appeal was described by David Grann in *The New Republic* this way: "In the wake of Bill Clinton's misconduct, McCain has become a reflection of our times, the focus of our desperate search for 'character' in a president to the exclusion of almost everything else—even actual political beliefs."

Primaries

In the American political process, the presidential candidates are selected for both the Republican and Democratic parties through primaries. In the primaries, voters cast ballots for delegates pledged to vote for a particular candidate at the party's convention, held in the summer of an election year. The Republican candidate for 2000 needs 1,034 delegates. McCain took to the streets of America in search of delegates.

McCain rode around the country in a bus he dubbed the "Straight Talk Express." He offered unprecedented access to the media, talking openly and candidly with reporters about the full range of his political agenda. He

McCain shakes hands with supporters at the conclusion of a rally in Livonia, Michigan, where he was campaigning for the state's upcoming presidential primary.

did this in vivid contrast with Clinton, who has been accused of polling before he makes a decision and "spinning" all his actions, or representing his decisions and behavior in the best possible light. McCain and his free-speaking ways also contrast with Bush, who limits access to the press and who has traditionally given scripted speeches and responses. Bush's campaign attacked McCain as a media darling, accusing the press of being soft on McCain because he gave them access.

But McCain stunned Bush in February 2000 when he won the New Hampshire primary, the first presidential primary of the year. For the first time, Bush's lock on the nomination seemed questionable. McCain's popularity surged, but Bush rallied and beat him in the South Carolina primary. McCain came back and beat Bush in the Michigan and Arizona primaries, doing particularly well with independent voters as well as with Democrats.

"Super Tuesday," March 7, 2000, was the decisive day for the McCain campaign. Super Tuesday was the single largest primary in the nation's history. The delegates were up for grabs in 16 states, including two of the largest states, California and New York,. Bush won decisively there, as well as in

10 other states. In his concession speech that night, McCain said that "we may meet again in the primaries a few days from now," implying that he might drop out of the race. However, he clearly asserted that "We will never give up this mission" to reform campaign finance laws.

McCain officially dropped out of the race for president on March 9. Speaking from his home in Arizona, McCain said the he was "suspending" his campaign. He congratulated Bush on his win, but stopped short of throwing his support—and his delegates—to the candidate. He said he was contemplating how he can "best continue to serve" his nation at this point in his political career. He claimed, "I love my party. It is my home," in part silencing the rumors that he might leave the party to run as the candidate of Ross Perot's Reform Party. Yet he cited that he had hoped his campaign would have been a "force for change in the Republican party." Vowing to return to Washington to renew the call for change, the scrappy McCain said he was "dedicated to the cause of reform," claiming that he "will never walk away from a fight for what I know is right and just for our country."

> "In the wake of Bill Clinton's misconduct, McCain has become a reflection of our times, the focus of our desperate search for 'character' in a president to the exclusion of almost everything else—even actual political beliefs."
> — David Grann,
> **The New Republic**

For now, McCain is considering how he can best continue to promote those causes he believes in with such passion, while remaining inside the political mainstream. In the eyes of many observers, America has not seen the last of John McCain.

MARRIAGE AND FAMILY

McCain has been married two times. He and his first wife, Carol, were married in 1965. She was divorced with two sons, Doug and Andy. McCain adopted the boys, and he and Carol had a daughter, Sidney, in 1966. John and Carol McCain divorced in 1980. That same year, McCain married Cindy Hensley. They have four children, Meghan, Jack, Jimmy, and Bridget. Bridget was an orphan who was born in Bangladesh. Cindy brought her to the U.S. for medical treatment when she was an infant, and the McCains adopted her.

Cindy McCain has come under media scrutiny of her own. She had back surgery in the early 1990s and was given prescription drugs for the pain. She became addicted to them. At one point, she broke into and stole drugs from the medical supply for a relief agency she was working with. John McCain said he never realized Cindy had become addicted, but her parents did. They confronted Cindy, and she agreed to get treatment. She was very open with the media about her problem when her husband announced his run for the presidency. She has never been that keen on the idea of being the First Lady, but she says that if she was, she knows what issues she would stress. "Adoption would be a main issue, along with foster care and women's health care. And I would hopefully be a good role model [on the drug issue]. I'm in recovery. If I can do it, then maybe they can do it, too. And maybe it would help somebody."

WRITINGS

Faith of My Fathers, 1999

AWARDS

Decorated Legion of Merit
Decorated Silver Star
Bronze Star
Purple Heart
Distinguished Flying Cross
Vietnamese Legion of Honor

FURTHER READING

Books

McCain, John. *Faith of My Fathers,* 1999
Timberg, Robert. *The Nightingale's Song,* 1995
Who's Who in America, 2000

Periodicals

Biography, Mar. 2000, p.80
Current Biography Yearbook 1989
Esquire, May 1998, p.94
Mother Jones, Nov./Dec. 1998, p.42
New Republic, May 13, 1996, p.23; May 24, 1999, p.24

New York Times, July 31, 1967, p.A1; Oct. 28, 1967, p.A1; Aug. 9, 1988, p.A16; Feb. 12, 1997, p.A1; Feb. 23, 2000, p.A1; Mar. 1, 2000, p.A1; Mar. 5, 2000, p.A1; Mar 8, 2000, p.A1

New York Times Magazine, May 25, 1997, p.32

New Yorker, Oct. 21, 1996, p.130

Newsweek, Feb. 14, 2000, p.22; Feb. 21, 2000, p.24; Feb. 28, 2000, p.76; Mar. 6, p.28; Mar. 20, 2000, p.28

People, Nov. 9, 1992, p.101; Oct. 4, 1999, p.139

Rolling Stone, Apr. 13, 2000, p.53

Time, Jan. 8, 1990, p.48; Oct. 11, 1999, p.39; Nov. 15, 1999, p.38

U.S. News and World Report, Mar. 28, 1983, p.40; Dec. 18, 1995, p.43; Sep. 27, 1999, p.26

ADDRESS

241 Russell Bldg.
Washington, DC 20510

WORLD WIDE WEB SITE

http://www.mccain2000.com

Walter Payton 1954-1999

American Professional Football Player
Former Running Back with the Chicago Bears
NFL Career Rushing Record Holder

BIRTH

Walter Jerry Payton was born in Columbia, Mississippi, on July 25, 1954, the second of three children born to Peter and Alyne Payton. Walter's brother, Eddie, was three years older, and his sister, Pamela, was one year younger. While Peter worked in a factory that produced parachutes and other military material, Alyne stayed home and took care of the children. The family lived in a modest three-room house until Payton was eight, when they moved into a brand-new home that was built with money Peter had saved from years of hard work.

YOUTH

Growing up in Columbia, Payton was always on the go and causing mischief. Every house on the block had a young boy, so he had plenty of playmates. Everything a child needed to have fun at that time was nearby—open fields, woods, a river, railroad tracks, and several factories. Whenever Payton was not in school, he was out looking for trouble. "I was jumpy and excitable and always loved to be going, doing, getting into something . . . mostly mischief," he recalled.

Summer days were the best. Payton and his friends would find something new to do every day—playing hide and seek in the barrels at the pickle factory one day, racing across a railroad trestle just ahead of an oncoming train another. It was a miracle no one was ever injured, but to the kids it all seemed like great fun. In Payton's mind, whenever he was told he could not do something, he had to do it once just to see what the big deal was.

"I was jumpy and excitable and always loved to be going, doing, getting into something . . . mostly mischief," Payton recalled about his younger days.

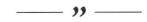

This led to plenty of punishment from his father, who was a strict disciplinarian. "I was a kid who invented trouble," Payton admitted. "I never got whipped for the same thing twice."

Religion played a large role in his childhood. His family attended the Chapel Baptist Church, and both his parents made sure that the children developed a deep religious faith. Still, for the active Payton, the long Sunday sermons were torture. After somehow managing to sit through Sunday school and the main service, he would burst from the church with his playmates and race home to watch *Tarzan*, his favorite childhood television show. The street remained quiet until *Tarzan* was over, when the air would fill with the whoops and shouts of the neighborhood boys imitating the TV character. "Sunday was a good day," Payton fondly recalled.

Though Payton did play Little League baseball for three years, sports did not play a big part in his early childhood. He was usually too busy doing other things — especially drumming — to spend much time playing sports. From an early age, he loved music in general and the drums in particular. Any hard surface was fair game for his drum practice. "He'd come through the house beating on anything he could put his hands on," his mother stated. "All he did was drum. When he'd start early in the morning, it was hard on me."

Payton's first exposure to football came through his membership in the Boy Scouts. Troop meetings would draw up to 100 kids for games of tag and football, and sometimes up to 50 would play a single game of football at one time. "With 20 or more guys on a team, you weren't sure whether or not you really wanted the ball," Payton remembered. "You couldn't see it anyway. You had to listen for it whooshing through the air over the sound of a stampede of potential tacklers. Talk about running out of sheer fear. But I quickly learned that I wanted the ball all the time. We had some wild games."

EDUCATION

School was always important to Payton, and to his family. He always did well in school, and he was often more interested in music than in sports. It was not until Payton entered John J. Jefferson High School that he played organized football for the first time. He did not go out for the team his freshman year, as he was afraid it would interfere with playing in the band, which was his first love. He was also on the track team as a long jumper, and he performed with a jazz-rock group after school. In addition, his brother Eddie was already a star on the football team, and Walter did not want his mother to have to worry about both of them getting hurt. After Eddie graduated, though, Walter decided to try out his sophomore season.

Things did not start well. Payton was a little scared at first by the equipment and uniforms, by having to follow in Eddie's footsteps, and by the often loud and intimidating coaching staff. He decided to play running back, but the first time he carried the ball in a scrimmage made him question that decision — he got turned around and ended up running the wrong way into the opposing team's end zone. That play turned out to be a fluke, of course. Payton quickly demonstrated to the coaches that he was a talented back who combined quickness with a punishing hit that often knocked over would-be tacklers. He started the team's first game against Purvis High and scored a 65-yard touchdown on his first carry. Later in the game, he scored a 75-yard touchdown. Not only did he make the league all-star team that first season, but he also managed to keep his spot in the marching band, playing his beloved drums.

In 1970, Jefferson was merged with Columbia High School to force the integration of white and African-American students. In 1954, in a landmark case, *Brown* v. *Board of Education*, the U.S. Supreme Court had struck down the "separate but equal" concept that had kept the schools —as well as movie theaters, restaurants, bathrooms, and drinking fountains—segregated by race. Yet even by 1970, when Walter Payton was in high school, it often took a court-ordered desegregation agreement to bring about integration in school districts. Tension was high in Mississippi at that time, as many people did not want to see the schools integrated. In his own way, Payton used his talent on the football field to ease those tensions and make integration a little bit easier. When fans of the Columbia Wildcats saw Payton, an African-American, score two touchdowns on runs of 65 and 95 yards each in his first game, they forgot about color for a minute and just appreciated the talent they were witnessing. "That did it for integration," said Payton's high school coach, Charles Boston. "The people didn't see a black boy running down the field. They saw a Wildcat."

Payton had two outstanding seasons for Columbia and was highly recruited by major colleges around the country prior to his high school graduation in 1972. After much soul-searching, he finally narrowed his choices to Kansas State University and nearby Jackson State,

When Payton was young, sometimes up to 50 kids would play a single game of football at one time. "With 20 or more guys on a team, you weren't sure whether or not you really wanted the ball," Payton remembered. "You couldn't see it anyway. You had to listen for it whooshing through the air over the sound of a stampede of potential tacklers. Talk about running out of sheer fear. But I quickly learned that I wanted the ball all the time. We had some wild games."

where his brother Eddie was already a star. He initially decided upon Kansas State, but on his way to catch his flight to visit the school, he stopped in Jackson to visit his brother. He loved the beautiful campus and was very impressed with Jackson State Coach Robert Hill, and he began to question his decision to attend Kansas State. More confused than ever, Payton skipped his flight to Kansas and returned home, which angered his parents. Frustrated with her youngest son's indecisiveness, Payton's mother made the decision for him. He would go to Jackson State.

Jackson State University

Payton fit in immediately at Jackson State. Living with his brother during his freshman year helped him ease into college life (although he and Eddie were very different and experienced quite a bit of sibling rivalry). As he had been in grade school and high school, Payton was a dedicated student *and* athlete. He wrote in his memoir *Sweetness* that he was determined "to dispel the myth that athletes in general and black athletes in particular don't have to work to get their diplomas and that they don't learn anything anyway." He worked hard at both, and with results.

At first, college football was harder than he had expected—he was amazed at the dedication and skill that the older players demonstrated. It did not take him long to adjust, however. Payton was one of just two freshmen to make the team's traveling squad for the first game against Prairie View. He did not get to play often in the early games, but he started seeing more action late in the season. During his first year, he ended up rushing for 614 yards and averaged an excellent 7.6 yards per carry. In addition to running back, he also punted and kicked for extra points.

During his sophomore year, Payton blossomed into a star. In the season's second game, he rewrote the National Collegiate Athletic Association (NCAA) record book when he ran for seven touchdowns and two 2-point conversions, scoring a total of 46 points. That's still a record for one game. The coach of the opposing school, Lane College, was impressed: "I don't care if he scored seven touchdowns in the schoolyard, it was damn fine running. We've stopped other good runners in this conference, but we couldn't stop him." Payton finished the season with 781 yards and 16 touchdowns, which helped Jackson State share first place in the Southwest Athletic Conference (SWAC) with Grambling.

"Sweetness"

Payton continued to improve as a ballplayer. His junior year, he ran for 1,139 yards and led the nation in scoring by racking up 24 touchdowns, 13 extra points, and 1 field goal. He was named Most Valuable Player and Offensive Player of the Year in the SWAC and made the Black All-America team. Jackson State again tied Grambling for the league championship. It was also during this time that Payton earned his famous nickname, "Sweetness." The name came from his "sweet" moves that made the opposition miss when they tried to tackle him. The nickname would stick with Payton throughout his career.

Payton (34) leaping past Reggie Doss (71) of the Los Angeles Rams for a gain of 10 yards, putting him over the 10,000-yard mark for rushing in the NFL, December 26, 1982

Payton dominated the gridiron again during his senior season and drew the national spotlight to Jackson State. He capped off an outstanding college career by running for 1,029 yards (in two fewer games than the previous season) and averaging 5.8 yards per carry. He finished his four years with 66 touchdowns and 464 points, both NCAA records. Even though he attended a small school, he was named College Player of the Year and All-American by many football publications. He was also the Most Valuable Offensive Player in the East-West Shrine Game, a postseason college football all-star game.

Most impressively, Payton made sure he did not neglect his studies while setting all those records. He graduated in three-and-a-half years with a bachelor's degree in communications, and even started taking courses toward a master's degree to specialize in the education of deaf children.

CAREER HIGHLIGHTS

Chicago Bears

Payton was ready to make the jump to the next level of competition. In January 1975 he was selected in the first round of the National Football League (NFL) draft by the Chicago Bears. He was the fourth player taken overall in the draft, so the expectations were high when he headed to Chicago for the first time.

Unfortunately, Payton did not make a good first impression in Chicago. He was supposed to attend a press conference at which the Bears would introduce their new star to the media and the public. He went to Chicago, but then he skipped the press conference upon his lawyer's advice when his lawyer was unable to attend it with him. It was the wrong thing to do. The Chicago media thought that he was either a spoiled college athlete or a backwoods hick who was not smart enough to make it in the big city. Payton and his lawyer, Bud Holmes, smoothed over most of the hurt feelings, but the hick image would stay with Payton for years. "I think that early on he didn't know how to act," a Chicago newspaper writer stated. "He was just a small-town kid suddenly thrust under lights in a big city, and because he was afraid of presenting the wrong image, he kept on the move and stayed evasive."

Once the Bears' fans saw Payton on the football field, though, all was forgiven. He started slowly his first season, rushing for 679 yards and seven touchdowns, as the Bears continued to struggle as a team and finished with a 4-10 record. With one year under his belt, however, Payton was ready to show the NFL just how talented he was. In the 1976 season, he ran for 1,390 yards and was named NFC Player of the Year by the *Sporting News*. Only a sprained ankle in the last game of the season kept him from edging out O.J. Simpson for the NFL rushing title. The Bears improved also, finishing 7-7 for the year.

A Powerful, Unstoppable Running Back

By this time, teammates and opponents alike were marveling about Payton's unique running style. He combined quick moves with raw power, and he simply refused to be tackled. He would fight for every inch, flailing his arms and driving his legs until the whistle blew, always trying to gain a little more ground. Throughout his career, after every carry, he would spot the ball several inches ahead of where he was really stopped. The referees almost always moved the ball back, but Payton estimates that he probably gained an additional 100 yards over the course of his career by moving the ball up. Anything he could do to give his team a competitive edge, he would do. He was known as much for his team-building, selfless attitude as for his powerful rushing. Not one to taunt the opposition with an end-zone dance, Payton would score a touch down, then hand the football to one of his offensive linesman, saying "they're the ones who do all the work." He could defend against players nearly twice his size. Once, against a powerful linebacker, he used his standard move, a forearm to the chin. The player, dazed, said, "Walter, what did you do that for?" "Because," the running back replied, "You were in the way."

Payton was known for his energy and his impishness. A teammate remembers the final game of the 1979 season. "We ran a sweep and the referee goes to spot the ball and Walter tries to untie his shoes," Ted Albrecht recalled. "Five plays later he was doing it again. He was always trying to keep it loose."

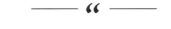

Payton wrote in his memoir **Sweetness** *that he was determined "to dispel the myth that athletes in general and black athletes in particular don't have to work to get their diplomas and that they don't learn anything anyway."*

By the beginning of his third season in the NFL, Payton was stronger and faster than he had been in college, and he was a true superstar in the making. That season, he ran for an astounding 1,852 yards and scored 16 touchdowns. It was the third-best season ever turned in by an NFL running back, trailing only Simpson and Jim Brown. Payton actually had a chance to break Simpson's record of 2,003 yards in the season's final game, but an icy field limited him to just 47 yards. His great year reached its peak in the season's tenth game, when Payton ran for 275 yards against the Minnesota Vikings—the most yards rushing ever gained in a single game. While the records were nice, Payton was even more excited that he finally helped lead the Bears into the playoffs with a 9-5 record. The team lost to Dallas 37-7 in the first round, but things still were looking up in Chicago. For his individual efforts, Payton was awarded almost every football honor imaginable, including NFL Most Valuable Player and UPI International Athlete of the Year.

In 1978, the Bears slipped to 7-9, but Payton again excelled. He became the first Chicago back to gain more than 1,000 yards in three straight seasons when he finished with 1,395. In 1979, after a strong draft of college

Payton, left, raising his hand in victory after setting a record to become the NFL's all-time rushing leader with 12,317 yards, October 7, 1984

players, the Bears finished 10-6, although they again lost in the first round of the playoffs. Payton kept rolling, posting 1,610 yards rushing and 17 touchdowns. All the promise of 1979 faded the next year, however, when the team got off to a terrible start and finished 7-9, missing the playoffs. Payton was one of the team's few bright spots that year. He finished with more than 1,000 yards for the fifth straight season and broke the Bears' career record for most yards gained, rushing and receiving combined.

In 1981, things bottomed out for the Bears. They finished 6-10, and head coach Neill Armstrong was fired at the end of the season. Payton finished with his lowest rushing total since his rookie season and was pounded on the field every week. "I took a beating," he said at the time. "The first week I could understand it; we had a rookie at tackle. But last week I took a beating and this week I took a beating. There's only so much you can take. If the rest of the season's going to be like this, the linemen can start scavenging for my arms and legs."

In 1982, tough and no-nonsense Mike Ditka took over as head coach of the Bears. A former Hall of Fame tight end with the Bears, Ditka vowed to rebuild the team's poor offense. Payton would be an important part of the rebuilding. "I thought Walter was one hell of a football player before I came to the Bears," Ditka stated. "I had great admiration for him. He was tough, always gave something extra when he was about to be tackled. . . . He's the very best football player I've ever seen. Period." Ditka's first season behind the bench was shortened by a seven-week player strike. With rookie quarterback Jim McMahon leading the way, the Bears only finished 3-6, but there were signs that Ditka's tough-minded approach was beginning to pay off. A highlight of that season for Payton came on December 26, 1982, when he reached a career high 10,000 rushing yards in a game against the Los Angeles Rams. Payton finished with 596 yards in the short season, and while he sometimes questioned why the Bears were passing more (which meant fewer carries for him), he decided to give Ditka's methods a chance.

He announced that 1987 would be his final season. For a player like Walter Payton, the decision was tough. Football was "something I love to do. Money isn't everything. Do you get married because of money? Do you have kids because of money? It's like something you have to fulfill in your life."

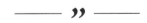

A New Rushing Record

The Bears began their climb to the top of the NFL in 1983, when Payton had one of his best seasons. The team finished 8-8, while Payton racked up 1,421 yards and 11 touchdowns. He also caught 53 passes for 607 yards to lead the Bears. In the team's sixth game of the season, playing against the Saints in New Orleans, Payton broke a record that most people considered unbreakable—Jim Brown's career rushing record of 12,312 yards. With a six-yard carry early in the second half of the game, Payton exceeded Brown's record. The game came to a brief stop as fans ran onto the field and Payton was congratulated by players and coaches on both teams. Everyone in the stadium knew they were witnessing a special moment. "Walter is still our best weapon," Ditka explained, "only now we get production out of him running, catching, throwing, and as a decoy." In 1984, the Bears improved again, this time to 10-6. The team won its first-round playoff game, but lost 23-0 to the San Francisco 49ers to fall just short of the Super Bowl.

Super Bowl XX

Just when it looked as if Payton might join the long list of great athletes who have wonderful careers but never win a championship, the Bears pulled it all together in 1985. Led by Payton, who finished with 1,551 yards rushing, 483 yards receiving, and 12 touchdowns, the Bears lost only one game during the regular season to finish 15-1. They were the huge favorites to win the Super Bowl, and they did not disappoint. With stars like Payton, McMahon, and William "The Refrigerator" Perry, as well as a cocky attitude that was best demonstrated in the team's "Super Bowl Shuffle" music video, the Bears steamrolled the New England Patriots 46-10. Payton finally had his Super Bowl ring.

Jarrett Payton gave the Hall of Fame induction speech for his father. "My dad played 13 seasons and missed only one game while breaking all the running back records," Jarrett noted. "Not only is my dad an excellent athlete, he's a role model. He's my biggest role model and my best friend."

The End of a Great Career

Payton would continue to play for two more seasons. In 1986, he rushed for 1,333 yards, but the Bears selected running back Neal Anderson in the draft because they knew Payton was getting older. Payton was somewhat bitter about the situation. He felt that the team was trying to force him out and was not giving him the respect he deserved. When the 1987 season opened, it was clear that Payton would have a reduced role on the team, and that was too much for the proud leader to bear. After several games, he broke down and cried in the locker room. "Sometimes, I feel I'm the problem here. A lot of time I feel I don't even belong here. These are feelings I've never had before. It's hard." He announced that 1987 would be his final season. For a player like Walter Payton, the decision was tough. Football was "something I love to do. Money isn't everything. Do you get married because of money? Do you have kids because of money? It's like something you have to fulfill in your life."

In his final regular season home game, Payton was given a stirring ovation by the Chicago fans, and it was announced that his uniform number 34 would be retired. It was a fitting end for one of the great careers in sports history. Payton finished with 16,726 career rushing yards and 110 rushing touchdowns, both of which are still NFL records. He also set or

Payton, center left, hugging his 12-year-old son, Jarrett, after being introduced as an inductee into the Pro Football Hall of Fame in Canton, Ohio, July 31, 1993

tied nine other NFL records during his career. There is no question that Payton is one of the greatest running backs of all time.

Hall of Fame

In 1993, Payton was rewarded for his terrific NFL career by being induct-ed into the Pro Football Hall of Fame in Canton, Ohio. While Payton had downplayed his induction, saying it was no big deal, the day became a memorable one when his young son, Jarrett Payton, gave the induction speech for his father. "My dad played 13 seasons and missed only one game while breaking all the running back records," Jarrett noted. "Not only is my dad an excellent athlete, he's a role model. He's my biggest role model and my best friend." The tribute moved Payton. "I was the first one to say I wouldn't [cry] and the first one to say how strong I was and everything else," he said that day. "But as it goes to show, a lot of time when you're among your peers, such as these great athletes, you try to be

Payton standing before the many "Get Well" cards he received from fans after announcing his illness, February, 1999

something you're not." In 1995, Payton was included among the first group of players from small colleges to be inducted into the College Football Hall of Fame.

Life After Football

Even while he was playing, Payton knew he would need something else to fall back on when his playing days were over. Toward this end, he founded Walter Payton Enterprises and became involved in a number of investments and businesses, including restaurants, timber, and real estate. He did so well in his investments that when he retired, he joined a group of investors that tried to become the first minority team owners in the NFL. That deal fell through, but Payton still had hopes of owning an NFL team someday. In 1996, Payton opened Walter Payton's Roundhouse, a restaurant in Chicago. In addition to his business interests, he was active in the community and in raising funds for charities in Chicago and Mississippi, especially those benefitting deaf or retarded children.

Retirement suited him, and he enjoyed his new life thoroughly. "If you could go back and change things, you might not be the person you are right now. There were times it was frustrating and there were times it was jubilant. Over all, it's been a lot of fun."

DEATH

Payton continued enjoying his post-football life until he began to suffer from indigestion in late 1998. After months of tests, Payton learned that he had primary sclerosing cholangitis, a rare disease in which the bile ducts of the liver become blocked. Later, he learned he also had bile duct cancer. In February 1999, Payton held a press conference in which he tearfully told the world about his condition. Fans by the thousands sent him cards and wishes for a full recovery. At first, he was placed on a waiting list for a donor liver, but the disease, and the chemotherapy and radiation to treat the cancer, ravaged Payton's body. He died on November 1, 1999, at the age of 45.

LEGACY

The Payton family had a public memorial service for the legendary football hero, attended by his many friends in football and the media. Former Bear's Coach Mike Ditka

——— " ———

"Many of you knew my father as a football player or businessman, said Jarrett Payton at his father's memorial service. "I knew him as dad. He was my hero. My mother, my sister, and I will miss him . . . but he is in a place where there is no sickness, no pain. The last 12 months have been extremely tough on me and my family. We learned a lot about love and life. Our greatest thanks goes out to the people of Chicago. You adopted my dad and made him yours. He loved you all."

——— " ———

recalled Payton as "the best runner, blocker, teammate, and friend I've ever seen. Truly the best football player I've ever seen." His thoughts were echoed by former NFL coach and television commentator John Madden, who said, "Walter Payton was the greatest. If you wanted yards you'd want Walter Payton. Who do you want to block? Walter Payton. If you wanted someone to catch, Walter Payton. I enjoyed him more than any other player." Paul Talgliabue, Commissioner of the NFL, said, "The tremendous grace and dignity he displayed in his final months reminded us again why "Sweetness" was the perfect nickname for Walter Payton." Payton's son Jarrett, now a college freshman, thanked the people of Chicago for embracing his father. "Many of you knew my father as a football player or businessman. I knew him as dad. He was my hero. My mother, my sister, and I will miss him . . . but he is in a place where there is no sickness, no pain. The last 12 months have been extremely tough on me and my family. We learned a lot about love and life. Our greatest thanks goes out to the people of Chicago. You adopted my dad and made him yours. He loved you all."

MARRIAGE AND FAMILY

Payton met Connie Norwood, the woman he would marry, in the spring of 1973 when she was a senior in high school. The following year she joined him as a student at Jackson State. The couple was engaged in January 1975, shortly after Payton was drafted by the Bears, and they were married on July 7, 1976. They had two children: son Jarrett, born in 1981, and daughter Brittney, born in 1984. In 1994, after 18 years of marriage, Payton and his wife announced that they planned to divorce, but they reconciled, and were together at the time of his death.

HOBBIES AND OTHER INTERESTS

One of Payton's main post-retirement passions was auto racing. An experienced driver, Payton began racing in 1988, joining the professional circuit in 1993. "I'm learning," he said after finishing at the back of the pack in his first race. "A lot of the guys I'm racing have been doing this a long time. I don't care if they take me seriously. I am. If they don't, they'll be behind me."

After competing on the race track for a few years, Payton decided to retire. But he remained close to the world of auto racing. In fact, he was a co-owner of the Payton/Coyne racing team, and spent many weekends watching his drivers compete in major races across the country.

WRITINGS

Sweetness, 1978

HONORS AND AWARDS

NFC Player of the Year (*Sporting News*): 1976
International Athlete of the Year (United Press International): 1977

NFL Most Valuable Player (Professional Football Writers of America): 1977
NFL Player of the Year (Associated Press): 1977
NFL Player of the Year (*Sport*): 1977
NFL Player of the Year (*Sporting News*): 1977
Pro Football Hall of Fame: 1993
College Football Hall of Fame: 1995
NFL's All-Time Leading Rusher: 16,726 career yards

FURTHER READING

Books

Koslow, Philip. *Walter Payton*, 1994 (juvenile)
Leder, Jane Mersky. *Walter Payton*, 1986 (juvenile)
Payton, Walter. *Sweetness*, 1978
Sufrin, Mark. *Payton*, 1988 (juvenile)
Who's Who in America, 1997

Periodicals

Chicago Sun-Times, Nov. 2, 1999, pA1; Nov. 8, 1999, p.A1
Chicago Tribune Nov. 2, 1999, p.A1; Nov. 9, 1999, p.A1
Current Biography Yearbook 1985
Ebony, Nov. 1980, p.58; Sep. 1986, p.92; July 1999, p.108
Jet, Nov. 18, 1985, p.54; Dec. 28, 1987, p.48; Feb. 22, 1999, p.52
Los Angeles Times, Nov. 2, 1999, p.A1
New York Times, Nov. 2, 1999, p.C23, C25
People, Apr. 19, 1999, p.73
Sport, Oct. 1984, p.31; Sep. 1998, p.22
Sporting News, Aug. 2, 1993, p.8
Sports Illustrated, Sep. 5, 1984, p.26; Oct. 15, 1984, p.44; Aug. 2, 1993, p.55

WORLD WIDE WEB SITES

http://www.payton34.com
http://www.chicagobears.com/lockerroom/hof/payton.html
http://www.chicagobears.com/lockerroom/hof/paytontribute.html

Freddie Prinze, Jr. 1976-

American Actor
Star of *I Know What You Did Last Summer, She's All That,* and *Down to You*

BIRTH

Freddie James Prinze, Jr. was born on March 8, 1976, in Los Angeles, California. His father was the well-known comedian Freddie Prinze, who was born Frederick Karl Pruetzel but changed his name when he decided to go into show business. His mother is Katherine Cochran, a real estate agent who lives in Las Vegas.

Freddie Prinze, Sr. was a comedian and actor who was best known for playing Chico Rodriguez, the Latino garage mechanic on the popular 1970s television sitcom, "Chico and the Man." He was widely admired for his talents as a comic actor, but he shot and killed himself when he was only 22. Many believe he was overwhelmed by the combined pressures of early celebrity, an impending divorce from his wife, and an addiction to prescription drugs. His death left Freddie Prinze, Jr. without a father at the age of 10 months.

YOUTH

In the wake of his father's death, Freddie Prinze, Jr. and his mother were the subjects of constant media attention. She decided that it would be difficult for her son to have a normal childhood in Los Angeles. So when he was four they moved to Albuquerque, New Mexico, where her parents lived. Freddie was raised in the middle-class Northeast Heights section of the city under the watchful eyes of his mother and grandparents. He spent most of his summers in Puerto Rico with his paternal grandmother, to whom he was also very close.

> "
> *As he grew older Prinze began to think more and more about losing his father. "I became very angry because almost everybody I knew had an old man except me."*
> "

"I went to school, to church, and I had a nice, quiet, normal childhood," Prinze recalls. He played Little League baseball, soccer, and took swimming lessons. He even found a substitute father: his best friend Chris's dad, Don Sandoval, who took him fishing and treated him like another son. Still, the issue of fathers became important to him. Prinze had long been shielded from the events surrounding his father's death, because he was so young at the time that he never really felt the loss. But as he grew older Prinze began to think more and more about his father. It was painful for him to see his friends' fathers pull into the driveway after a long day at work, or take their kids on weekend outings. "I became very angry because almost everybody I knew had an old man except me," he says.

The media's interest in the Prinze family died down for a while after they moved to New Mexico. But it resurfaced when Prinze was about 11, forcing him to deal with the reality of his father's death. Ron DeBlasio, his father's former manager, finally sat young Freddie down and told him the whole story. He explained why Freddie Prinze, Sr. had started abusing the drugs that had been prescribed by his doctor and what happened the night he shot himself. Knowing the truth didn't make life any easier for Prinze, but it taught him a lesson about the dangers of too much success at a young age.

Freddie's mother had done everything in her power to get him away from Hollywood and the entertainment industry. Still, his interest in acting was obvious from the start. "He had a special talent, always playing make-believe and acting things out," Don Sandoval recalls.

When he was young, Prinze used to listen to albums and watch videotapes of his father's stand-up comedy routines. "That was my way of being close to him. I would practice the voice and memorize the routines. I had it down perfectly and I loved doing it."

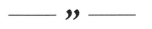

EARLY MEMORIES

When he was young, Prinze used to listen to albums and watch videotapes of his father's stand-up comedy routines. "That was my way of being close to him. I would practice the voice and memorize the routines. I had it down perfectly and I loved doing it."

EDUCATION

Prinze attended Manzano Day School as an elementary student and three different high schools. He spent his freshman year at El Dorado High School, his sophomore year at Sandia High, and then transferred to La Cueva High in his junior year. He changed schools not only because he was having trouble finding friends and fitting in with his peers, but also because of the media attention that continued to surround him as the son of a famous comedian who had committed suicide.

Prinze was not a good student. He often skipped classes, and rarely studied unless something really captured his imagination. His 12th grade English teacher still remembers how he loved reading aloud from the classic Greek drama, *Oedipus Rex*. But he spent most of his time living in a fantasy world. An avid reader of comic books, Prinze identified closely with "The X-Men," a team of mutant superheroes who were regarded as outcasts but who used their special abilities to do good in the world. Sometimes he would hide in the wrestling room during lunch, when he knew no one else would be there, and pretend he was a superhero named

Prinze with the cast of I Know What You Did Last Summer.

Prism, or act out scenes from his favorite movies. "I was considered really weird," he says, "and people kind of kept their distance." He tried playing sports, only to discover that he had little athletic talent. Instead, he would run the length of the soccer field, fighting off imaginary attacks from his X-Men rivals and trying to dodge magnetic blasts. "Even back then I was acting; I just didn't know it yet," he says.

Prinze graduated from La Cueva High School in 1994. He soon recognized his family's increasing financial hardships and the limited opportunities that existed in Albuquerque. So, he decided to move to Los Angeles and pursue an acting career because it was the only thing he was any good at. Although his mother had tried to discourage him from following in his father's footsteps, she supported his decision once it was clear that his mind was made up. Only two months after graduation, he set off for Los Angeles in a broken down Jeep.

FIRST JOBS

Because he had so little money, Prinze moved in with family friends and worked at their restaurant in Van Nuys. He took acting classes during the day and started going to auditions. Many people tried to persuade him to change his name so that he wouldn't be compared to his father, but he refused. "I told them my name was something my father wanted to give me, and he wasn't able to give me a lot," Prinze explains.

After a few months, Prinze landed his first acting job: a four-line role in the ABC sitcom, "Family Matters." Then he got a role in a television movie called "Detention: Siege at Johnson High," in which he played the go-between who helps the police capture a psychotic gunman. The high ratings this show received reflected well on the 19-year-old actor, and soon his agent was sending him out to audition for more prestigious roles. His first lead was in an ABC Afterschool Special called "Too Soon for Jeff," in which he portrayed a high school senior who is forced to grow up in a hurry when his girlfriend gets pregnant. He was supposed to audition for a supporting role, but he bluffed his way into an audition for the role of Jeff and ended up getting it.

CAREER HIGHLIGHTS

To Gillian On Her 37th Birthday

In 1996 Prinze made his film debut in *To Gillian on Her 37th Birthday*. It was about a widower (Peter Gallagher) whose obsession with his deceased wife (Michelle Pfeiffer) threatens to ruin his relationship with his teenage daughter (Claire Danes), who desperately needs his guidance. Prinze played the daughter's punk boyfriend, complete with tattoos and multiple body piercings.

The most difficult part for Prinze was kissing Claire Danes on screen. She was a far more experienced actor, and he'd had relatively little experience with girls in high school. To make matters worse, he had developed a serious crush on her during the filming. He was so nervous about the kissing scene that he was afraid he might throw up. Fortunately, Danes sensed his discomfort and went out of her way to help him relax. As a result, the scenes between Prinze and Danes came alive in a very natural way, and the two ended up becoming close friends.

Appearing in a feature-length film with established actors gave Prinze's self-confidence a real boost. It also brought him the kind of attention that most young actors only dream about. Soon he was being asked to audition for major film roles on a regular basis, and people started telling him he was going to be a big star like his father. But Prinze shrugged it off. He knew what could happen if he didn't keep his ego under control and his life firmly grounded in reality.

The House of Yes

Prinze's second film, *The House of Yes* (1997), was an independent dark comedy about a dysfunctional family. It starred Geneviève Bujold, Parker Posey, Rachel Leigh Cook, and Tori Spelling. Posey played Jackie-O, a young woman who believes that she is Jacqueline Kennedy Onassis. Her twin brother, Marty (Josh Hamilton), brings home his new fiancée, Lesly (Tori Spelling), and Prinze plays Anthony, the naive younger brother who has ideas of his own about Lesly. When it came time to film his love scene with Spelling, Prinze was again overcome with nervousness. "I did everything wrong you could do wrong," he admits. At one point, he missed her mouth altogether and kissed her eye.

> *When it came time to film his love scene with Spelling, Prinze was again overcome with nervousness. "I did everything wrong you could do wrong," he admits. At one point, he missed her mouth altogether and kissed her eye.*

The role of Anthony was unlike anything Prinze had ever done before, and he loved the challenge of playing someone so completely different from himself. He once described Anthony as being "not completely insane, but you know he's going to snap eventually." He also learned a great deal from Parker Posey, a talented actress who is known as "the Indie Queen" for her many roles in independent films. Prinze describes her as "one of the top three actors I'll ever work with in my life."

The House of Yes premiered at the Sundance Film Festival and was nominated for numerous awards. After its release, some of the most powerful agents in Hollywood began calling Prinze. He finally ended up signing with Creative Artists, widely regarded as the best agency in town. This film was his biggest break so far, and it remains his favorite project to this day.

Prinze attending the premiere of the film
I Still Know What You Did Last
Summer.

I Know What You Did Last Summer

When Prinze was in fourth grade, he had read the Lois Duncan novel on which his next big film was based. "I was terrified for a month and didn't want to sleep or anything," he recalls. *I Know What You Did Last Summer* tells the story of four teenagers who accidentally run over and kill a stranger after a night of partying. Rather than going to the police, they decide to get rid of the body and try to forget the whole incident. A year later, they return to the town where the crime occurred, and their lives become a nightmare when one of them receives an anonymous note that says, "I know what you did last summer."

Prinze played the role of Ray Bronson, a kid from the wrong side of the tracks who hasn't had the privileged upbringing shared by his girlfriend Julie (Jennifer Love Hewitt) and her friends. Like Prinze himself in high school, Ray wants to fit in. He's the one who is driving the night the accident occurs, and the events that follow transform him from an innocent boy into a man.

I Know What You Did Last Summer was Prinze's first teen thriller. It was such a big hit at the box office in 1997 that the producers immediately began developing a sequel. Prinze and Jennifer Love Hewitt were joined in the sequel by the pop singer Brandy (from the television series "Moesha") and Mekhi Phifer, who had appeared in Brandy's video for "The Boy Is Mine." *I Still Know What You Did Last Summer* (1998) follows Julie as she goes off to college, where her relationship with Ray begins to fall apart. Soon, she and her roommate, Karla (Brandy) take off on an all-expenses paid trip to the Bahamas. They take along Karla's boyfriend Tyrell (Phifer) and another classmate, Will (Matthew Settle). But soon, their dream vacation turns into a nightmare.

I Still Know What You Did Last Summer received mixed reviews, but teenage audiences still flocked to see it. It brought Freddie Prinze, Jr. national attention, but he was still seen primarily in supporting roles or as a member of an ensemble cast.

She's All That

Prinze's first leading role was in the romantic comedy *She's All That,* about a high school prom king who asks the nerdiest girl in the class to be his queen. Zack Siler (Prinze) is the class president, a star athlete, and the most popular boy in his school — the exact opposite of what Prinze was like when he was that age. He makes a bet with his friends that he can turn an ugly duckling named Laney Boggs (Rachel Leigh Cook) into a prom queen. The film is a modern version of the Pygmalion myth in which boy meets girl, tries to re-make her in his own image, and ends up falling in love with who she truly is. But the plot struck so close to home for Prinze that he broke down and cried after filming the scene in which Laney finds out that she is nothing more than the subject of a bet.

> **Prinze has not yet given up on his dream of playing a superhero — or a cowboy, or even a bad guy. "There are so many roles out there that I haven't even gotten to touch," he says.**

She's All That opened on January 29, 1999. It was the 22nd anniversary of the death of Freddie Prinze, Sr., and it was a triumphant moment for his 22-year-old son. In addition to making Prinze a star, it won him and Cook an MTV Movie Award nomination for Best On-Screen Duo.

More Recent Films

Prinze followed his success in *She's All That* with strong supporting roles in *Sparkler* and *Wing Commander,* both of which were released in 1999. *Sparkler* is about three young men who are on their way to Las Vegas to win enough at the gambling casinos to pay the rent on their L.A. apartment. They meet a housewife from a trailer park who has left her husband and is looking for a new life. This quirky independent film never made it to the theaters but was very successful in the home video market. *Wing Commander,* based on the CD-ROM game series, is a science fiction action movie in which three rebellious space pilots fight an alien race that plans to destroy the earth. It gave Prinze his first opportunity to perform his own stunt sequences, which included flying around on wires in a heavy space suit.

Next up was *Down to You* (2000), a lightweight romantic comedy set on a college campus. Prinze plays a New York City college student named Al Connelley who meets the love of his life, an art student named Imogen (Julia Stiles), while picking songs on a jukebox. They soon start dating, things get serious, and then Al must deal with the possibility of losing the love of his life. Response to the movie, from both critics and fans, was only lukewarm.

———— **"** ————

Prinze is the first to admit that he lacks his father's comic gift. "The hardest thing in the world is to make people laugh, and my father was just brilliant. I couldn't write a joke for anything!"

———— **"** ————

Upcoming Projects

Prinze has recently worked on several new projects. One is *Head Over Heels*, the story of an art restorer (Monica Potter) who finds herself attracted to someone who appears to be the perfect man (Prinze). While spying on him to see if he's as good as he seems to be, she thinks she sees him committing a murder. In her search for the truth, she learns some important lessons about friendship and falling in love. The next is *Boys and Girls*, a romantic comedy in which Prinze plays a young man named Ryan whose relationship with his girlfriend Jennifer (Claire Forlani) becomes complicated. Both of these films are scheduled for release in late summer 2000.

Next up is *Summer Catch*, the story of a romance between a poor local boy and a wealthy young woman who spends the summer in his Cape Cod hometown. Prinze plays a minor-league ballplayer trying to earn his way to the big time. *Summer Catch* is scheduled to begin filming in mid-2000. He also plans to appear in *I Know What You Did Last Summer 3*, which is still in pre-production. And Prinze has not yet given up on his dream of playing a superhero—or a cowboy, or even a bad guy. "There are so many roles out there that I haven't even gotten to touch,"he says.

MAJOR INFLUENCES

Freddie Prinze, Sr. has had a huge impact on his son's life. In fact, one of the most satisfying things about Prinze's career choice is that it has brought him closer to the father he never had a chance to know. Now that he has

Prinze and Julia Stiles in Down to You.

acted in television sitcoms and become a Hollywood celebrity, Prinze has a better understanding of what his father's life was like. But he is the first to admit that he lacks his father's comic gift. "The hardest thing in the world is to make people laugh, and my father was just brilliant. I couldn't write a joke for anything!" he says.

Prinze may have gotten his foot in Hollywood's door because of his father's name, but since then, he has stood firmly on his own. In fact, it bothers him that people still ask him about the circumstances surrounding his father's death, rather than focusing on the contributions he made during his life. He particularly dislikes it when people predict that he'll end up the same way his father did. "My dad did his thing, and it didn't work out for him," Prinze says. "I'm doing my thing, and it's working out a lot better."

FAVORITE MOVIES

Prinze lists several favorite movies including *Ferris Bueller's Day Off* and *Pretty in Pink,* which he describes as "an entire generation's encyclopedia of feelings." But his favorite movie of all time is *Who Framed Roger Rabbit?* "If every film was like that," he says, "I'd live at the theater."

HOME AND FAMILY

For four years, Prinze had a very close relationship with Kimberly McCullough, an actress who played Robin Scorpio on the soap opera "General Hospital." They broke up recently, and he now lives alone in the house he bought in Toluca Lake, not far from Hollywood.

Having a family is definitely part of Prinze's plan for the future. "I know one day I'm going to be the best father in the world. Not having a father makes me want to be a great one." He still keeps a photograph of his dad and a framed copy of his hit comedy album, *Looking Good,* on the wall of his home.

"I know one day I'm going to be the best father in the world. Not having a father makes me want to be a great one."

HOBBIES AND OTHER INTERESTS

Prinze has always stayed away from Hollywood clubs and parties, and he avoids using drugs and alcohol because he is so aware of what they did to his father. He describes himself as "a total dork" who would rather stay home reading comic books and playing high-tech computer games, at which he excels. His favorite game is Star Crash, although he also loves more active games that require strategic thinking, such as paintball.

CREDITS

Television

"Family Matters," 1995
"Detention: Siege at Johnson High," 1995
"Too Soon for Jeff," 1996

Films

To Gillian on Her 37th Birthday, 1996
The House of Yes, 1997
I Know What You Did Last Summer, 1997

I Still Know What You Did Last Summer, 1998
She's All That, 1999
Sparkler, 1999
Wing Commander, 1999
Vig, 1999
Down to You, 2000

HONORS AND AWARDS

Hottie of the Year (Teen Choice Awards): 1999 Choice Actor — Film

FURTHER READING

Books

Catalano, Grace. *Freddie Prinze, Jr.: He's All That,* 1999
Jordan, Victoria. *Freddie Prinze, Jr.: A Biography,* 2000
Shapiro, Marc. *Freddie Prinze, Jr.: The Unofficial Biography,* 1999

Periodicals

Chicago Tribune, Jan. 28, 1999, Tempo section, p.1
In Style, Jan. 1999, p.81
Los Angeles Times, Dec. 24, 1995, p.42; Jan. 20, 2000, Calendar Section, p.6
People, Nov. 18, 1996, p.135; Nov. 30, 1998, p.33; May 10, 1999, p.197
Premiere, Feb. 1999, p.68
Seventeen, Nov. 1997, p.126; Feb. 2000, p.98
TV Guide, Dec. 13, 1997, p.46
USA Weekend, Jan. 30, 2000, p.10
Vanity Fair, Jan. 2000, p.57

ADDRESS

Creative Artists Agency
9830 Wilshire Blvd.
Beverly Hills, CA 90212

WORLD WIDE WEB SITE

http://us.imdb.com/Bio?Prinze+Jr.,+Freddie

NA Steganography:
Approach to Cryptography
Viviana I. Risca

Results

BRIEF ENTRY

Viviana Risca 1982-

Romanian-American Student and Winner of the 2000
Intel Science Talent Search

EARLY YEARS

Viviana Risca was born on December 6, 1982, in Bucharest,
Romania. Her parents, Mihai and Mihaela Risca, are both en-
gineers who left Romania in 1991 to find work in the United
States. In 1992 Viviana and her younger sister, Anca, boarded
a plane to join their parents in Port Washington, New York.

EDUCATION

Before she came to the U.S., Risca attended a public elementary school in Romania. She arrived in the U.S. knowing how to say only a few phrases in English, things like "Where's the bathroom?" and "How do I get home?" Within a few days, she found herself in a third grade classroom at the Grundy Avenue School in Holbrook, New York. Her school in Romania had emphasized hard work and doing what she was told, so she was able to apply this same disciplined approach to learning English. She progressed rapidly, and within a few years her language skills were as good as those of her classmates.

As a ninth grader at Paul D. Schreiber High School in Port Washington, Risca became deeply interested in scientific research when she learned about DNA—the material that carries genetic information in all life forms. That same year she applied to a special science program at Schreiber High that teaches students how to perform sophisticated research. She started the program as a sophomore, meeting with a faculty adviser four times a week and spending at least an hour a day learning how to hypothesize, experiment, and draw valid conclusions. It was also during her sophomore year that Risca earned highest honors at the Long Island Science Fair, where she received the Director's Award.

By the time she was 16, Risca had not only mastered the English language but scored 100% on all math and science Regents exams, which are tough statewide exams given to New York students. She also scored a near-perfect 1580 (out of 1600) on the SAT. During her senior year at Schreiber High School, she also won an achievement award from the National Council of Teachers of English for her skills as a writer. As a published poet and managing editor of her high school's literary magazine, Risca began to worry about what she would major in when she got to college. If she pursued a double major in biology and computer science, she might not have time to take courses in art and literature. "I think it is really important to be well-rounded, and to do as much as possible, and do what you love," she says.

MAJOR ACCOMPLISHMENTS

Students participating in Schreiber's special research program normally spend the summer before 11th grade at a university or hospital working directly with professional mentors in their field. Risca was invited to do research with Dr. Carter Bancroft, a judge who had been impressed by her entry in the Long Island Science Fair. She worked with him on a DNA project over the summer at Mt. Sinai School of Medicine, where he is a researcher. Although most of his research assistants had been graduate students or postdoctoral fellows, Dr. Bancroft says that Risca "seemed like a natural."

The project on which Bancroft wanted Risca's help involved steganography, which dates back 500 years. Here, Bancroft explains the process. "Our technique is based upon the concept of 'steganography,' which dates from 1499 and literally means 'covered writing.' Steganography basically involves putting a secret message into a form such that it can be concealed by hiding it among a large number of objects to which it is physically similar." In other words, the secret message would be hidden by changing its form, then concealing it by placing it among a lot of similar and seemingly innocent objects. During World War II, for example, German spies would take pages of printed material, photograph them, shrink the photographs down to the size of microdots, then conceal them as periods in innocent-looking letters that were sent through the mail. What Bancroft was interested in was whether DNA could be used as a medium for steganography.

> *When asked to describe her project, Risca shrugged it off as "a simple idea." "I was able to hide a message in a molecule of DNA and then combine that molecule with a lot of other DNA so that somebody who doesn't know how to find it will be unable to know which of those molecules has the message."*

For her part of the project, Risca started by designing a synthetic DNA strand. She then created a code for the English alphabet using DNA, by assigning each letter a certain sequence of three out of the four DNA chemicals. Next, she encrypted (turned into code) the message "JUNE 6 INVASION: NORMANDY," a famous secret message that was used in World War II. She inserted the message in the gene sequence of the synthetic DNA strand and then flanked it with two secret "primer" DNA sequences, which act like "keys" to the code. The message is indistinguishable from the background material in which it's placed, so that only someone who knows the primers, or keys, can find the message. Bancroft compares this to incorporating a thread into a carpet made up of 30 million threads of DNA. The primers act as a "hook," enabling someone to pull out the right thread from the surrounding carpet. Because discovering the primers involves choosing from among a trillion trillion options, the code is essentially unbreakable.

*The top three winners in the Intel Science Talent Search 2000.
From left to right: third-place winner Feng Zhang, a senior from Theodore
Roosevelt High School in Des Moines, Iowa; first-place winner Viviana Risca,
a senior at Schreiber High School in Port Washington, NY; and second place-
winner Jayce Getz, a senior at Big Sky High School in Missoula, Mont.*

Winning the Intel Science Talent Search

Risca and more than 1,500 other high school students across the United States submitted their research projects to the Intel Science Talent Search (STS), America's oldest and most prestigious pre-college science scholarship competition. Formerly known as the Westinghouse Science Talent Search and often referred to as the "junior Nobel Prize" because five previous winners have gone on to win the Nobel award, the Intel competition selects 40 finalists on the basis of their research ability, scientific originality, and creative thinking. Top scientists from a variety of disciplines review and judge the finalists, and the top ten receive college scholarships.

At age 17, Viviana Risca walked away with the top prize in the 2000 Intel Science Search. Two of the other finalists were also students at Schreiber

High School—a real tribute to the school's special science research program. Risca won a $100,000 college scholarship. Since she describes herself as a "worrywart" who started obsessing about how much college would cost when she was still in elementary school, the Intel prize should go a long way toward easing her fears.

When asked to describe her project, Risca shrugged it off as "a simple idea." "I was able to hide a message in a molecule of DNA and then combine that molecule with a lot of other DNA so that somebody who doesn't know how to find it will be unable to know which of those molecules has the message," she explains. Her method provides a way of "copyrighting" an organism that has been genetically engineered by hiding the name of the person or the company that created it inside the DNA of the organism.

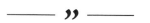

Risca paints, writes poetry, and enjoys visiting art museums. "It's really sad when scientists have the macho attitude that literature is for the weak," she adds.

Future Plans

Beginning in the fall of 2000, Risca will attend Stanford University in Palo Alto, California. She plans to major in molecular biology or biochemistry, and she also plans to complete either a minor or a second major in computer science, physics, or math.

HOBBIES AND OTHER INTERESTS

Despite her talents as a scientific researcher, Risca also enjoys the arts as well. She paints, writes poetry, and enjoys visiting museums to view Japanese pottery. "I couldn't do without having an artistic side to my life," she said. "It's really sad when scientists have the macho attitude that literature is for the weak."

HONORS AND AWARDS

Young Women of Achievement Award (National Organization for Women): 1998
Young Woman Achiever Award (Long Island Fund for Women and Girls): 1999, for excellence in math and science
Achievement Award in Writing (National Council of Teachers of English): 1999
Intel Science Talent Search: 2000

FURTHER READING

Periodicals

New York Times, Mar. 14, 2000, p.B5; Mar. 22, 2000, p.B2
Science News, Mar. 18, 2000, p. 181
USA Today, Mar. 14, 2000, p.D10

ADDRESS

Science Talent Search
Science Service
1719 N Street, N.W.
Washington, D.C. 20036

WORLD WIDE WEB SITE

http://www.intel.com/education/sts

Briana Scurry 1971-
American Soccer Player
Goalkeeper for the 1996 Olympic Gold Medal
Winners and the 1999 World Cup Champions

BIRTH

Briana Collette Scurry was born on September 7, 1971, in
Minneapolis, Minnesota. Her parents are Ernest and Robbie
Scurry. Briana was the youngest of their nine children; she
has three older brothers and five older sisters.

338

YOUTH

Before Briana was born, the Scurry family lived in Galveston, Texas. But in 1960, their house was wiped out by a hurricane. So Ernest and Robbie decided to move north, away from hurricane alley. They settled in Minneapolis, Minnesota. But soon after Briana was born, their house began to sink. It had been built on land that was created from a filled-in lake, and the ground was starting to give way. Soon, their house was sinking and tipping like the Leaning Tower of Pisa. "Every other year we needed two truckloads of dirt to fill in the hole" beneath the house, says her father. "We decided we were going to find a place where the houses didn't sink."

When Briana was about five, the Scurry family moved from Minneapolis to Dayton, Minnesota, a predominantly white suburb about 25 miles south. "In the four-town radius where I lived we were the only African-American family," Scurry says. "But I never got singled out. My parents never let me think I was alone in anything. They taught me that I could do whatever I wanted to do." Both her parents and her early teammates helped Scurry feel like she fit in. "Whatever sport I played, I was pretty much the only black kid on the team, so I'm used to it. It never bothered me because I was well-received by my teammates coming up through the ranks. I also thank my parents because they taught me to be well-adjusted, view the situation around me, and be friends with everyone regardless of color."

"In the four-town radius where I lived we were the only African-American family. But I never got singled out. My parents never let me think I was alone in anything. They taught me that I could do whatever I wanted to do."

There was another reason, too, that the family moved from Minneapolis to Dayton. "The reason we moved was my parents wanted me to get a better education," Scurry once said. "In actuality, I don't think I would have had nearly the opportunities to play multiple sports in high school if we hadn't moved. It opened up more opportunities, and it molded me." In fact, it's unlikely that Scurry would have become a soccer player if her family had stayed in inner-city Minneapolis. In the U.S. today, soccer is predominantly a suburban and white sport. There are very few soccer fields in urban environments, where the majority of African-Americans and Hispanics live. In fact, Scurry has said that there was only one soccer field in inner-city Minneapolis when she was growing up. "Soccer is similar to hockey in that it's not a sport played in the inner cities or places where a lot of African-Americans live," she says. "It's a matter of geography. If you brought soccer into the inner cities, it would be as popular as the other sports. In other countries, they have soccer, and that's it. In this country, there are so many different choices."

> "Whatever sport I played, I was pretty much the only black kid on the team, so I'm used to it. It never bothered me because I was well-received by my teammates coming up through the ranks. I also thank my parents because they taught me to be well-adjusted, view the situation around me, and be friends with everyone regardless of color. But I am proud of my heritage, and I take very seriously my role of showing African-American youth and people in general that we can excel in any sport or anything."

Becoming Involved in Sports

Sports have been a big part of Scurry's life since she was a young child. "I was hooked on sports pretty early," she says. She brought home fliers from the Dayton-Champlin Youth Association offering a wide range of choices, and she would pick just about every sport they offered. "I think I took home every flyer they put out," she said. "Football, floor hockey, soccer, basketball, track. You get a flyer, you take it home, and for 15 bucks, you can play the sport. I think I've played everything, except tennis." Her first love, though, was football. She played cornerback and wide receiver on an all-boys team in fourth and fifth grades. But when it was time to move up to a heavier weight class, her mother wouldn't let her continue to play.

So Scurry switched to soccer when she was about 11 or 12. Again she played on an all-boys team, because there weren't any local girls' teams at that time. At first, the coach put her in the goal because he was afraid she would get hurt out on the field. "They threw me in there because I was the only girl on the team. They loved me because nobody else wanted to play in goal. . . . I liked it because I liked flopping around on the ground." After about a year, she switched to a girls' travel team. She also decided that she didn't like being in the goal—she wanted to score. So she switched to forward for several seasons. Later, she switched back to the goal.

At age 14, Scurry was selected for the Olympic Development Program's state team. The Olympic Development Program (ODP) identifies and trains top players to create a pool of potential talent for the Olympic team. For the next two years she was invited to the ODP's regional camps, but she was never selected for their regional team. These experiences later had a profound effect on her self-confidence, Scurry has said. Because she was never selected for the team, "ODP left me believing I didn't compare with elite players."

Still, Scurry would dream about being in the Olympics, imagining herself making a dramatic save in an Olympic shootout and then winning the gold medal. People around her in Minnesota were skeptical. But her mother never doubted her. "When Briana sets her mind on something, she becomes very determined," Robbie Scurry said. "When someone says she can't do something, she will work extra hard to prove that she can. I didn't doubt it for a minute when she talked of being in the Olympics someday."

EDUCATION

Scurry attended the local public schools. A good student, she continued to excel in sports also. At Anoka High School, she was a varsity athlete in five sports: soccer, basketball, softball, track, and floor hockey. Her top sports, though, were basketball, where she was named All-State, and soccer, where she was named All-American. In her senior season with the Anoka Tornadoes, she recorded 12 shutouts, meaning that in 12 games she prevented the other team from scoring—the crowning achievement for a goalie. She also led her team, the Anoka Tornadoes, to their only state soccer title. As a senior, Scurry was named the top goalkeeper in her state.

When she finished high school in 1989, Scurry turned down several basketball and track scholarship offers to NCAA Division I schools. Instead, she took a scholarship offer to play goalie for the University of Massachusetts Minutemaids. She decided on U-Mass, in part, because its coach, Jim Rudy, was considered one of the best goalkeeping coaches in the country.

College Years

At U-Mass Scurry studied political science and played goalkeeper for the Minutemaids. Rudy, her coach, was impressed with her speed and athleticism. But he saw more than that. "Composure," he said. "I watched her

*Scurry, right, with Carla Overbeck after winning their
Olympic Gold Medals in 1996*

and, even if she was rattled, you didn't see it. That's a great place to start
with a goalkeeper. Most goalkeepers, if there's a mistake, they show it to
their teammates, which is bad. But even worse, they show it to the other
team. It shows you're reachable. She played here four years and opponents couldn't ever touch her, even under pressure."

Scurry attended college during a period of transition in women's sports.
Before the 1970s, most schools offered few athletic programs for their female students. In 1972, a federal law was passed, called Title IX, that required schools to provide equal funding to athletic programs for men and
women. Then, only one per cent of high school women considered themselves athletes; now, that number is more like 43 percent. Since Title IX,
things have changed slowly. More athletic programs have been added at
high schools and colleges, which have created a pool of talented female
adult athletes. But there haven't been a lot of opportunities for these athletes after they finished school — no teams to play on, no league to play
in, and no one to pay them. So even the top female athletes who played
sports in college couldn't continue after they graduated. In many sports,
that's still true today.

In soccer, there was one national women's team. But Scurry still didn't believe that she was good enough for it. In fact, she studied political science because she planned to go to law school and become a lawyer. "I really never had any aspirations to play on the national team. When my coach at U-Mass informed me that I had the potential, I didn't believe him," she once said. An incident in 1992 reinforced her self-doubts. She played in an exhibition game against the U.S. national team at the 1992 Olympic Festival. Before the game she was approached by Pete DiCicco, who was then the goalkeepers' coach for the national team and is now the team's head coach. DiCicco patted her on the shoulder and said, "I'm going to be watching you today." That made Scurry so nervous that she gave up three goals in the first 15 minutes. Pulled out of the game before halftime, she was sure that she had blown her chances for ever making it to the national team.

During her four years with the U-Mass Minutemaids Scurry became an All-American, posting a record of 48-12-4. In 1993, in her final season, she gave up less than half a goal per game and was named National College Goalkeeper of the Year. That year, she also led her team to the NCAA Division I Soccer Final Four against the University of North Carolina Tar Heels. The UNC team included Mia Hamm and Kristine Lilly, two players from the women's national team; it was coached by Anson Dorrance, who at that time was also the head coach of the women's national team. Although Scurry's Minutemaids lost to the Tar Heels 4-1, Scurry played an excellent game, making 25 saves. After the game, she was walking through the UNC stadium when she saw Hamm and Dorrance walking toward her. According to Scurry, "Mia passes me and says, 'Hey Keeper, great game.' So I walked over, shook her hand, and whispered in her ear, 'Thanks, but tell him that, would ya?' Mia whispered back, 'He already knows'." (For more information on Hamm, see the entry in *Biography Today Sports*, Vol. 2.)

> "When Briana sets her mind on something, she becomes very determined. When someone says she can't do something, she will work extra hard to prove that she can. I didn't doubt it for a minute when she talked of being in the Olympics someday."
> — Robbie Scurry

The following Monday, Scurry was back at school contemplating her future when her coach called her into his office and told her that she'd been asked to try out for the U.S. national soccer team. "I was ecstatic," Scurry says. "Here I was, an unknown, not in the ODP loop. My family had no clout. But I was going to the national team's training camp anyway." By that point, she had used up her four years of college athletic eligibility. But she hadn't completed the coursework for her degree. Over the next two years, she finished up her classes while also playing soccer with the national team. She graduated from the University of Massachusetts in the spring of 1995 with a bachelor's degree in political science.

CAREER HIGHLIGHTS

Scurry became a starter on the U.S. women's national soccer team in 1994. Since then, she has played in the Olympics and in two World Cup competitions, as well as many other international matches. She's been an integral part of the U.S. team during an exciting time in its history.

———— " ————

"I really never had any aspirations to play on the national team. When my coach at U-Mass informed me that I had the potential, I didn't believe him."

———— " ————

Since early in this century, men's soccer has featured two different international competitions: the Olympics and the World Cup. For the World Cup, countries from around the world form national teams composed of their best players. These teams compete in qualifying matches, and the top 24 teams advance to the World Cup competition, which takes place over a month every four years. The World Cup is the most popular sporting event in the world. But women's soccer is a fairly recent addition to these international competitions. The U.S. women's national team was just formed in 1985. The first Women's World Cup was held in China in 1991, and the U.S. team won that competition. The Olympics added women's soccer in 1996. So Scurry joined the U.S. team at a particularly exhilarating time—shortly before the second Women's World Cup and the first women's Olympic soccer competition.

Joining the Women's National Soccer Team

The U.S. women's coach Anson Dorrance had been watching Scurry's progress for several years. After her outstanding college season in 1993, he invited her to attend a training camp run by the U.S. team. She quickly impressed the coaches with her speed, agility, and intelligence. She was asked to join the team as the number four goalkeeper, but she didn't stay in that spot for long. She was so eager to learn and improve that by 1994 she had moved up to the number one goalkeeper's spot. According to Tony DiCicco, who moved up from assistant to head coach when Dorrance stepped down in 1994, "Training a goalkeeper is an evolutionary process. . . . I look for two things in a goalkeeper: athleticism and mental skills, and [Scurry] epitomizes both. I can teach techniques and tactics, but the other two are the most difficult to affect."

Scurry soon proved that she had earned her spot as the starting keeper on the U.S. national team. She started playing in exhibition tournaments against other top international teams and quickly became known for her spectacular diving saves. She earned a shutout in her first start, playing against Portugal at the 1994 Algarve Cup. That same year, she posted a record of 11-1-0 with 7 shutouts in 12 starts and was named Most Valuable Player at the 1994 Chiquita Cup. In 1995, she started 15 games and posted a record of 11-2-2, including 9 shutouts. At the time, Scurry still seemed to worry about her lack of experience in international play. "My biggest need is reading the game," she said. "I haven't had a lot of opportunity to do that. . . . I want to bring my goalkeeping up a level so I have to make fewer diving saves." But DiCicco was confident in her skills. "Briana is just a great all around athlete, and I really enjoy her competitive nature," DiCicco said at the time. "Although she is one of the younger and least-experienced players on the team, she is supremely confident in goal and has earned the respect of her older teammates. Sure, there are some things we can work on, but over the long haul, she can become the best woman goalkeeper in the world." Soon, Scurry would be well on her way to earning that title.

Women's World Cup 1995

In 1995, the U.S. team flew to Sweden for the second Women's World Cup. It proved to be a disappointment for the team. As the winners of the first Women's World Cup in 1991, they were the defending champions, and they were optimistic about their chances. For their first four games they tied China 3-3 and then won their next three, beating Denmark 2-1, Australia 4-1, and Japan 4-1. For their fifth game, though, they ran into trouble against Norway in the semifinals. The U.S. lost 1-0 when Norway scored on a corner kick that was headed into the goal. The U.S. went on to win its final game, beating China 2-0 and taking third place and the bronze medal.

For Scurry, the 1995 World Cup left her with two important lessons. The first was an issue of strength. When Norway scored on that corner kick, Scurry had been blocked from reaching the ball by the Norwegians. She

just wasn't strong enough to muscle through their line of opposing players. "They were pushing me around," she later said. "I just wasn't big
enough. So I hit the weight room and gained 15 pounds going into the
Olympics. It helped me immensely." At 5'8", she increased her weight
from 135 to 150 pounds and worked out in the weight room to turn that
added weight into powerful muscles. The second was an issue of emotional response. At the end of the game, the Norwegian players fell to the
ground and started crawling around the field in a routine they called the
Train. "It was harmless but humiliating," Scurry later said. "I burned it
into my head so I wouldn't forget it later."

Olympics 1996

Scurry was part of the U.S. national team that played in the 1996 Summer
Olympics in Atlanta, Georgia, for the first Olympic games that included
women's soccer. It was a great series for the U.S. team and particularly for
Scurry. She started and played every minute of her team's five games and
only allowed three goals in all that time. For the first three games, the
U.S. beat Denmark 3-0 and Sweden 2-1, and tied China 0-0. The fourth
game, the semifinals match, was particularly satisfying for Scurry, when
they beat Norway 2-1 in overtime. With that game, Scurry finally felt vin-
dicated for her team's loss the previous year in the World Cup. Although
she had kept her composure in 1995 when her team lost, Scurry burst
into tears after the U.S. beat Norway in 1996. The U.S. team went on to
beat China 2-1 in the championship game, winning the gold.

After that game, many people expressed frustration because NBC, the TV
network broadcasting the Olympics, had shown only a few minutes of
the championship game. The network obviously didn't think many viewers cared about women's soccer. Yet 76,481 fans turned out to watch the
U.S. victory over China, the first women's soccer medal in Olympic history. It was a milestone for women's sports, the largest crowd ever—anywhere in the world—to see a women's soccer event, and the largest
crowd in the U.S. to see any women's sporting event.

The 1996 Olympics included one silly note for Scurry. Shortly before the
beginning of the games, Scurry received a call from a reporter at *Sports
Illustrated* magazine. The reporter asked what she would do if her team
won the gold medal. Well, it was early in the morning, and she was sleepy,
so she said the first thing that popped into her head—that she would run
naked through the streets. Then she forgot all about it, until the magazine
printed her comment just before the beginning of the Olympic games. Of
course, then all the other reporters started asking her about it, especially

*Scurry blocking a shot as teammate Joy Fawcett (14) helps defend Brazil's
Prentinha during the first half of the Women's World Cup
soccer semifinal game, July 4, 1999*

when the U.S. won the gold. Scurry was determined to keep her word—
and equally determined that no one would watch. So she grabbed a friend
late one night, brought a video camera, and drove to a deserted street. She
whipped off her clothes in the car and then ran down the block and back.
Her friend taped it, to be able to prove that she really did it. Now that she
has the proof, Scurry keeps the tape locked up at home.

Style of Play

Scurry's style of play has evolved a lot over the years as she has matured as
a keeper. When she was younger, in her college days, she used to stay close
to the goal line. She would rely on her ability as a shot blocker, using reflex-
es to make spectacular saves to stop the ball. Now she has the confidence
to roam more freely around the box, to stop offensive plays before they turn
into shots on goal, to anticipate her opponents' moves, and to organize her
team's defense. "The modern game requires more from the goalkeeper, and
she has increased her range because she has the athleticism to do it," says
DiCicco. Team co-captain and defensive player Carla Overbeck would
agree. "She's the best goalkeeper in the world," Overbeck once said.
"Having her back there has a calming effect on all of us."

Scurry's composed and reserved demeanor is somewhat unusual in a sport where many male keepers clearly show their anger and disgust with their own defensive teammates. But for Scurry, her low-key behavior is intentional. "I don't want the other team to see me upset, because I like to win the psychological battle in a game. Being ice cold is the way I do it." That approach gets results, according to Jim Rudy, her coach from U-Mass: "Playing against Briana is like rock climbing a slab of marble. There are no weaknesses in her game."

Training for the World Cup

Scurry and the other players on the women's national soccer team became such awesome athletes through hard work and training. Between big events like the World Cup or the Olympics, they play together as a team in competitions against the top international teams in stadiums around the world. But they also have a training camp in Orlando, Florida, where the team spends five or six months working together to get ready for the big events. It's tough for the players to be away from their homes and families for extended periods like that. Many are married, and two—Carla Overbeck and Joy Fawcett—are mothers of young children. Their kids spend a lot of time at the training camp with them, with a nanny on duty to help out.

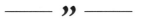

"She's the best goalkeeper in the world. Having her back there has a calming effect on all of us."—Carla Overbeck, team co-captain and defensive player

In Florida, their training complex has four soccer fields, offices, and apartments and houses nearby. The team members live together in small groups, sharing companionship and fun. They start their workouts early in the morning, to avoid some of the intense midday Florida heat and humidity. Their workouts include drills in speed, endurance, strength, conditioning, and specific soccer skills. In addition to practice, they have team meetings and do a lot of weight lifting. Still, there's a lot of down time, for hanging out with roommates and analyzing what worked and what didn't in practice. Equally important, they're building team cohesiveness, taking individual players and forming them into one tight team. They have a sports psychologist who helps them work on team-building exercises— things like forming two teams, holding hands, and then trying to get the whole team through a hula hoop without letting go of each other. These

WORLD CUP TRAINING

This series of killer sprints is just one part of the team's regular training routine, as reported by Scurry's teammate, Julie Foudy, and her co-writer, David Hirshey, in *Women's Sports and Fitness*:

For Speed

20 x 20s	Sprint 20 yards and jog back. Rest 15 seconds. Repeat 20 times.
15 x 40s	Sprint 40 yards. Rest 20 seconds. Repeat 15 times.
10 x 60s	Sprint 60 yards. Rest 20 seconds. Repeat 10 times.
10 x 120s	Sprint 120 yards (the length of a soccer field) in 17 seconds and run back in less than 30 seconds. Rest 30 seconds. Repeat 10 times.

For Endurance

Stinkers	Sprint 50 yards out and back 3 times in a row in under one minute. Rest one and a half minutes. Repeat 3 times.
Stinkettes	Sprint 25 yards out and back 6 times in a row in under one minute and five seconds. Rest one and a half minutes. Repeat 3 times.
Suicides	Run 5 yards out and back, then increase to running 10, 15, 20, and 25 yards out and back. Rest 25 seconds. Repeat it all 10 times.

team-building exercises seem goofy, but they offer lessons in communication, leadership, unity, and trust. "We come down here for five months, and there are not going to be any surprises for us when the Cup comes," Scurry says. "A lot of teams just start playing together the last few weeks, and that's way too little. No time to do the million and one things you have to do to get ready."

Women's World Cup 1999

All that hard work and training paid off when the U.S. team arrived at the 1999 Women's World Cup. Hosted by the United States, the World Cup featured 16 teams playing 32 matches over the course of three weeks in

Scurry blocking the penalty kick by China that led to the
U.S. Women's World Cup victory, 1999

eight major stadiums around the country, in Illinois, Massachusetts, New Jersey, Maryland, Oregon, and California. Each team would play an opening round of three games, and then the top teams would go on to the quarterfinals, semifinals, and finals. From the beginning, the U.S. was favored to win the Cup.

The United States women's national soccer team played its first game of the 1999 World Cup against Denmark in Giants Stadium in New Jersey. There were 78,972 fans in attendance, which set a new record for the most fans ever to attend a women's sporting event. Both teams were unnerved, at first, by the noisy, supportive crowd. But at the 17-minute mark, forward and superstar Mia Hamm showed a little of her trademark fancy footwork, using her right foot to push the ball past a defender and then switching to her left foot to rocket the ball into the roof of the net. It was a great start to a fast-moving offensive game that showcased the team's relentless attacking style. The U.S. won their first match 3-0, with a shutout for Scurry. The team went on to win their next four games, beating Nigeria 7-1, Korea 3-0, Germany 3-2, and Brazil 2-0. Scurry's play was particularly key in the semifinal match against Brazil. While the team had relied primarily on offense in the previous games, Scurry was pushed to her limit by the unswerving pressure of the Brazilian team. Still, she posted another shutout and was named the Most Spectacular Player of the game. "I definitely think today was my best effort in my five years playing on the team," she said. "Any game where I can do my part and get my team in the final of the Women's World Cup is my best game."

The U.S. team went on to the finals, playing China for the World Cup championship at the Rose Bowl stadium in Pasadena, California, in front of 90,185 fans, another new record for women's sports. The two teams were evenly matched, and they both played an aggressive but controlled game. Both defensive lines were so strong that despite numerous opportunities, neither team was able to score during regulation play (90 minutes). The game went into two 15-minute overtime periods, and play was intense as both teams tried for the winning goal. Still, neither team was able to score during either the first or the second overtime, and the game went into a penalty kick shoot-out. For each team, five players would come up one at a time to the line, 12 feet out, and have a chance to shoot on goal. For the U.S., the shooters would be Carla Overbeck, Joy Fawcett, Kristine Lilly, Mia Hamm, and Brandi Chastain. The pressure was enormous, both on the shooters and on Scurry and the Chinese goalkeeper, Gao

"I don't want the other team to see me upset, because I like to win the psychological battle in a game. Being ice cold is the way I do it."

Hong. And the odds favor the shooters. Scurry had confidence in her teammates' abilities to make their shots, so winning the game would mean that she would have to outsmart the Chinese kickers. "I knew I just had to make one save, because my teammates would make their shots."

The two teams alternated shots, with China going first. The first four kickers—two for each team—all found the goal. But then China's third shooter, midfielder Liu Ying, came up to the line. "I saw her body language when she was walking up to the penalty spot," Scurry said. "She didn't look like she really wanted to be there. Her shoulders were slumped, and she looked tired. I thought, 'This is the one.'" She was sure that this was the one goal she would be able to block. As Liu approached the ball, Scurry sprang forward and to her left, blocking the shot. So when the U.S. made their third goal, they were now up one. Both China and the U.S. made their fourth shots, and then China made a goal on its fifth shot. Now it was up to the final U.S. shooter, Brandi Chastain. If she made the shot, the U.S. would win the game. Chastain walked up to the line and barely hesitated before drilling it into the goal. "I didn't hear any noise. I didn't look at the [Chinese goalkeeper]," she later said. "As soon as the whistle blew, I just stepped up and hit it. I just kind of lost my mind." In a moment of delirious happiness, she fell to her knees and pulled off her shirt, stripping down to her sports bra. The crowd roared, and her teammates piled on top of her in celebration. The U.S. beat China 5-4 in overtime.

Afterward, there was a minor controversy about the game. When Scurry blocked Liu Ying's kick, she moved forward just before the kick. In soccer, that's an illegal move—until the ball is kicked, the keeper can't move forward. But the referee hadn't called Scurry on the play, so the results stood.

Response from the Fans

The response from fans was just overwhelming, as they erupted in celebration. The fun continued afterward, too, at a victory bash that night, at a parade at Disney World, and at appearances on TV and around the country. In fact, the fans' response during and after the Cup was so intense that many journalists tried to explain the team's appeal. Fans had jammed into the stadiums throughout the tournament. Attendance in 1999 marked a phenomenal change over previous years. For the 1995 World Cup there were 112,000 tickets, in total, sold to all the matches, whereas over 658,000 people attended the 1999 events. In fact, they had as many fans in 1999 at their practices as they did at their games at the 1995 World Cup. The team members were mobbed everywhere they went—they even needed police escorts to get on and off the field. The fans were also different than those at most sporting events. Instead of being primarily male, there were many adult women and young girls, including a lot of young soccer players and their parents—a reflection of the over 100,000 girls who began playing soccer between 1990 and 1997.

One reason for the team's great success with the fans is certainly the quality of the play. Analysts agreed that their professional style of play proved beyond a shadow of a doubt that they deserved all the respect, admiration, and financial support earned by male athletes. Many commentators wondered if this would be the beginning of true equality in men's and women's sports, if this would signal the era when women athletes would be taken as seriously as men. But another reason for the team's success with fans is the athletes themselves. Many observers have noted how different these athletes are from some of their male counterparts. While many male professional athletes are considered arrogant, egotistical, and ungrateful, the women's soccer players are considered friendly, gracious, and grateful for their fans. Brandi Chastain explained their attitude by saying, "When we were kids, we didn't have women soccer players to look up to. That's why everyone on this team is so accessible." In many ways, this team was a celebration of all female athletes. As Mia Hamm said, "We came to understand that this World Cup wasn't just about us making it to Pasadena and winning. This is an historic event far beyond any single result. If we lose sight of that, everything we did would be for nothing."

Future Plans

For the time being, Scurry will continue with the U.S. national soccer team, at least through the 2000 Olympics in Australia. But she has also said that she would like to return to her earlier love of basketball and try out for the Women's National Basketball Association. "I could probably do this until I'm 40, but I don't want to," she said. "I'm going to train hard and see if [the WNBA is] in the cards for me."

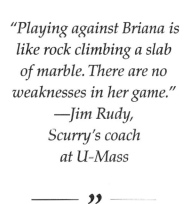

"Playing against Briana is like rock climbing a slab of marble. There are no weaknesses in her game."
—Jim Rudy,
Scurry's coach
at U-Mass

ON BEING A ROLE MODEL

Being an inspiration to young kids is important to Scurry. "I am proud of my heritage, and I take very seriously my role of showing African-American youth and people in general that we can excel in any sport or anything." As the only African-American starter on her team (the only other black player is Saskia Webber, also a goalkeeper), Scurry hopes to inspire young black athletes to try the game—especially since so few have traditionally played the sport. "We need more African-Americans in this game. Besides me, there are very few, so it's important for me to help get the word out. Soccer's a great sport that offers great opportunities. Our kids need to know that."

HOME AND FAMILY

Scurry recently moved to a home in the suburbs outside Detroit. "I could have moved anywhere I wanted to, but I chose Detroit because I like it here. I like the winter and snow, and after living in Minnesota and Massachusetts, I know what's coming." Scurry is single, and she has talked about how hard it is to start a relationship, since her schedule takes her out of town so much.

HOBBIES AND OTHER INTERESTS

In 1995, Scurry learned that there is more to life than soccer. While she was playing soccer in Sweden in the World Cup, her sister Robbie's son became seriously ill. Her then 10-year-old nephew Jerome, who suffers from leukemia, developed an infection of the pancreas and nearly died. Her sister didn't tell Briana the bad news until after the last game. Briana quickly flew home and gave her bronze medal from the World Cup to Jerome, who was still in the hospital at that point. Fortunately, Jerome is now in remission. But Scurry learned what it's like to love and cherish a seriously ill child. Now she works for the Make-a-Wish Foundation, which grants wishes for sick kids. She has also been a contributor to AIDS causes in honor of a friend with HIV.

HONORS AND AWARDS

National College Goalkeeper of the Year: 1993
World Cup Soccer: 1995, Bronze Medal; 1999, Gold Medal
Olympic Soccer: 1996, Gold Medal

FURTHER READING

Books

Miller, Marla. *All-American Girls: The U.S. Women's National Soccer Team,* 1999

Periodicals

Chicago Tribune, June 21, 1999, Sports section, p.12
Emerge, Oct. 1999, p.62
Los Angeles Times, June 15, 1999, Sports section, p.1; July 5, 1999, p.D1
Miami Herald, July 9, 1999, p.D7
Minneapolis Star Tribune, May 2, 1995, p.C1
New York Times, May 20, 1999, p.C25; June 18, 1999, p.D6; June 19, 1999, p.B15; June 26, 1999, p.B17; June 27, 1999, p.21; July 5, 1999, p.D1; July 11, 1999, p.1
Newsweek, July 19, 1999, p.46

People, July 26, 1999, p.52

Seattle Times, July 10, 1999, p.B1

Soccer America, July 19, 1999

Sports Illustrated, July 5, 1999, p.100; July 12, 1999, p.36; July 19, 1999, p.38

Sports Illustrated for Kids, Nov. 1996, p.36

St. Paul Pioneer Press, July 14, 1996, p.N9

Time, June 28, 1999, p.62; July 19, 1999, pp.58 and 64

USA Today, June 4, 1999, p.C22

Women's Sports and Fitness, July 1999, p.75

ADDRESS

U.S. Soccer
1801 South Prairie
Chicago, IL 60615

WORLD WIDE WEB SITES

http://www.womensoccer.com/biogs/scurry.html
http://www.soccer.com
http://wwc99.fifa.com/english/competition/usastars1.html

George Thampy 1987-

American Student and Winner of the 2000 National Spelling Bee

EARLY YEARS

George Abraham Thampy was born on August 16, 1987, in Houston, Texas. His parents, Bina and K. George Thampy, had emigrated to the United States from southern India before he was born. His mother, who works full time home schooling her children, holds graduate degrees in urban planning and social science. His father is a biochemist and a physician who is currently a fellow in endocrinology at the School of Medicine at Washington University in St. Louis. The family first moved to the St. Louis area when George was five; they now live in Maryland Heights, a St. Louis suburb. The second of seven children, George has three brothers and three sisters: Eapen, Laila, Mallika, Matthew, Lukose, and Nina.

Even as a very young child, according to his mother, George had "a way with words." He learned to read at the age of three, and one day he was reading the newspaper when he came across an article about the National Spelling Bee. He pointed to the picture of the trophy and said he wanted to win it, so his parents bought him a copy of a study booklet containing 3,500 words commonly used in the first rounds of spelling bees. George immediately began memorizing it.

As a recent immigrant from India's Kerala state, Bina Thampy couldn't pronounce many of the words, much less coach her son. She was also very busy home schooling her other children. So George learned the words on his own. Soon he was ready to tackle Webster's Third New International Dictionary, which had more than 460,000 words.

> *"Home schooling is good for me," George says. "I don't think it's for everybody. It will only work if your parents love you like they love me, and they are committed to you and committed to providing you with the best education for so many years."*

EDUCATION

Thampy's parents made the decision to home school their children when they lived in Houston. They were worried about the safety of the local public schools, which had installed metal detectors to prevent students from bringing in weapons. This was not the kind of learning environment the Thampys wanted for their children, so Bina Thampy decided to make a full-time commitment to educating them at home. She teaches them languages, economics, and social science, while her husband works with them on math and science in the evenings. The Thampy children have taken field trips with other home-schooled students to museums, farms, and even their father's endocrinology lab.

"Home schooling is good for me," George says. "I don't think it's for everybody. It will only work if your parents love you like they love me, and they are committed to you and committed to providing you with the best education for so many years."What he likes best about home schooling is the fact that it gives him more flexibility in terms of what he wants to learn. "I can do something else — like Latin," he says. Sometimes he is taught in a group with his other siblings, but often he is taught individually. He also does in-depth research via the Internet on subjects that interest him.

MAJOR ACCOMPLISHMENTS

Geography Whiz

In addition to his fascination with words, George showed an early aptitude for geography, which he learned by reading *National Geographic* magazine and studying his mother's huge collection of maps. He shared this interest with his older brother Eapen and his younger sister Mallika, both of whom won their home state's geography bee and competed for the national championship. In 1997 it was George's turn to win the Missouri Geography Bee, giving him his first taste of competition at the national level.

In May 2000, Thampy came in second at the National Geography Bee, sponsored by the National Geographic Society. He won a $15,000 college scholarship. He took second place because he was able to name only one of the three largest sections of Denmark (Jutland, Sjaelland, and Fyn). Considering the fact that he started preparing for the geography bee only four months before the finals, his second-place finish was a triumph.

The National Spelling Bee

Thampy entered his first spelling bee at the age of six. Just a few years later, in 1998, he won the St. Louis Post-Dispatch Spelling Bee, his home state's highest competition. He advanced to the National Spelling Bee, sponsored by the Scripps Howard media organization, and came in fourth. The next year, 1999, he again won his state's spelling championship and went on to the national competition in Washington, where he came in third. Still hoping to win the top prize, he continued to study spelling guides and word lists from previous competitions for three or four hours a night.

In 2000 he qualified for the National Spelling Bee a third time, and this time he won, taking home the $10,000 first prize while his parents and five of his siblings cheered him on. But it wasn't the money that motivated him. "It was really the words," George says, "and there were 400,000 of them" — referring to the number of entries in the official dictionary used

Thampy with his parents after winning the Scripps Howard Spelling Bee.

at the spelling bee. In fact, he once told a reporter that he would be just as happy to learn a new word during a competition as he would be to win it.

Thampy had to out-spell 248 other students from kindergarten to eighth grade to win the top prize. He had to spell "fondu," "waiver," "serendipity," "ersatz," "surfactant," "vesicant," "annelid," "trophobiosis," "psilosis," "quodlibet," "eudaemonic," "ditokous," and "propaedeutic." The word that made him a champ, however, was "demarche," which means "a step or a maneuver," but it wasn't the most difficult he encountered during the competition. During an earlier round he had been asked to spell "emmetropia," the condition of refraction of light in the eye. George didn't know what it meant or whether it had one "m" or two. How did he come up with the correct spelling? "God put it in my head," he says.

A Victory for Home Schoolers

According to his parents, the key to George's victory wasn't the time he spent preparing but the hours he spent as a home-schooled student. "We teach these children the art of studying," his father says. "If I give him a new thing today, I'm confident he'll become a master of it in a very short period of time with very little help." His father would come home from work every day with new words for George to spell, and both his parents practiced with him on a regular basis.

———— " ————

According to his parents, the key to George's victory was the time he spent as a home-schooled student. "We teach these children the art of studying," his father says. "If I give him a new thing today, I'm confident he'll become a master of it in a very short period of time with very little help."

———— " ————

Although Thampy was only the second home schooler to win the National Spelling Bee, his two closest rivals in the 2000 contest had also been home schooled. George's success, along with that of other home-schooled students in similar high-pressure national competitions, has been a real boost for the home-schooling movement. About one-and-a-half million children are currently being home schooled in the U. S., a number that is increasing by at least seven percent a year.

For Thampy, the best part of winning was being invited to throw out the opening pitch at a St. Louis Cardinals' game at Busch Stadium. He also got to sit in the dugout with the players and to meet Mark McGwire, who autographed one of his bats for George to take home. In addition, he appeared on the "Today" show and on "Good Morning America," as well as on news shows on ABC, MSNBC, CNN, and the Fox News Channel.

HOBBIES AND OTHER INTERESTS

Aside from spelling and geography, Thampy's interests include stamp and coin collecting, baseball, playing the flute, and flying kites. He is a member of his church youth group and the Boy Scouts, and he spends much of his time reading and playing with his laptop computer, on which he has created a 20,000-word database he uses to prepare for spelling competitions. He likes to challenge his father in chess and, not surprisingly, he is a whiz at crossword puzzles and other word games. He particularly enjoys coming up with palindromes—words or phrases that are spelled the same backward and forward.

HONORS AND AWARDS

Scripps Howard National Spelling Bee Winner: 2000

FURTHER READING

Periodicals

New York Times, June 2, 2000, p.A15
St. Louis Post-Dispatch, June 2, 2000, p.A1; June 11, 2000, p. C1; July 31, 2000, West Post section, p.7

ADDRESS

Scripps Howard National Spelling Bee
P. O. Box 5380
Cincinnati, OH 45201

WORLD WIDE WEB SITE

http://www.spellingbee.com

CeCe Winans 1964 -

American Gospel Singer
Winner of Eight Grammy Awards as Half of the
Duo "BeBe and CeCe"and as a Solo Artist

BIRTH

Priscilla (CeCe) Winans was born on October 8, 1964, in Detroit, Michigan. She was the eighth child and long-awaited first daughter in a family of ten children. Her father, David Winans, was a barber and gospel singer who often took extra jobs to make ends meet. Her mother, Delores Winans, was a medical transcriptionist and gospel singer. Her seven older brothers are David II, Ronald, Carvin, Marvin, Michael, Daniel, and Benjamin (BeBe). She also has two younger sisters, Angelique and Debbie. The entire family, alone or in various groups, are professional musicians. They are known as "The First Family of Gospel Music."

YOUTH

Faith, family, and music were the foundation of CeCe Winans's childhood and of her future success as a singer. From babyhood, Priscilla was called CeCe. Though no one remembers why, CeCe guesses that it's short for "Sister," the name her paternal grandmother gave her as the first girl in the family. Her parents, both devout Christians, met as singers in a Detroit gospel chorale in 1950. With ten children and a modest income, the family had little material comfort. But, as Winans recalled: "My parents worked hard to create a home environment in which love took priority over things. Discipline was second to love. Laughter ran a close third. We didn't have a lot of the things we wanted, but there was always more than enough of the things we needed."

> "My parents worked hard to create a home environment in which love took priority over things. Discipline was second to love. Laughter ran a close third. We didn't have a lot of the things we wanted, but there was always more than enough of the things we needed."

The family flooded their small, three-bedroom home with activity, music, and friends. What's more, they enjoyed a second home at the Mack Avenue Church of God in Christ, which had been founded by David Winans's grandfather. "When we weren't at church service on Tuesday, Friday, and Sunday, we were attending summer church camps, going to revivals, or off somewhere either singing or rehearsing in the young people's choir," Winans remembered. For young CeCe, church was a comfortable place where she could hang out with friends from similar backgrounds. Above all, she could share her Christian faith through song.

Non-religious music was forbidden in the Winans's household—along with parties, dancing, make-up, and movie-going. But passionate gospel music flowed through their lives. Winans remembered constant music: "Mom humming a tune from church, Dad praying in song, or one of my seven brothers banging out a tune of his own creation on the piano. . . . There was singing throughout the day and into the night. After teasing one another back and forth about whose head was shaped the funniest, who was the clumsiest, whose feet stank the most from their gym shoes, and who had holes in their underwear, we'd sing ourselves to sleep." Each Christmas, the family rented an auditorium to treat their friends and relatives to their rousing, spiritual music. These concerts ultimately helped to launch the Winans's musical careers.

—————— " ——————

Winans remembers constant music from her childhood: "Mom humming a tune from church, Dad praying in song, or one of my seven brothers banging out a tune of his own creation on the piano. . . . There was singing throughout the day and into the night. After teasing one another back and forth about whose head was shaped the funniest, who was the clumsiest, whose feet stank the most from their gym shoes, and who had holes in their underwear, we'd sing ourselves to sleep."

—————— " ——————

Winans made her solo debut in her great-grandfather's church at age seven singing the gospel song "Fill My Cup, Lord." Young CeCe wept as she sang, not out of religious feeling, but from shyness and fear. "I was just happy that it was over when it was over," she remembered. "But the strange warmth that came over me when I finished wasn't just relief. It was like a presence that came over me, a warm embrace from something outside of me." The song became her signature solo at the annual church convocation.

But Winans was extremely shy, terrified of performing. "Growing up a girl in a house with seven brothers will make you become either aggressive and outspoken or quiet and retiring," she remarked. Her defense was to withdraw into a private world of play. There, she would spend hours dressing and undressing her dolls and styling their hair. The arrival of her younger sisters gave Winans playmates and soul mates, but did not lessen her reserve or seriousness. "With two sisters below me and seven brothers above me, I felt squeezed in the middle with the responsibility to be mature," she recalled. "Those two girls were looking to me as an example, and those seven brothers were . . . testing my strength and my resolve."

The Winans brothers' idea of fun was to be wild and physical, and they delighted in teasing their sisters, and each other, unmercifully. Constant razzing and raucous arguments rang through the Winans home. "Fights

Winans with producer Fred Hammond.

always broke out about who drank the last bit of Kool-Aid, who broke what, who ripped whose pair of pants, or whose turn it was to sleep on the floor," Winans said. Nevertheless, the children took to heart their parents' strong lesson "to love one another, to support one another and to remember God," Winans said. "To be real—that was the main thing—and to always put God first." Although she has said that she has not outgrown—merely overcome—her shyness, Winans's reliance on her family and faith in God became the bedrock of her success as a singer.

EDUCATION

Winans attended Detroit's Mumford High School, where she was a loner with few friends. "My conservative upbringing kept me from hanging out with a lot of people," she said. "It wasn't just my longer-than-usual skirts and dresses, I'm sure. I was a city girl who didn't wear make-up or nail polish, who never wore the flashy earrings that were the rage at the time, and who didn't wear revealing blouses. . . . Movies were out and parties were forbidden by my folks. I was different."

Singing in the Mumford choir, however, boosted Winans's confidence and gave her an important outlet for her time and energy. "Singing in the school choir was the only place where I was not just different. I was special," she remembered. "There, the special quality of my alto voice meant that I was frequently chosen to sing special parts. I came as close as I ever would to being popular, to being one of the gang, and to being accepted, because being able to sing gave me an edge in the competitive world of adolescents."

Church also continued to be an important home away from home during Winans's high-school years. By then, her family had joined a new congregation, the Shalom Temple, where she sang in the young people's choir and took on a new role, directing some songs. Her fellow-choir members — including her sisters and brother, BeBe — teased that she was too small to be seen over singers' heads. But she didn't mind their good-natured taunts. "We were family," she said. "They were all pariahs at school like me and needed a place to belong. When we were together at church, we reminded ourselves that no matter what students at school thought about us, we were normal teenagers."

In addition to singing, Winans stood out during these years for her excellent typing ability. With this skill, she planned for a career as a court stenographer (a highly skilled typist who records the proceedings in a court of law). "Aspiring to be a court stenographer may not sound particularly grand," she observed. "But for a little girl from Detroit who had never ventured too far from her Pentecostal, close-knit family, becoming a court stenographer was a stretch of the soul, a profession, a good, steady job, and a way out of poverty."

Winans graduated from Mumford High School in 1981, then studied cosmetology for a brief time. Her plan was to work as a hairstylist in order to earn money for her court-stenography courses. But, to her surprise, she was hired as a singer on the "PTL Show," a Christian TV program broadcast nationally from North Carolina. After she left the "PTL Show" in 1984, she continued studying cosmetology and earned her beautician's license at the Virginia Farrell Cosmetology School in Detroit.

FIRST JOBS

Winans was just 17 when she and her brother BeBe were invited to audition for the gospel chorus of the "PTL Show." She was excited. "I knew I was on the verge of becoming something, but I didn't have a clue as to what," she recalled. "All I knew was that I didn't want to be a court stenographer any longer." She and her brother spent three years singing on the show, where they gained invaluable experience singing before a live audience and in front of television cameras.

Their first big break came in 1984 when they were chosen to sing a cover of "Love Lifts Us Up," a pop song from the soundtrack of the movie *An Officer and a Gentleman*. Revised as "Lord, Lift Us Up," the song was wildly popular with the show's audience and was later included on a "PTL" album. It became BeBe and CeCe's first radio hit and attracted invitations to perform around the country.

Filled with newfound confidence, Winans discovered that singing professionally brought her joy and contentment. She also liked working with her brother. "Despite some awkwardness in the beginning, BeBe and I were beginning to enjoy singing together," she recalled. "We had been singing together long enough to know each other's style. . . . Best of all, we were family. As family, we trusted each other and were comfortable with each other. This was the important part."

"Singing in the school choir was the only place where I was not just different. I was special. There, the special quality of my alto voice meant that I was frequently chosen to sing special parts. I came as close as I ever would to being popular, to being one of the gang, and to being accepted, because being able to sing gave me an edge in the competitive world of adolescents."

MARRIAGE AND FAMILY

Winans met her future husband, Alvin Love II, at a family bowling outing while she was on a visit home to Detroit from North Carolina. "I thought he was cute, but . . . the last thing on my mind was a relationship," she recalled. "I certainly didn't have time to be in a relationship. I was too busy singing and traveling." But a few months later, Love joined Winans's brothers on a visit to North Carolina. Before leaving, he told her he wanted to marry her. They were married on June 23, 1984, when she was only 19 years old. "Now I get nervous when I think about [marrying at 19]," she admitted. "I really could have messed up. But certain people in my life [my parents and pastor] had to be at peace with the situation. Thank God I had the wisdom to know that." Her husband, a former sales executive with Xerox, eventually became her business manager, and then her personal manager. "He has proven to be a loving father and husband," she said. "We've grown together, and we've learned to do what we've needed to keep this marriage, family, and this music career going." Their son Alvin Lemar III was born

BeBe and CeCe Winans in 1991.

on June 20, 1985. Their daughter Ashley Rose was born on September 5, 1987. The Love family lives in Nashville, Tennessee. Winans is extremely proud of and focused on her husband and two children. Of all the awards she has received in her career, she has said, "none would compare with the reward of being a wife and mother."

During her first few years of marriage, before her singing career was firmly established, Winans was a businesswoman with her own hair-styling salon in Detroit. Eventually, 14 stylists rented space in her shop. "I had to toughen up and learn the hard lessons of being an entrepreneur," she recalled. "Learning the delicate art of hiring and firing people who worked for me would come in handy years later when as an artist I had to summon the courage to hire and fire managers, lawyers and band members."

CAREER HIGHLIGHTS

For the past 15 years, Winans has had a successful career in gospel music, both as a duo with BeBe and as a solo act. Critics have credited CeCe and BeBe for attracting new audiences to gospel music by infusing it with the sounds of contemporary popular music. Some traditionalists claim that the Winans sound is not religious enough. But listeners loved it. BeBe and CeCe Winans were among the first gospel artists to score high on the gospel music sales charts, as well as rhythm and blues (R&B) or pop-music ones.

In her solo career, CeCe has continued to expand the musical horizons of her work. She also has widened her own scope, branching out as a television host, actress, and author. Regardless of which musical style or medium she chooses, Winans remains faithful to her Christian messages of faith, joy, and love. She has described work as not a career, but a calling. "It's a mission that we're on," she said of herself and her family. "I believe we'll always glorify God and carry the message of God's love."

Beginnings

In spite of a lifetime spent singing in church and with her family, Winans never dared to believe she could support herself with singing. "But music started kicking off," she said. "And God made it real clear that this was where I was supposed to be."

Her four brothers Marvin, Carvin, Ronald and Michael were the first of her clan to win wide acclaim, first as the "Testimonial Singers," then as "The Winans." They were the main attraction for audiences at the family's annual Christmas concerts at Detroit's Mercy College. But soon "Winans Part II"—made up of CeCe and brothers BeBe, Daniel, and Michael—were also wowing the crowd. Andrae Crouch, a gospel star who helped "The Winans" to succeed, noticed the younger siblings and hired them as his back-up singers.

Success with Brother BeBe

In late 1985, BeBe and CeCe signed their first recording contract, with the Christian-music label, Sparrow Records. Their album, *Introducing BeBe and CeCe Winans*, released in 1987, featured two songs that scored high on both Inspirational and R&B charts: "For Always" and "I.O.U. Me." The latter, like many of the album's songs, was written and co-produced by BeBe. Winans credits him and co-producer Keith Thomas with creating a unique sound. "BeBe's lyrics and background-vocals arrangements combined with Keith's hit-making genius for pop music . . . [made] a sound that was contemporary, hip, smooth, and striking," she noted. That sound won the pair the award for Best New Artists at the 1987 Christian music Dove Awards. CeCe also earned her first Grammy for Best Soul Gospel Performance—Female for the song "For Always."

The duo's second album, *Heaven* (1988), soared to even greater heights of success. It became the first gospel album to reach Billboard magazine's R&B Top10 and only the second to go gold, following the distinguished lead of Aretha Franklin's *Amazing Grace* 16 years earlier. CeCe and BeBe were recognized with four Grammy awards as well as an Image Award from the National Association for the Advancement of Colored People (NAACP)—the first of several.

It was at a ceremony for the NAACP award that Winans met pop super-star Whitney Houston. Their meeting, Winans said, "was the start of a wonderful friendship marked by visits, phone calls, laughter, cheering for each other, and praying for each other." The two also went on to become collaborators, notably in their duet "Count on Me," from Houston's soundtrack for the 1996 film *Waiting to Exhale*. The single scored as number one on Billboard's R&B charts and in pop's Top Ten shortly after its release.

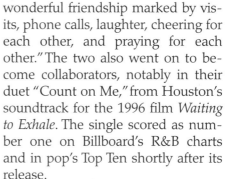

> For her solo album debut, Winans chose to record traditional gospel songs. "Not because I disliked contemporary gospel, far from it. I was ready to get back to a part of my background that I always cherished, and I wanted desperately to share that part with the rest of the world."

On their next album, *Different Lifestyles* (1991), BeBe and CeCe again blended slick production values and popular music styles with traditional messages. Again, their contemporary, soulful sound attracted both R&B and gospel fans. Guest singers like Houston, rap star Hammer, and Luther Vandross, who also arranged some songs, helped propel the CD to the top of both charts and into the platinum sales category. It won the 1992 Grammy Award for Best Contemporary Soul Gospel Album.

In 1993 BeBe and CeCe returned to the spirit of their family's annual holiday concerts with a seasonal album, *First Christmas*. Their next effort, *Relationships*, released in 1994, produced another cluster of cross-over hit singles and reached gold album status. But Winans recalled that, following the concert tour for the album, she "knew it was time to do something different. BeBe and I both knew it." After five albums and seven Grammys, countless concerts and many appearances on television—including "Sesame Street" and "The Tonight Show"—Winans and her brother decided to pursue their own separate paths. "Neither of us be-

Whitney Houston and Winans perform a duet at the 1996 Grammy Awards.

lieved that the duo BeBe and CeCe was over," she said. "But I think God decided that it was time for both of us to minister on another level."

CeCe Solo

For her solo album debut, Winans chose to record traditional gospel songs. "Not because I disliked contemporary gospel, far from it," she explained. "I was ready to get back to a part of my background that I always cherished, and I wanted desperately to share that part with the rest of the world." Though her name alone is on the cover, family is everywhere evident on *Alone in His Presence* (1995). Her sisters sing background on several songs, her brother-in-law Cedric Caldwell is producer, and her mother joins in a duet of "Great Is Thy Faithfulness." Winans has said that the highlight of the album is singing with her mom.

Alone in His Presence became a Top Five gospel hit and even cracked Billboard's mainstream pop chart. The album received the Grammy Award for Best Contemporary Soul Gospel Album in 1996. The same year, Winans became the first black woman to win the Dove Award for Best Female

Vocal Artist. Winans remarked: "There was a time in my life when I thought I couldn't perform if I didn't have BeBe next to me. But in 1995 God showed me differently."

Winans's second solo CD, *Everlasting Love*, reached the top of the gospel charts and furthered her reach into the R&B audience. She described it as "all-the-way urban inspiration, filled with contemporary hip-hop, R&B sounds as my way of reaching the world." Perhaps inevitably, some critics complained that this time Winans had truly "sold out." Nevertheless, she is firm that her new recordings still are gospel music. "Lauryn Hill wrote and produced one of my songs called 'On that Day,' so you're gonna get that [popular] flavor," she said. "But the message in every song is consistent. It's about the Good News. A couple of my songs say Jesus and a lot don't. My songs speak the gospel messages of love, of being encouraged."

> "Every time I sang, I had to be pushed to do it, and every year I cried when the time came for me to sing 'Fill My Cup, Lord.' Now I'm glad my family and friends pushed me. I'm glad they pushed me into my purpose. I discovered that God had a call on my life, and what God was calling me to do had nothing to do with becoming famous, or signing record contracts, or getting rich. That call had to do with spreading the news of the reality of God."

As a solo performer, CeCe has begun to share her messages of love and encouragement on screen, stage, and in print, as well as through music. As the host of "CeCe's Place," an hour-long Christian music and talk show on the Odyssey Channel, she reaches more than 1,500 cable and satellite systems. She also has taken a number of non-singing acting roles on programs like "Touched By an Angel." Off-Broadway, she joined gospel star Shirley Caesar in the play *Born to Sing*, by Vy Higgensen. Finally, her autobiographical-inspirational book, *On a Positive Note*, details her childhood and early career and emphasizes the roles of faith and family in her musical success.

With the 1999 launch of her own record label, CW Wellspring Entertainment, Winans is poised to take her career to even greater heights. Her first Wellspring release was her own CD, *Alabaster Box*, which appeared in 1999. Featuring "Fill My Cup, Lord," her first solo as a seven-year-old in her great-grandfather's church, the album brings CeCe Winans's faith-filled career full circle.

"Every time I sang, I had to be pushed to do it, and every year I cried when the time came for me to sing 'Fill My Cup, Lord'," Winans said. "Now I'm glad my family and friends pushed me. I'm glad they pushed me into my purpose. I discovered that God had a call on my life, and what God was calling me to do had nothing to do with becoming famous, or signing record contracts, or getting rich. That call had to do with spreading the news of the reality of God."

HOBBIES AND OTHER INTERESTS

Winans has created a non profit organization called Sharing the Vision, designed to help young people. Among its several programs are "My Sister's Keeper," which provides weekly support groups for women aged 13 to 30. It also offers mentoring services, community outreach and positive social activities. Another program, Teen Save, aims to prevent teen suicide and to reach out to communities. And Camp CeCe provides a Christian camp experience for young people.

RECORDINGS

Recordings with BeBe Winans

"Lord, Lift Us Up," 1983
Introducing BeBe and CeCe Winans, 1987
Heaven, 1988
Different Lifestyles, 1991
First Christmas, 1993
Relationships, 1994
Greatest Hits, 1996

Solo Recordings

Alone in His Presence, 1996
Everlasting Love, 1998
The Gift, 1998
Alabaster Box, 1999

WRITINGS

On a Positive Note, 1999 (with Renita J. Weems)

HONORS AND AWARDS

Grammy Award (The Recording Academy): 1987, Best Gospel Performance, Female, for "For Always"; 1989, Best Gospel Performance, Female, for "Don't Cry"; 1991, Best Contemporary Soul Gospel Album, for *Different Lifestyles*, (with BeBe Winans); 1995, Best Contemporary Soul Gospel Album, for *Alone in His Presence*

Stellar Gospel Music Award: 1988, Best New Gospel Artist (with BeBe Winans)

Dove Award (Gospel Music Association): 1988, New Artist of the Year (with BeBe Winans); 1990 (5 awards), Group of the Year (with BeBe Winans), Pop/Contemporary Album, for *Heaven* (with BeBe Winans), Pop/Contemporary Recorded Song, for "Heaven"(with BeBe Winans), Contemporary/Gospel Recorded Song, for "With My Whole Heart" (with BeBe Winans), Contemporary/Gospel Recorded Song, for "Addictive Love" (with BeBe Winans); 1992, Group of the Year (with BeBe Winans); 1996 (2 awards), Female Vocalist of the Year and Traditional Recorded Gospel Song, for "Great Is Thy Faithfulness"; 1997 (3 awards), Female Vocalist of the Year, Special Event Album, for *Tribute: The Songs of Andrae Crouch* (with various artists), Contemporary/Gospel Recorded Song, for "Take Me Back"; 1998 (2 awards), Special Event Album, for *God with Us: A Celebration of Christmas Carols and Classics* (with various artists), Contemporary/Gospel Recorded Song, for "Lord, Lift Us Up" (with BeBe Winans)

NAACP Image Award (National Association for the Advancement of Colored People): 1990, Best Gospel Artist (with BeBe Winans); 1992, Best Gospel Artist (with BeBe Winans)

Soul Train Music Award (Soul Train Magazine): 1990, Best Gospel Album, for *Heaven* (with BeBe Winans); 1999 (2 awards), Lady of Soul Award and Best Gospel Album, for *The Gift*

FURTHER READING

Books

*Contemporary Black Biography,*Vol.14, 1997
Winans, CeCe, with Renita J. Weems. *On a Positive Note,*1999

Periodicals

Ebony, Dec. 1991, p.52; Nov. 1998, p.132
Essence, Dec. 1992, p.80; June, 1999, p.76

Interview, Feb. 1995, p.94
Jet, Jan. 25, 1993, p.24; Oct. 9, 1995, p.58
People, July 3, 1989, p. 44; Jan. 15, 1996, p.26

ADDRESS

CW Wellspring Entertainment
230 Franklin Road
Franklin, Tennessee 37064

WORLD WIDE WEB SITES

http://www.CeCeWinans.com
http://www.sharingthevision.org

Photo and Illustration Credits

Christina Aguilera/Photos: Yariv Milchan; AFP/CORBIS; AP/Wide World Photos.

Lance Armstrong/Photos: AP/Wide World Photos.

K.A. Applegate/Covers: ANIMORPHS: THE MESSAGE; ANIMORPHS: THE DECISION; EVERWORLD: ENTER THE ENCHANTED; ANIMORPHS: THE REUNION all courtesy of Scholastic.

Backstreet Boys/Photos: Copyright © Bill Davila/Retna; Copyright © Bill Davila/Retna; AP/Wide World Photos; Copyright © Kelly Swift/Retna.

Daisy Bates/Photos: Bettmann/CORBIS (pages 68, 71, and 75); Photographs by Will Counts (pages 72, 79, 80, and 83); AP/ Wide World Photos (pages 76 and 85).

Harry Blackmun/Photos: Collection, The Supreme Court Historical Society/ Joseph D. Lavenburg; AP/Wide World Photos; Collection, The Supreme Court Historical Society/Richard Strauss, Smithsonian Institute.

George W. Bush/Photos: George Bush Presidential Library; AP/Wide World Photos.

Carson Daly/Photos: Phil Smrek; copyright © Tara Canova/Retna.

Ron Dayne/Photo: AP/Wide World Photos.

Henry Louis Gates, Jr./Photos: AP/Wide World Photos. Covers: THE SIGNIFYING MONKEY: A THEORY OF AFRICAN-AMERICAN LITERARY CRITICISM by Henry Louis Gates, Jr., copyright © 1988 by Henry Louis Gates, Jr. Used by permission of Oxford University Press, Inc.; THIRTEEN WAYS OF LOOKING AT A BLACK MAN copyright © 1997 Henry Louis Gates, Jr. Cover design by Frank D'Astolfo. Vintage Books, a division of Random House, Inc.

Doris Haddock/Photos: Copyright © Reuters NewMedia Inc./CORBIS; AP/Wide World Photos.

Jennifer Love Hewitt/Photos: Copyright © Mitchell Garber/CORBIS; Larry Watson/FOX; Craig Blankenhorn/FOX.

Chamique Holdsclaw/Photos: Greg Shamus; Patrick Murphy-Racey; Mitchell Layton.

Katie Holmes/Photos: Lorenzo Agius (*Teaching Mrs. Tingle*).

Charlayne Hunter-Gault/Photos: TM & copyright © 1999 CNN, A Time Warner Co./Mark Hill; Courtesy of *The Atlanta Journal-Constitution*; AP/Wide World Photos.

Johanna Johnson/Photos: Courtesy Make-A-Wish Foundation; AP/Wide World Photos.

Craig Kielburger/Photos: Courtesy Free The Children and Fred Kielburger.

John Lasseter/Photos: AP/Wide World Photos; copyright © The Walt Disney Company. All Rights Reserved; copyright © Disney/Pixar; copyright © Disney Enterprises, Inc./Pixar Animation Studios; copyright © The Walt Disney Company. All Rights Reserved.

Peyton Manning/Photos: AP/Wide World Photos.

Ricky Martin/Photos: AP/Wide World Photos; copyright © Ernie Paniccioli/Retna (Menudo).

John McCain/Photos: Courtesy Office of Sen. John McCain; AP/Wide World Photos. Cover: FAITH OF MY FATHERS copyright © 1999 by John McCain and Mark Salter. Jacket design by Andy Carpenter. Jacket photos courtesy of the McCain family.

Walter Payton/Photos: AP/Wide World Photos; CBS.

Freddie Prinze, Jr./Photos: Barry Wetcher; copyright © Jay Blakesberg/ Retna; copyright © Steve Granitz/Retna.Viviana Risca/Photo: AP/Wide World Photos.

Briana Scurry/Photos: AP/Wide World Photos.

George Thampy/Photos: Copyright © AFP/CORBIS; AP/Wide World Photos.

CeCe Winans/Photos: Michael Gomez; Capital Entertainment; AP/Wide World Photos.

Appendix

This Appendix contains updates for selected individuals profiled in previous volumes of the regular series and the special subject series of *Biography Today*.

* YASIR ARAFAT *

In 2000 Arafat was once again in the news as he and Israeli Prime Minister Ehud Barak held a summit with President Bill Clinton to hammer out an end to the Palestinian-Israeli conflict. Their meeting ended without an accord. In September 2000, fighting broke out over control of a section of Jerusalem that both Jews and Muslims hold sacred. Arafat and Barak then met in Paris with Secretary of State Madeleine Albright to try to work out an accord, but the talks broke down before an agreement could be reached. As of early October, the fighting continued and threatened the fragile peace and Arafat's control over the Palestinians of Israel.

* LANCE ARMSTRONG *

After winning his second straight Tour de France in July 2000, Armstrong prepared to compete in the Olympics in Sydney. But while training in France, Armstrong was hit by a car, breaking a vertebra in his neck. He came back from the injury to compete in two races in the Olympics. In his first event, a 240 km race, he finished 13th. Next, he competed in the 33-mile time trial and won a bronze medal for third place. Armstrong was philosophical about his finish. "I came to win the gold medal, but I did everything I could," he said. "I'm glad the race is over and I can enjoy myself," he added. Each year, he celebrates the occasion of his diagnosis of cancer, and his subsequent win in his battle with the disease. "Every year we have a party or have some special time with friends and family," he said. "They've occurred all over the world. This time it will be in Sydney. I had hoped to make it a double celebration, but I can't complain."

* GEORGE W. BUSH *

In October 2000, George W. Bush and Al Gore met in a series of three debates moderated by Jim Lehrer of PBS. Both candidates deviated from the time limits placed for questions, responses, and rebuttals, in debates that encompassed their views on all the major issues of the campaign, including Social Security, taxes, education, foreign policy, and Medicare. After the debates, both parties declared victory for their candidates.

As the election neared, the race was too close to call. On November 7, 2000, U.S. voters turned out for what proved to be one of the most extraordinary presidential elections in history. Long after the polls closed, the race was still too close to call. On the morning of November 8, Americans awoke to the news that the race between Bush and Gore was so close that the new president had yet to be determined. With 99% of the vote counted, Gore had won the popular vote, with 48,707,413, to Bush's 48,609,640. But the electoral vote stood at 255 for Gore and 246 for Bush, and neither candidate had garnered the 270 electoral votes needed to win.

The election came down to the race in Florida, which, with its 25 electoral votes, would bring victory to either candidate. Yet the vote was so close — less than .5% of the popular vote separated the two candidates — that it triggered an automatic recount. That recount took place on November 9, amid charges of possible voting irregularities. This prompted the Democratic Party to demand a follow-up recount by hand in four counties and to call for unspecified "legal actions" in reaction to the irregularities.

As of November 9, these questions regarding the Florida election were unresolved, and the 43rd President of the United States had yet to be determined.

* BRANDI CHASTAIN *

Chastain and the U.S. women's soccer team took the silver medal at the 2000 Olympics in Sydney in September 2000. They lost the final game to Norway, 3-2, a team that has always been a tough opponent. After the game, Chastain said she and her team were proud of what they'd accomplished. "I think you could see that in everybody's eyes. We're very, very proud of what we accomplished. And I hope everybody who watches the fame understands it wasn't easy." She now plans to play in the first season of the new women's professional soccer league, the WUSA.

* BILL CLINTON *

As Bill Clinton prepared to leave office after six years as President, he sought to define his legacy to the office. Anxious to be remembered for something beyond the Monica Lewinsky scandal and the impeachment proceedings, Clinton spent his last year traveling around the world and hosting summit meetings with world leaders. He also lent his political clout to Al Gore's campaign for the presidency, and to his wife's campaign for the Senate in New York. After he leaves the White House in January 2001, he plans to spend most of his time in Arkansas overseeing the construction of his presidential library. How the future will evaluate the presidency of Bill Clinton remains to be seen.

* HILLARY CLINTON *

In February, First Lady Hillary Clinton announced that she would run as the Democratic candidate for Senator for the state of New York. She and President Clinton had purchased a house in New York, so she had established residency in the state. When she announced her candidacy, her Republican opponent was Rudolph Giuliani, the mayor of New York City. But Giuliani dropped out of the race in May, after he learned that he had cancer. Clinton then faced New York Congressman Rick Lazio in the election. Polling leading up to the election predicted that the race was very close. On election day, New Yorkers chose Clinton, by a margin of 12 points, over Lazio. Hillary Clinton now plans to move to Washington and take her seat in the Senate and become the only First Lady in history to win elective office.

* CHRISTOPHER PAUL CURTIS *

On January 17, 2000, Christopher Paul Curtis became the first writer in history to receive both the Newbery Award and the Coretta Scott King Award for his new book, *Bud, Not Buddy*. "I'm just overwhelmed," said the writer. Set during the Great Depression of the 1930s, *Bud, Not Buddy* tells the story of 10-year-old Bud Caldwell, an orphan living in foster homes and orphanages in Flint, Michigan. The story follows Bud's adventures as he runs away in search of the man he thinks is his father.

Curtis is still getting used to his fame. "I still have a moment of disbelief when I'm introduced as a Newbery of Coretta Scott King winner," he says. But his devotion to spreading the importance of reading and writing to young people hasn't changed. He wants to encourage kids, especially African-American kids, to write. "I can only suggest that librarians and teachers take the same attitude I take when speaking to a group of eighth graders. Sure, some of them could care less what I have to say. Some of them will find it boring. But if one out of a group of 100 can be reached and made to think, 'Hey, if this guy can, maybe I can,' then it has been a great day for me."

* BILL GATES *

In 2000, Bill Gates and his company, Microsoft, were in the news because of a federal lawsuit. In 1998, Microsoft was sued by the U.S. Justice Department for unfair business practices. The suit alleged that Microsoft's inclusion of it Internet Explorer web browser on its Windows 98 operating system did not allow other Internet browsers, such as Netscape Navigator, to compete fairly for their share of the market. Because Microsoft's operating system, Windows, is used on 90% of all PCs, Microsoft was said to have an unfair advantage. The suit alleged that the company's business practices pressured PC manufacturers to use only Microsoft products. At issue was whether Microsoft had violated federal anti-trust laws, which protect business competition by outlawing price fixing and by prohibiting companies from using their economic power to create monopolies, where a single company has exclusive control of a product. The case against Microsoft was brought by the Justice Department on behalf of Netscape and other competitors, who alleged that Microsoft had engaged in monopolistic practices to drive them out of business.

Gates testified during the trial, providing a videotaped deposition that was played in court. Legal observers said he appeared either combative or bored and that he avoided answering questions. The judge noted that Gates was not "particularly responsive," and some analysts said that his testimony was a turning point in the trial because it weakened the credibility of the company's case.

In June 2000, the trial concluded when Microsoft was found to be in violation of U.S. anti-trust laws. Federal judge Michael Penfield Jackson ruled that Microsoft must be broken up into two companies. One company would center on Windows technology, the operating system used on most of the personal computers in the world. The other company would center on the rest of the Microsoft products, like Word, PowerPoint, Excel, Outlook, and others. In his ruling, the judge said that he found Microsoft to be "untrustworthy," and he said that "credible evidence" existed that indicated that Microsoft continued to use its monopolistic strength to damage rivals.

The judgment also imposed restrictions on how Microsoft could conduct business. For example, it required that Microsoft set up a pricing schedule for Windows, and it also prevented the company from setting limits on how a computer manufacturer can place Windows on the machines they sell.

After Judge Jackson's ruling, Gates immediately condemned it as "an unwarranted and unjustified intrusion," and Microsoft promptly filed a legal appeal. In October, they won a round in the appeal process when the U.S. Supreme Court refused to hear the appeal directly. Instead, the Supreme Court sent the case back to a federal appeals court. The federal appeals court will then rule on the Microsoft appeal. At this time, the final disposition of the anti-trust case against Microsoft is still undecided.

* AL GORE *

In August 2000, Al Gore was named the Democratic Party's nominee for President. Earlier in the year, he had fought off former Senator Bill Bradley, who had challenged Gore in the primaries. Gore won each of the primaries, and by Super Tuesday in March, had enough delegates to win the nomination. After the convention, Gore received a lift in the polls that closed the gap between him and Bush, who had led by as much as 10% in polls conducted during the summer of 2000.

In October, Gore faced Republican challenger George W. Bush in three televised debates moderated by Jim Lehrer of PBS. Both candidates deviated from the time limits placed for questions, responses, and rebuttals, in debates that encompassed their views on all the major issues of the campaign, including Social Security, taxes, education, foreign policy, and Medicare. After the debates, both parties declared victory for their candidates.

As the election neared, the race was too close to call. On November 7, 2000, U.S. voters turned out for what proved to be one of the most extraordinary presidential elections in history. Long after the polls closed, the race was still too close to call. On the morning of November 8, Americans awoke to the news that the race between Bush and Gore was so close that the new president had yet to be determined. With 99% of the vote counted, Gore had won the popular vote, with 48,707,413, to Bush's 48,609,640. But the electoral vote stood at 255 for Gore and 246 for Bush, and neither candidate had garnered the 270 electoral votes needed to win.

The election came down to the race in Florida, which, with its 25 electoral votes, would bring victory to either candidate. Yet the vote was so close — less than .5% of the popular vote separated the two candidates — that it triggered an automatic recount. That recount took place on November 9, amid charges of possible voting irregularities. This prompted the Democratic Party to demand a follow-up recount by hand in four counties and to call for unspecified "legal actions" in reaction to the irregularities.

As of November 9, these questions regarding the Florida election were unresolved, and the 43rd President of the United States had yet to be determined.

* MIA HAMM *

At the 2000 Olympics in Sydney, Australia, Hamm and the U.S. Women's Team placed second, losing the final match and the gold medal to Norway in a hard-fought 3-2 loss that went in to sudden death overtime. After the loss, Hamm told her teammates, "Hold your head high—and be proud." Her thoughts were echoed by the team's coach, April Heinrichs, who said, "They won the silver medal, but their game was golden tonight." Hamm and many of the women on the U.S. team plan to play in the first professional women's league, the WUSA. And she has her eyes on the team's next encounter with Norway, the only team to beat the U.S. in a World Cup or Olympics. That match will take place in the 2003 World Cup. "I want to be back," said Hamm about that next matchup. "You hate for it to end like this."

* MICHAEL JOHNSON *

At the 2000 Olympics in Sydney, Australia, Michael Johnson won his second gold medal in the 400-meter race, becoming the first man to win the event in back-to-back Olympics. He won the race in a time of 43.84 seconds, off the world record but with a comfortable lead over his nearest competitor. Johnson won gold again as the anchor of the American 4 x 400-meter relay team, in a win that was marked by the typical graciousness of this athlete. "It felt great being able to end it running with a great group of guys," he said of the relay team. "I actually enjoy working as part of a team." Johnson's plans for the future are uncertain at this time. He's said that Sydney was definitely his last Olympics, and he doesn't plan to compete in the World Championships again. But he might continue to compete in a few events in the upcoming season.

* STEPHEN KING *

In the summer of 1999, Stephen King was hit by a car in a serious accident that nearly ended his writing career. He sustained a broken hip, pelvis, ribs, and thighbone. He was first confined to bed and then a wheelchair, and doctors believe he will never have full use of his right leg again. After months of surgeries and a slow recuperation, King was back writing, and ready to take on a new technology. He published a book titled *Riding the Bullet* in March 2000, exclusively in electronic form. In July, he self-published another new book, *The Plant*, also only in an electronic version, asking his on-line readership to pay him for the book at the rate of $1 per chapter. He claimed he would stop writing if he did not receive payments from 75% of those readers who had downloaded that first chapter. Within a week, he had received payment of over $115,000 from his on-line readers. It would seem that despite his life-threatening accident, King is as creative and innovative as ever.

* JULIE KRONE *

Julie Krone was honored by her peers in horse racing by being named to the National Museum of Racing and Hall of Fame in August 2000. She is the first woman ever to be so honored. The diminutive Krone, 4'11", stepped on a crate to reach the podium and deliver her acceptance speech. "I wish I could put every single one of you on the back of a horse at the one-eighth pole so you could have the feeling of communicating with an animal you love so much," she said. "I got to do that every day of my life." To her young fans, she had this to say: "I want this to be a lesson to all kids everywhere. If the stable is closed, climb the fence."

* WINONA LaDUKE *

As she did in 1996, Winona LaDuke ran as Ralph Nader's vice presidential candidate for the Green Party in 2000. In the November 7 election, the Green Party received approximately 3% of the vote nationwide. LaDuke continues to live and work on the White Earth reservation in northern Minnesota.

* DAN MARINO *

After a professional football career that lasted 17 years, Dan Marino retired from the Miami Dolphins and pro ball in 2000. In his 17 years with the Dolphins, he led his team to the playoffs 10 times, but a Super Bowl win remained elusive. His final season was particularly disappointing, as he was plagued with an injury that weakened his ability. In his last game, the Dolphins collapsed in a humiliating 62-7 defeat to Jacksonville. Marino said it was the worst loss of his life. Yet he retires with more touchdowns and yards than any other quarterback in the history of the game.

* SLOBODAN MILOSEVIC *

On October 5, 2000, the people of Yugoslavia rose up against their leader of 13 years, Slobodan Milosevic, and removed him from power. Milosevic had rarely appeared in public since Serbia had been defeated by NATO forces in 1999. When opposition parties called for elections in 2000, he reluctantly agreed. On September 24, 2000, the Serbian people voted for Vojisla Kostunica to be their president by a large majority over Milosevic. Yet Milosevic, who still controlled the media and the military, refused to accept the mandate. Over the next two weeks, he sought to have the election overturned. Then, on October 5, hundreds of thousands of Serbs took to the streets of Belgrade. They took over the media and burned the Parliamentary buildings, demanding that Milosevic leave and Kostunica be declared president. The police, formerly loyal to Milosevic, let the demonstrators proceed. On October 6, Milosevic shocked the world by resigning from the presidency. The U.S. and the nations of the West have voiced support for Kostunica, and certain economic sanctions against Yugoslavia were lifted. Now Kostunica must lead a country still devastated economically by Milosevic's policies and by the NATO bombing. And as of mid-October, the whereabouts and fate of Milosevic remain unknown.

* DOT RICHARDSON *

After nearly being eliminated from medal contention, Dot Richardson and the women's Olympic softball team won the gold medal in the 2000 Olympic games in Sydney, Australia. The team was one game from elimination when it won its last five games to clinch the medal. The U.S. team played Japan in its last game, which went into extra winnings and resulted in a 2-1 victory for the Americans. Richardson was happy, and relieved. "It's been a very tough and battling and challenging mission that we've had to overcome," she said. "The world sensed the excitement. And that's so cool." Richardson now plans to return to her practice as an orthopedic surgeon.

* J.K. ROWLING *

The much-anticipated fourth volume in J.K. Rowling's "Harry Potter" series appeared in 2000, as fans all over the world thrilled to the new adventures of Harry. *Harry Potter and the Goblet of Fire* was released at Midnight on July 8th, and many bookstores had parties to celebrate. Kids and adults dressed up as characters from the series. Some bookstores had cauldrons full of oatmeal, and live owls, in honor of the new book.

The book was a publishing phenomenon. Scholastic Books, publisher of the American edition of the "Harry Potter" books, made an initial printing of 3.8 million books, the largest initial press run in history. Nearly 3 million sold in the first weekend. Scholastic announced that it would print another 3 million copies the week after the initial release. Still topping the bestseller charts, all the "Harry Potter" books have become a beloved fixture on bookshelves all over the world.

And in the summer of 2000, the cast was chosen for the movie version of the first book, *Harry Potter and the Sorcerer's Stone*. The actor who will play Harry is 11-year old English schoolboy Daniel Radcliffe, chosen from more than 40,000 aspiring actors. Fans young and old can catch the film version sometime in 2001.

Rowling's success is a source of both surprise and gratitude. Her books have sold over 25 million copies, in 28 languages. She began a book tour immediately after her current book, and she enjoyed meeting her many fans. She signed autographs for hours and chatted with her readers. "It's a real joy," she says.

* CHARLES SCHULZ *

On February 13, 2000, just weeks after he announced that he was ending his comic strip "Peanuts," Charles Schulz died of colon cancer. He was mourned all over the world, where millions of fans had spent many years chuckling at the adventures of Charlie Brown, Linus, Lucy, and all the "Peanuts" gang. The last original strip, which ran on the day he died, was a farewell, in which Schulz said, "Charlie Brown, Snoopy, Linus, Lucy. . . how can I ever forget them?" Schultz had written the strip for nearly 50 years at the time of his death.

* AMY VAN DYKEN *

Swimming in what she knew would be her final Olympics, Amy Van Dyken won two more gold medals to end her swimming career with seven Olympic first-place finishes. Van Dyken won her medals in the 400-meter freestyle relay and the 400-meter medley relay. Her final event was the 50-meter freestyle, where she placed fourth. Afterwards, she lingered in the pool. "It's the last time I'll see the pool as a competitor," she said. "It's hard, you know. I was a lot more emotional that I thought I would be."

Van Dyken has no immediate plans, now that her full-time swimming career is over. She plans to get married in February 2001 to Denver Broncos' punter Tom Rouen. And she hasn't hung up her swimsuit for good, either. She's thinking of trying the triathlon, a sport that combines swimming, biking, and running. "I'm a great bike rider," she says. "Not as good as I have to be, though. The running part is bad, but I always have to do things the hard way."

* SERENA WILLIAMS *

Serena Williams and her sister Venus became the first sisters to win an Olympic gold medal in tennis, winning the final in women's doubles easily against Miriam Oremans and Kristie Boogert of the Netherlands with a score of 6-1, 6-1. The match was characterized by the powerful serves and volleys that both Serena and Venus Williams possess. After their win, they threw their rackets in the air and screamed with delight. The match was the 22nd in a row for the Williams sisters, and it was Venus's second gold medal of the Olympics (see below).

* VENUS WILLIAMS *

Venus Williams became a tennis superstar in 2000. In July, she defeated Lindsay Davenport to win the women's singles at the prestigious Wimbledon tournament in England. She followed that with another win against Davenport at the U.S. Open in September. Later that month, she competed in her first Olympics, where she won two gold medals. She defeated Russian player Elena Dementieva in the women's singles final for her first gold medal. Then she and sister Serena defeated the women's doubles team of Miriam Oremans and Kristie Boogert of the Netherlands to win the gold medal in doubles, 6-1, 6-1. Venus and Serena are the first sisters ever to win the women's Olympic doubles, and Venus is the first women since Helen Wills in 1924 to win the gold in both singles and doubles in the same year.

* OPRAH WINFREY *

Oprah Winfrey continued her dominance in the media by becoming a partner in the media conglomerate Oxygen, which includes television, publishing, and Internet content, and by publishing her own magazine, "O." The magazine is off to an incredible start, and it is considered one of the most successful magazine launches in history.

* TIGER WOODS *

In 2000, Tiger Woods had one of the most successful seasons in the history of golf. He won nine overall tournaments, including two majors, the U.S. Open and the PGA Champsionship. He was rated number one in the world and topped the leader board with an astonishing $8,286,821, the largest amount earned in pro golf in history.

* BORIS YELTSIN *

After holding the office of President of Russia for seven years, Boris Yeltsin finally stepped down from power in 2000. His ability to govern had been challenged for several years, and his political power was waning. In the spring of 2000, Vladimir Putin was elected to the office of President of Russia. Yeltsin is now in retirement and living in the country.

* STEVE YOUNG *

After 15 years in pro football, most of them as quarterback of the San Francisco 49ers, Steve Young decided to retire in 2000. He had sustained several serious concussions in the last several years, and his neurologist told him it was dangerous to continue to play. Young retires as the highest-rated passer in the NFL, the winner of two MVP awards, and a Super Bowl winner. "I really believe he's one of the top five players ever to play the game at his position," said former 49ers offensive coordinator Mike Shanahan, now coach of the Denver Broncos. Young, who recently married and is expecting a child with his wife, is considering a future in either politics or broadcasting.

How to Use the Cumulative Index

Our indexes have a new look. In an effort to make our indexes easier to use, we've combined the Name and General Index into a new, cumulative General Index. This single ready-reference resource covers all the volumes in *Biography Today*, both the general series and the special subject series. The new General Index contains complete listings of all individuals who have appeared in *Biography Today* since the series began. Their names appear in bold-faced type, followed by the issue in which they appear. The General Index also includes references for the occupations, nationalities, and ethnic and minority origins of individuals profiled in *Biography Today*.

We have also made some changes to our specialty indexes, the Places of Birth Index and the Birthday Index. To consolidate and to save space, the Places of Birth Index and the Birthday Index will no longer appear in the January and April issues of the softbound subscription series. But these indexes can still be found in the September issue of the softbound subscription series, in the hardbound Annual Cumulation at the end of each year, and in each volume of the special subject series.

General Series

The General Series of *Biography Today* is denoted in the index with the month and year of the issue in which the individual appeared. Each individual also appears in the Annual Cumulation for that year.

Special Subject Series

The Special Subject Series of *Biography Today* are each denoted in the index with an abbreviated form of the series name, plus the number of the volume in which the individual appears. They are listed as follows.

Adams, Ansel .... Artist V.1	(Artists Series)
Cooney, Barbara .... Author V.8	(Author Series)
Harris, Bernard.............. Science V.3	(Scientists & Inventors Series)
Jeter, Derek.................... Sport V.4	(Sports Series)
Peterson, Roger Tory .... WorLdr V.1	(World Leaders Series: Environmental Leaders)
Sadat, Anwar .... WorLdr V.2	(World Leaders Series: Modern African Leaders)
Wolf, Hazel................. WorLdr V.3	(World Leaders Series: Environmental Leaders 2)

Updates

Updated information on selected individuals appears in the Appendix at the end of the *Biography Today* Annual Cumulation. In the index, the original entry is listed first, followed by any updates.

Arafat, Yasir . . Sep 94; Update 94; Update 95; Update 96; Update 97; Update 98; Update 00
Gates, Bill ... Apr 93; Update 98; Update 00
Griffith Joyner, Florence .... Sport V.1; Update 98
Sanders, Barry.......... Sep 95; Update 99
Spock, Dr. Benjamin.... Sep 95; Update 98
Yeltsin, Boris .... Apr 92; Update 93; Update 95; Update 96; Update 98; Update 00

General Index

This index includes names, occupations, nationalities, and ethnic and minority origins that pertain to individuals profiled in *Biography Today*.

Olajuwon, Hakeem . . . . Sep 95
Oleynik, Larisa . . . . Sep 96
Oliver, Patsy Ruth . . . . WorLdr V.1
Olsen, Ashley . . . . Sep 95
Olsen, Mary Kate . . . . Sep 95
Olympics
  Ali, Muhammad . . . . Sport V.2
  Armstrong, Lance . . . . . . Sep 00; Update 00
  Bailey, Donovan . . . . Sport V.2
  Baiul, Oksana . . . . Apr 95
  Bird, Larry . . . . Jan 92; Update 98
  Blair, Bonnie . . . . Apr 94
  Boulmerka, Hassiba . . . . Sport V.1
  Chastain, Brandi . . . . . Sport V.4; Update 00
  Devers, Gail . . . . Sport V.2
  Evans, Janet . . . . Jan 95; Update 96
  Ewing, Patrick . . . . Jan 95
  Griffith Joyner, Florence . . . . Sport V.1;
    Update 98
  Hamm, Mia . . . . Sport V.2; Update 00
  Harding, Tonya . . . . Sep 94
  Hasek, Dominik . . . . Sport V.3
  Hill, Grant . . . . Sport V.1
  Jansen, Dan . . . . Apr 94
  Johnson, Michael . . . . Jan 97; Update 00
  Joyner-Kersee, Jackie . . . Oct 92; Update 96;
    Update 98
  Kerrigan, Nancy . . . . Apr 94
  Kwan, Michelle . . . . Sport V.3
  Lewis, Carl . . . . Sep 96
  Lipinski, Tara . . . . Apr 98
  Lobo, Rebecca . . . . Sport V.3
  Miller, Shannon . . . . Sep 94; Update 96
  Moceanu, Dominique . . . . Jan 98
  Pippig, Uta . . . . Sport V.1
  Richardson, Dot . . . . . Sport V.2; Update 00
  Roba, Fatuma . . . . Sport V.3
  Robinson, David . . . . Sep 96
  Rudolph, Wilma . . . . Apr 95
  Sanchez Vicario, Arantxa . . . . Sport V.1
  Scurry, Briana . . . . Jan 00
  Stockton, John . . . . Sport V.3
  Street, Picabo . . . . Sport V.3
  Summitt, Pat . . . . Sport V.3
  Swoopes, Sheryl . . . . Sport V.2
  Van Dyken, Amy . . . . Sport V.3; Update 00
  Williams, Serena . . . . . Sport V.4; Update 00
  Williams, Venus . . . . Jan 99; Update 00
  Yamaguchi, Kristi . . . . Apr 92
  Zmeskal, Kim . . . . Jan 94

O'Neal, Shaquille . . . . Sep 93
Oppenheimer, J. Robert . . . . Science V.1
painters
  see artists
Pak, Se Ri . . . . Sport V.4
Pakistanis
  Bhutto, Benazir . . . . Apr 95; Update 99
  Masih, Iqbal . . . . Jan 96
Palestinian
  Arafat, Yasir . Sep 94; Update 94;Update 95;
    Update 96; Update 97; Update 98; Update
    00
Parkinson, Jennifer . . . . Apr 95
Parks, Gordon . . . . Artist V.1
Parks, Rosa . . . . Apr 92; Update 94
Pascal, Francine . . . . Author V.6
Paterson, Katherine . . . . Author V.3
Patrick, Ruth . . . . Science V.3
Pauley, Jane . . . . Oct 92
Pauling, Linus . . . . Jan 95
Paulsen, Gary . . . . Author V.1
Payton, Walter . . . . Jan 00
Peet, Bill . . . . Author V.4
Pei, I.M. . . . . Artist V.1
Pelé . . . . Sport V.1
Perlman, Itzhak . . . . Jan 95
Perot, H. Ross . . . . Apr 92; Update 93;
  Update 95; Update 96
Perry, Luke . . . . Jan 92
Peterson, Roger Troy . . . . WorLdr V.1
Petty, Richard . . . . Sport V.2
philanthropist
  McCarty, Oseola . . . . Jan 99; Update 99
Phoenix, River . . . . Apr 94
photographers
  Adams, Ansel . . . . Artist V.1
  Bourke-White, Margaret . . . . Artist V.1
  Land, Edwin . . . . Science V.1
  Leibovitz, Annie . . . . Sep 96
  Parks, Gordon . . . . Artist V.1
Pike, Christopher . . . . Sep 96
pilot
  Van Meter, Vicki . . . . Jan 95
Pine, Elizabeth Michele . . . . Jan 94
Pinkney, Jerry . . . . Author V.2
Pinkwater, Daniel . . . . Author V.8
Pinsky, Robert . . . . Author V.7
Pippen, Scottie . . . . Oct 92
Pippig, Uta . . . . Sport V.1
Pitt, Brad . . . . Sep 98

411

Places of Birth Index

The following index lists the places of birth for the individuals profiled in *Biography Today*. Places of birth are entered under state, province, and/or country.

Birthday Index

June (continued)

		Year
23	Rudolph, Wilma	1940
	Thomas, Clarence	1948
25	Carle, Eric	1929
	Gibbs, Lois	1951
26	Harris, Bernard	1956
	Jeter, Derek	1974
	LeMond, Greg	1961
27	Babbitt, Bruce	1938
	Dunbar, Paul Laurence	1872
	Perot, H. Ross	1930
28	Elway, John	1960
30	Ballard, Robert	1942

July

		Year
1	Brower, David	1912
	Calderone, Mary S.	1904
	Diana, Princess of Wales	1961
	Duke, David	1950
	Lewis, Carl	1961
	McCully, Emily Arnold	1939
2	Bethe, Hans A.	1906
	George, Jean Craighead	1919
	Marshall, Thurgood	1908
	Petty, Richard	1937
	Thomas, Dave	1932
5	Watterson, Bill	1958
6	Bush, George W.	1946
	Dalai Lama	1935
	Dumitriu, Ioana	1976
7	Chagall, Marc	1887
	Heinlein, Robert	1907
	Kwan, Michelle	1980
	Stachowski, Richie	1985
8	Hardaway, Anfernee "Penny"	1971
	Sealfon, Rebecca	1983
9	Farmer, Nancy	1941
	Hanks, Tom	1956
	Hassan ll	1929
	Krim, Mathilde	1926
	Sacks, Oliver	1933
10	Ashe, Arthur	1943
	Boulmerka, Hassiba	1969
11	Cisneros, Henry	1947
	White, E.B.	1899
12	Cosby, Bill	1937
	Johnson, Johanna	1983
	Yamaguchi, Kristi	1972
13	Ford, Harrison	1942
	Stewart, Patrick	1940

15	Aristide, Jean-Bertrand	1953
	Ventura, Jesse	1951
16	Johnson, Jimmy	1943
	Sanders, Barry	1968
18	Glenn, John	1921
	Lemelson, Jerome	1923
	Mandela, Nelson	1918
19	Tarvin, Herbert	1985
20	Hillary, Sir Edmund	1919
21	Chastain, Brandi	1968
	Reno, Janet	1938
	Riley, Dawn	1964
	Williams, Robin	1952
22	Calder, Alexander	1898
	Dole, Bob	1923
	Hinton, S.E.	1948
23	Haile Selassie	1892
24	Abzug, Bella	1920
	Krone, Julie	1963
	Moss, Cynthia	1940
	Wilson, Mara	1987
25	Payton, Walter	1954
26	Berenstain, Jan	1923
28	Davis, Jim	1945
	Pottter, Beatrix	1866
29	Burns, Ken	1953
	Creech, Sharon	1945
	Dole, Elizabeth Hanford	1936
	Jennings, Peter	1938
	Morris, Wanya	1973
30	Hill, Anita	1956
	Moore, Henry	1898
	Schroeder, Pat	1940
31	Cronin, John	1950
	Reid Banks, Lynne	1929
	Rowling, J. K.	1965

August

		Year
1	Brown, Ron	1941
	Coolio	1963
	Garcia, Jerry	1942
2	Baldwin, James	1924
	Healy, Bernadine	1944
3	Roper, Dee Dee	
	Savimbi, Jonas	1934
4	Gordon, Jeff	1971
5	Ewing, Patrick	1962
	Jackson, Shirley Ann	1946

Biography Today

General Series

Biography Today **General Series** includes a unique combination of current biographical profiles that teachers and librarians — and the readers themselves — tell us are most appealing. The **General Series** is available as a 3-issue subscription; hardcover annual cumulation; or subscription plus cumulation.

Within the **General Series**, your readers will find a variety of sketches about:

- Authors
- Musicians
- Political leaders
- Sports figures
- Movie actresses & actors
- Cartoonists
- Scientists
- Astronauts
- TV personalities
- and the movers & shakers in many other fields!

ONE-YEAR SUBSCRIPTION
- 3 softcover issues, 6" x 9"
- Published in January, April, and September
- 1-year subscription, $56
- 150 pages per issue
- 10-12 profiles per issue
- Contact sources for additional information
- Cumulative General, Places of Birth, and Birthday Indexes

HARDBOUND ANNUAL CUMULATION
- Sturdy 6" x 9" hardbound volume
- Published in December
- $57 per volume
- 450 pages per volume
- 30-36 profiles — includes all profiles found in softcover issues for that calendar year
- Cumulative General, Places of Birth, and Birthday Indexes
- Special appendix features current updates of previous profiles

SUBSCRIPTION AND CUMULATION COMBINATION
- $99 for 3 softcover issues plus the hardbound volume

"Biography Today will be useful in elementary and middle school libraries and in public library children's collections where there is a need for biographies of current personalities. High schools serving reluctant readers may also want to consider a subscription."
— *Booklist,* American Library Association

"Highly recommended for the young adult audience. Readers will delight in the accessible, energetic, tell-all style; teachers, librarians, and parents will welcome the clever format, intelligent and informative text. It should prove especially useful in motivating "reluctant" readers or literate nonreaders."
— *MultiCultural Review*

"Written in a friendly, almost chatty tone, the profiles offer quick, objective information. While coverage of current figures makes *Biography Today* a useful reference tool, an appealing format and wide scope make it a fun resource to browse." — *School Library Journal*

"The best source for current information at a level kids can understand."
— Kelly Bryant, School Librarian, Carlton, OR

"Easy for kids to read. We love it! Don't want to be without it."
— Lynn McWhirter, School Librarian, Rockford, IL

1992

Paula Abdul
Andre Agassi
Kirstie Alley
Terry Anderson
Roseanne Arnold
Isaac Asimov
James Baker
Charles Barkley
Larry Bird
Judy Blume
Berke Breathed
Garth Brooks
Barbara Bush
George Bush
Fidel Castro
Bill Clinton
Bill Cosby
Diana, Princess of Wales
Shannen Doherty
Elizabeth Dole
David Duke
Gloria Estefan
Mikhail Gorbachev
Steffi Graf
Wayne Gretzky
Matt Groening
Alex Haley
Hammer
Martin Handford
Stephen Hawking
Hulk Hogan
Saddam Hussein
Lee Iacocca
Bo Jackson
Mae Jemison
Peter Jennings
Steven Jobs
Pope John Paul II
Magic Johnson
Michael Jordon
Jackie Joyner-Kersee
Spike Lee
Mario Lemieux
Madeleine L'Engle
Jay Leno
Yo-Yo Ma
Nelson Mandela
Wynton Marsalis
Thurgood Marshall
Ann Martin
Barbara McClintock
Emily Arnold McCully
Antonia Novello
Sandra Day O'Connor
Rosa Parks

Jane Pauley
H. Ross Perot
Luke Perry
Scottie Pippen
Colin Powell
Jason Priestley
Queen Latifah
Yitzhak Rabin
Sally Ride
Pete Rose
Nolan Ryan
H. Norman
  Schwarzkopf
Jerry Seinfeld
Dr. Seuss
Gloria Steinem
Clarence Thomas
Chris Van Allsburg
Cynthia Voigt
Bill Watterson
Robin Williams
Oprah Winfrey
Kristi Yamaguchi
Boris Yeltsin

1993

Maya Angelou
Arthur Ashe
Avi
Kathleen Battle
Candice Bergen
Boutros Boutros-Ghali
Chris Burke
Dana Carvey
Cesar Chavez
Henry Cisneros
Hillary Rodham Clinton
Jacques Cousteau
Cindy Crawford
Macaulay Culkin
Lois Duncan
Marian Wright Edelman
Cecil Fielder
Bill Gates
Sara Gilbert
Dizzy Gillespie
Al Gore
Cathy Guisewite
Jasmine Guy
Anita Hill
Ice-T
Darci Kistler
k.d. lang
Dan Marino
Rigoberta Menchu
Walter Dean Myers

Martina Navratilova
Phyllis Reynolds Naylor
Rudolf Nureyev
Shaquille O'Neal
Janet Reno
Jerry Rice
Mary Robinson
Winona Ryder
Jerry Spinelli
Denzel Washington
Keenen Ivory Wayans
Dave Winfield

1994

Tim Allen
Marian Anderson
Mario Andretti
Ned Andrews
Yasir Arafat
Bruce Babbitt
Mayim Bialik
Bonnie Blair
Ed Bradley
John Candy
Mary Chapin Carpenter
Benjamin Chavis
Connie Chung
Beverly Cleary
Kurt Cobain
F.W. de Klerk
Rita Dove
Linda Ellerbee
Sergei Fedorov
Zlata Filipovic
Daisy Fuentes
Ruth Bader Ginsburg
Whoopi Goldberg
Tonya Harding
Melissa Joan Hart
Geoff Hooper
Whitney Houston
Dan Jansen
Nancy Kerrigan
Alexi Lalas
Charlotte Lopez
Wilma Mankiller
Shannon Miller
Toni Morrison
Richard Nixon
Greg Norman
Severo Ochoa
River Phoenix
Elizabeth Pine
Jonas Salk
Richard Scarry
Emmitt Smith

Will Smith
Steven Spielberg
Patrick Stewart
R.L. Stine
Lewis Thomas
Barbara Walters
Charlie Ward
Steve Young
Kim Zmeskal

1995

Troy Aikman
Jean-Bertrand Aristide
Oksana Baiul
Halle Berry
Benazir Bhutto
Jonathan Brandis
Warren E. Burger
Ken Burns
Candace Cameron
Jimmy Carter
Agnes de Mille
Placido Domingo
Janet Evans
Patrick Ewing
Newt Gingrich
John Goodman
Amy Grant
Jesse Jackson
James Earl Jones
Julie Krone
David Letterman
Rush Limbaugh
Heather Locklear
Reba McEntire
Joe Montana
Cosmas Ndeti
Hakeem Olajuwon
Ashley Olsen
Mary-Kate Olsen
Jennifer Parkinson
Linus Pauling
Itzhak Perlman
Cokie Roberts
Wilma Rudolph
Salt 'N' Pepa
Barry Sanders
William Shatner
Elizabeth George
  Speare
Dr. Benjamin Spock
Jonathan Taylor
  Thomas
Vicki Van Meter
Heather Whitestone
Pedro Zamora

1996

Aung San Suu Kyi
Boyz II Men
Brandy
Ron Brown
Mariah Carey
Jim Carrey
Larry Champagne III
Christo
Chelsea Clinton
Coolio
Bob Dole
David Duchovny
Debbie Fields
Chris Galeczka
Jerry Garcia
Jennie Garth
Wendy Guey
Tom Hanks
Alison Hargreaves
Sir Edmund Hillary
Judith Jamison
Barbara Jordan
Annie Leibovitz
Carl Lewis
Jim Lovell
Mickey Mantle
Lynn Margulis
Iqbal Masih
Mark Messier
Larisa Oleynik
Christopher Pike
David Robinson
Dennis Rodman
Selena
Monica Seles
Don Shula
Kerri Strug
Tiffani-Amber Thiessen
Dave Thomas
Jaleel White

1997

Madeleine Albright
Marcus Allen
Gillian Anderson
Rachel Blanchard
Zachery Ty Bryan
Adam Ezra Cohen
Claire Danes
Celine Dion
Jean Driscoll
Louis Farrakhan
Ella Fitzgerald

Harrison Ford
Bryant Gumbel
John Johnson
Michael Johnson
Maya Lin
George Lucas
John Madden
Bill Monroe
Alanis Morissette
Sam Morrison
Rosie O'Donnell
Muammar el-Qaddafi
Christopher Reeve
Pete Sampras
Pat Schroeder
Rebecca Sealfon
Tupac Shakur
Tabitha Soren
Herbert Tarvin
Merlin Tuttle
Mara Wilson

1998

Bella Abzug
Kofi Annan
Neve Campbell
Sean Combs (Puff
    Daddy)
Dalai Lama (Tenzin
    Gyatso)
Diana, Princess of Wales
Leonardo DiCaprio
Walter E. Diemer
Ruth Handler
Hanson
Livan Hernandez
Jewel
Jimmy Johnson
Tara Lipinski
Oseola McCarty
Dominique Moceanu
Alexandra Nechita
Brad Pitt
LeAnn Rimes
Emily Rosa
David Satcher
Betty Shabazz
Kordell Stewart
Shinichi Suzuki
Mother Teresa
Mike Vernon
Reggie White
Venus Williams
Kate Winslet

1999

Ben Affleck
Jennifer Aniston
Maurice Ashley
Kobe Bryant
Bessie Delany
Sadie Delany
Sharon Draper
Sarah Michelle Gellar
John Glenn
Savion Glover
Jeff Gordon
David Hampton
Lauryn Hill
King Hussein
Lynn Johnston
Shari Lewis
Oseola McCarty
Mark McGwire
Slobodan Milosevic
Natalie Portman
J. K. Rowling
Frank Sinatra
Gene Siskel
Sammy Sosa
John Stanford
Natalia Toro
Shania Twain
Mitsuko Uchida
Jesse Ventura
Venus Williams

2000

Christina Aguilera
K.A. Applegate
Lance Armstrong
Backstreet Boys
Daisy Bates
Harry Blackmun
George W. Bush
Carson Daly
Ron Dayne
Henry Louis Gates, Jr.
Doris Haddock
    (Granny D)
Jennifer Love Hewitt
Chamique Holdsclaw
Katie Holmes
Charlayne Hunter-Gault
Johanna Johnson
Craig Kielburger
John Lasseter
Peyton Manning
Ricky Martin

John McCain
Walter Payton
Freddie Prinze, Jr.
Viviana Risca
Briana Scurry
George Thampy
CeCe Winans

Biography Today

Subject Series

For ages 9 and above

Expands and complements the General Series and targets specific subject areas . . .

Our readers asked for it! They wanted more biographies, and the *Biography Today* **Subject Series** is our response to that demand. Now your readers can choose their special areas of interest and go on to read about their favorites in those fields. Priced at just $38 per volume, the following specific volumes are included in the *Biography Today* **Subject Series**:

- **Artists Series**
- **Author Series**
- **Scientists & Inventors Series**
- **Sports Series**
- **World Leaders Series**
  Environmental Leaders
  Modern African Leaders

FEATURES AND FORMAT

- Sturdy 6" x 9" hardbound volumes
- Individual volumes, $39 each
- 200 pages per volume
- 12 profiles per volume — targets individuals within a specific subject area
- Contact sources for additional information
- Cumulative General, Places of Birth, and Birthday Indexes

NOTE: There is *no duplication of entries* between the **General Series** of *Biography Today* and the **Subject Series.**

AUTHOR SERIES

"A useful tool for children's assignment needs." — *School Library Journal*

"The prose is workmanlike: report writers will find enough detail to begin sound investigations, and browsers are likely to find someone of interest." — *School Library Journal*

SCIENTISTS & INVENTORS SERIES

"The articles are readable, attractively laid out, and touch on important points that will suit assignment needs. Browsers will note the clear writing and interesting details." — *School Library Journal*

"The book is excellent for demonstrating that scientists are real people with widely diverse backgrounds and personal interests. The biographies are fascinating to read." — *The Science Teacher*

SPORTS SERIES

"This series should become a standard resource in libraries that serve intermediate students." — *School Library Journal*

ENVIRONMENTAL LEADERS #1

"A tremendous book that fills a gap in the biographical category of books. This is a great reference book." — *Science Scope*

Artists Series

VOLUME 1
Ansel Adams
Romare Bearden
Margaret Bourke-White
Alexander Calder
Marc Chagall
Helen Frankenthaler
Jasper Johns
Jacob Lawrence
Henry Moore
Grandma Moses
Louise Nevelson
Georgia O'Keeffe
Gordon Parks
I.M. Pei
Diego Rivera
NormanRockwell
Andy Warhol
Frank Lloyd Wright

Author Series

VOLUME 1
Eric Carle
Alice Childress
Robert Cormier
Roald Dahl
Jim Davis
John Grisham
Virginia Hamilton
James Herriot
S.E. Hinton
M.E. Kerr
Stephen King
Gary Larson
Joan Lowery Nixon
Gary Paulsen
Cynthia Rylant
Mildred D. Taylor
Kurt Vonnegut, Jr.
E.B. White
Paul Zindel

VOLUME 2
James Baldwin
Stan and Jan Berenstain
David Macaulay
Patricia MacLachlan
Scott O'Dell

Jerry Pinkney
Jack Prelutsky
Lynn Reid Banks
Faith Ringgold
J.D. Salinger
Charles Schulz
Maurice Sendak
P.L. Travers
Garth Williams

VOLUME 3
Candy Dawson Boyd
Ray Bradbury
Gwendolyn Brooks
Ralph Ellison
Louise Fitzhugh
Jean Craighead George
E.L. Konigsburg
C.S. Lewis
Fredrick McKissack
Patricia McKissack
Katherine Paterson
Anne Rice
Shel Silverstein
Laura Ingalls Wilder

VOLUME 4
Betsy Byars
Chris Carter
Caroline Cooney
Christopher Paul Curtis
Anne Frank
Robert Heinlein
Marguerite Henry
Melissa Mathison
Bill Peet
Lois Lowry
August Wilson

VOLUME 5
Sharon Creech
Michael Crichton
Karen Cushman
Tomie de Paola
Lorraine Hansberry
Karen Hesse
Brian Jacques
Gary Soto
Richard Wright
Laurence Yep

VOLUME 6
Lloyd Alexander
Paula Danziger

Nancy Farmer
Zora Neale Hurston
Shirley Jackson
Angela Johnson
Jon Krakauer
Leo Lionni
Francine Pascal
Louis Sachar
Kevin Williamson

VOLUME 7
William H. Armstrong
Patricia Reilly Giff
Langston Hughes
Stan Lee
Julius Lester
Robert Pinsky
Todd Strasser
Jacqueline Woodson
Patricia C. Wrede
Jane Yolen

VOLUME 8
Amelia Atwater-Rhodes
Barbara Cooney
Paul Laurence Dunbar
Ursula K. Le Guin
Farley Mowat
Naomi Shihab Nye
Daniel Pinkwater
Beatrix Potter
Ann Rinaldi

Scientists & Inventors Series

VOLUME 1
John Bardeen
Sylvia Earle
Dian Fossey
Jane Goodall
Bernadine Healy
Jack Horner
Mathilde Krim
Edwin Land
Louise & Mary Leakey
Rita Levi-Montalcini
J. Robert Oppenheimer
Albert Sabin
Carl Sagan
James D. Watson

VOLUME 2
Jane Brody
Seymour Cray
Paul Erdös
Walter Gilbert
Stephen Jay Gould
Shirley Ann Jackson
Raymond Kurzweil
Shannon Lucid
Margaret Mead
Garrett Morgan
Bill Nye
Eloy Rodriguez
An Wang

VOLUME 3
Luis Alvarez
Hans A. Bethe
Gro Harlem Brundtland
Mary S. Calderone
Ioana Dumitriu
Temple Grandin
John L. Gwaltney
Bernard Harris
Jerome H. Lemelson
Susan Love
Ruth Patrick
Oliver Sacks
Richie Stachowski

VOLUME 4
David Attenborough
Robert Ballard
Ben Carson
Eileen Collins
Biruté Galdikas
Lonnie Johnson
Meg Lowman
Forrest Mars Sr.
Akio Morita
Janese Swanson

Sports Series

VOLUME 1

Hank Aaron
Kareem Abdul-Jabbar
Hassiba Boulmerka
Susan Butcher
Beth Daniel
Chris Evert
Ken Griffey, Jr.
Florence Griffith Joyner
Grant Hill
Greg Lemond
Pelé
Uta Pippig
Cal Ripken, Jr.
Arantxa Sanchez Vicario
Deion Sanders
Tiger Woods

VOLUME 2

Muhammad Ali
Donovan Bailey
Gail Devers
John Elway
Brett Favre
Mia Hamm
Anfernee "Penny"
    Hardaway
Martina Hingis
Gordie Howe
Jack Nicklaus
Richard Petty
Dot Richardson
Sheryl Swoopes
Steve Yzerman

VOLUME 3

Joe Dumars
Jim Harbaugh
Dominik Hasek
Michelle Kwan
Rebecca Lobo
Greg Maddux
Fatuma Roba
Jackie Robinson
John Stockton
Picabo Street
Pat Summitt
Amy Van Dyken

VOLUME 4

Wilt Chamberlain
Brandi Chastain
Derek Jeter
Karch Kiraly
Alex Lowe
Randy Moss
Se RiPak
Dawn Riley
Karen Smyers
Kurt Warner
Serena Williams

World Leaders Series

VOLUME 1: Environmental Leaders 1

Edward Abbey
Renee Askins
David Brower
Rachel Carson
Marjory Stoneman
    Douglas
Dave Foreman
Lois Gibbs
Wangari Maathai
Chico Mendes
Russell Mittermeier
Margaret and Olaus
    Murie
Patsy Ruth Oliver
Roger Tory Peterson
Ken Saro-Wiwa
Paul Watson
Adam Werbach

VOLUME 2: Modern African Leaders

Mohammed Farah
    Aidid
Idi Amin
Hastings Kamuzu Banda
Haile Selassie
Hassan II
Kenneth Kaunda
Jomo Kenyatta
Mobutu Sese Seko
Robert Mugabe
Kwame Nkrumah
Winnie Mandela
Julius Kambarage
    Nyerere
Anwar Sadat
Jonas Savimbi
Léopold Sédar Senghor
William V. S. Tubman

VOLUME 3: Environmental Leaders 2

John Cronin
Dai Qing
Ka Hsaw Wa
Winona LaDuke
Aldo Leopold
Bernard Martin
Cynthia Moss
John Muir
Gaylord Nelson
Douglas Tompkins
Hazel Wolf